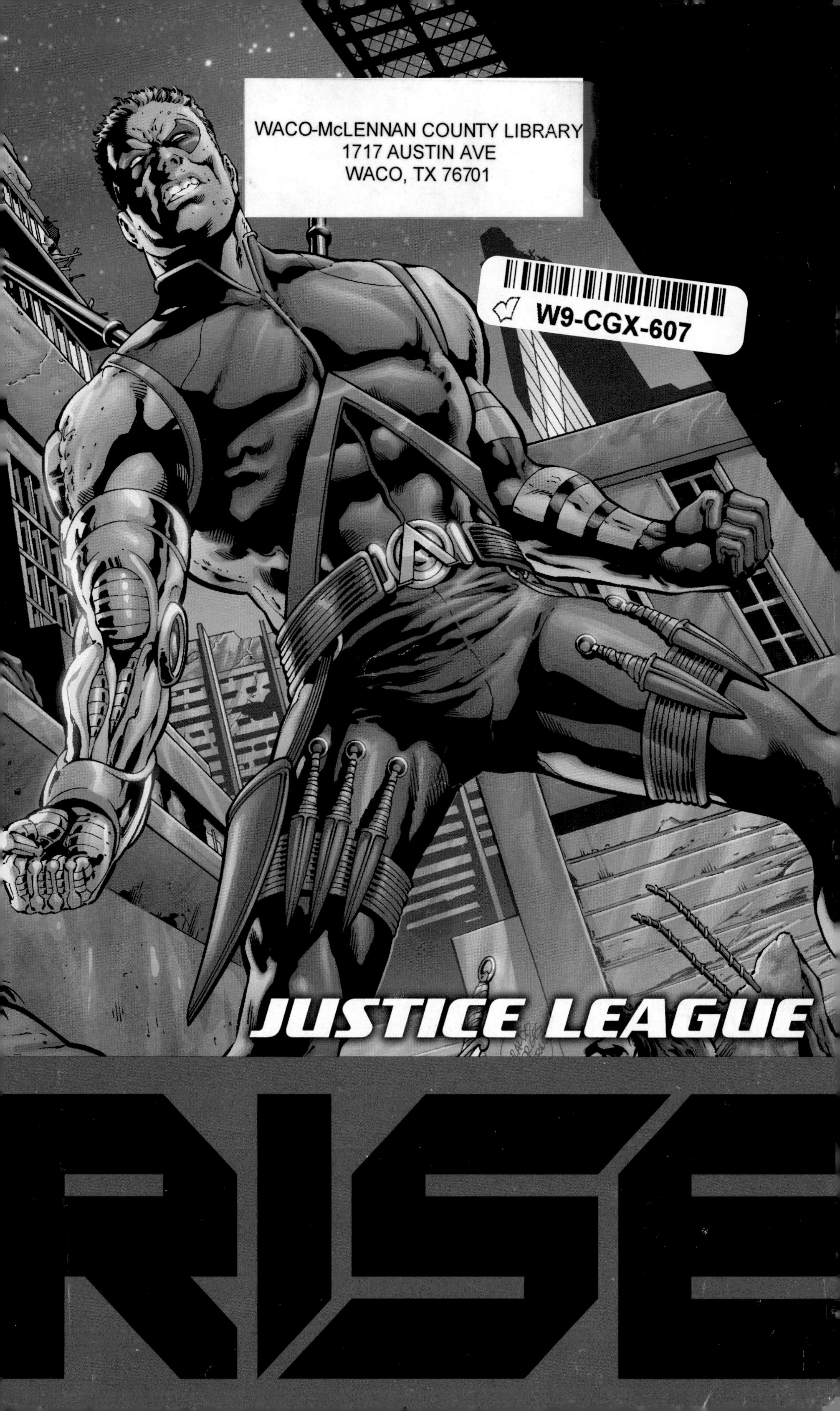
JUSTICE LEAGUE
RISE

AND

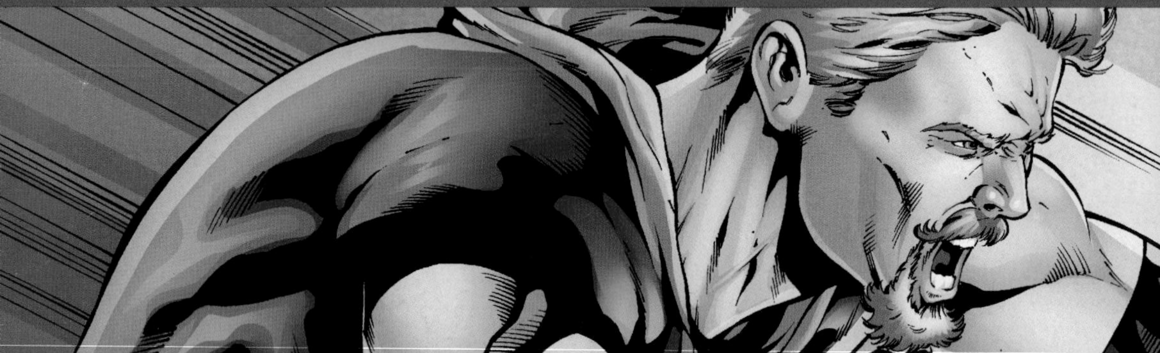

FALL

JUSTICE LEAGUE
RISE AND FALL

J.T. Krul Writer

Diogenes Neves Mike Mayhew Fabrizio Fiorentino Federico Dallocchio
Geraldo Borges Kevin Sharpe Sergio Arino Fabio Jansen Pencillers

Mike Mayhew Vicente Cifuentes Ruy José Federico Dallocchio
Marlo Alquiza Mark McKenna John Dell Scott Hanna Inkers

Nei Ruffino Andy Troy Michael Atiyeh Hi-Fi Colorists

John J. Hill Sal Cipriano Rob Clark Jr. Letterers

Mike Mayhew & Andy Troy Cover artists

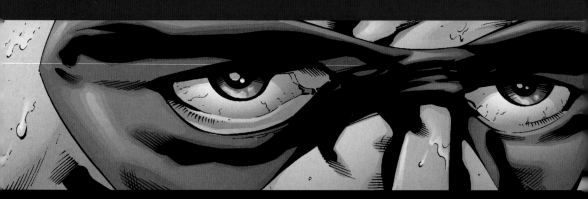

Adam Schlagman Eddie Berganza Brian Cunningham Editors-original series / Sean Ryan Associate Editor-original series
Bob Harras Group Editor-Collected Editions / Robbin Brosterman Design Director-Books

DC COMICS
Diane Nelson President / Dan DiDio and Jim Lee Co-Publishers / Geoff Johns Chief Creative Officer
Patrick Caldon EVP-Finance and Administration / John Rood EVP-Sales, Marketing and Business Development
Amy Genkins SVP-Business and Legal Affairs / Steve Rotterdam SVP-Sales and Marketing / John Cunningham VP-Marketing
Terri Cunningham VP-Managing Editor / Alison Gill VP-Manufacturing / David Hyde VP-Publicity / Sue Pohja VP-Book Trade Sales
Alysse Soll VP-Advertising and Custom Publishing / Bob Wayne VP-Sales / Mark Chiarello Art Director

JUSTICE LEAGUE: RISE AND FALL

DC Comics, 1700 Broadway, New York, NY 10019
A Warner Bros. Entertainment Company
Printed by RR Donnelley, Salem, VA, USA. 2/17/12. First printing.

SC ISBN: 978-1-4012-3014-2

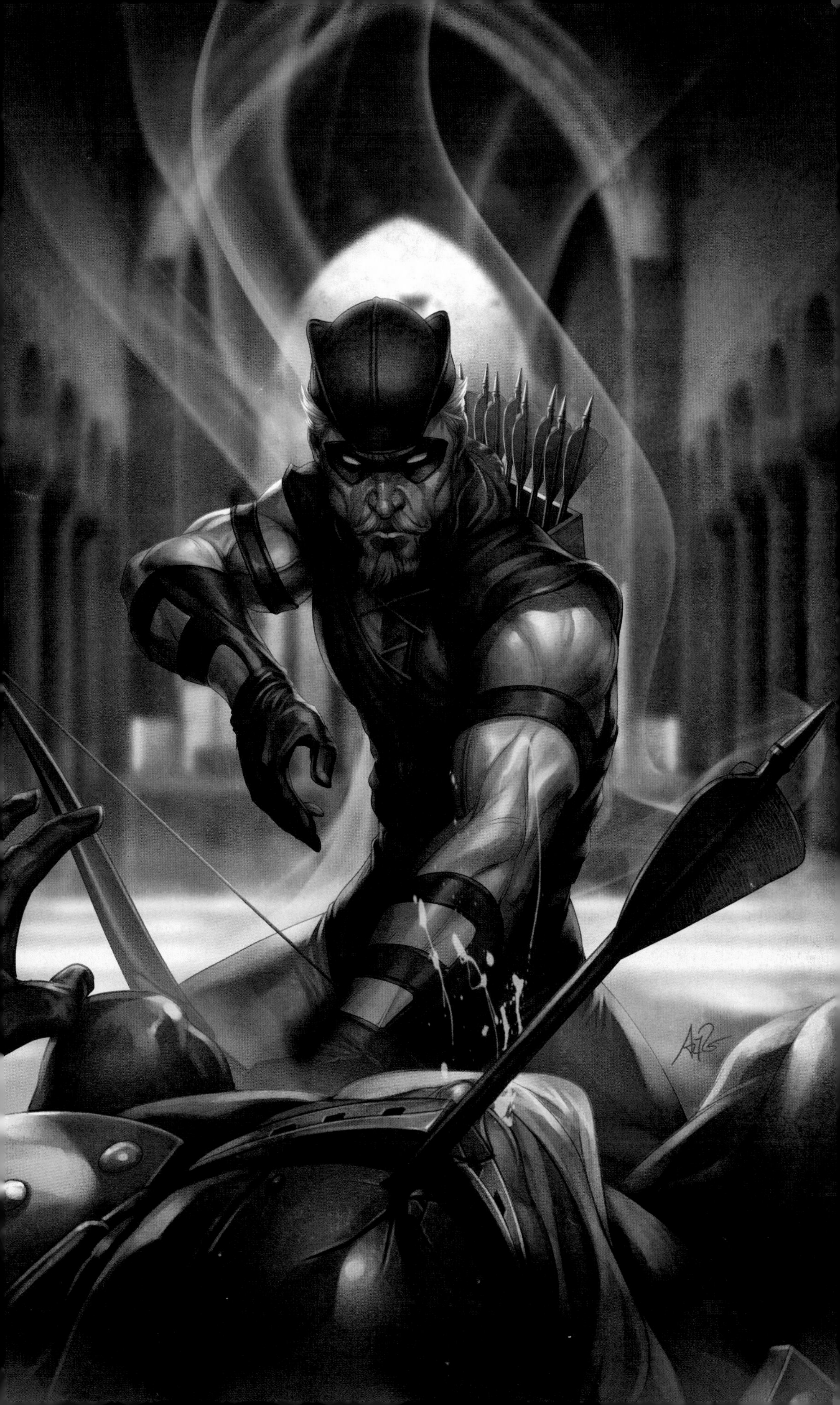

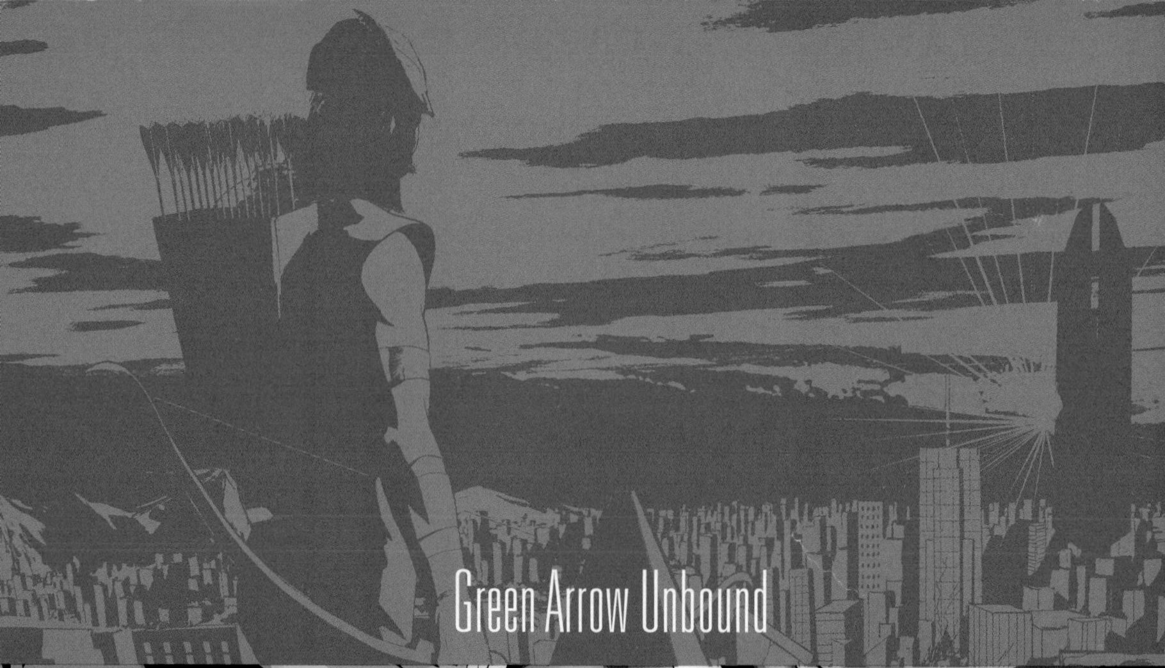

Green Arrow Unbound

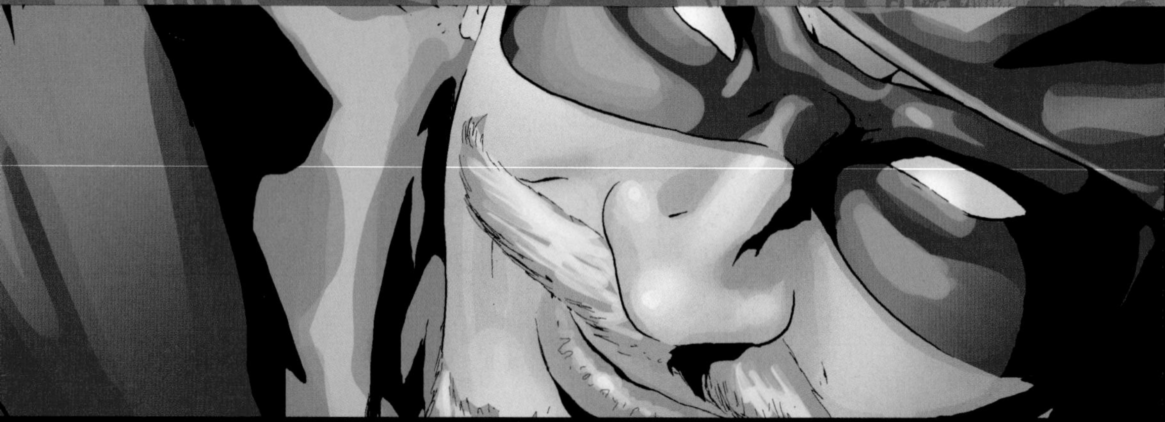

Cover by Stanley "Art Germ" Lau

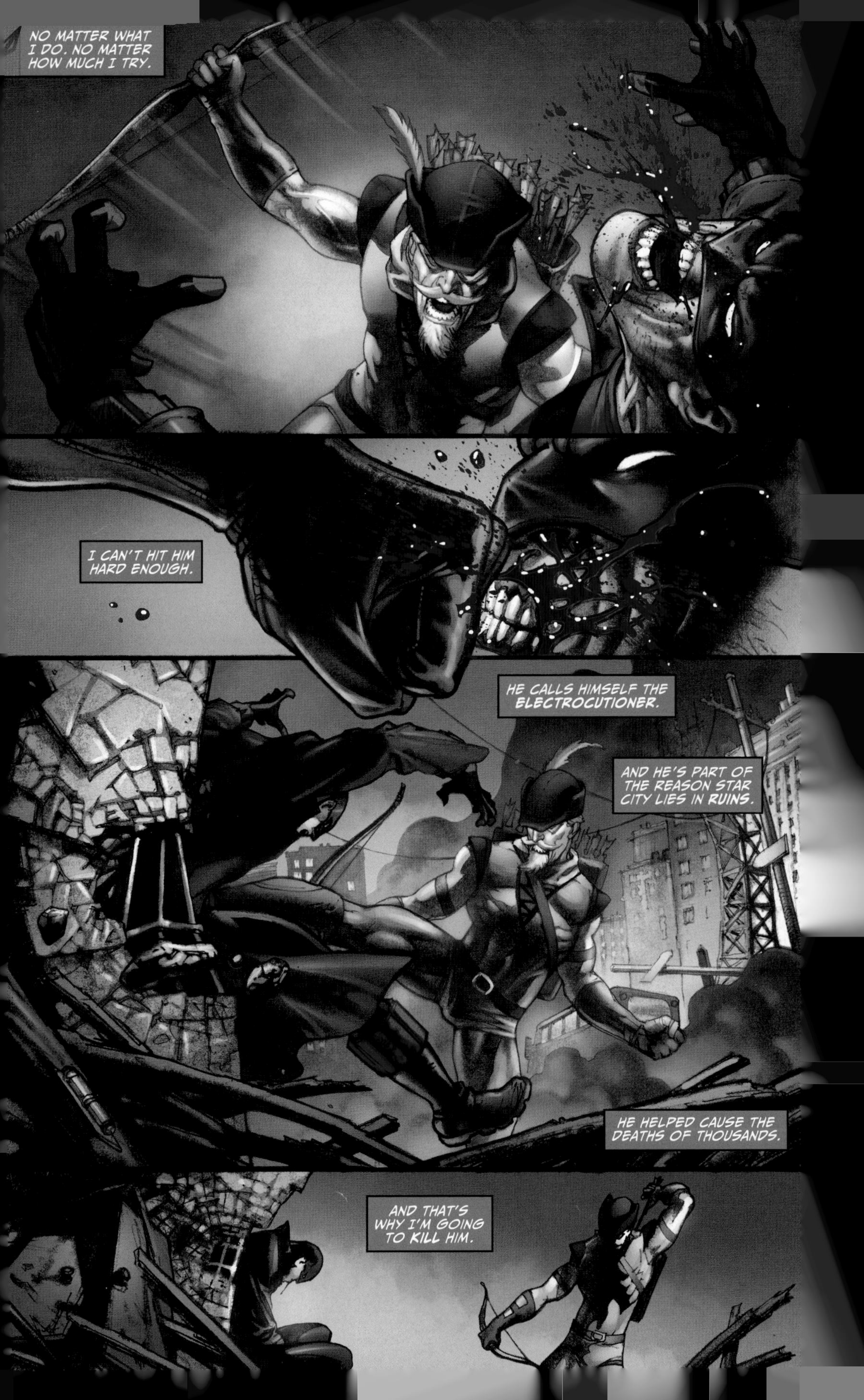
NO MATTER WHAT I DO. NO MATTER HOW MUCH I TRY.
I CAN'T HIT HIM HARD ENOUGH.
HE CALLS HIMSELF THE ELECTROCUTIONER.
AND HE'S PART OF THE REASON STAR CITY LIES IN RUINS.
HE HELPED CAUSE THE DEATHS OF THOUSANDS.
AND THAT'S WHY I'M GOING TO KILL HIM.

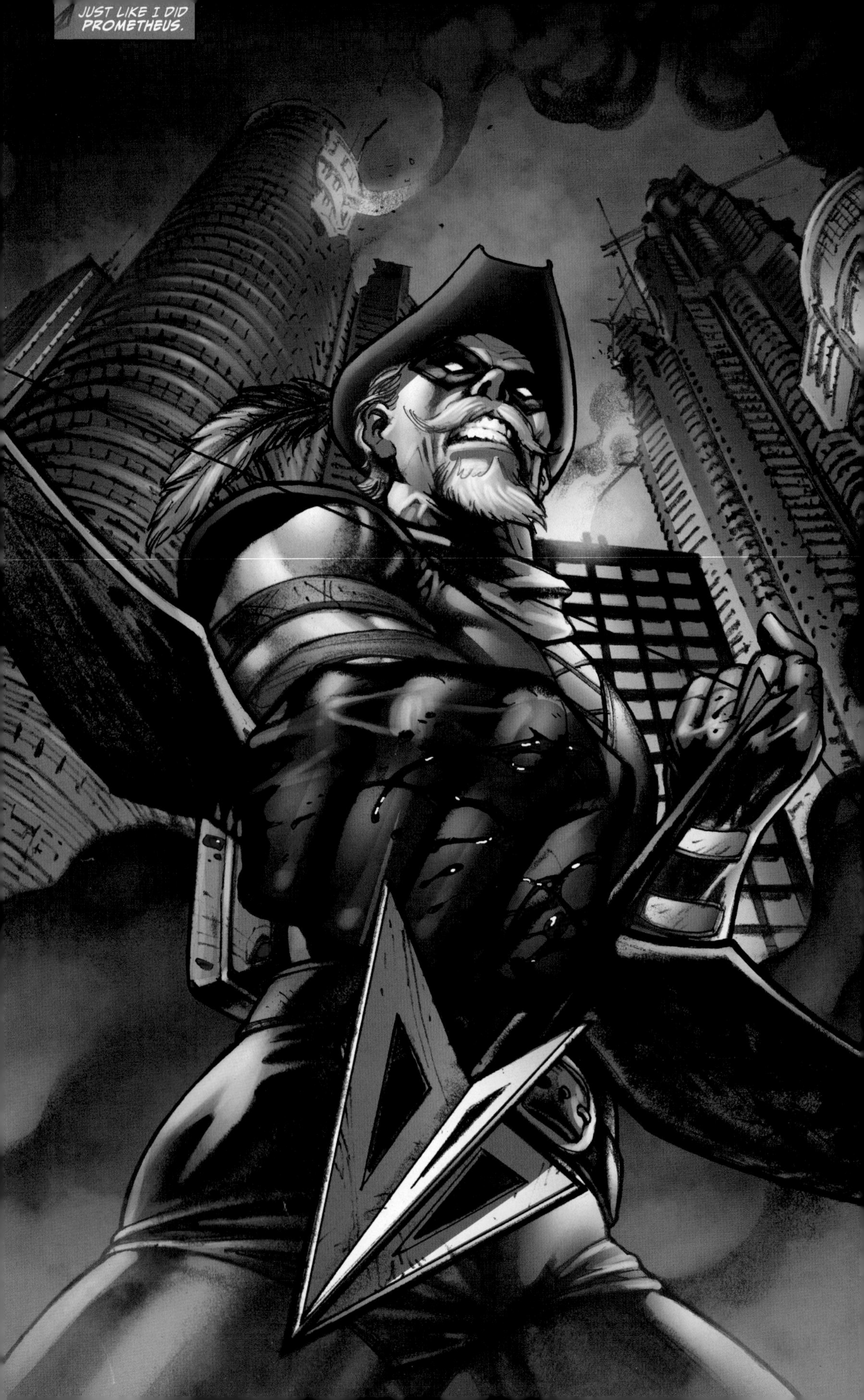
JUST LIKE I DID PROMETHEUS.

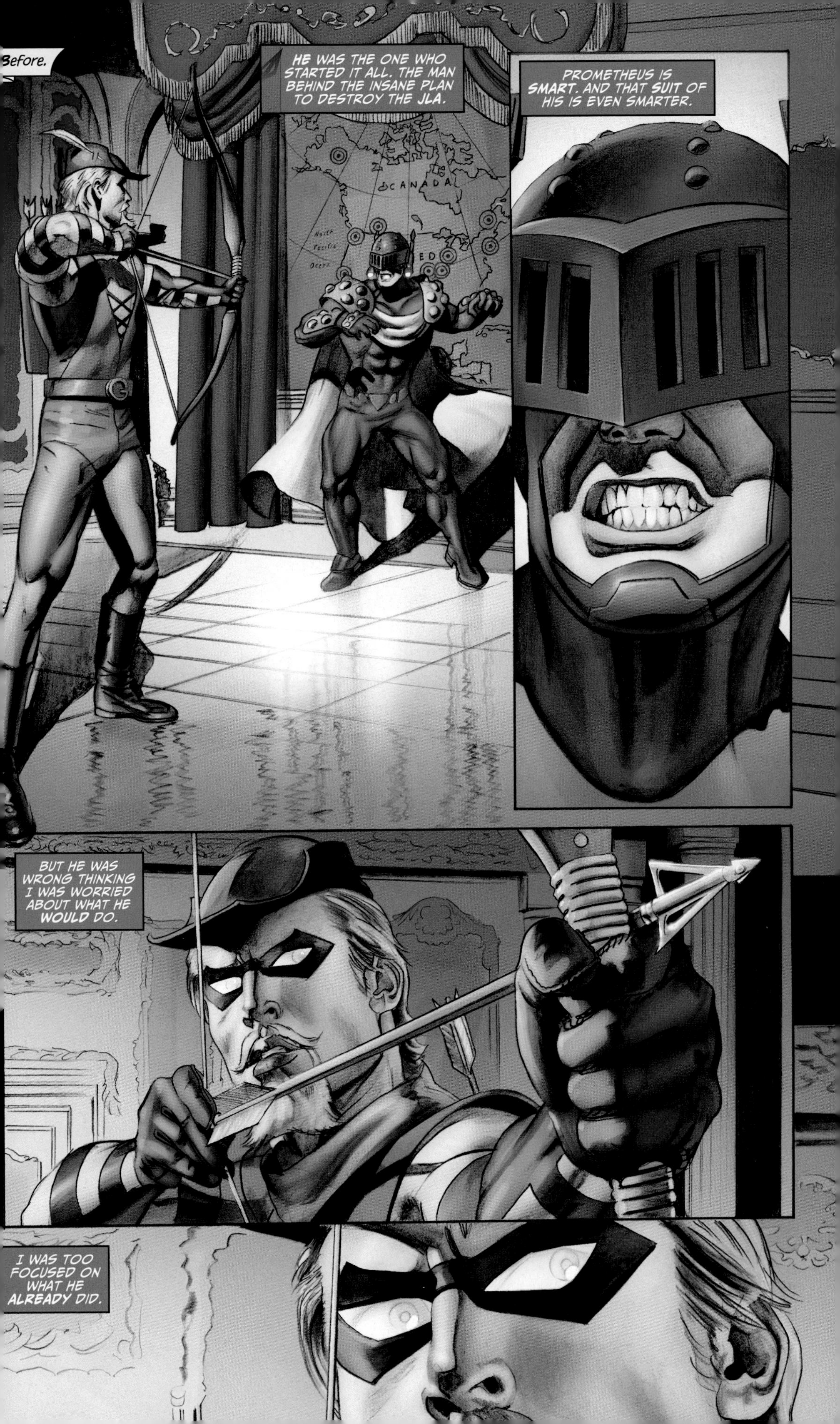
Before.
HE WAS THE ONE WHO STARTED IT ALL. THE MAN BEHIND THE INSANE PLAN TO DESTROY THE JLA.
CANADA
North Pacific Ocean
PROMETHEUS IS SMART. AND THAT SUIT OF HIS IS EVEN SMARTER.
BUT HE WAS WRONG THINKING I WAS WORRIED ABOUT WHAT HE WOULD DO.
I WAS TOO FOCUSED ON WHAT HE ALREADY DID.

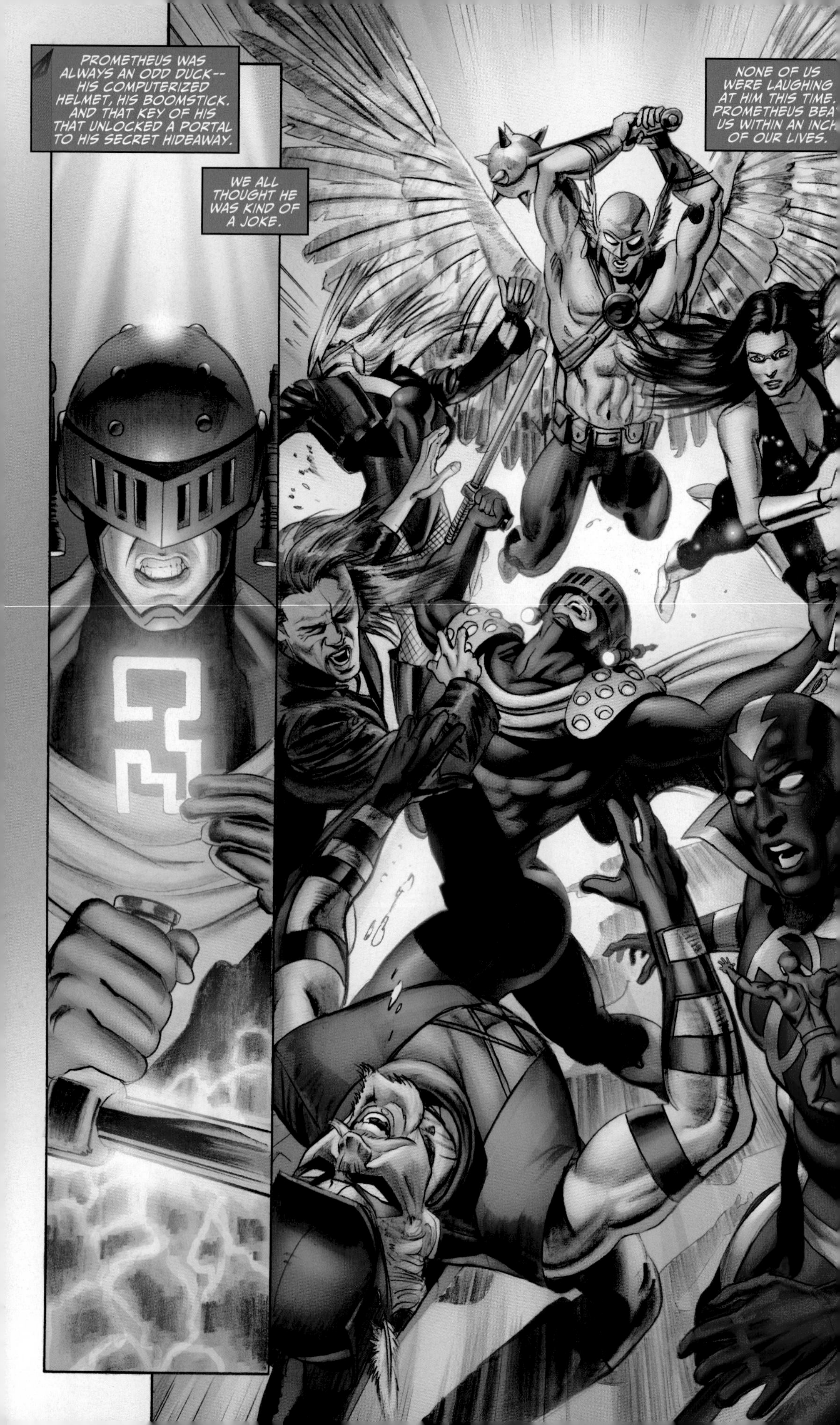

PROMETHEUS WAS ALWAYS AN ODD DUCK-- HIS COMPUTERIZED HELMET, HIS BOOMSTICK. AND THAT KEY OF HIS THAT UNLOCKED A PORTAL TO HIS SECRET HIDEAWAY.
WE ALL THOUGHT HE WAS KIND OF A JOKE.
NONE OF US WERE LAUGHING AT HIM THIS TIME. PROMETHEUS BEAT US WITHIN AN INCH OF OUR LIVES.

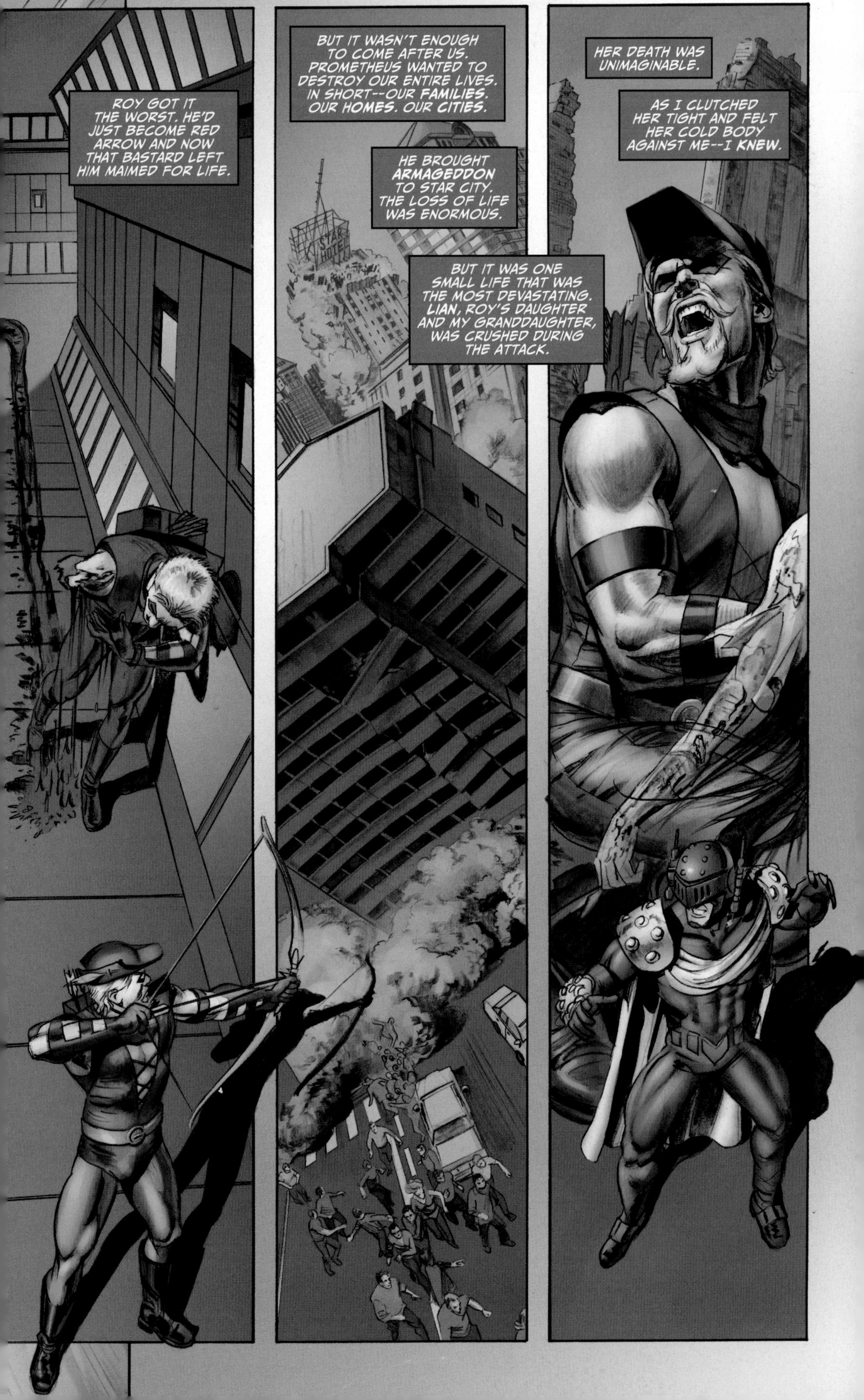
ROY GOT IT THE WORST. HE'D JUST BECOME RED ARROW AND NOW THAT BASTARD LEFT HIM MAIMED FOR LIFE.
BUT IT WASN'T ENOUGH TO COME AFTER US. PROMETHEUS WANTED TO DESTROY OUR ENTIRE LIVES. IN SHORT--OUR FAMILIES. OUR HOMES. OUR CITIES.
HE BROUGHT ARMAGEDDON TO STAR CITY. THE LOSS OF LIFE WAS ENORMOUS.
BUT IT WAS ONE SMALL LIFE THAT WAS THE MOST DEVASTATING. LIAN, ROY'S DAUGHTER AND MY GRANDDAUGHTER, WAS CRUSHED DURING THE ATTACK.
HER DEATH WAS UNIMAGINABLE.
AS I CLUTCHED HER TIGHT AND FELT HER COLD BODY AGAINST ME--I KNEW.

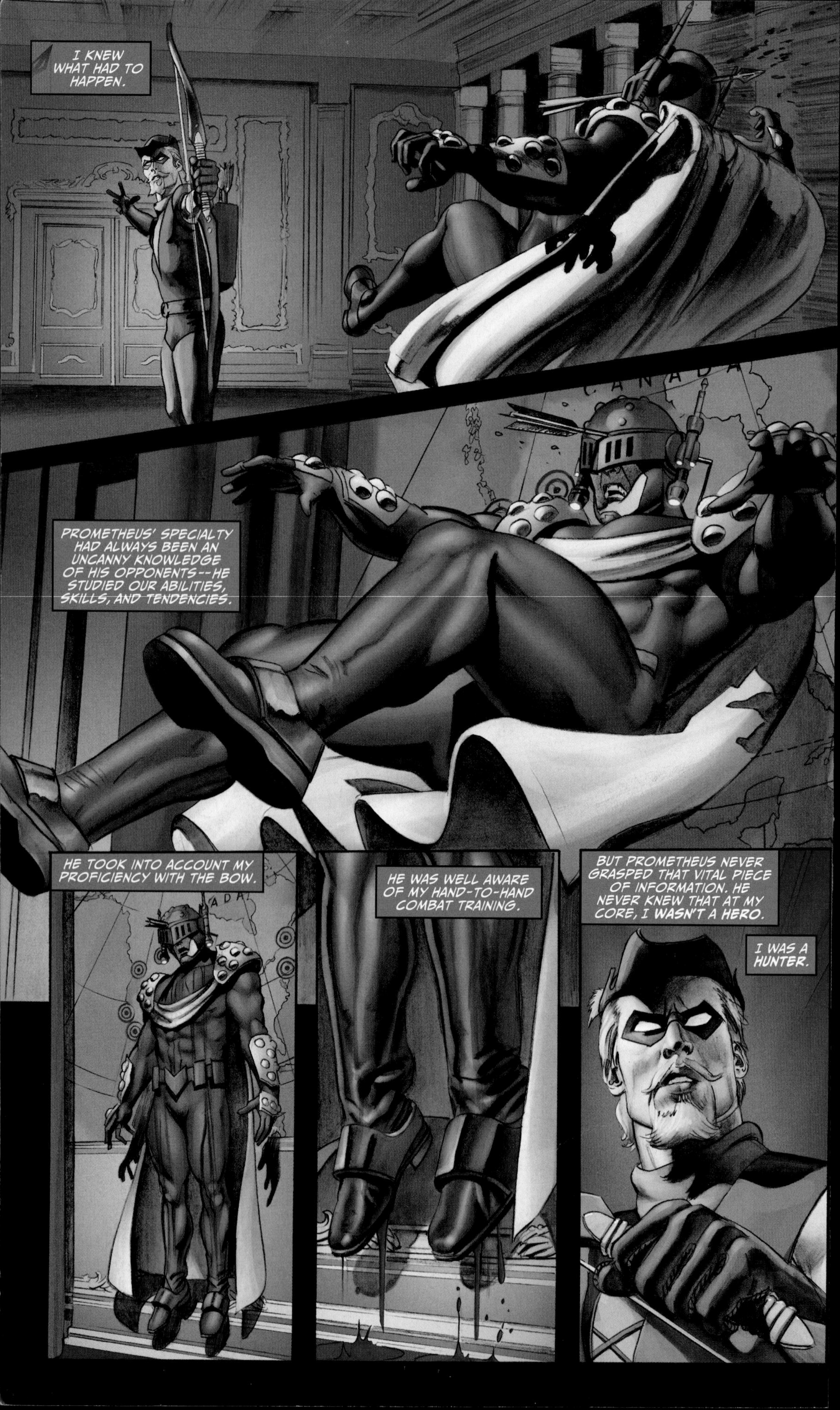
I KNEW WHAT HAD TO HAPPEN.
CANADA
PROMETHEUS' SPECIALTY HAD ALWAYS BEEN AN UNCANNY KNOWLEDGE OF HIS OPPONENTS--HE STUDIED OUR ABILITIES, SKILLS, AND TENDENCIES.
HE TOOK INTO ACCOUNT MY PROFICIENCY WITH THE BOW.
HE WAS WELL AWARE OF MY HAND-TO-HAND COMBAT TRAINING.
BUT PROMETHEUS NEVER GRASPED THAT VITAL PIECE OF INFORMATION. HE NEVER KNEW THAT AT MY CORE, I WASN'T A HERO.
I WAS A HUNTER.

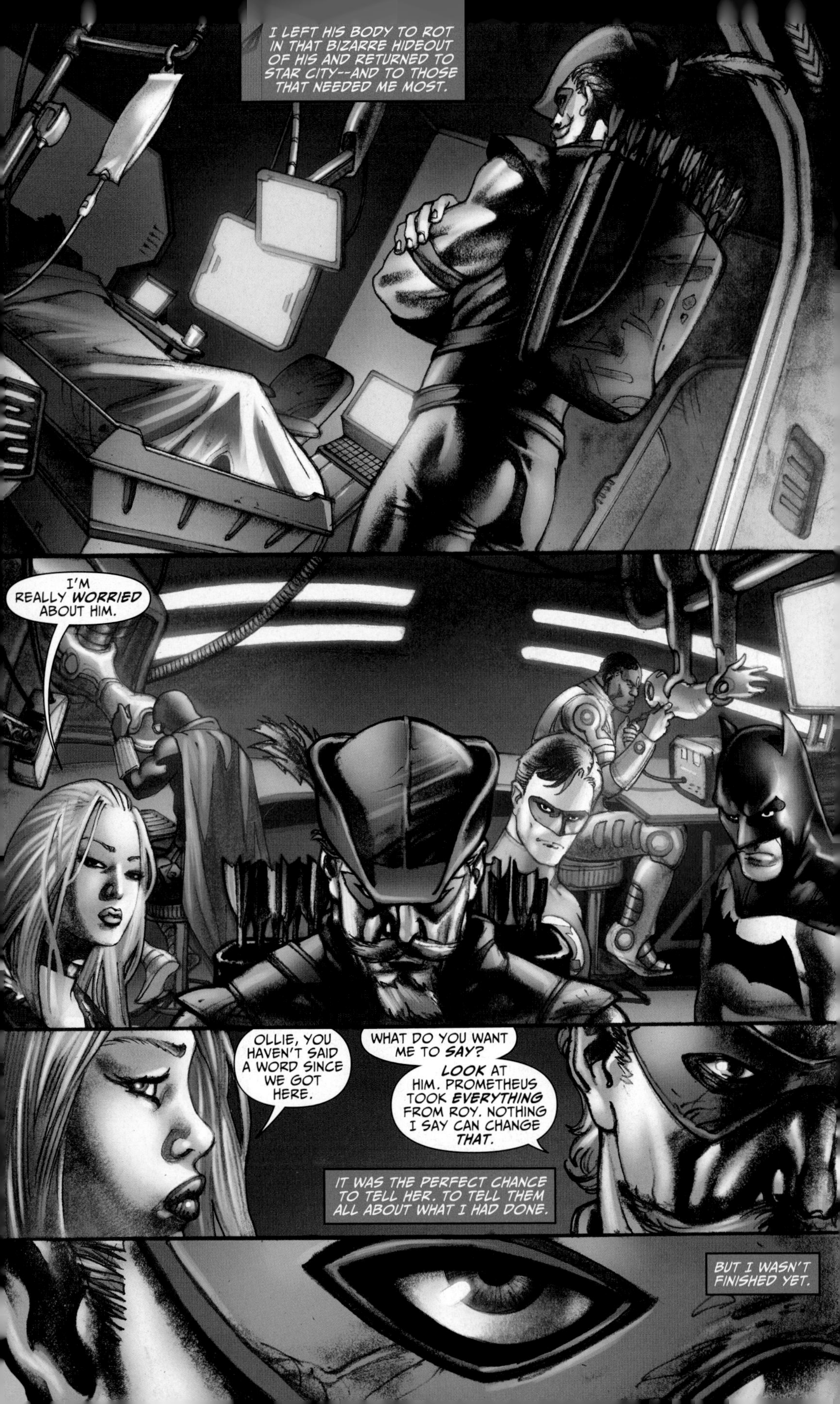
I LEFT HIS BODY TO ROT IN THAT BIZARRE HIDEOUT OF HIS AND RETURNED TO STAR CITY--AND TO THOSE THAT NEEDED ME MOST.
I'M REALLY WORRIED ABOUT HIM.
OLLIE, YOU HAVEN'T SAID A WORD SINCE WE GOT HERE.
WHAT DO YOU WANT ME TO SAY?
LOOK AT HIM. PROMETHEUS TOOK EVERYTHING FROM ROY. NOTHING I SAY CAN CHANGE THAT.
IT WAS THE PERFECT CHANCE TO TELL HER. TO TELL THEM ALL ABOUT WHAT I HAD DONE.
BUT I WASN'T FINISHED YET.

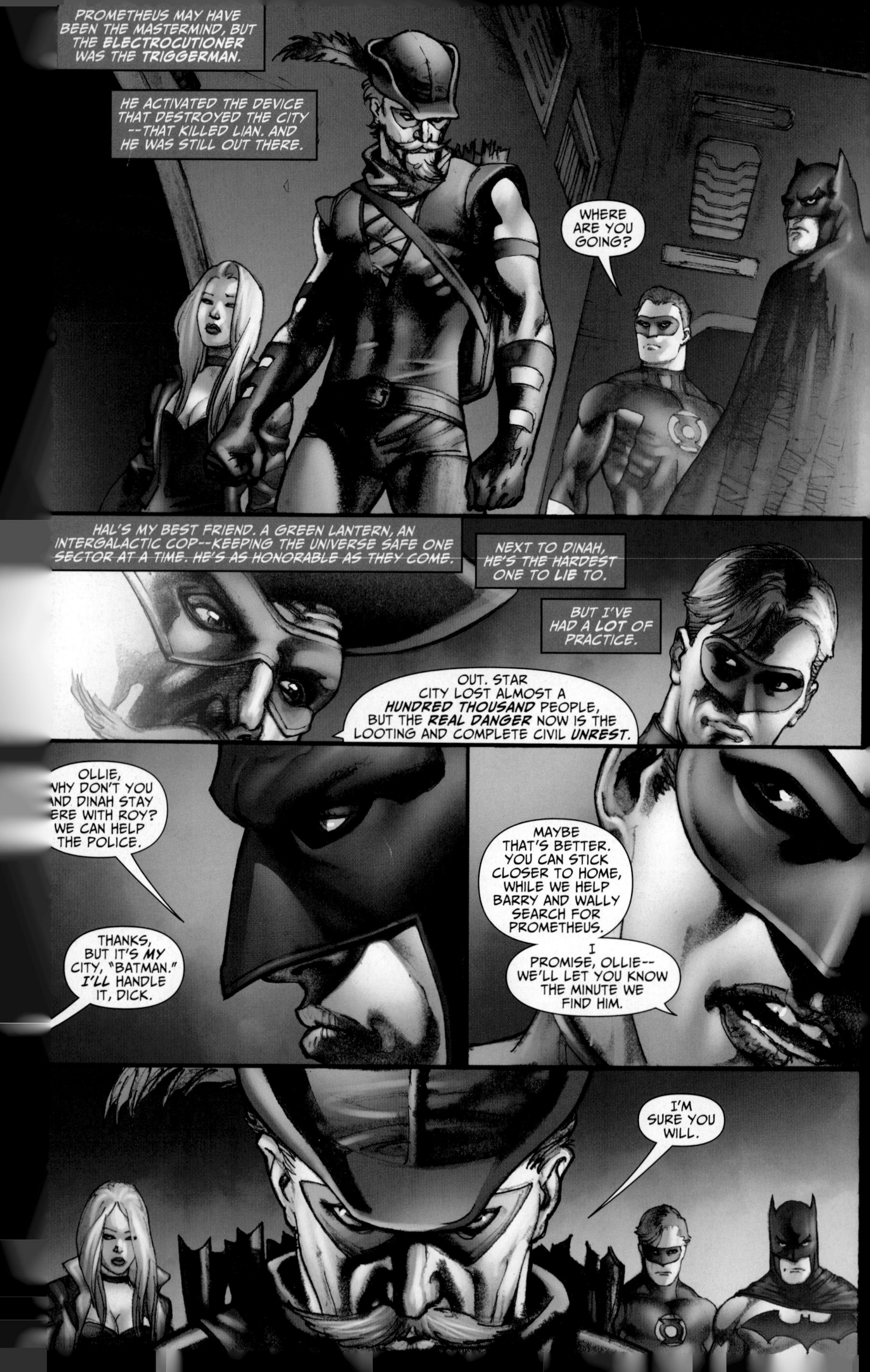
PROMETHEUS MAY HAVE BEEN THE MASTERMIND, BUT THE ELECTROCUTIONER WAS THE TRIGGERMAN.
HE ACTIVATED THE DEVICE THAT DESTROYED THE CITY --THAT KILLED LIAN. AND HE WAS STILL OUT THERE.
WHERE ARE YOU GOING?
HAL'S MY BEST FRIEND. A GREEN LANTERN, AN INTERGALACTIC COP--KEEPING THE UNIVERSE SAFE ONE SECTOR AT A TIME. HE'S AS HONORABLE AS THEY COME.
NEXT TO DINAH, HE'S THE HARDEST ONE TO LIE TO.
BUT I'VE HAD A LOT OF PRACTICE.
OUT. STAR CITY LOST ALMOST A HUNDRED THOUSAND PEOPLE, BUT THE REAL DANGER NOW IS THE LOOTING AND COMPLETE CIVIL UNREST.
OLLIE, WHY DON'T YOU AND DINAH STAY HERE WITH ROY? WE CAN HELP THE POLICE.
MAYBE THAT'S BETTER. YOU CAN STICK CLOSER TO HOME, WHILE WE HELP BARRY AND WALLY SEARCH FOR PROMETHEUS.
THANKS, BUT IT'S MY CITY, "BATMAN." I'LL HANDLE IT, DICK.
I PROMISE, OLLIE-- WE'LL LET YOU KNOW THE MINUTE WE FIND HIM.
I'M SURE YOU WILL.

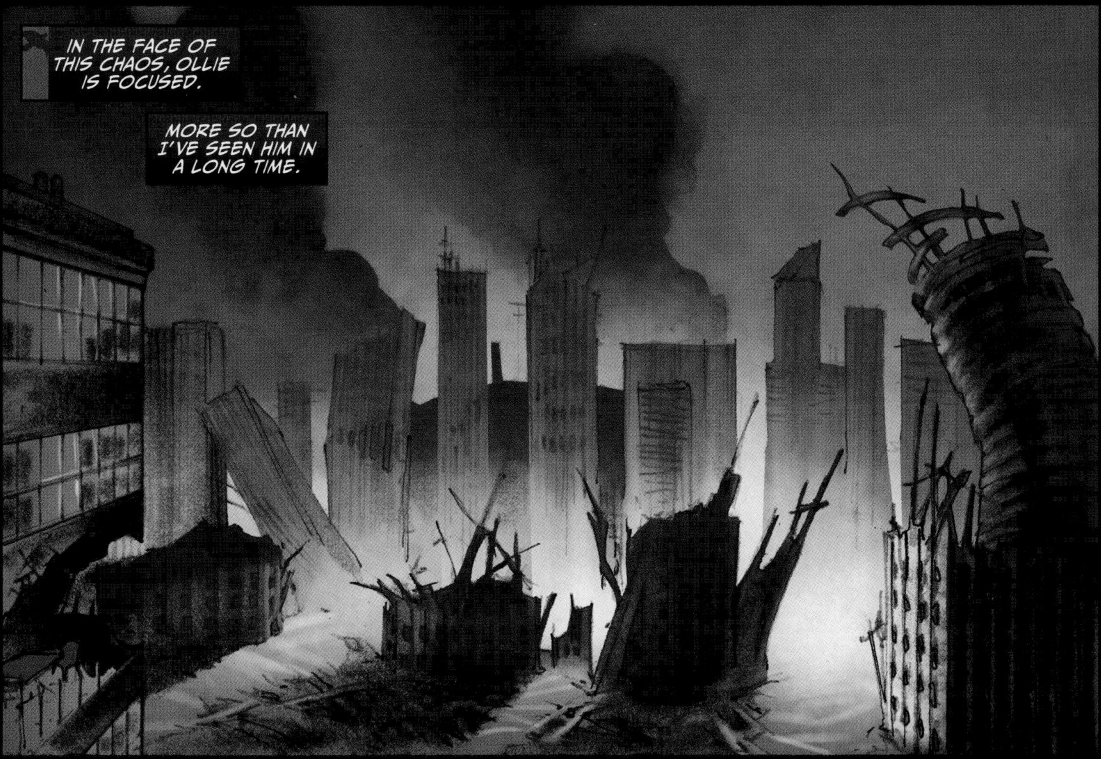
IN THE FACE OF THIS CHAOS, OLLIE IS FOCUSED.
MORE SO THAN I'VE SEEN HIM IN A LONG TIME.

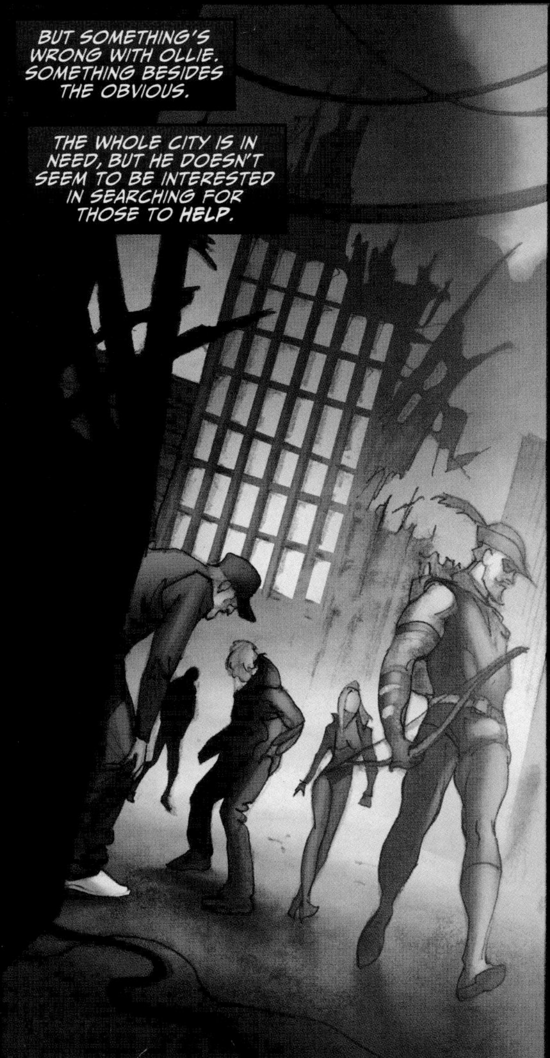
BUT SOMETHING'S WRONG WITH OLLIE. SOMETHING BESIDES THE OBVIOUS.
THE WHOLE CITY IS IN NEED, BUT HE DOESN'T SEEM TO BE INTERESTED IN SEARCHING FOR THOSE TO **HELP**.

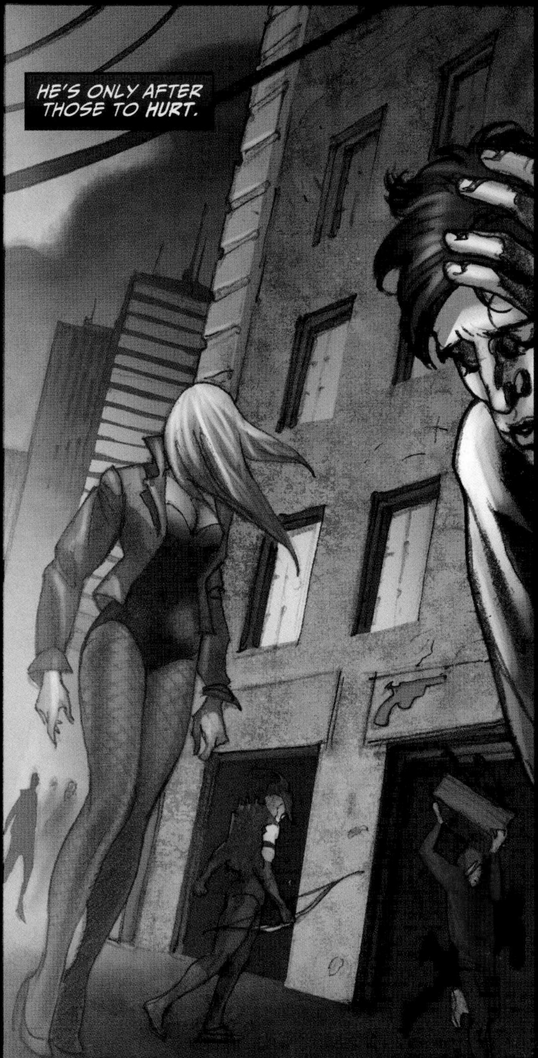
HE'S ONLY AFTER THOSE TO **HURT**.

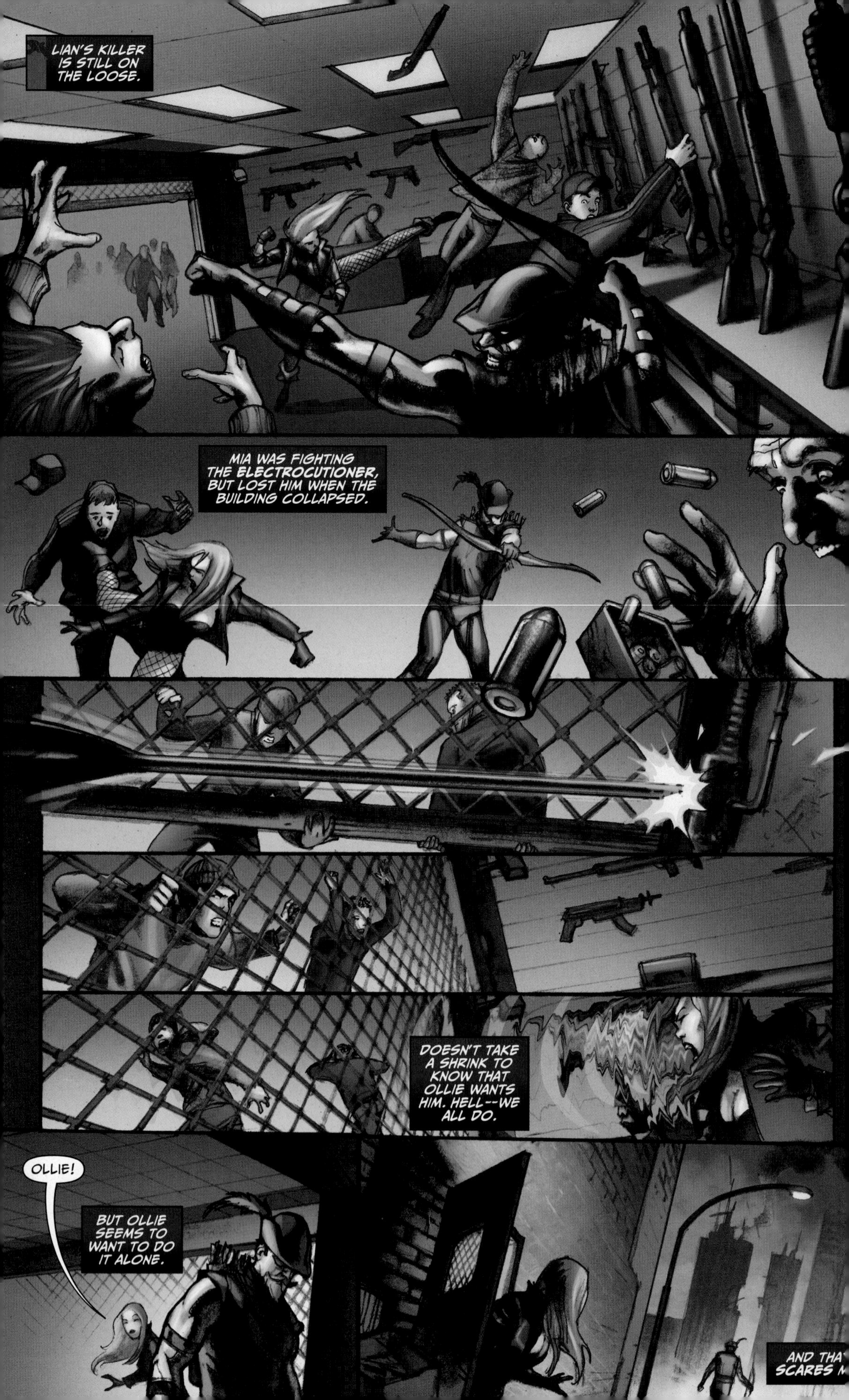
LIAN'S KILLER IS STILL ON THE LOOSE.
MIA WAS FIGHTING THE ELECTROCUTIONER, BUT LOST HIM WHEN THE BUILDING COLLAPSED.
DOESN'T TAKE A SHRINK TO KNOW THAT OLLIE WANTS HIM. HELL--WE ALL DO.
OLLIE!
BUT OLLIE SEEMS TO WANT TO DO IT ALONE.

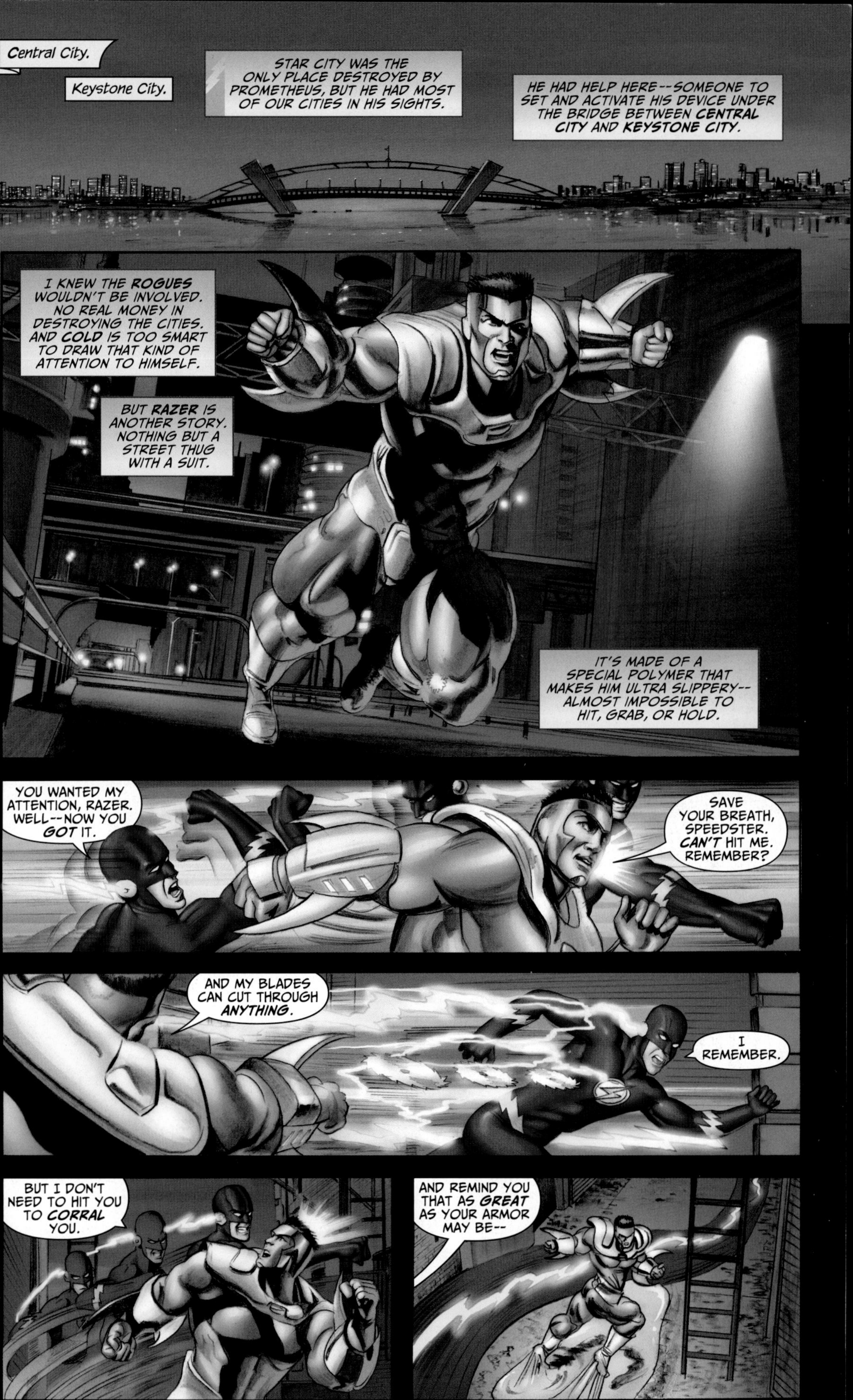

Central City.
Keystone City.
STAR CITY WAS THE ONLY PLACE DESTROYED BY PROMETHEUS, BUT HE HAD MOST OF OUR CITIES IN HIS SIGHTS.
HE HAD HELP HERE--SOMEONE TO SET AND ACTIVATE HIS DEVICE UNDER THE BRIDGE BETWEEN CENTRAL CITY AND KEYSTONE CITY.
I KNEW THE ROGUES WOULDN'T BE INVOLVED. NO REAL MONEY IN DESTROYING THE CITIES. AND COLD IS TOO SMART TO DRAW THAT KIND OF ATTENTION TO HIMSELF.
BUT RAZER IS ANOTHER STORY. NOTHING BUT A STREET THUG WITH A SUIT.
IT'S MADE OF A SPECIAL POLYMER THAT MAKES HIM ULTRA SLIPPERY--ALMOST IMPOSSIBLE TO HIT, GRAB, OR HOLD.
YOU WANTED MY ATTENTION, RAZER. WELL--NOW YOU GOT IT.
SAVE YOUR BREATH, SPEEDSTER. CAN'T HIT ME. REMEMBER?
AND MY BLADES CAN CUT THROUGH ANYTHING.
I REMEMBER.
BUT I DON'T NEED TO HIT YOU TO CORRAL YOU.
AND REMIND YOU THAT AS GREAT AS YOUR ARMOR MAY BE--

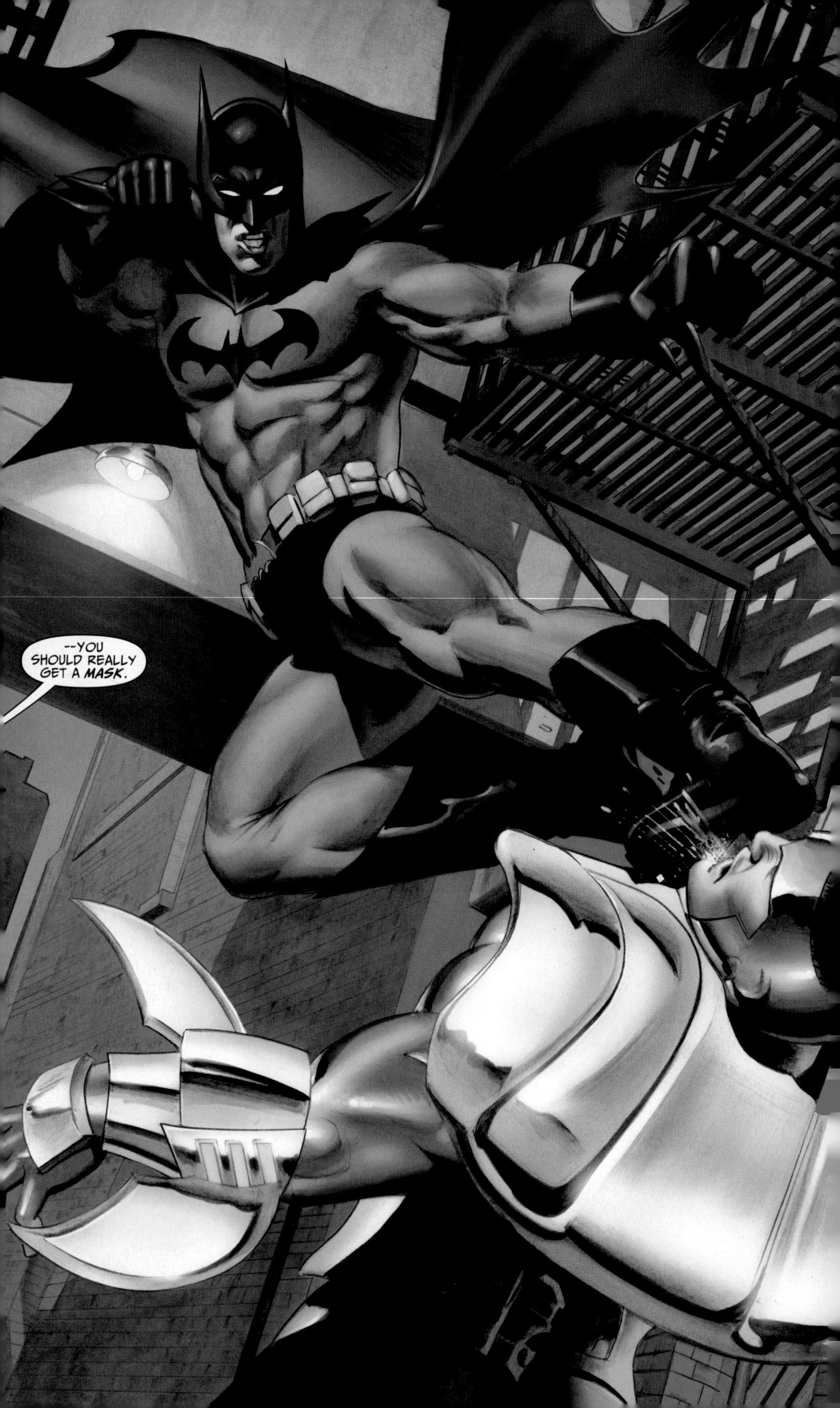
--YOU SHOULD REALLY GET A MASK.

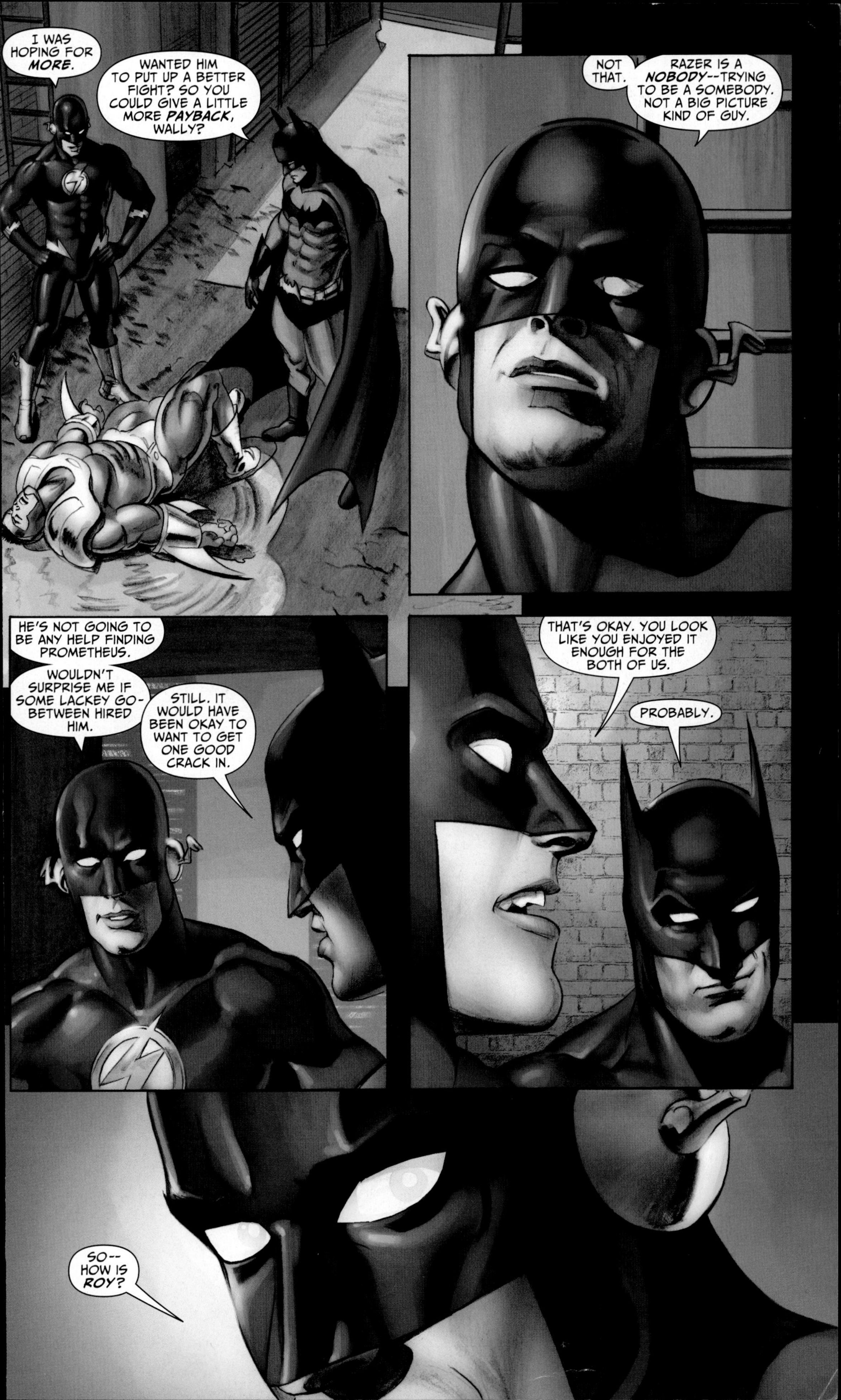

I WAS HOPING FOR **MORE**.
WANTED HIM TO PUT UP A BETTER FIGHT? SO YOU COULD GIVE A LITTLE MORE **PAYBACK**, WALLY?
NOT THAT.
RAZER IS A **NOBODY**--TRYING TO BE A SOMEBODY. NOT A BIG PICTURE KIND OF GUY.
HE'S NOT GOING TO BE ANY HELP FINDING PROMETHEUS.
WOULDN'T SURPRISE ME IF SOME LACKEY GO-BETWEEN HIRED HIM.
STILL. IT WOULD HAVE BEEN OKAY TO WANT TO GET ONE GOOD CRACK IN.
THAT'S OKAY. YOU LOOK LIKE YOU ENJOYED IT ENOUGH FOR THE BOTH OF US.
PROBABLY.
SO--HOW IS **ROY**?

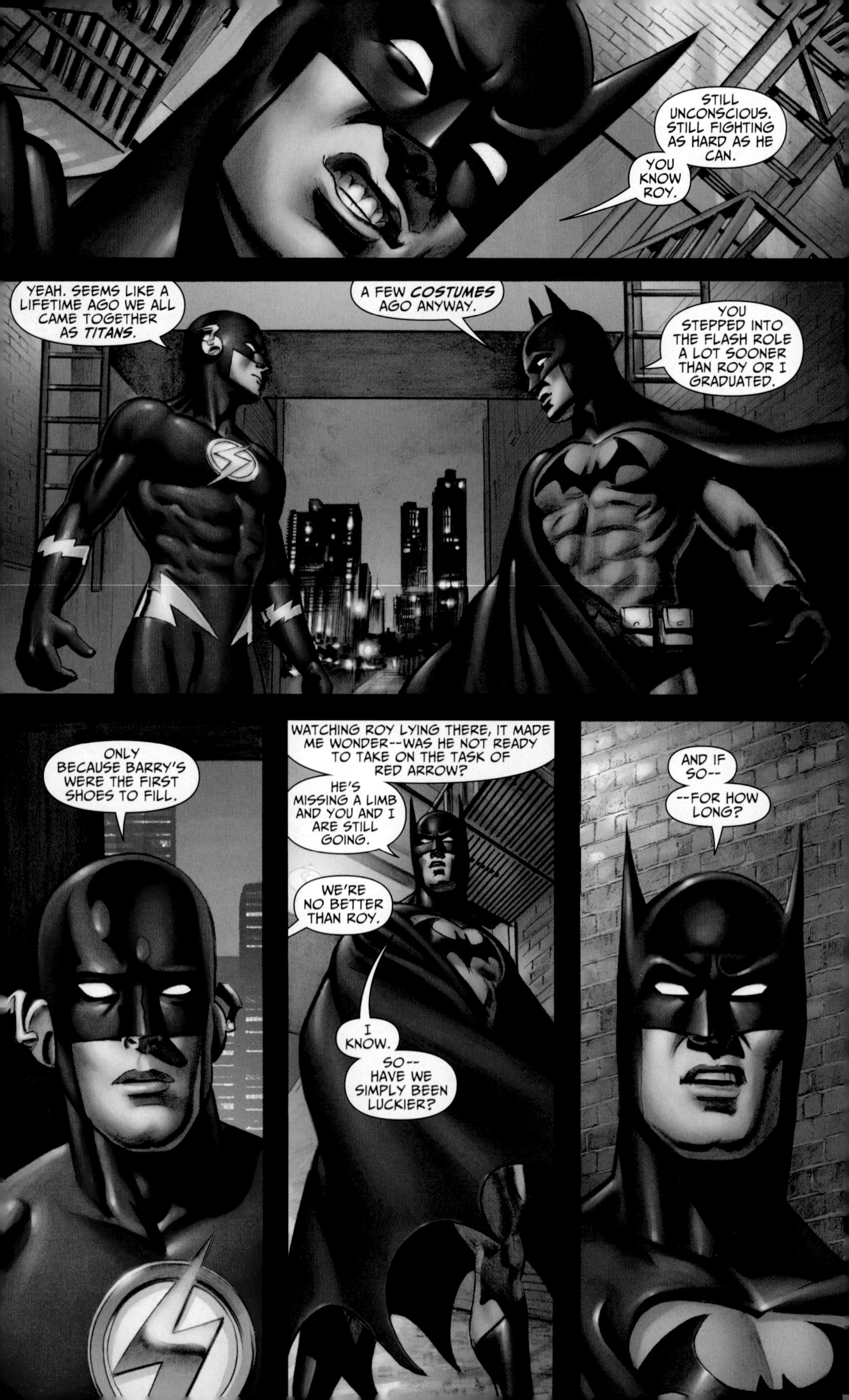
STILL UNCONSCIOUS. STILL FIGHTING AS HARD AS HE CAN.
YOU KNOW ROY.
YEAH. SEEMS LIKE A LIFETIME AGO WE ALL CAME TOGETHER AS *TITANS*.
A FEW *COSTUMES* AGO ANYWAY.
YOU STEPPED INTO THE FLASH ROLE A LOT SOONER THAN ROY OR I GRADUATED.
ONLY BECAUSE BARRY'S WERE THE FIRST SHOES TO FILL.
WATCHING ROY LYING THERE, IT MADE ME WONDER--WAS HE NOT READY TO TAKE ON THE TASK OF RED ARROW?
HE'S MISSING A LIMB AND YOU AND I ARE STILL GOING.
WE'RE NO BETTER THAN ROY.
I KNOW.
SO-- HAVE WE SIMPLY BEEN LUCKIER?
AND IF SO--
--FOR HOW LONG?

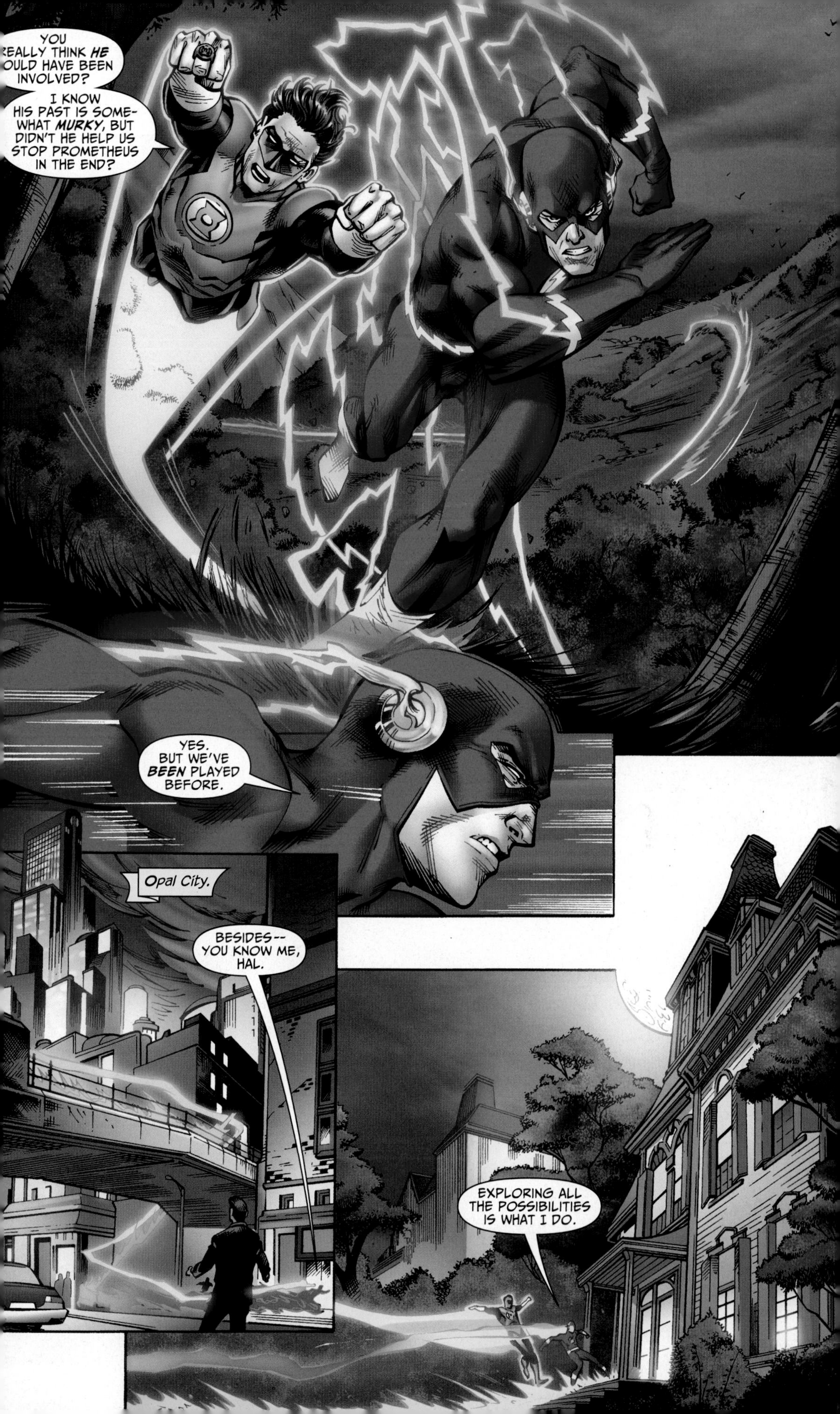
YOU
REALLY THINK HE
COULD HAVE BEEN
INVOLVED?
I KNOW
HIS PAST IS SOME-
WHAT MURKY, BUT
DIDN'T HE HELP US
STOP PROMETHEUS
IN THE END?
YES.
BUT WE'VE
BEEN PLAYED
BEFORE.
Opal City.
BESIDES--
YOU KNOW ME,
HAL.
EXPLORING ALL
THE POSSIBILITIES
IS WHAT I DO.

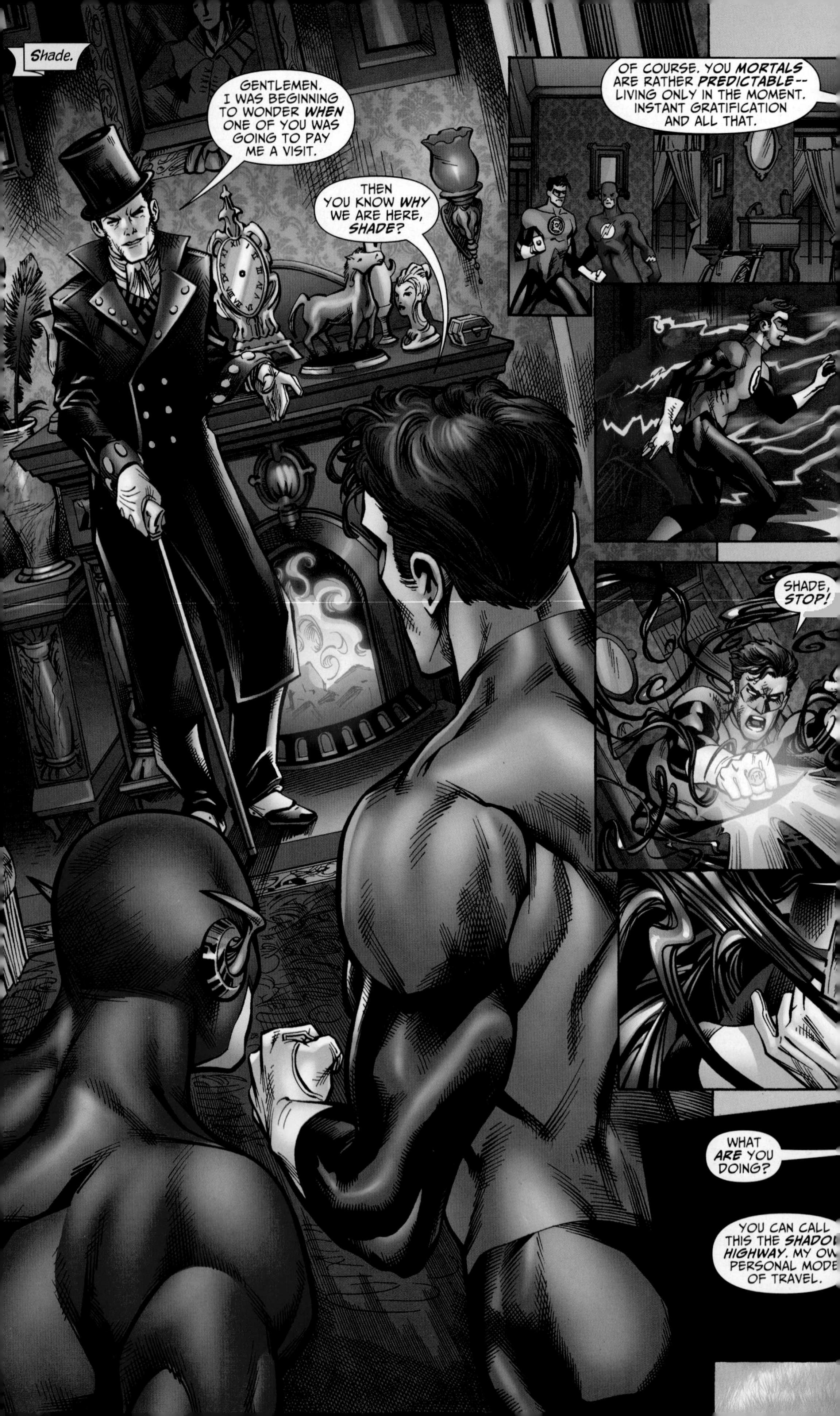
Shade.
GENTLEMEN. I WAS BEGINNING TO WONDER WHEN ONE OF YOU WAS GOING TO PAY ME A VISIT.
THEN YOU KNOW WHY WE ARE HERE, SHADE?
OF COURSE. YOU MORTALS ARE RATHER PREDICTABLE-- LIVING ONLY IN THE MOMENT. INSTANT GRATIFICATION AND ALL THAT.
SHADE, STOP!
WHAT ARE YOU DOING?

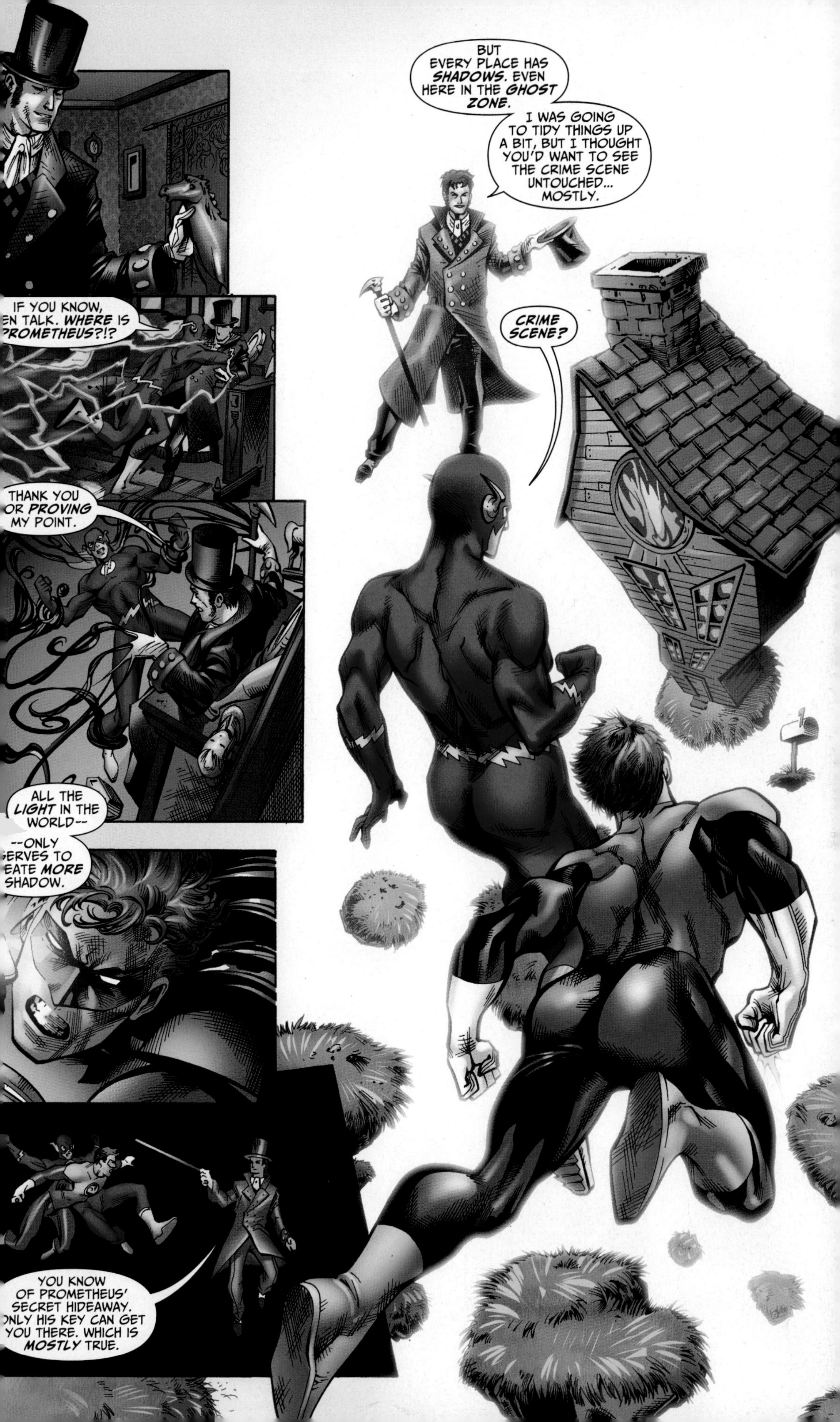

BUT EVERY PLACE HAS SHADOWS. EVEN HERE IN THE GHOST ZONE.
I WAS GOING TO TIDY THINGS UP A BIT, BUT I THOUGHT YOU'D WANT TO SEE THE CRIME SCENE UNTOUCHED... MOSTLY.
CRIME SCENE?
IF YOU KNOW, EN TALK. WHERE IS PROMETHEUS?!?
THANK YOU OR PROVING MY POINT.
ALL THE LIGHT IN THE WORLD--
--ONLY ERVES TO EATE MORE SHADOW.
YOU KNOW OF PROMETHEUS' SECRET HIDEAWAY. NLY HIS KEY CAN GET YOU THERE. WHICH IS MOSTLY TRUE.

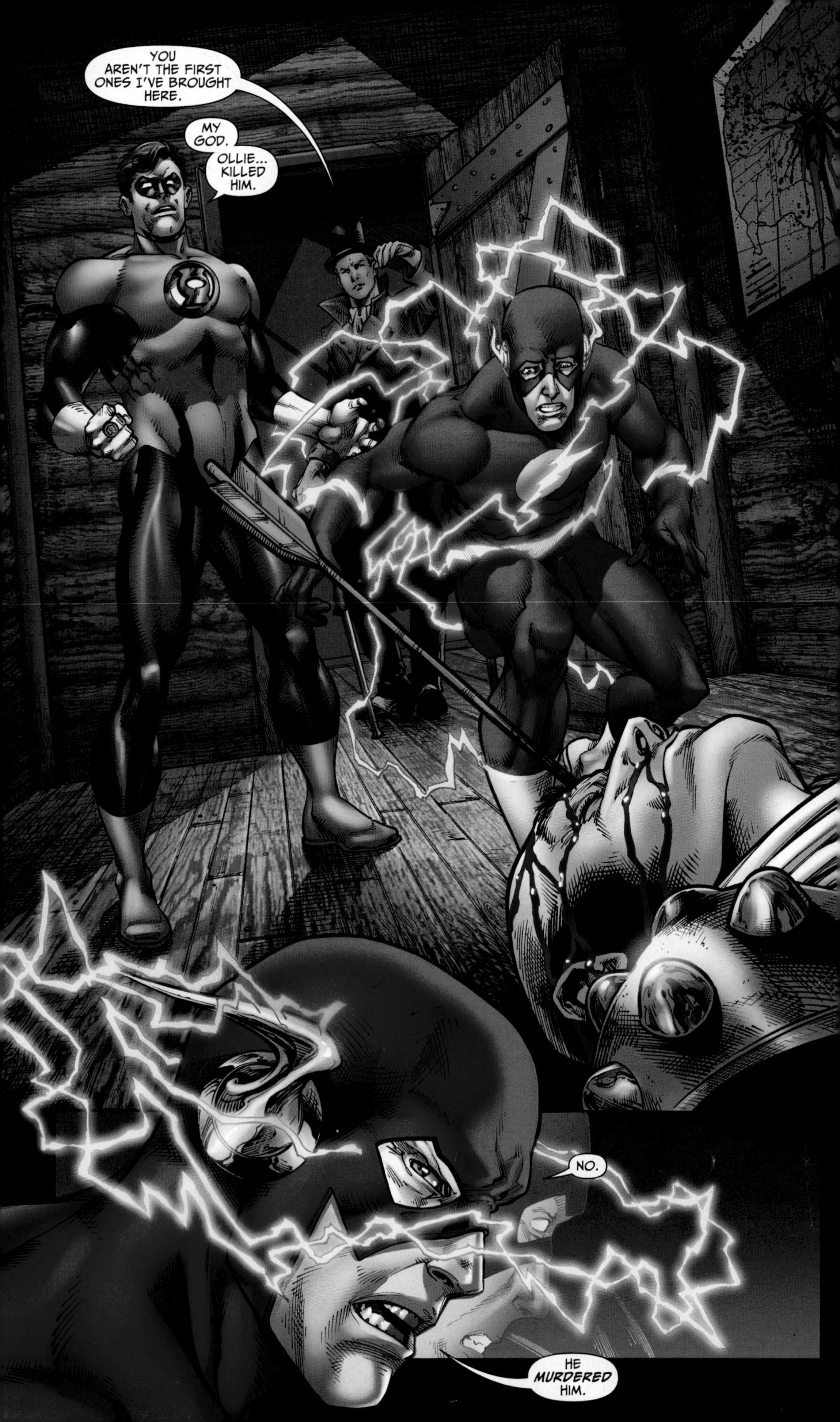
YOU AREN'T THE FIRST ONES I'VE BROUGHT HERE.
MY GOD. OLLIE... KILLED HIM.
NO.
HE MURDERED HIM.

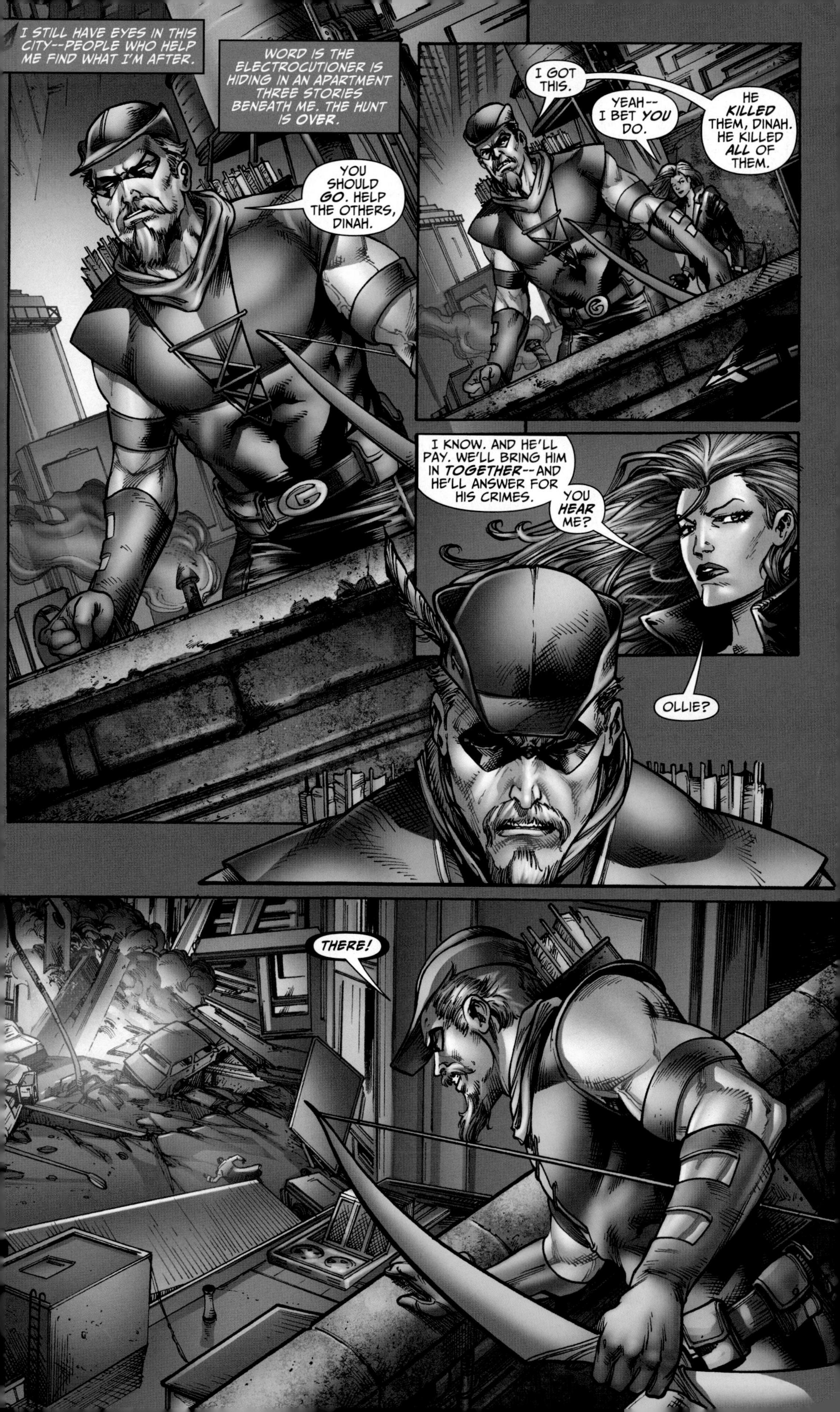

I STILL HAVE EYES IN THIS CITY--PEOPLE WHO HELP ME FIND WHAT I'M AFTER.
WORD IS THE ELECTROCUTIONER IS HIDING IN AN APARTMENT THREE STORIES BENEATH ME. THE HUNT IS OVER.
YOU SHOULD GO. HELP THE OTHERS, DINAH.
I GOT THIS.
YEAH-- I BET YOU DO.
HE KILLED THEM, DINAH. HE KILLED ALL OF THEM.
I KNOW. AND HE'LL PAY. WE'LL BRING HIM IN TOGETHER--AND HE'LL ANSWER FOR HIS CRIMES.
YOU HEAR ME?
OLLIE?
THERE!

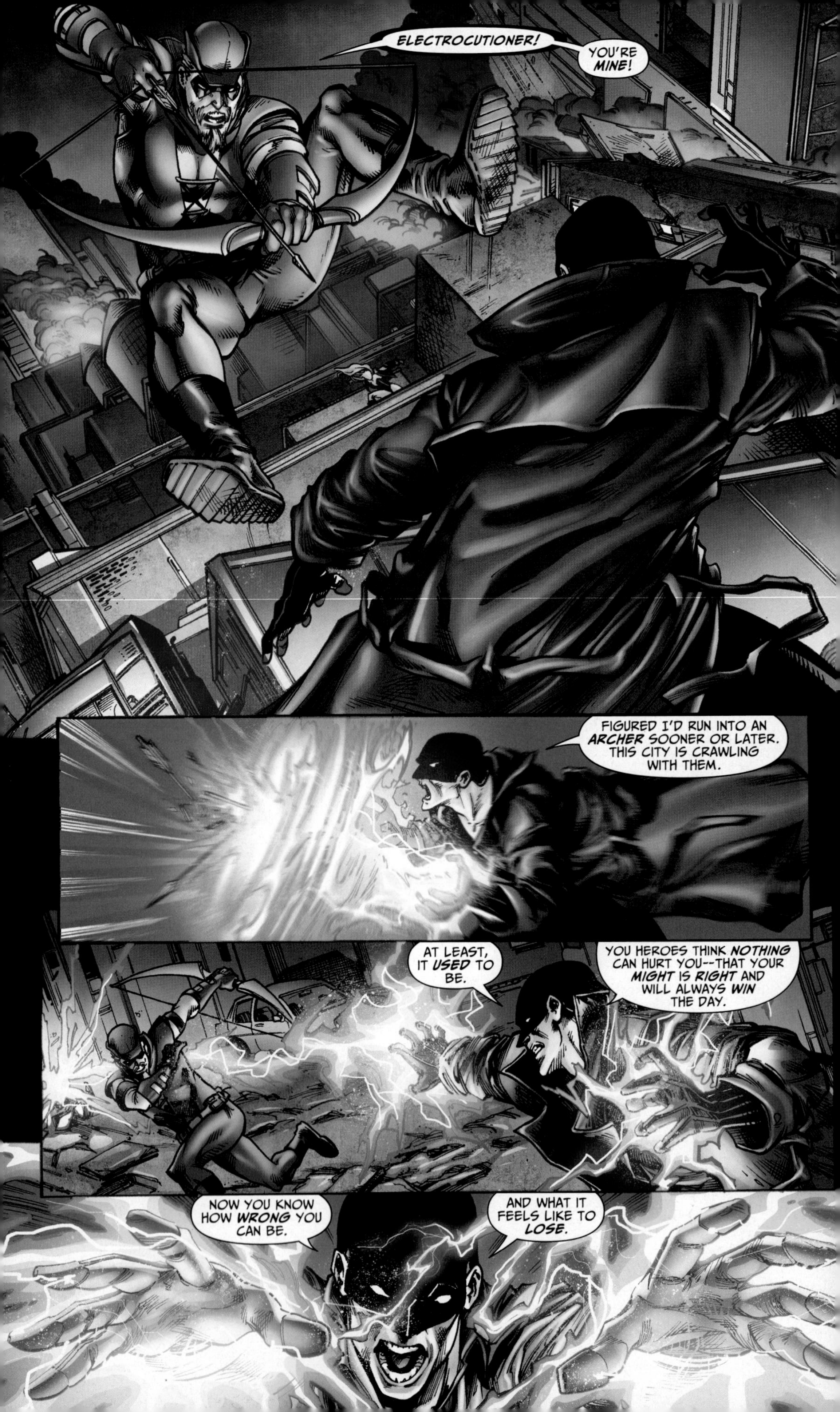
ELECTROCUTIONER!
YOU'RE MINE!
FIGURED I'D RUN INTO AN ARCHER SOONER OR LATER. THIS CITY IS CRAWLING WITH THEM.
AT LEAST, IT USED TO BE.
YOU HEROES THINK NOTHING CAN HURT YOU--THAT YOUR MIGHT IS RIGHT AND WILL ALWAYS WIN THE DAY.
NOW YOU KNOW HOW WRONG YOU CAN BE.
AND WHAT IT FEELS LIKE TO LOSE.

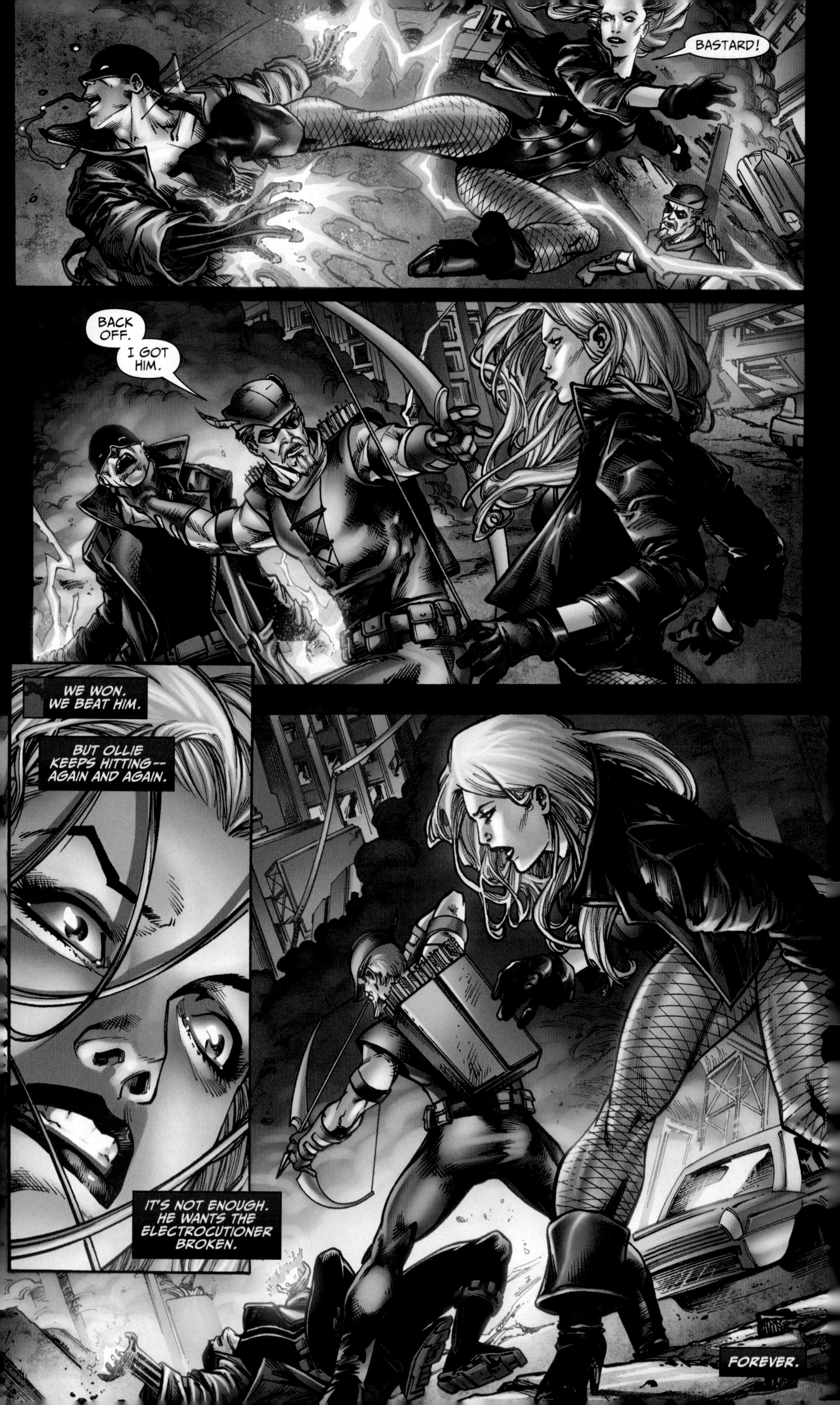
BASTARD!
BACK OFF.
I GOT HIM.
WE WON. WE BEAT HIM.
BUT OLLIE KEEPS HITTING-- AGAIN AND AGAIN.
IT'S NOT ENOUGH. HE WANTS THE ELECTROCUTIONER BROKEN.
FOREVER.

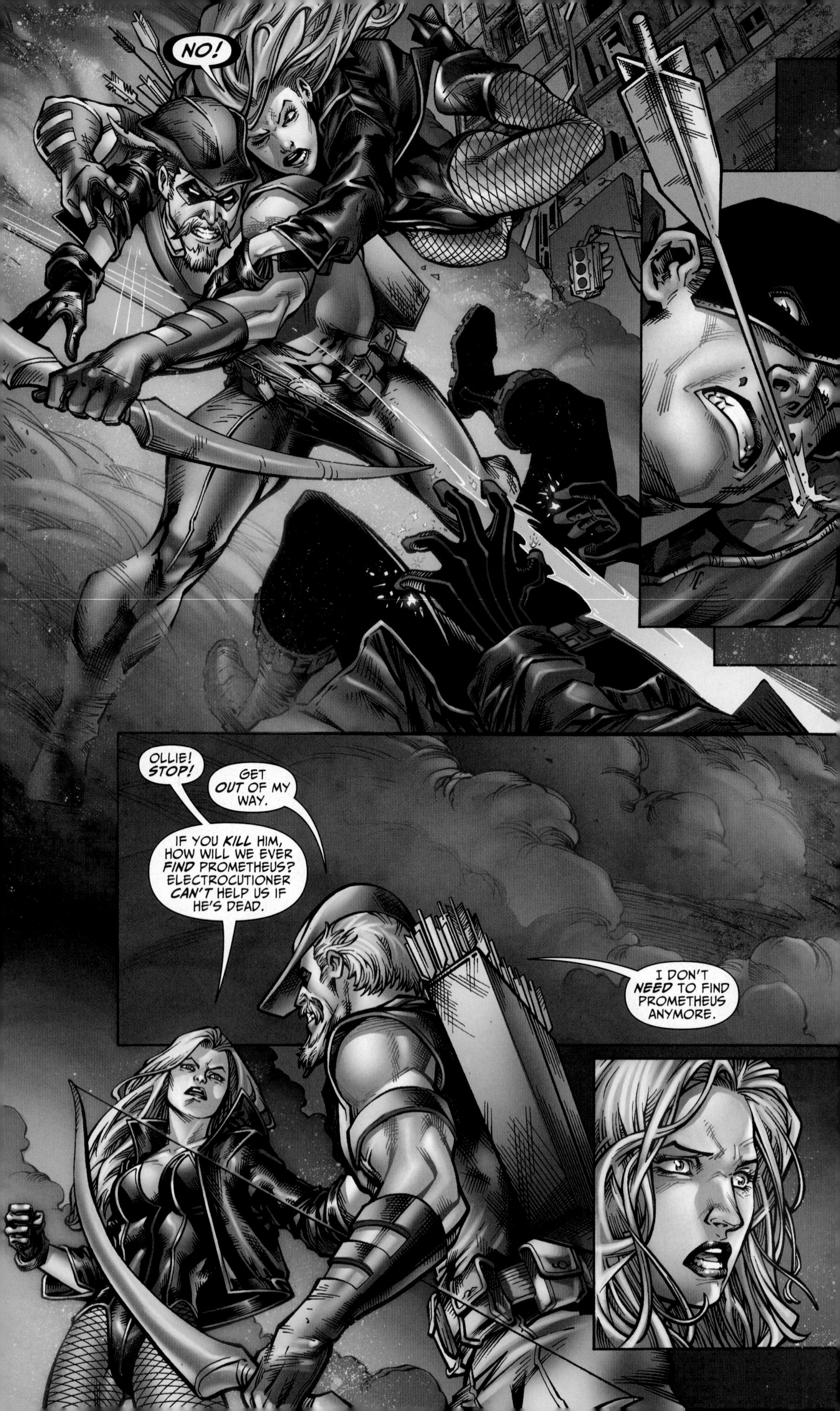
NO!
OLLIE! STOP!
GET OUT OF MY WAY.
IF YOU KILL HIM, HOW WILL WE EVER FIND PROMETHEUS? ELECTROCUTIONER CAN'T HELP US IF HE'S DEAD.
I DON'T NEED TO FIND PROMETHEUS ANYMORE.

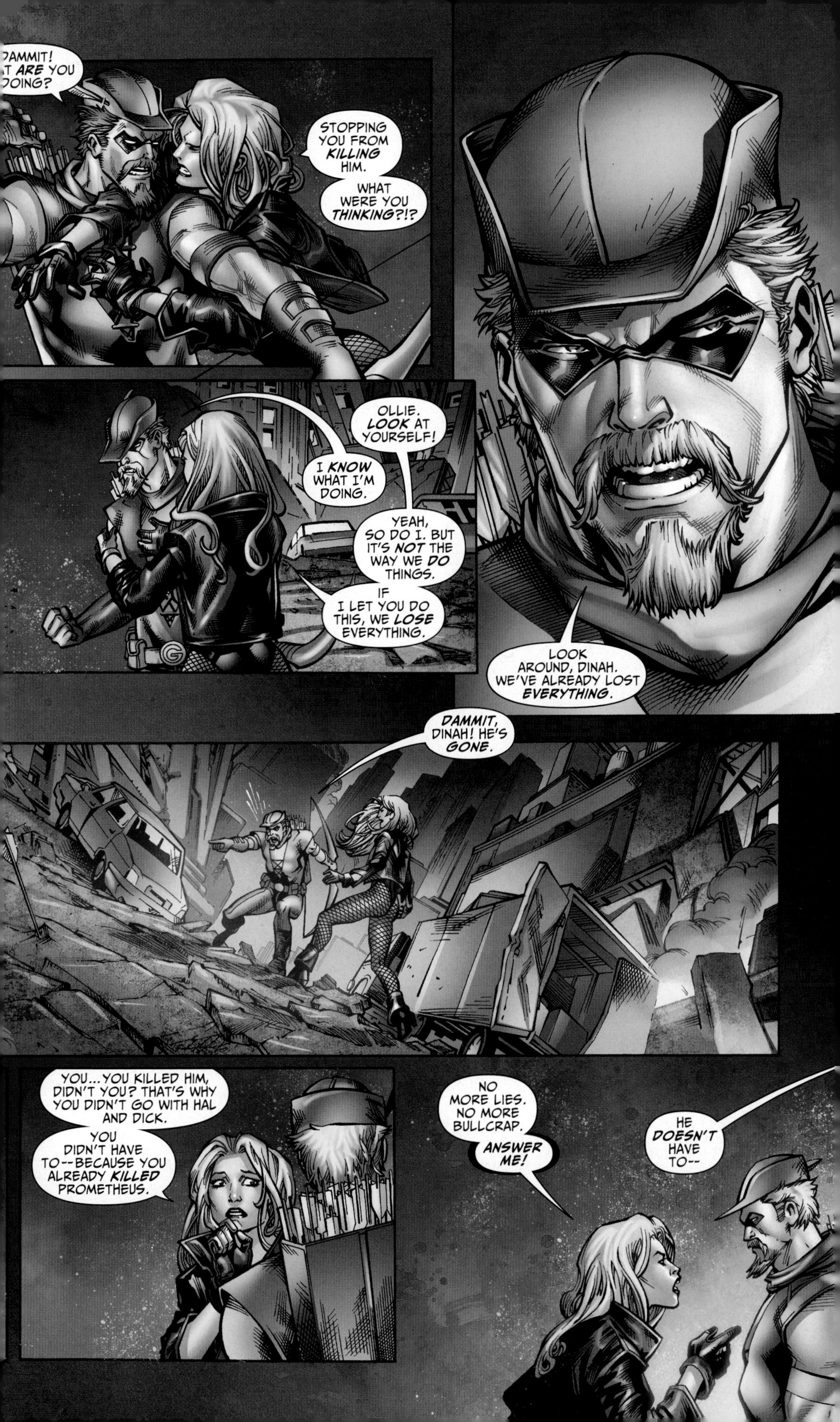
DAMMIT! AT ARE YOU DOING?
STOPPING YOU FROM KILLING HIM.
WHAT WERE YOU THINKING?!?
OLLIE. LOOK AT YOURSELF!
I KNOW WHAT I'M DOING.
YEAH, SO DO I. BUT IT'S NOT THE WAY WE DO THINGS.
IF I LET YOU DO THIS, WE LOSE EVERYTHING.
LOOK AROUND, DINAH. WE'VE ALREADY LOST EVERYTHING.
DAMMIT, DINAH! HE'S GONE.
YOU...YOU KILLED HIM, DIDN'T YOU? THAT'S WHY YOU DIDN'T GO WITH HAL AND DICK.
YOU DIDN'T HAVE TO--BECAUSE YOU ALREADY KILLED PROMETHEUS.
NO MORE LIES. NO MORE BULLCRAP.
ANSWER ME!
HE DOESN'T HAVE TO--

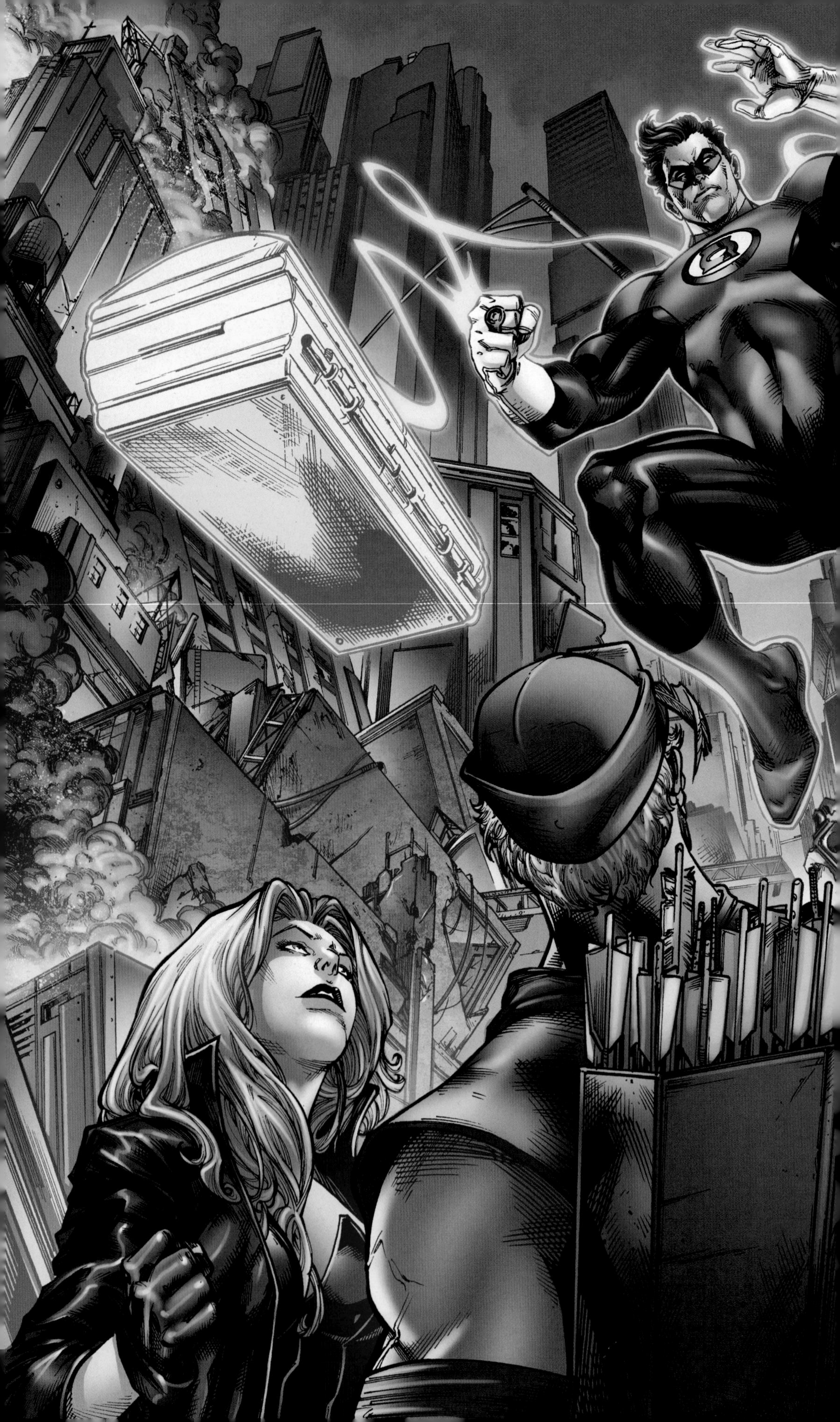

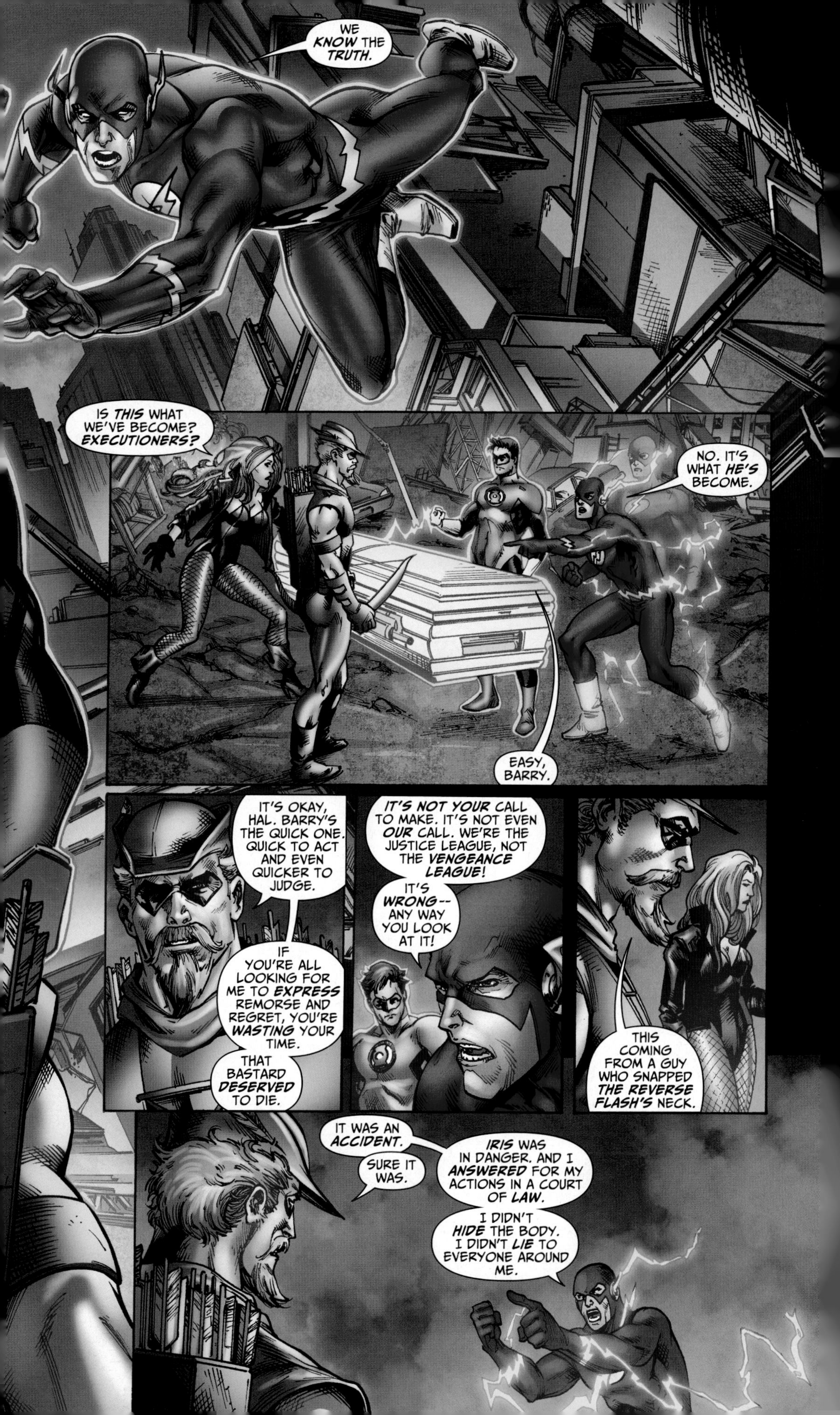
WE KNOW THE TRUTH.
IS THIS WHAT WE'VE BECOME? EXECUTIONERS?
NO. IT'S WHAT HE'S BECOME.
EASY, BARRY.
IT'S OKAY, HAL. BARRY'S THE QUICK ONE. QUICK TO ACT AND EVEN QUICKER TO JUDGE.
IF YOU'RE ALL LOOKING FOR ME TO EXPRESS REMORSE AND REGRET, YOU'RE WASTING YOUR TIME.
THAT BASTARD DESERVED TO DIE.
IT'S NOT YOUR CALL TO MAKE. IT'S NOT EVEN OUR CALL. WE'RE THE JUSTICE LEAGUE, NOT THE VENGEANCE LEAGUE!
IT'S WRONG-- ANY WAY YOU LOOK AT IT!
THIS COMING FROM A GUY WHO SNAPPED THE REVERSE FLASH'S NECK.
IT WAS AN ACCIDENT.
SURE IT WAS.
IRIS WAS IN DANGER. AND I ANSWERED FOR MY ACTIONS IN A COURT OF LAW.
I DIDN'T HIDE THE BODY. I DIDN'T LIE TO EVERYONE AROUND ME.

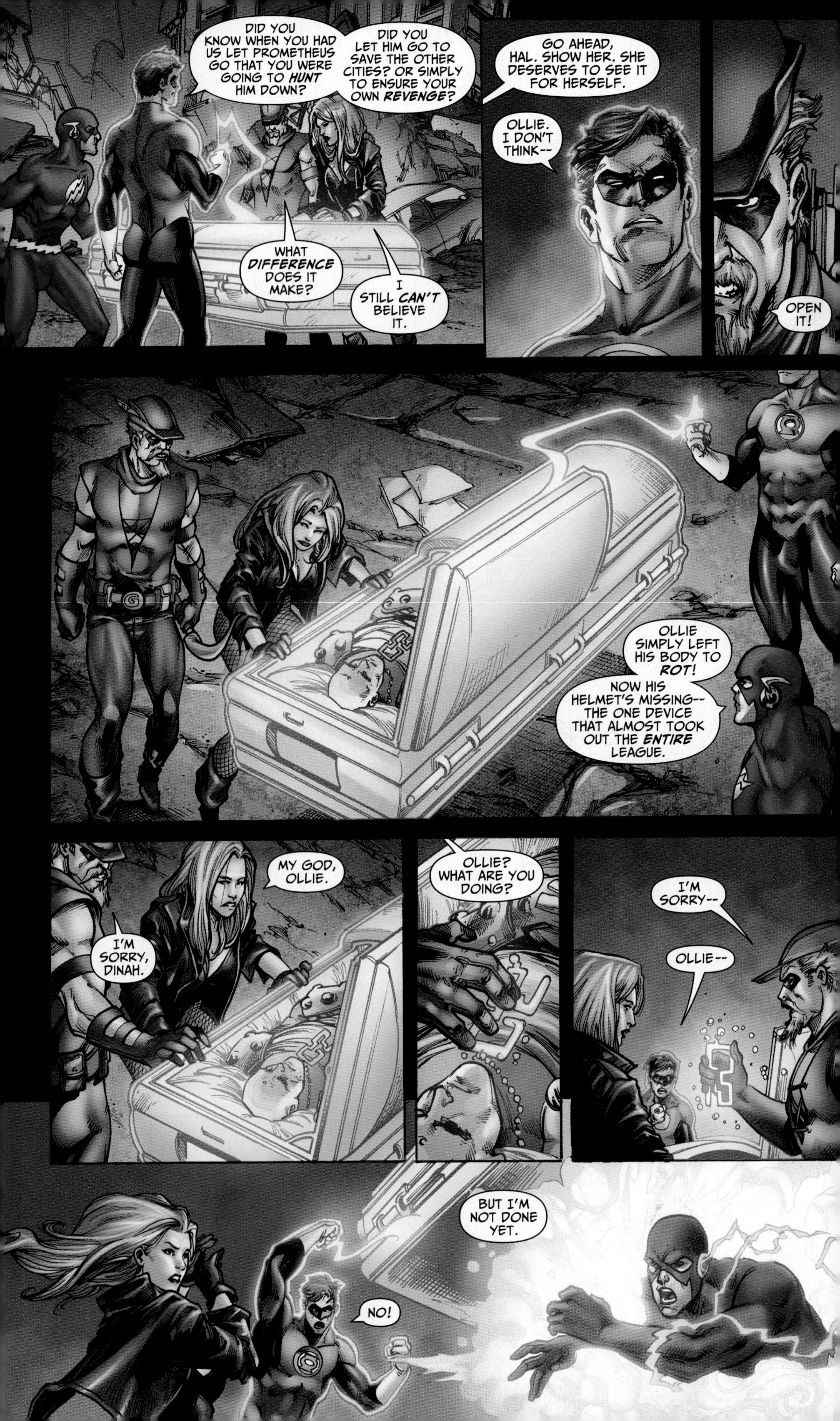
DID YOU KNOW WHEN YOU HAD US LET PROMETHEUS GO THAT YOU WERE GOING TO HUNT HIM DOWN?
DID YOU LET HIM GO TO SAVE THE OTHER CITIES? OR SIMPLY TO ENSURE YOUR OWN REVENGE?
WHAT DIFFERENCE DOES IT MAKE?
I STILL CAN'T BELIEVE IT.
GO AHEAD, HAL. SHOW HER. SHE DESERVES TO SEE IT FOR HERSELF.
OLLIE. I DON'T THINK--
OPEN IT!
OLLIE SIMPLY LEFT HIS BODY TO ROT!
NOW HIS HELMET'S MISSING-- THE ONE DEVICE THAT ALMOST TOOK OUT THE ENTIRE LEAGUE.
MY GOD, OLLIE.
I'M SORRY, DINAH.
OLLIE? WHAT ARE YOU DOING?
I'M SORRY--
OLLIE--
BUT I'M NOT DONE YET.
NO!

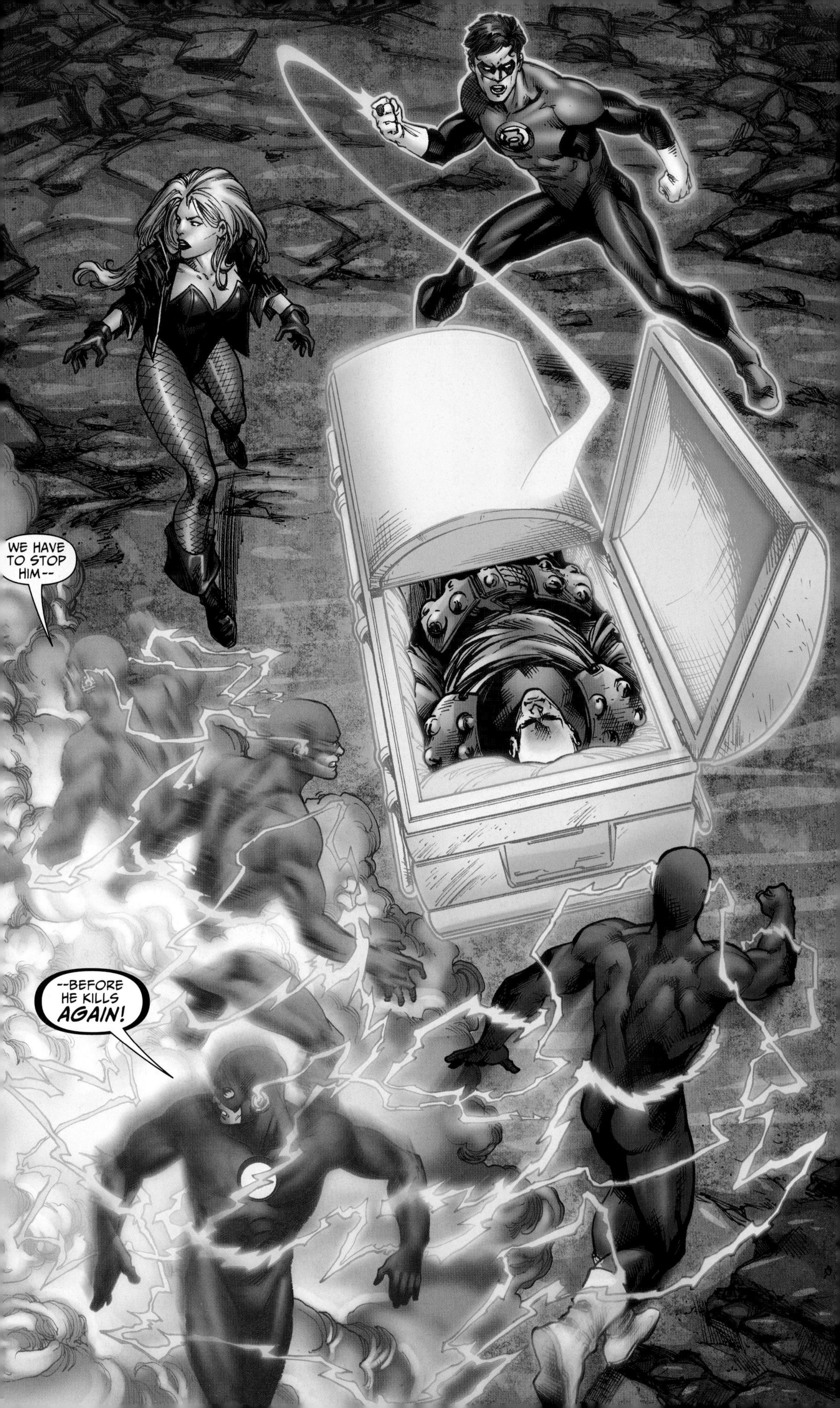
WE HAVE TO STOP HIM--
--BEFORE HE KILLS AGAIN!

March 10, 2010

The Star Gazette

75¢

Local Forecast: Sunny
High, 79, Low 61

HELPLESS HEROES

By: Evan Gibson

What do you call a hero who fails?

Human.

That's what we saw today standing before the devastation of Star City. The dust has yet to fully settle following the worst attack in our city's history, but Green Arrow brought out all the heroes to mourn with the citizens of Star City over the tremendous loss of life. So far, the estimated death toll from the bizarre seismic quake stands at just over 80,000, with more bodies being pulled from the wreckage every day.

To say that the destruction is widespread does not begin to describe what happened to Star City. Its heart has been literally ripped out, as the entire center of the city now lies in ruins. Almost five miles across at its widest point, not a building or structure still stands. All that remains is a landscape of broken concrete, bent steel, and shattered glass.

Multiple sources have confirmed reports that a massive electronic transformer array caused the destruction — a device put into place by a technologically savvy psychopath known only as Prometheus. What he wanted is still unknown, but it turns out that Star City wasn't the only target in his crosshairs. Similar devices were found in cities all over the country — Gotham, Metropolis, Central City, Coast City and about a half-dozen other locations. The Superhero commu-

nity managed to stop the other attacks, but in Star City they were too late.

Today at ground zero, I stood with the masses, watching the heroes — Superman, Batman, Wonder Woman, Green Lantern and countless others. Some I've heard of and others I've never seen before. Side-by-side they stood silently . Perhaps that was what made the scene so unnerving — their stillness. Like Green Arrow, they all appeared humbled before the horrific sight. We live our lives believing in our

heroes — believing in their ability to keep us safe from the threats all around us. But today, all I saw was the abject helplessness in their eyes. What does that say when the greatest gathering of superheroes fills one with a sense of woe instead of awe? Today served as a reminder that superheroes cannot always save the day.

Prometheus is still at large, but the tone of the speeches wasn't about retribution. It was about remembrance. For days, citizens have been congregating at the south face of the disaster zone — lighting candles, posting

pictures, and tying ribbons in memory of those who died. It was as if Star City was forming its own wailing wall — built on the blood and tears of its people. Today was the first official on-site address since the attack, and while many public officials spoke, Green Arrow was the one people seemed most eager to hear.

Words failed most of the people I tried to interview about the attack. They were numb and morose as they spoke of lost loved ones, shattered lives, and hopeless futures. But the sight of the Emerald Archer brought emotions out of even the most re-

served soul. Even before the longtime resident of Star City stepped onto the platform, opinions in the crowd were mixed regarding Green Arrow. Some consider him a bastion of justice in our troubled city, while others see him as an outlaw — causing more trouble than he's worth.

"He does what nobody else in this city can," said Fran Berkshire — a sixty-year resident from Huntington View. "I've lived in Star City my entire life. I know what it used to be like before Green Arrow arrived, and I know what it's like now. I'm not saying he's the nicest

fellow I ever met, but I can sit on my front porch at night and it's all because of him."

Roger Benson sees it differently. "He's a menace, pure and simple. Look at this city. Everything was fine before he came to town. Sure we had our share of crime, but what city doesn't? At least it was the kind of crime the police could handle." Roger is among a section of the populace that casts blame on the Emerald Archer for the current devastation. "Thanks to him, we attracted a whole collection of masked villains and assassins. Let's face it, trouble follows that guy like a magnet – as long as Green Arrow is in Star City, this kind of thing is going to happen over and over again. How long before we say enough is enough?"

Green Arrow's brash persona and abrasive personality are almost as legendary in Star City as is his skill with a bow and arrow, but none of that was on display when he stepped up to the microphone. "Like you, Star City is my home," he said. "We have all lost during this terrible attack. Lost friends. Lost loved ones. Lost family. Our grief may tear at our hearts, but it is also what gives us strength – and brings us together. I was not able to stop this terrible tragedy from occurring, but I promise you all today – Prometheus will never harm any of you ever again."

Strong words for sure, but such declarations have been made in the past —many times as the righteous have vowed to ensure the safety of the innocent.

Do I believe him? I do. Right now, I have to believe him. For in the face of such evil, the best one can hope for is faith. That is what I will choose, because the alternative is too horrifying.

Words: J.T. Krul ♦ Art: Mike Mayhew ♦ Color: Andy Troy ♦ Design: Steve Wands

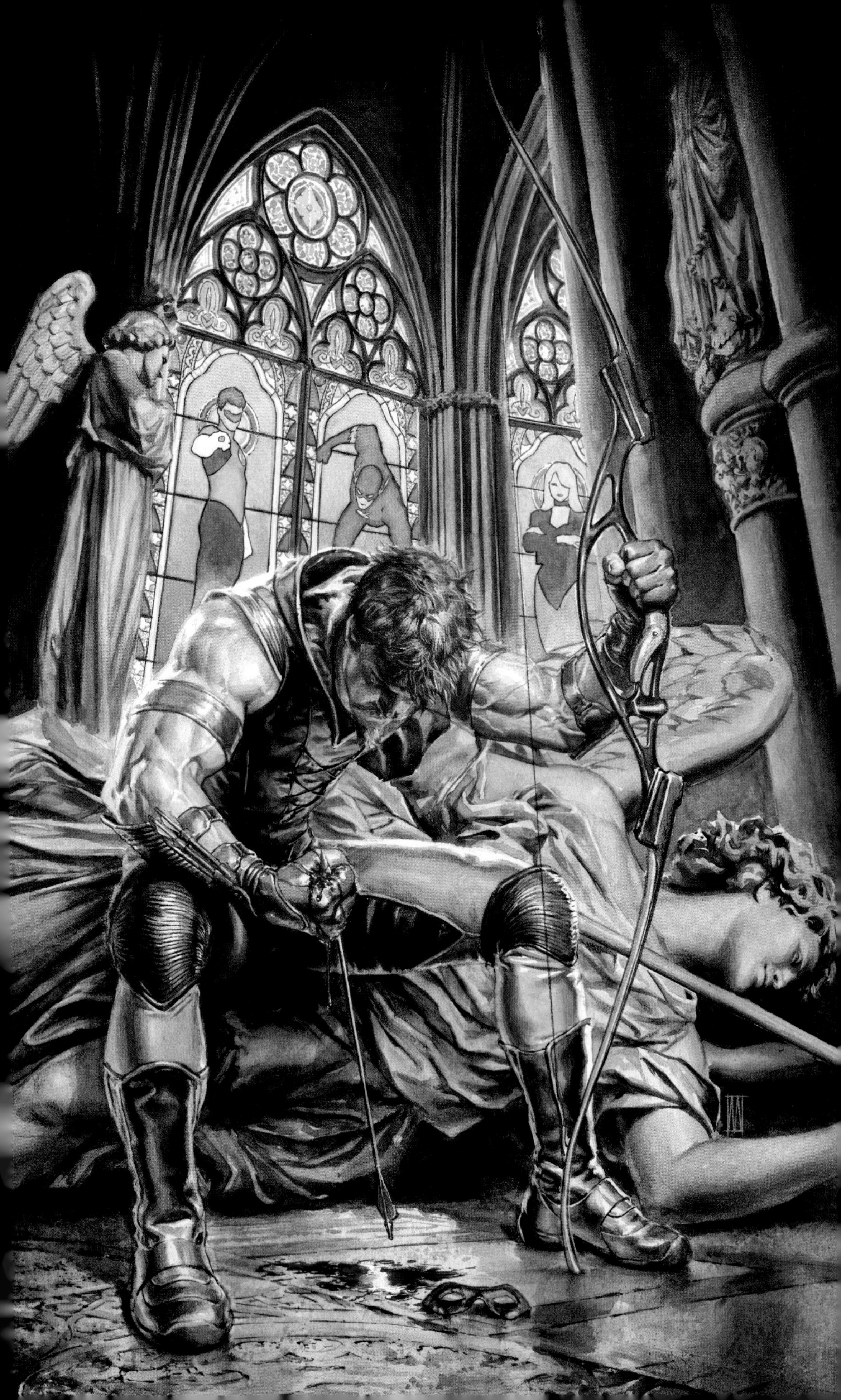

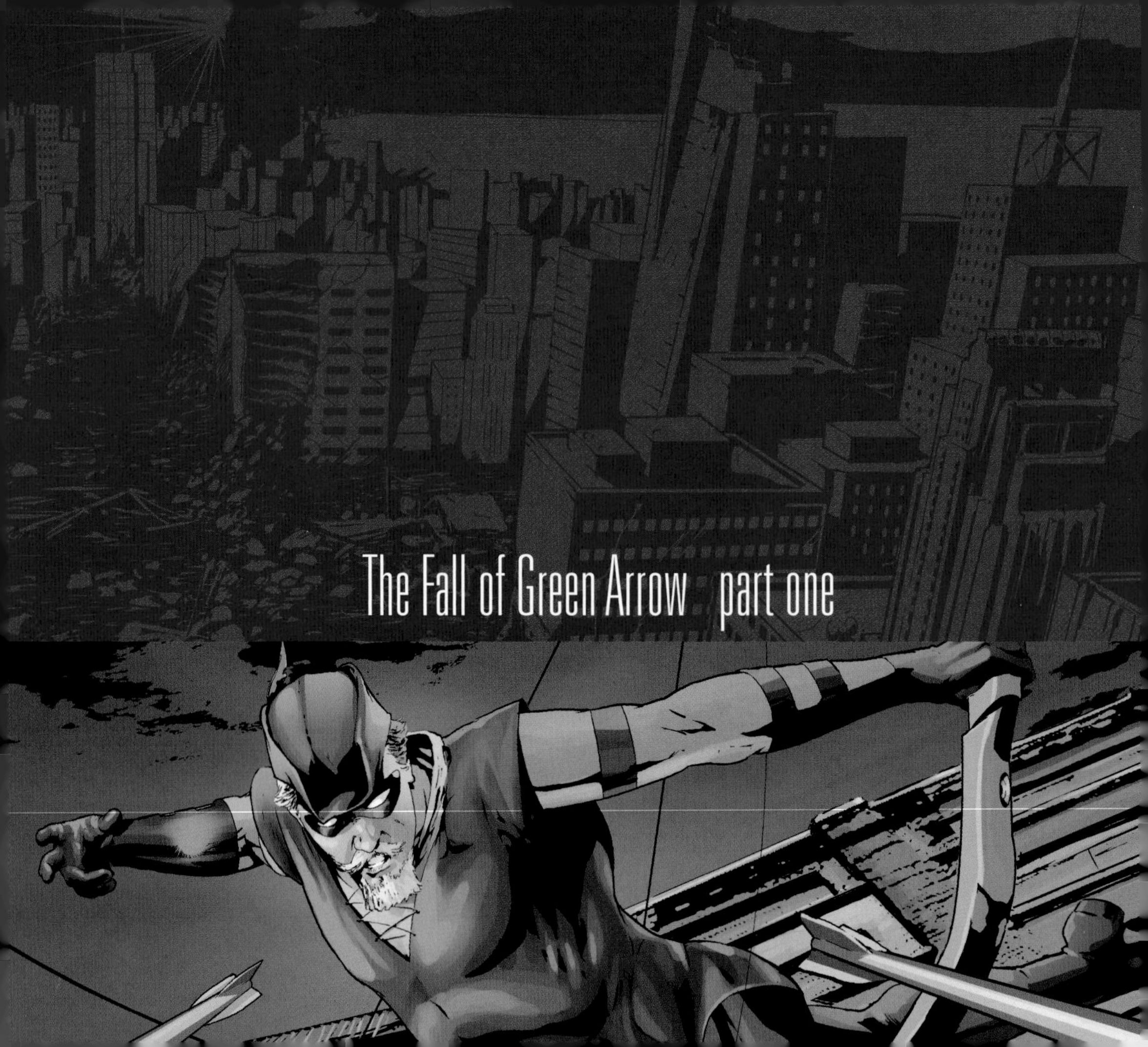
The Fall of Green Arrow part one

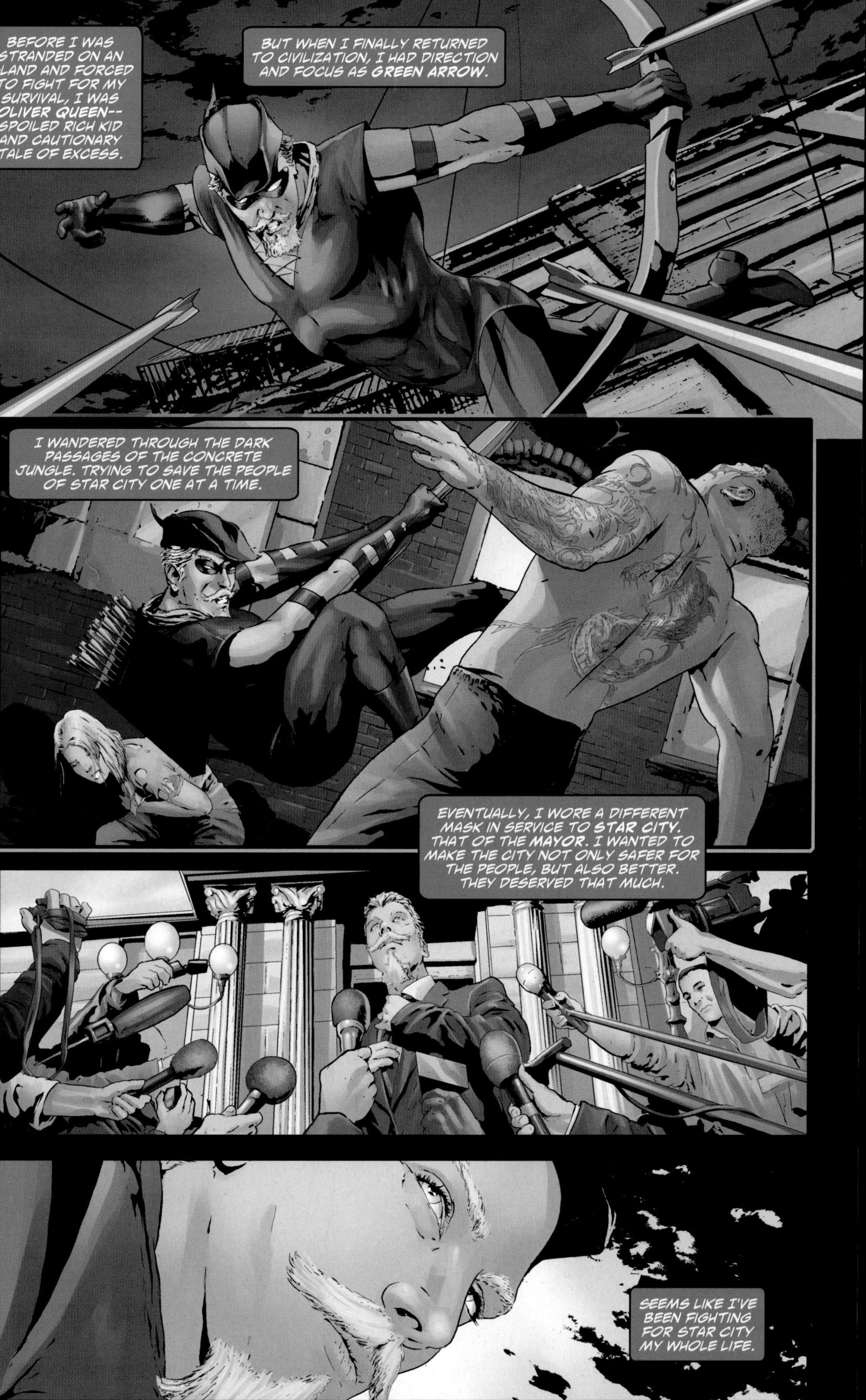
BEFORE I WAS STRANDED ON AN ISLAND AND FORCED TO FIGHT FOR MY SURVIVAL, I WAS OLIVER QUEEN-- SPOILED RICH KID AND CAUTIONARY TALE OF EXCESS.
BUT WHEN I FINALLY RETURNED TO CIVILIZATION, I HAD DIRECTION AND FOCUS AS GREEN ARROW.
I WANDERED THROUGH THE DARK PASSAGES OF THE CONCRETE JUNGLE. TRYING TO SAVE THE PEOPLE OF STAR CITY ONE AT A TIME.
EVENTUALLY, I WORE A DIFFERENT MASK IN SERVICE TO STAR CITY. THAT OF THE MAYOR. I WANTED TO MAKE THE CITY NOT ONLY SAFER FOR THE PEOPLE, BUT ALSO BETTER. THEY DESERVED THAT MUCH.
SEEMS LIKE I'VE BEEN FIGHTING FOR STAR CITY MY WHOLE LIFE.

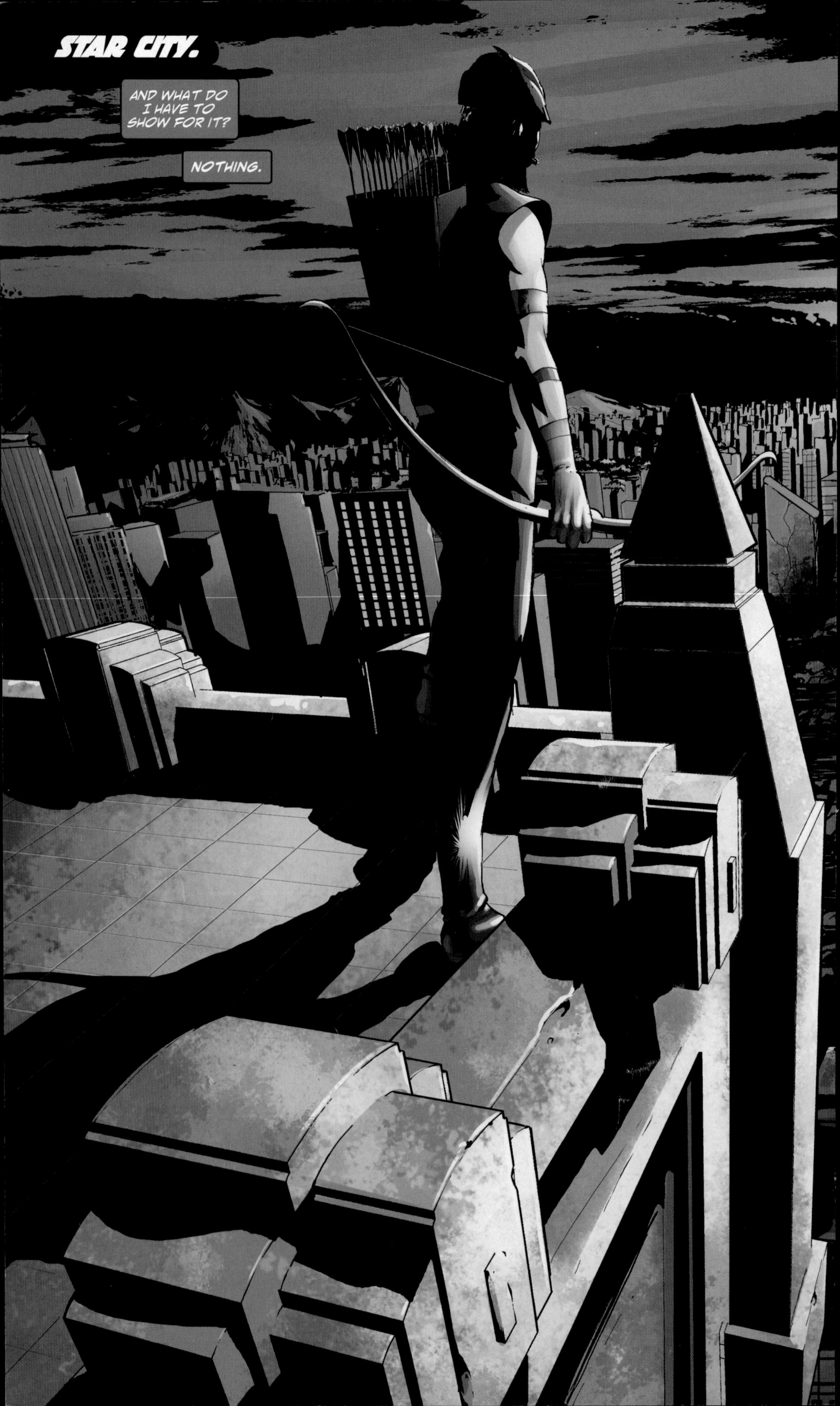
STAR CITY.
AND WHAT DO I HAVE TO SHOW FOR IT?
NOTHING.

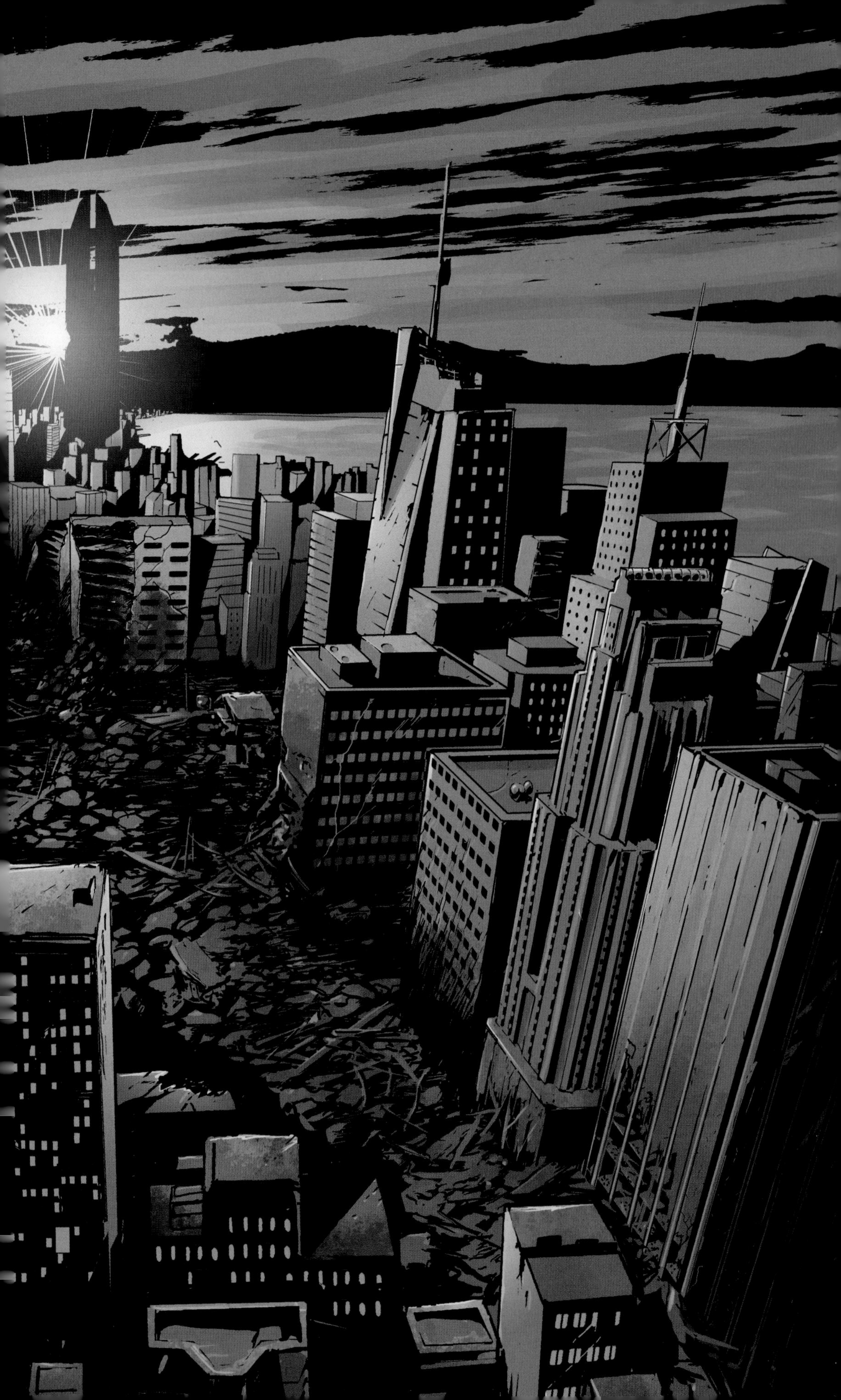

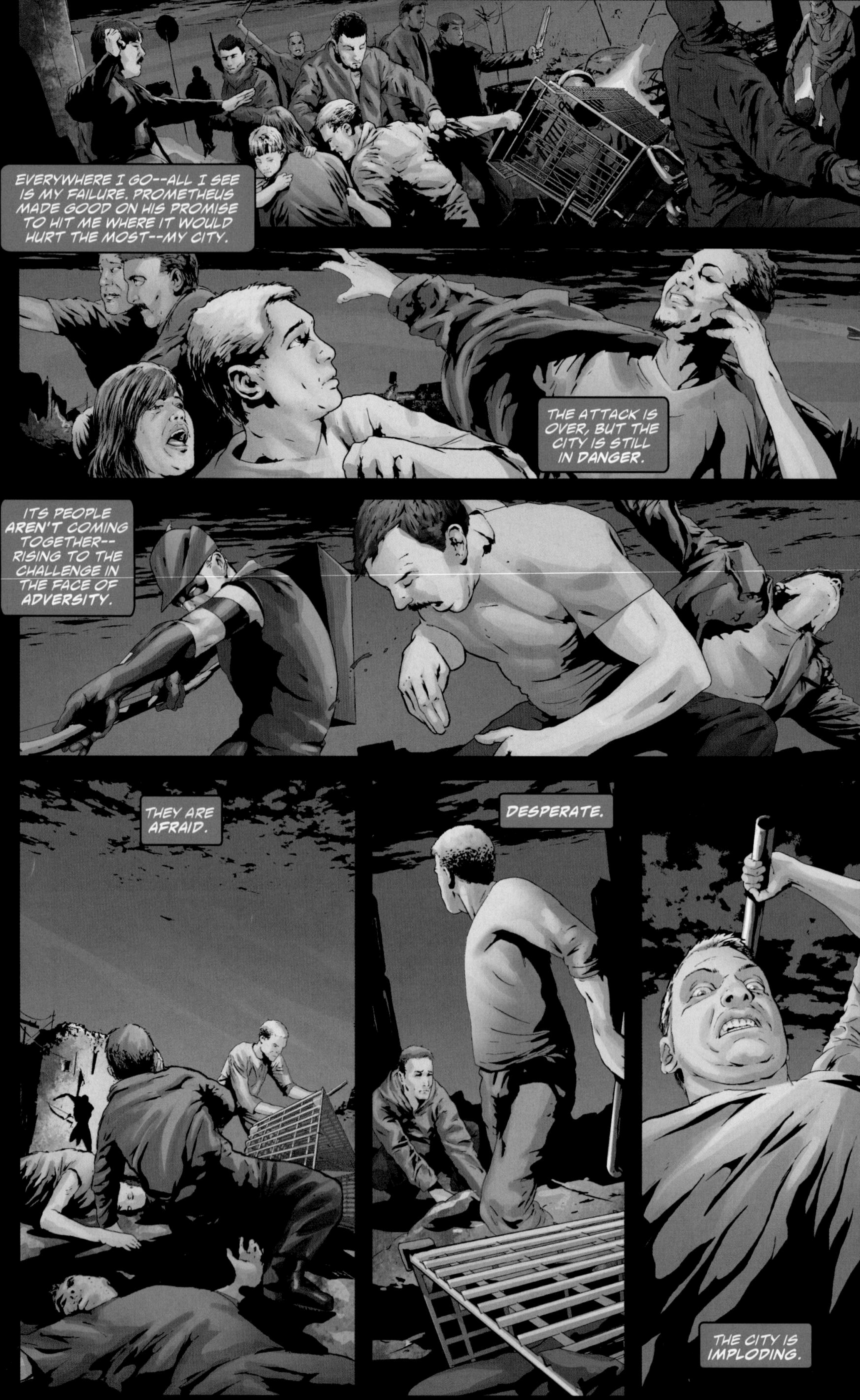
EVERYWHERE I GO--ALL I SEE IS MY FAILURE. PROMETHEUS MADE GOOD ON HIS PROMISE TO HIT ME WHERE IT WOULD HURT THE MOST--MY CITY.
THE ATTACK IS OVER, BUT THE CITY IS STILL IN DANGER.
ITS PEOPLE AREN'T COMING TOGETHER--RISING TO THE CHALLENGE IN THE FACE OF ADVERSITY.
THEY ARE AFRAID.
DESPERATE.
THE CITY IS IMPLODING.

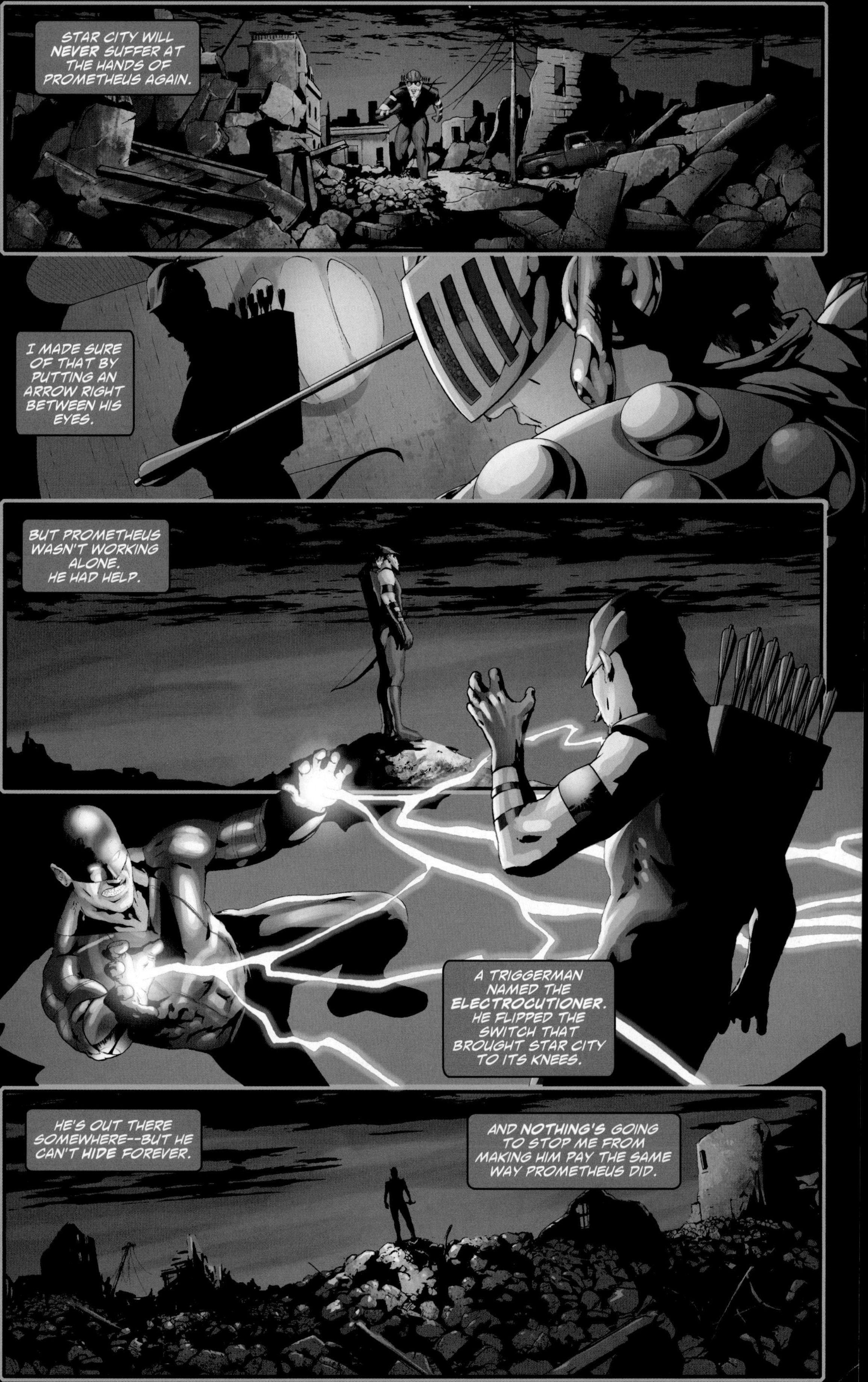
STAR CITY WILL NEVER SUFFER AT THE HANDS OF PROMETHEUS AGAIN.
I MADE SURE OF THAT BY PUTTING AN ARROW RIGHT BETWEEN HIS EYES.
BUT PROMETHEUS WASN'T WORKING ALONE. HE HAD HELP.
A TRIGGERMAN NAMED THE ELECTROCUTIONER. HE FLIPPED THE SWITCH THAT BROUGHT STAR CITY TO ITS KNEES.
HE'S OUT THERE SOMEWHERE--BUT HE CAN'T HIDE FOREVER.
AND NOTHING'S GOING TO STOP ME FROM MAKING HIM PAY THE SAME WAY PROMETHEUS DID.

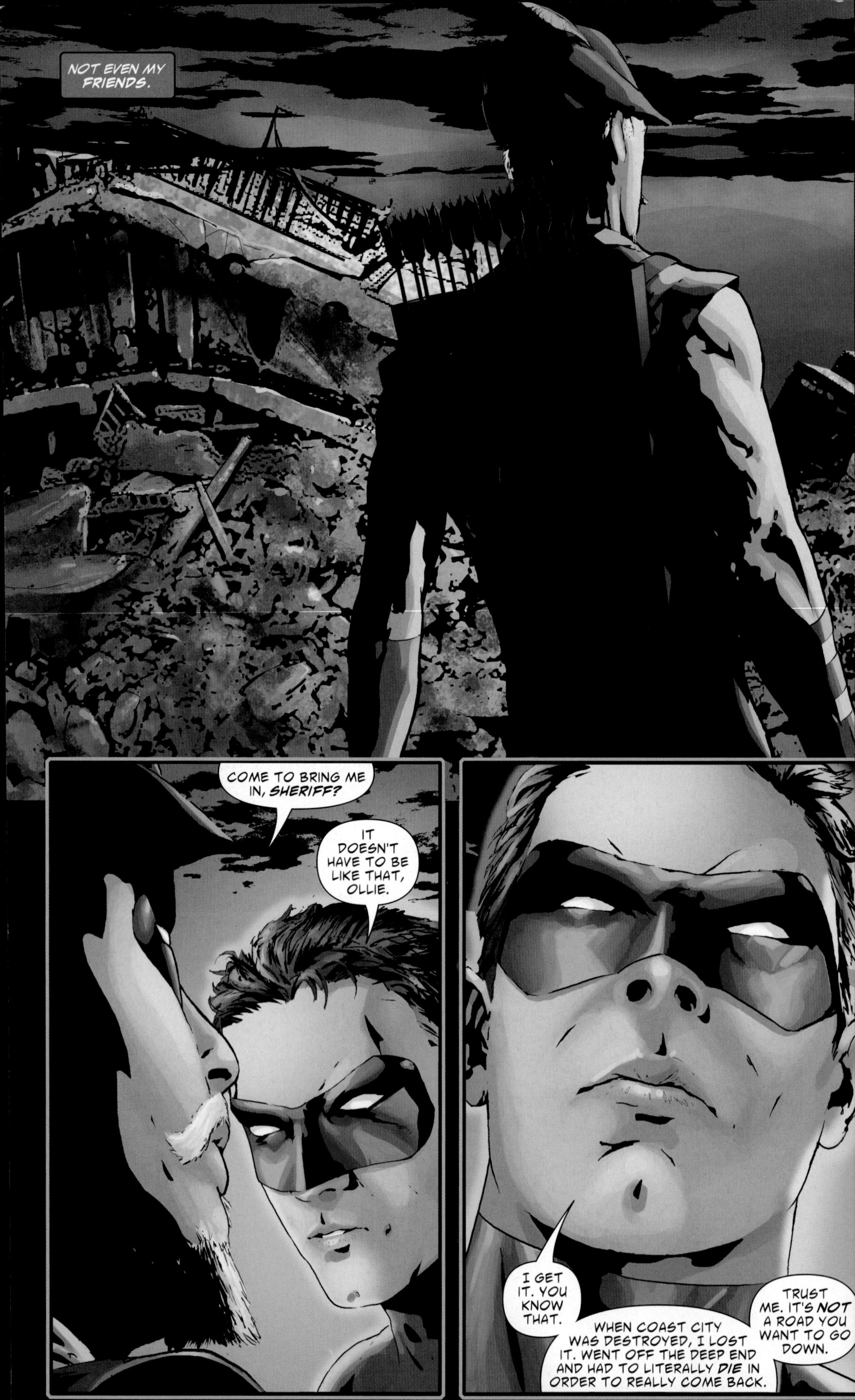
NOT EVEN MY FRIENDS.
COME TO BRING ME IN, SHERIFF?
IT DOESN'T HAVE TO BE LIKE THAT, OLLIE.
I GET IT. YOU KNOW THAT.
WHEN COAST CITY WAS DESTROYED, I LOST IT. WENT OFF THE DEEP END AND HAD TO LITERALLY DIE IN ORDER TO REALLY COME BACK.
TRUST ME. IT'S NOT A ROAD YOU WANT TO GO DOWN.

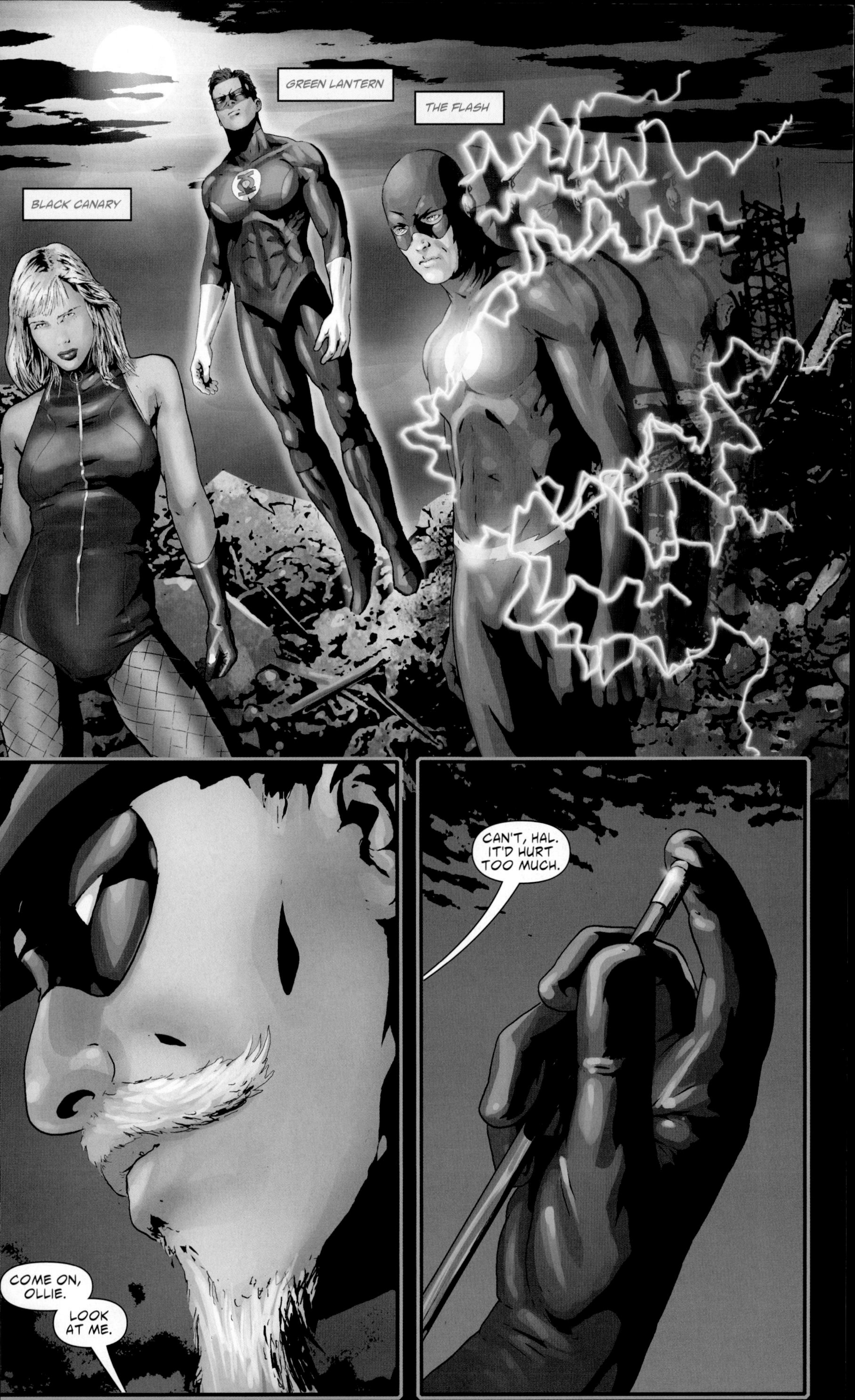
GREEN LANTERN
THE FLASH
BLACK CANARY
COME ON, OLLIE.
LOOK AT ME.
CAN'T, HAL. IT'D HURT TOO MUCH.

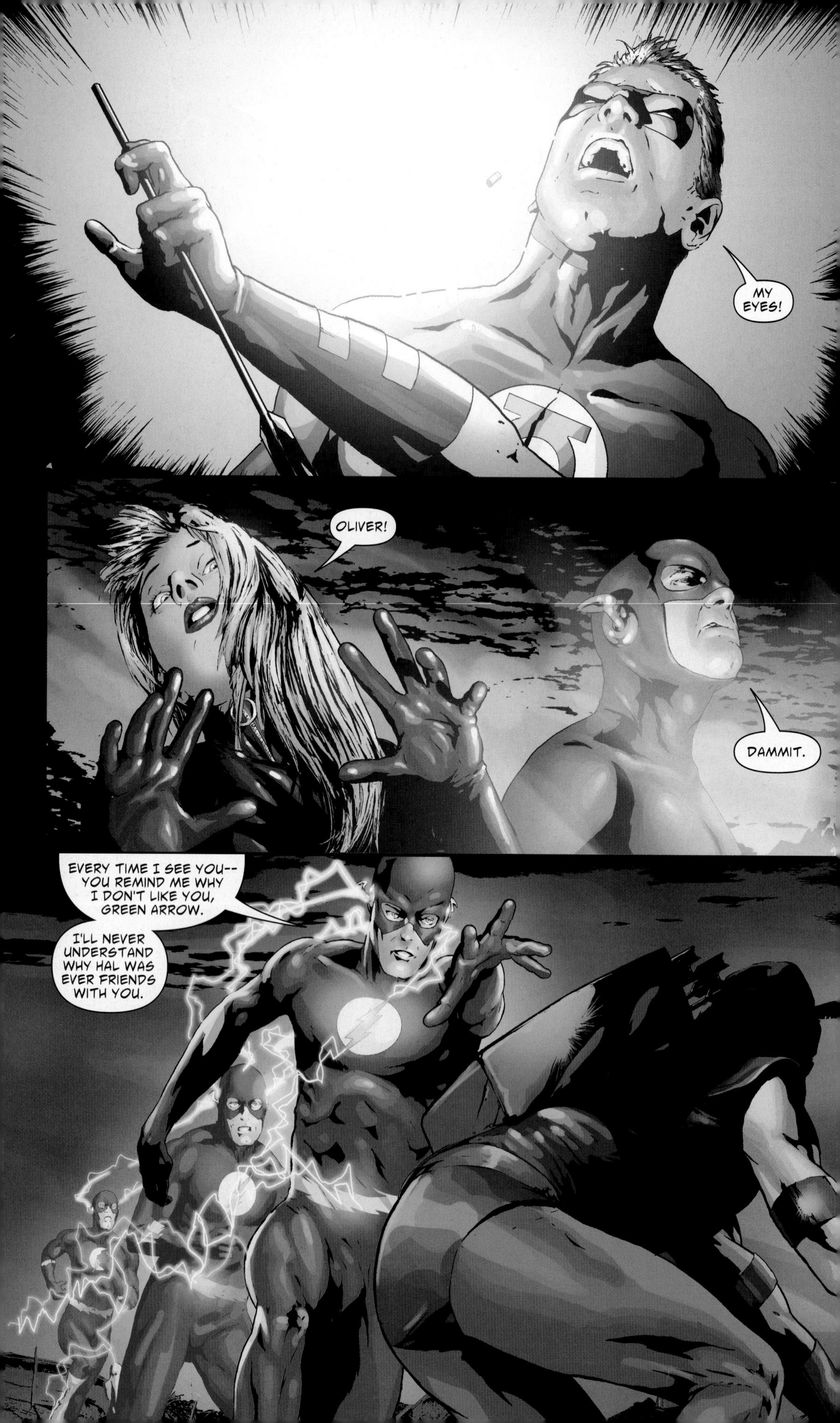
MY EYES!
OLIVER!
DAMMIT.
EVERY TIME I SEE YOU-- YOU REMIND ME WHY I DON'T LIKE YOU, GREEN ARROW.
I'LL NEVER UNDERSTAND WHY HAL WAS EVER FRIENDS WITH YOU.

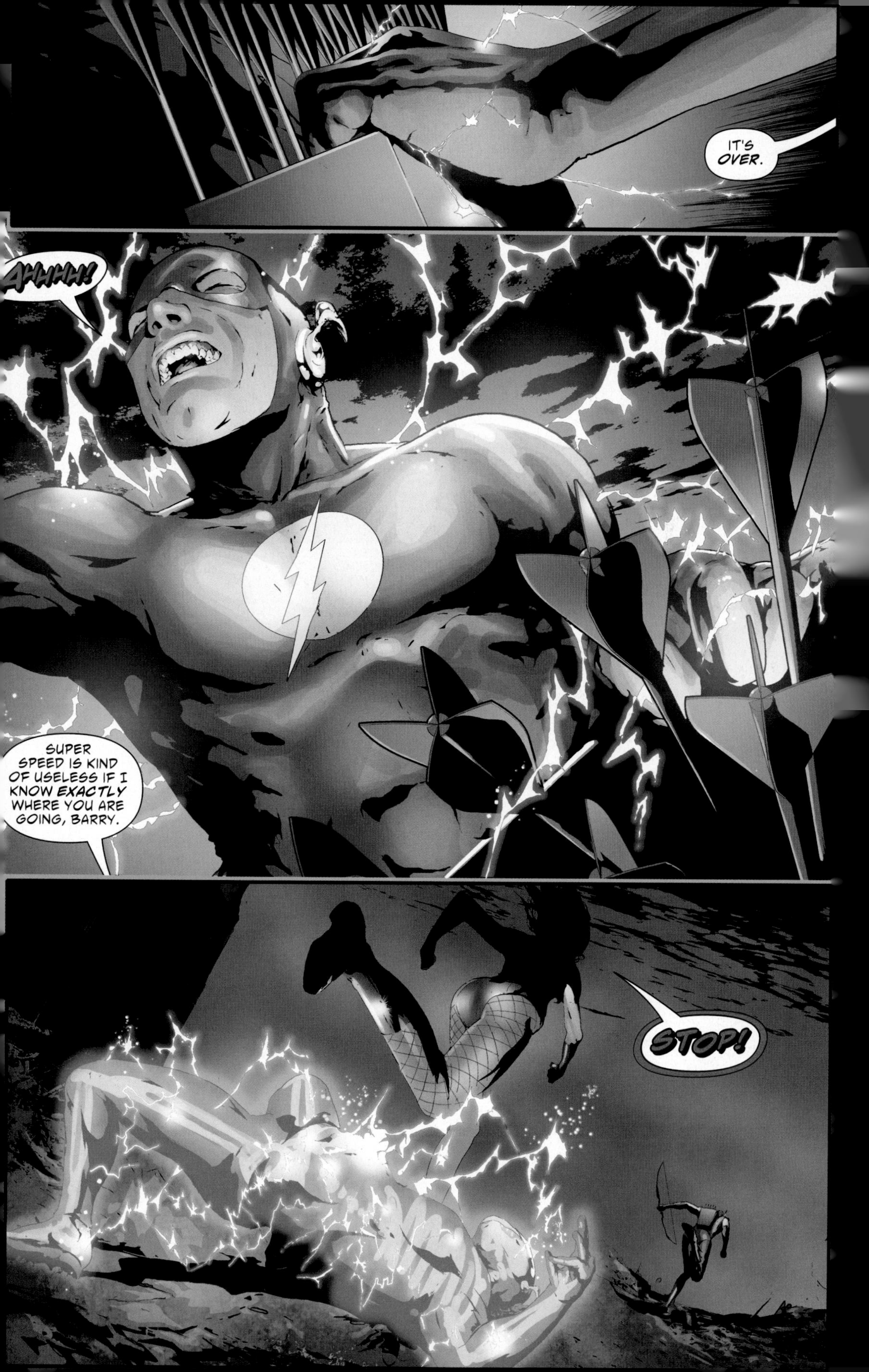
IT'S OVER.
AHHHH!
SUPER SPEED IS KIND OF USELESS IF I KNOW EXACTLY WHERE YOU ARE GOING, BARRY.
STOP!

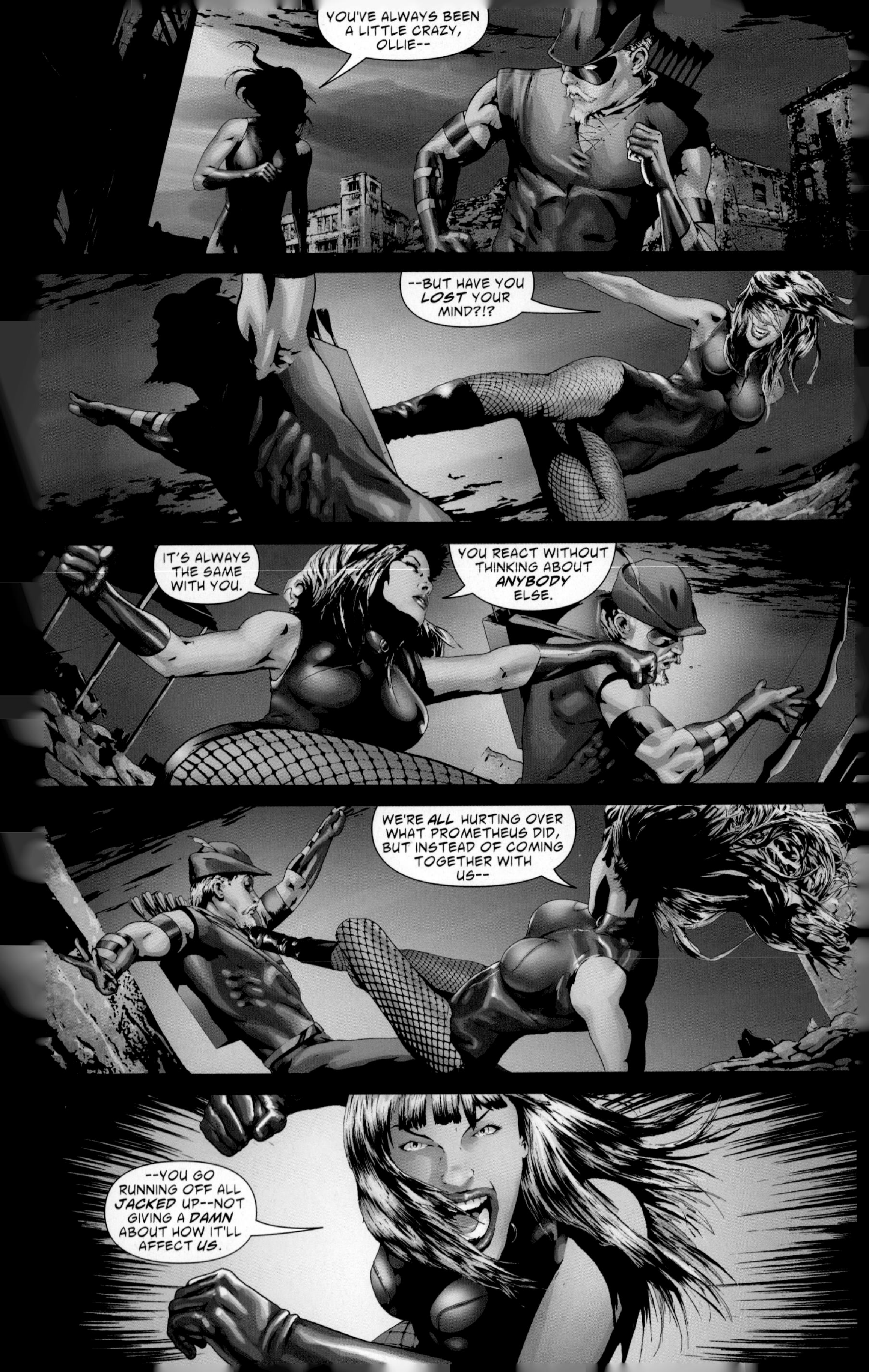
YOU'VE ALWAYS BEEN A LITTLE CRAZY, OLLIE--
--BUT HAVE YOU LOST YOUR MIND?!?
IT'S ALWAYS THE SAME WITH YOU.
YOU REACT WITHOUT THINKING ABOUT ANYBODY ELSE.
WE'RE ALL HURTING OVER WHAT PROMETHEUS DID, BUT INSTEAD OF COMING TOGETHER WITH US--
--YOU GO RUNNING OFF ALL JACKED UP--NOT GIVING A DAMN ABOUT HOW IT'LL AFFECT US.

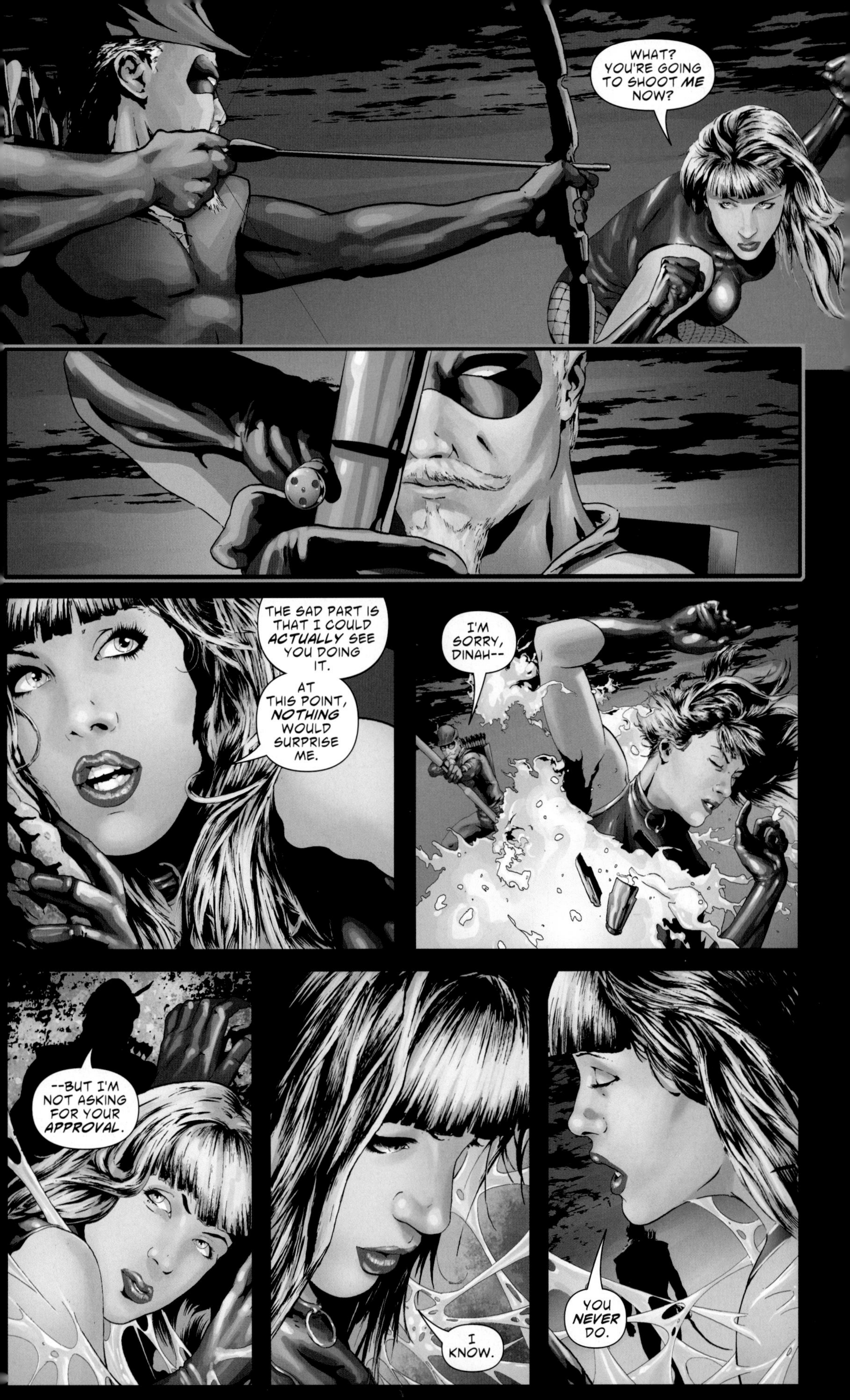
WHAT? YOU'RE GOING TO SHOOT *ME* NOW?
THE SAD PART IS THAT I COULD *ACTUALLY* SEE YOU DOING IT.
AT THIS POINT, *NOTHING* WOULD SURPRISE ME.
I'M SORRY, DINAH--
--BUT I'M NOT ASKING FOR YOUR *APPROVAL*.
I KNOW.
YOU *NEVER* DO.

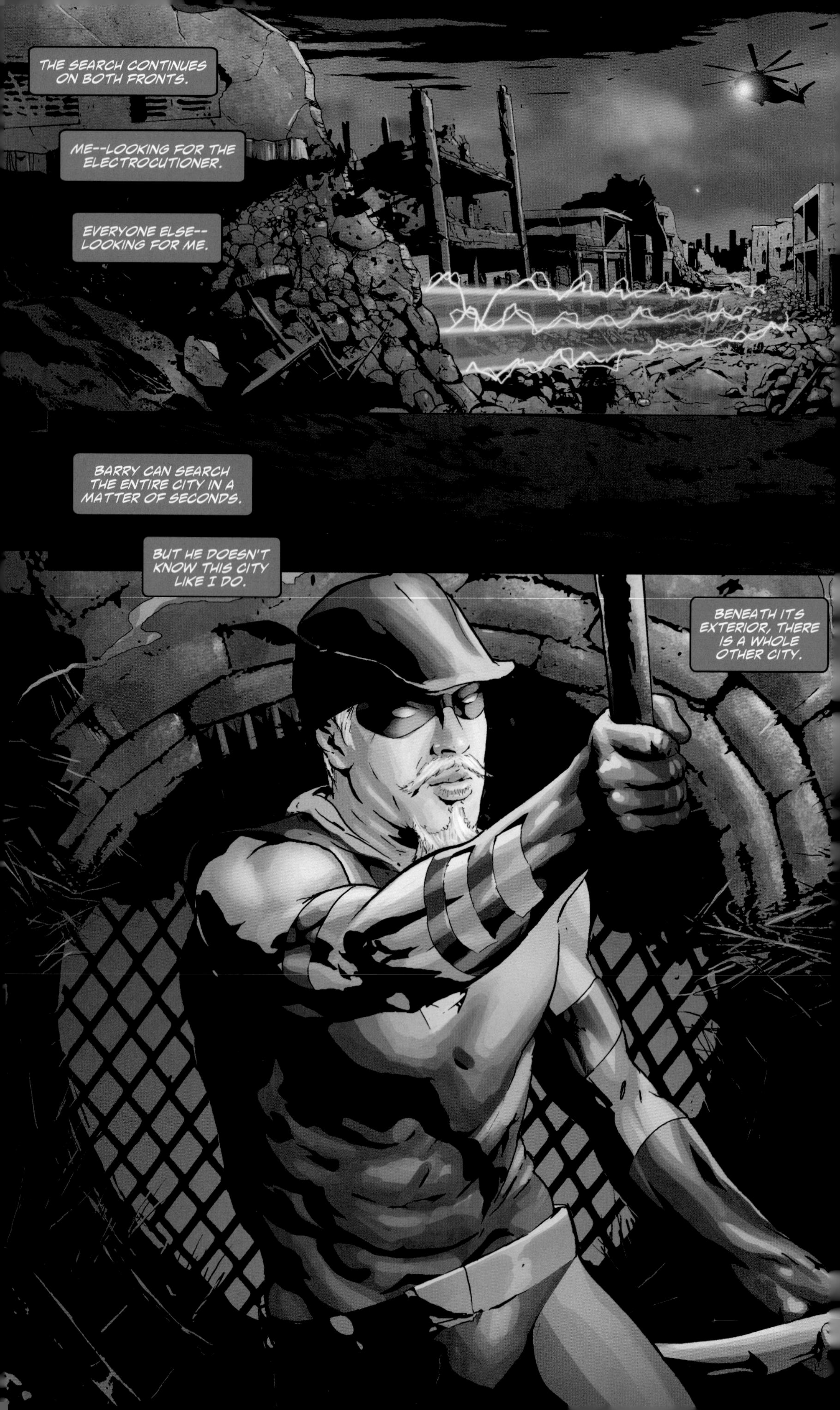
THE SEARCH CONTINUES ON BOTH FRONTS.
ME--LOOKING FOR THE ELECTROCUTIONER.
EVERYONE ELSE--LOOKING FOR ME.
BARRY CAN SEARCH THE ENTIRE CITY IN A MATTER OF SECONDS.
BUT HE DOESN'T KNOW THIS CITY LIKE I DO.
BENEATH ITS EXTERIOR, THERE IS A WHOLE OTHER CITY.

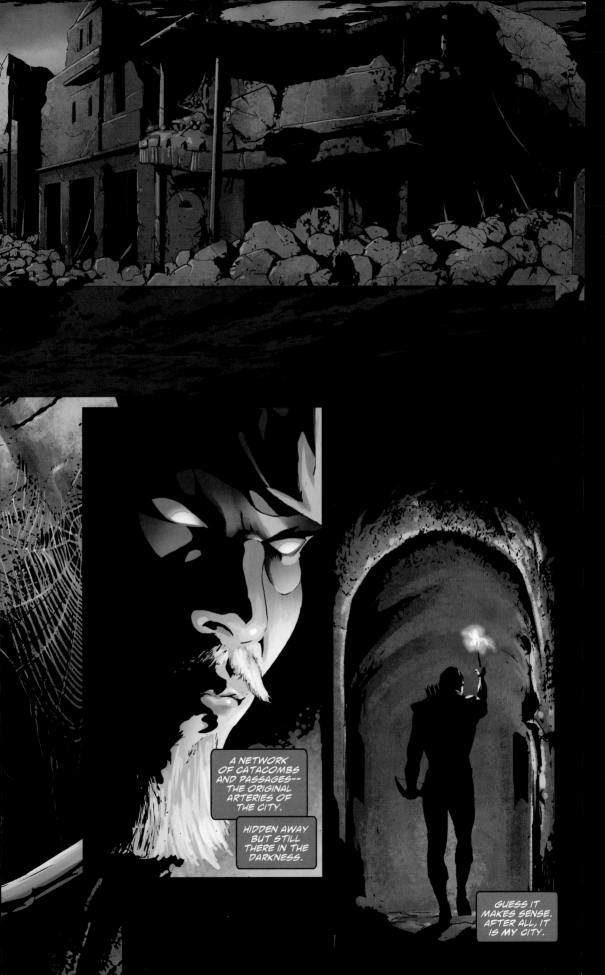

A NETWORK OF CATACOMBS AND PASSAGES-- THE ORIGINAL ARTERIES OF THE CITY.

HIDDEN AWAY BUT STILL THERE IN THE DARKNESS.

GUESS IT MAKES SENSE. AFTER ALL, IT IS MY CITY.

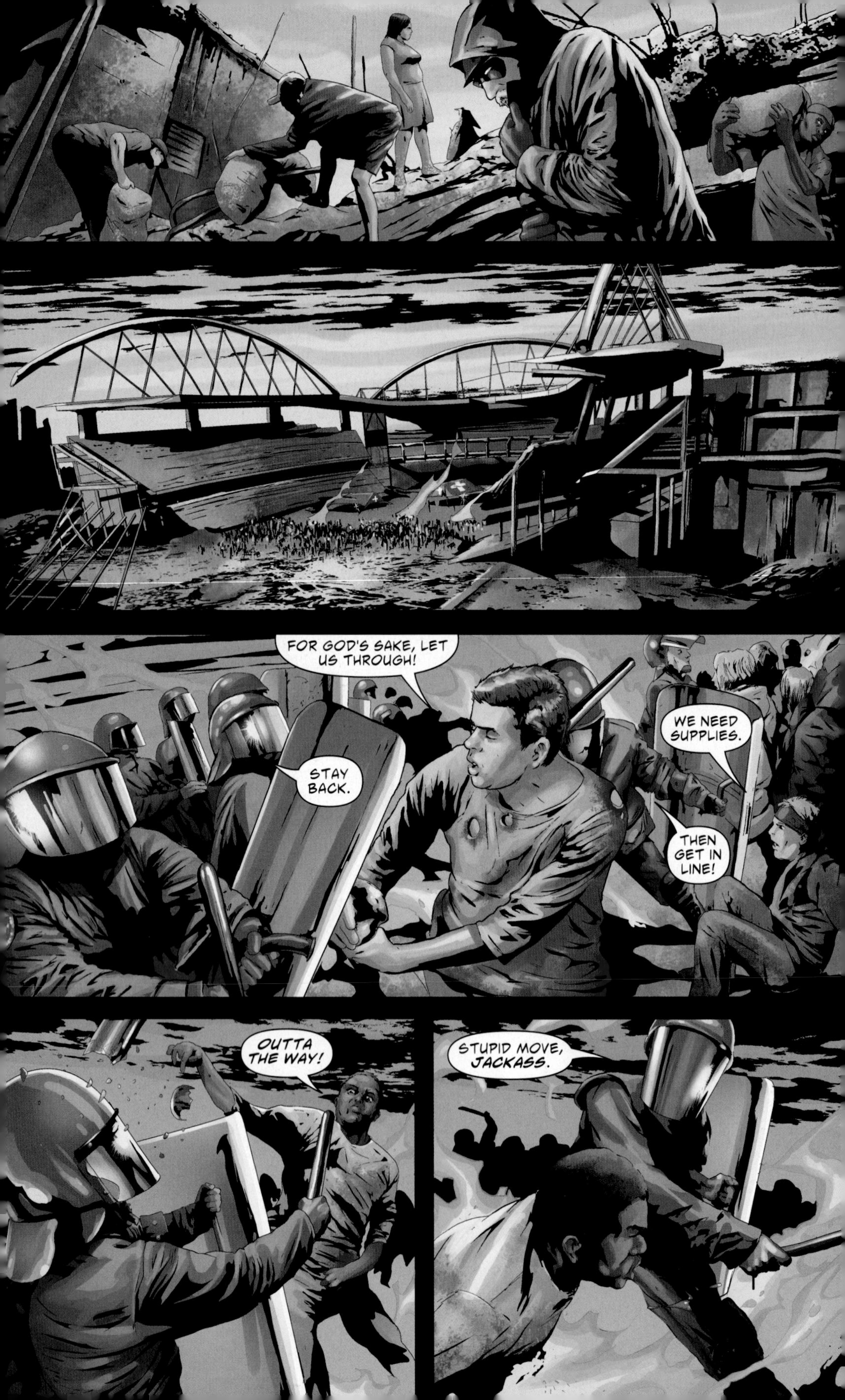
FOR GOD'S SAKE, LET US THROUGH!
STAY BACK.
WE NEED SUPPLIES.
THEN GET IN LINE!
OUTTA THE WAY!
STUPID MOVE, JACKASS.

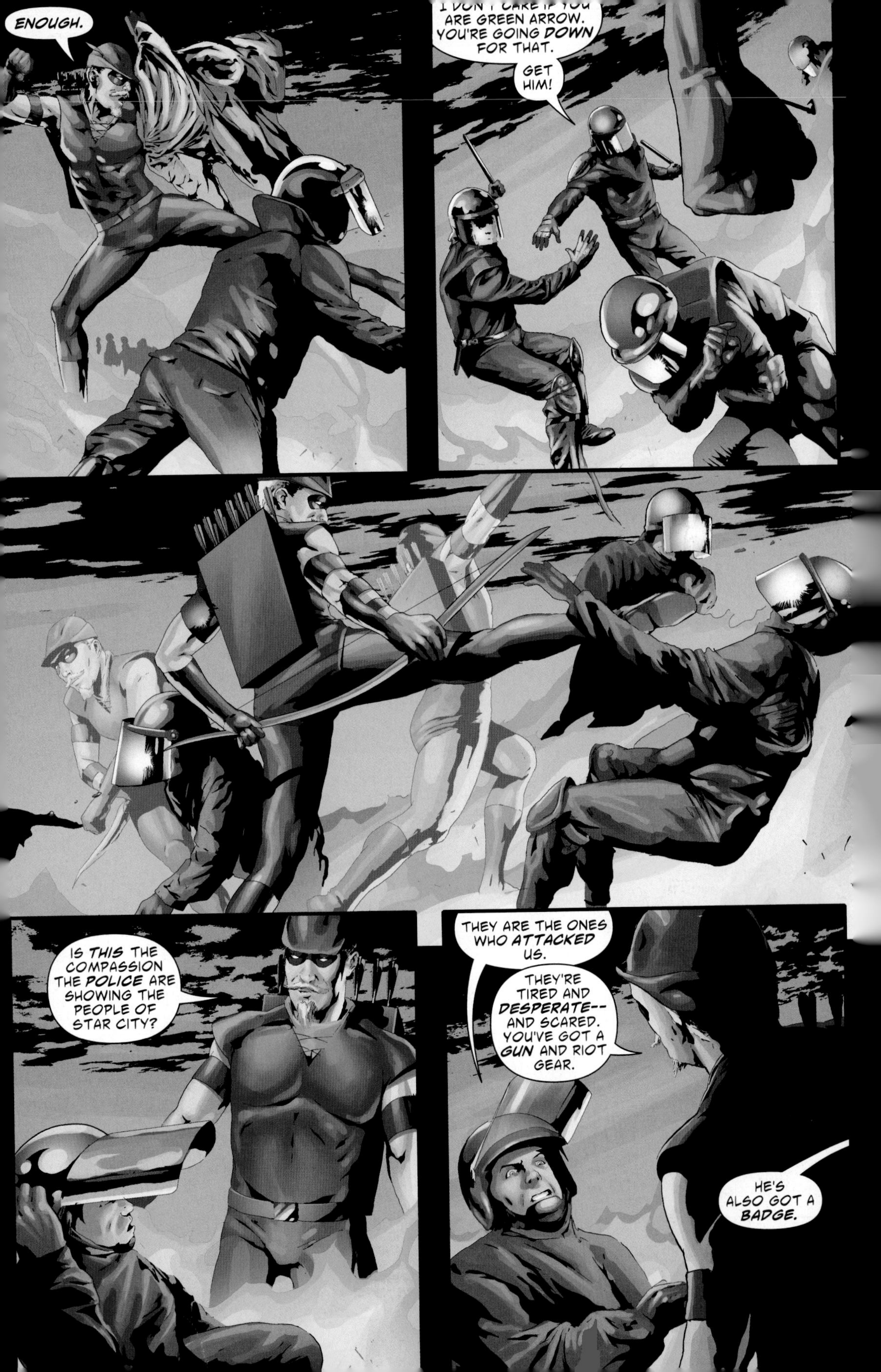
ENOUGH.
ARE GREEN ARROW. YOU'RE GOING DOWN FOR THAT.
GET HIM!
IS THIS THE COMPASSION THE POLICE ARE SHOWING THE PEOPLE OF STAR CITY?
THEY ARE THE ONES WHO ATTACKED US.
THEY'RE TIRED AND DESPERATE-- AND SCARED. YOU'VE GOT A GUN AND RIOT GEAR.
HE'S ALSO GOT A BADGE.

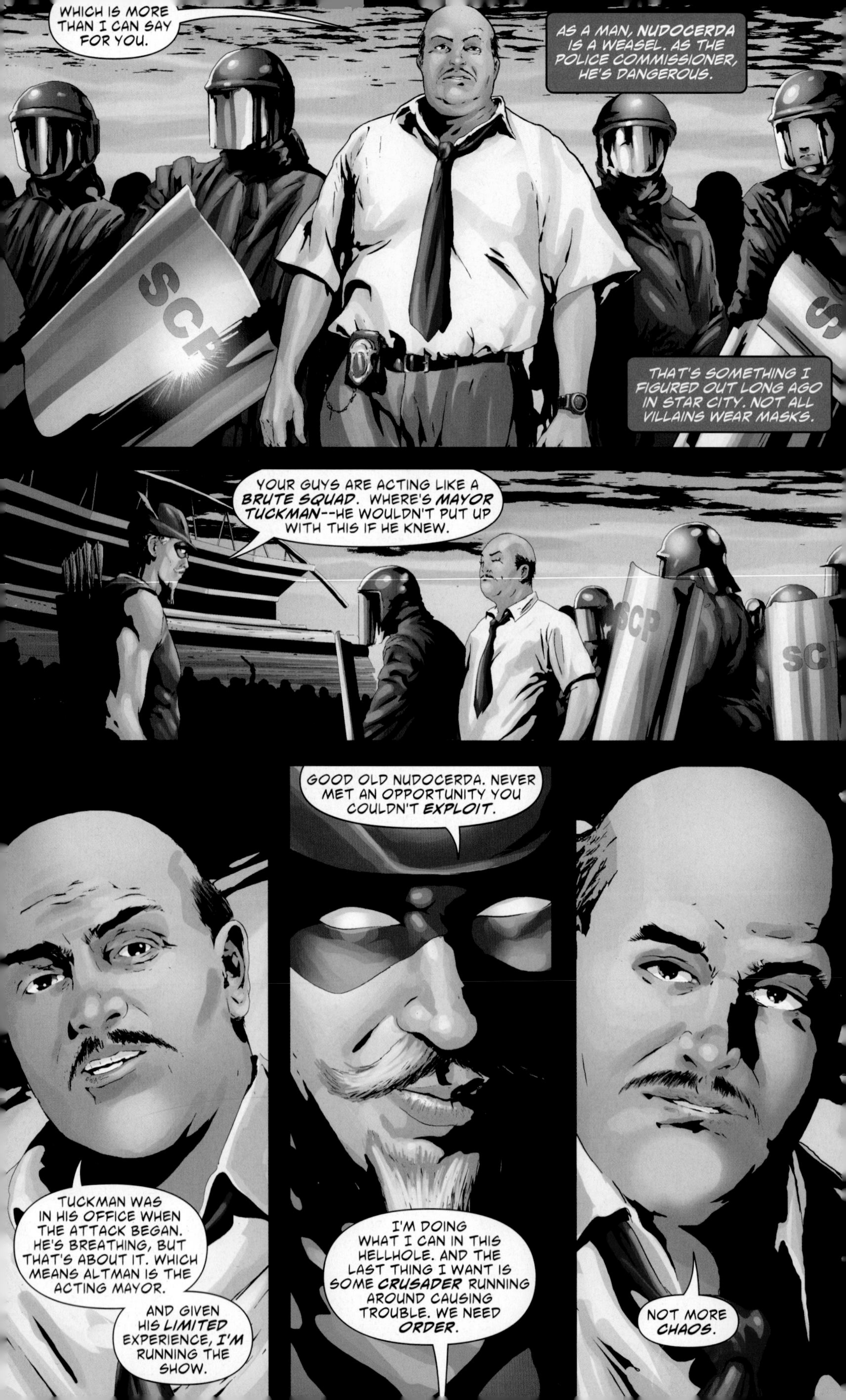
WHICH IS MORE THAN I CAN SAY FOR YOU.
AS A MAN, NUDOCERDA IS A WEASEL. AS THE POLICE COMMISSIONER, HE'S DANGEROUS.
THAT'S SOMETHING I FIGURED OUT LONG AGO IN STAR CITY. NOT ALL VILLAINS WEAR MASKS.
SCP
YOUR GUYS ARE ACTING LIKE A BRUTE SQUAD. WHERE'S MAYOR TUCKMAN--HE WOULDN'T PUT UP WITH THIS IF HE KNEW.
TUCKMAN WAS IN HIS OFFICE WHEN THE ATTACK BEGAN. HE'S BREATHING, BUT THAT'S ABOUT IT. WHICH MEANS ALTMAN IS THE ACTING MAYOR.
AND GIVEN HIS LIMITED EXPERIENCE, I'M RUNNING THE SHOW.
GOOD OLD NUDOCERDA. NEVER MET AN OPPORTUNITY YOU COULDN'T EXPLOIT.
I'M DOING WHAT I CAN IN THIS HELLHOLE. AND THE LAST THING I WANT IS SOME CRUSADER RUNNING AROUND CAUSING TROUBLE. WE NEED ORDER.
NOT MORE CHAOS.

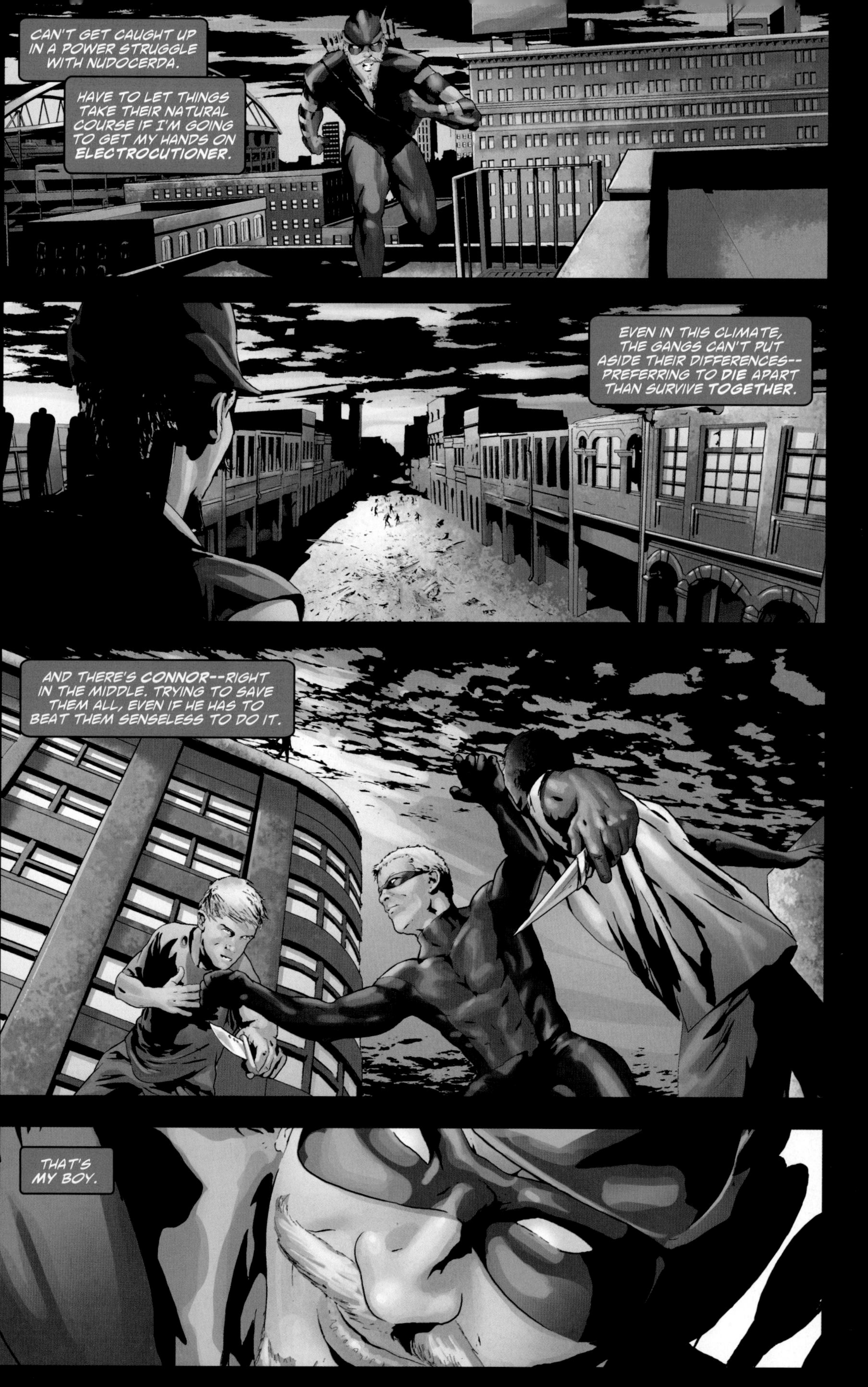
CAN'T GET CAUGHT UP IN A POWER STRUGGLE WITH NUDOCERDA.
HAVE TO LET THINGS TAKE THEIR NATURAL COURSE IF I'M GOING TO GET MY HANDS ON ELECTROCUTIONER.
EVEN IN THIS CLIMATE, THE GANGS CAN'T PUT ASIDE THEIR DIFFERENCES-- PREFERRING TO DIE APART THAN SURVIVE TOGETHER.
AND THERE'S CONNOR--RIGHT IN THE MIDDLE. TRYING TO SAVE THEM ALL, EVEN IF HE HAS TO BEAT THEM SENSELESS TO DO IT.
THAT'S MY BOY.

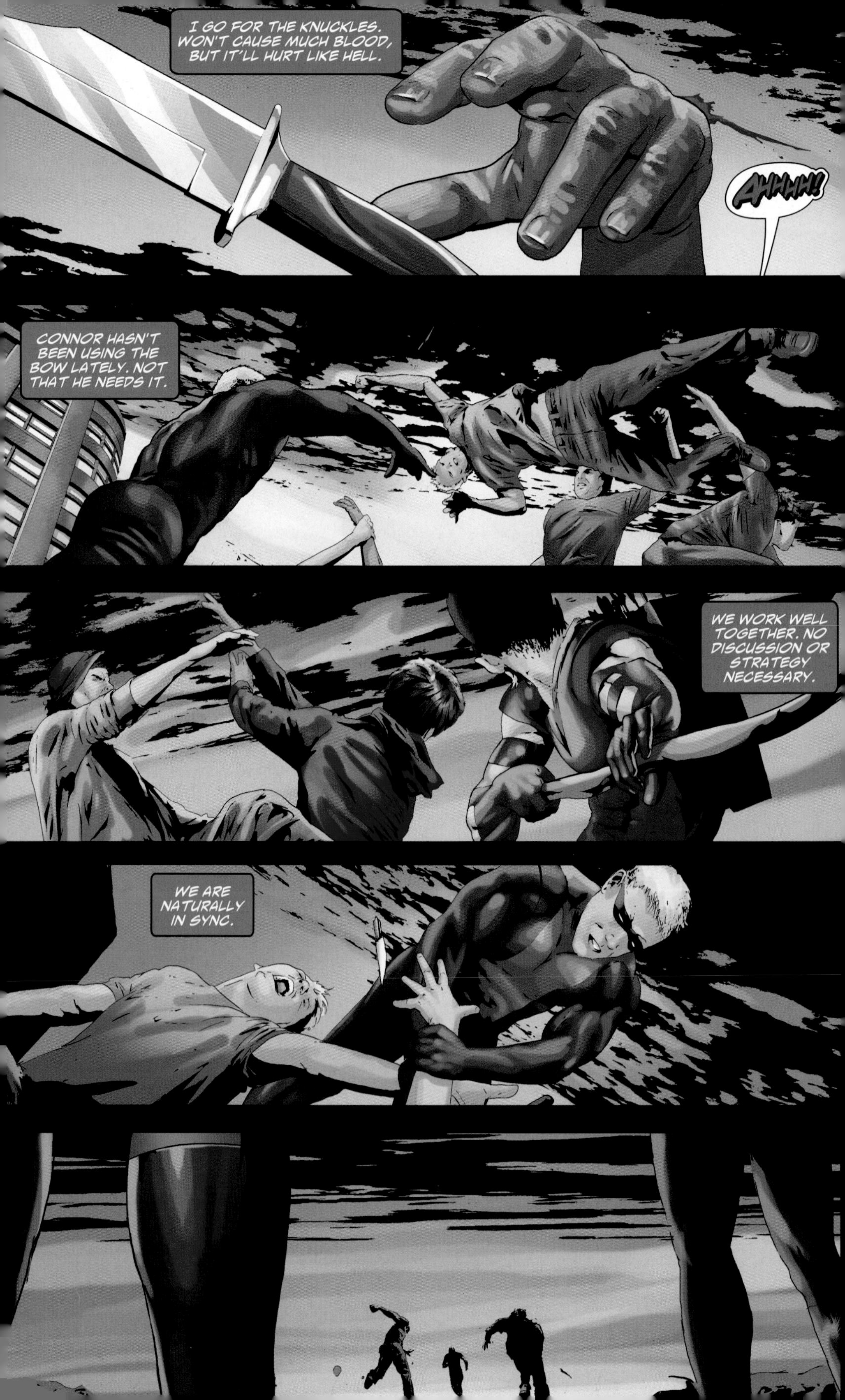
I GO FOR THE KNUCKLES. WON'T CAUSE MUCH BLOOD, BUT IT'LL HURT LIKE HELL.
AHHHH!
CONNOR HASN'T BEEN USING THE BOW LATELY. NOT THAT HE NEEDS IT.
WE WORK WELL TOGETHER. NO DISCUSSION OR STRATEGY NECESSARY.
WE ARE NATURALLY IN SYNC.

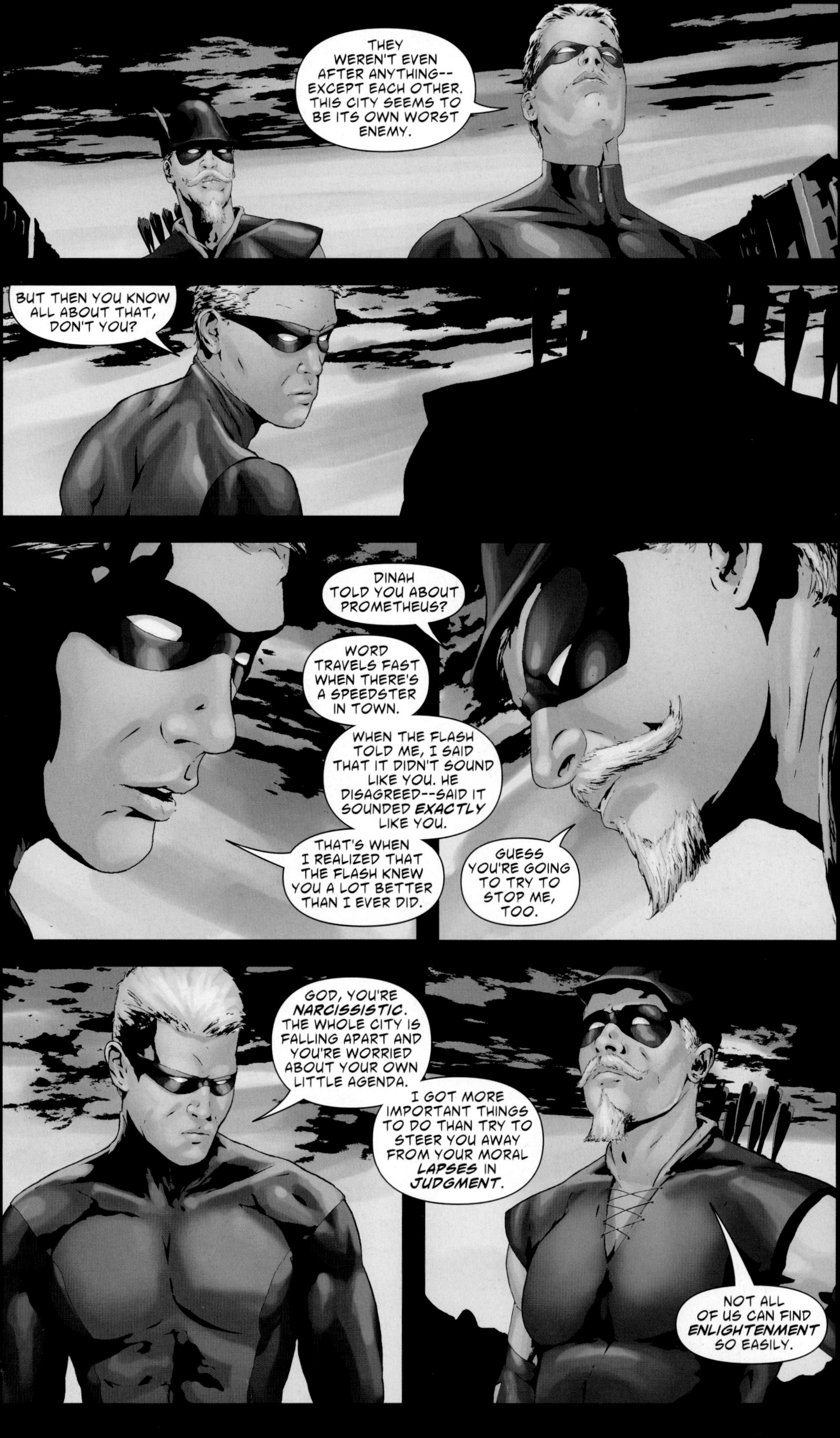
THEY WEREN'T EVEN AFTER ANYTHING-- EXCEPT EACH OTHER. THIS CITY SEEMS TO BE ITS OWN WORST ENEMY.
BUT THEN YOU KNOW ALL ABOUT THAT, DON'T YOU?
DINAH TOLD YOU ABOUT PROMETHEUS?
WORD TRAVELS FAST WHEN THERE'S A SPEEDSTER IN TOWN.
WHEN THE FLASH TOLD ME, I SAID THAT IT DIDN'T SOUND LIKE YOU. HE DISAGREED--SAID IT SOUNDED EXACTLY LIKE YOU.
THAT'S WHEN I REALIZED THAT THE FLASH KNEW YOU A LOT BETTER THAN I EVER DID.
GUESS YOU'RE GOING TO TRY TO STOP ME, TOO.
GOD, YOU'RE NARCISSISTIC. THE WHOLE CITY IS FALLING APART AND YOU'RE WORRIED ABOUT YOUR OWN LITTLE AGENDA.
I GOT MORE IMPORTANT THINGS TO DO THAN TRY TO STEER YOU AWAY FROM YOUR MORAL LAPSES IN JUDGMENT.
NOT ALL OF US CAN FIND ENLIGHTENMENT SO EASILY.

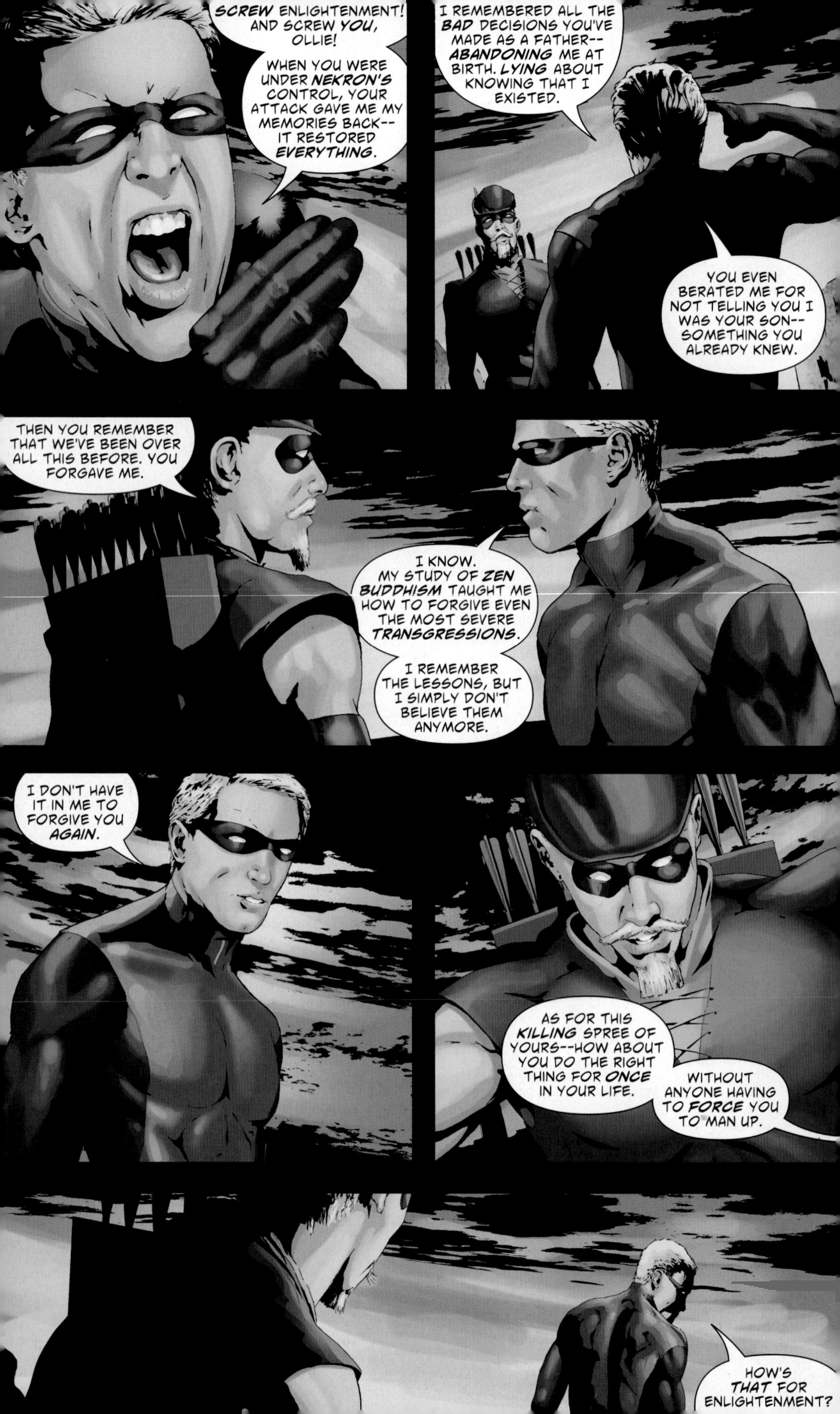
SCREW ENLIGHTENMENT! AND SCREW YOU, OLLIE!
WHEN YOU WERE UNDER NEKRON'S CONTROL, YOUR ATTACK GAVE ME MY MEMORIES BACK-- IT RESTORED EVERYTHING.
I REMEMBERED ALL THE BAD DECISIONS YOU'VE MADE AS A FATHER-- ABANDONING ME AT BIRTH. LYING ABOUT KNOWING THAT I EXISTED.
YOU EVEN BERATED ME FOR NOT TELLING YOU I WAS YOUR SON-- SOMETHING YOU ALREADY KNEW.
THEN YOU REMEMBER THAT WE'VE BEEN OVER ALL THIS BEFORE. YOU FORGAVE ME.
I KNOW. MY STUDY OF ZEN BUDDHISM TAUGHT ME HOW TO FORGIVE EVEN THE MOST SEVERE TRANSGRESSIONS.
I REMEMBER THE LESSONS, BUT I SIMPLY DON'T BELIEVE THEM ANYMORE.
I DON'T HAVE IT IN ME TO FORGIVE YOU AGAIN.
AS FOR THIS KILLING SPREE OF YOURS--HOW ABOUT YOU DO THE RIGHT THING FOR ONCE IN YOUR LIFE.
WITHOUT ANYONE HAVING TO FORCE YOU TO MAN UP.
HOW'S THAT FOR ENLIGHTENMENT?

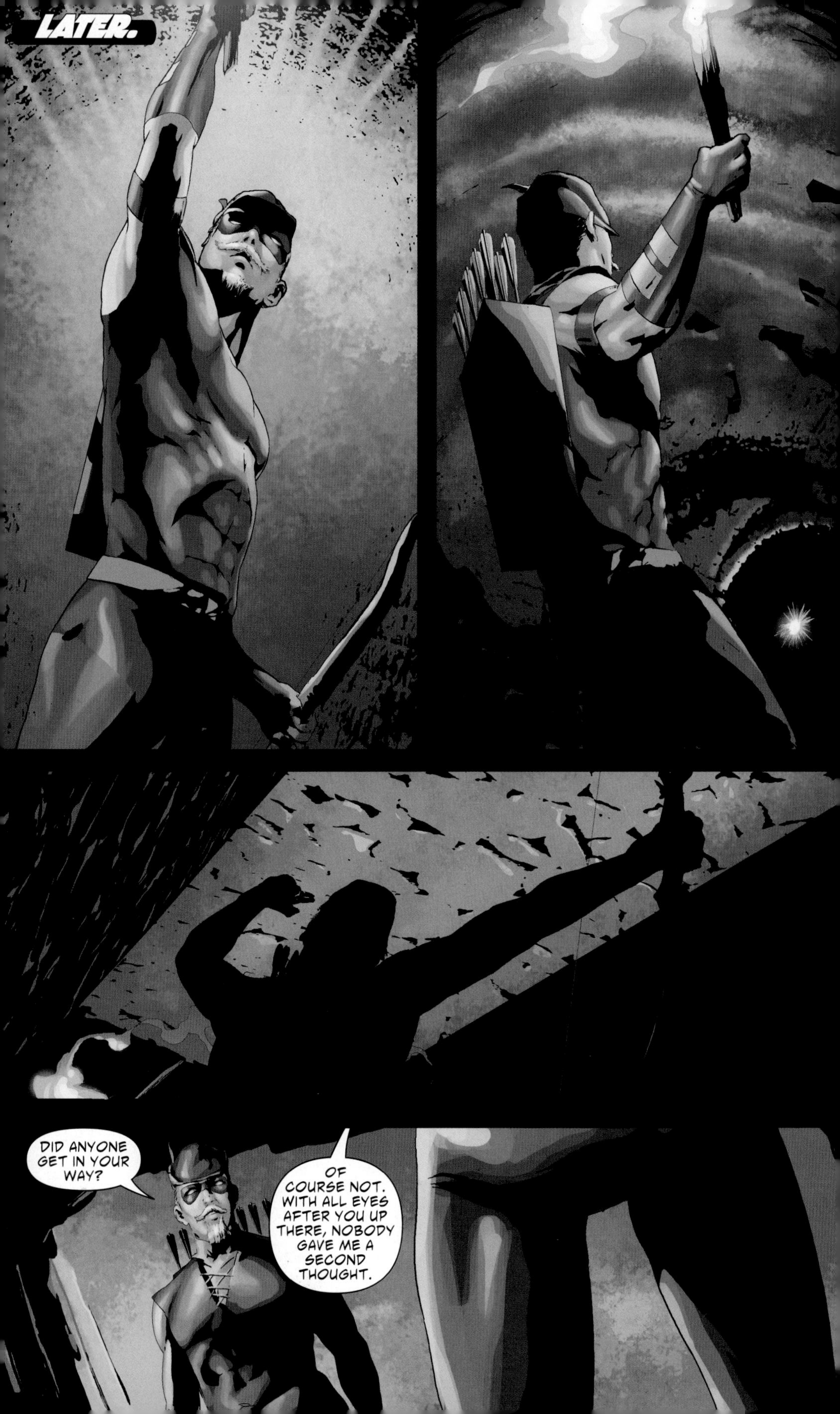
LATER.
DID ANYONE GET IN YOUR WAY?
OF COURSE NOT. WITH ALL EYES AFTER YOU UP THERE, NOBODY GAVE ME A SECOND THOUGHT.

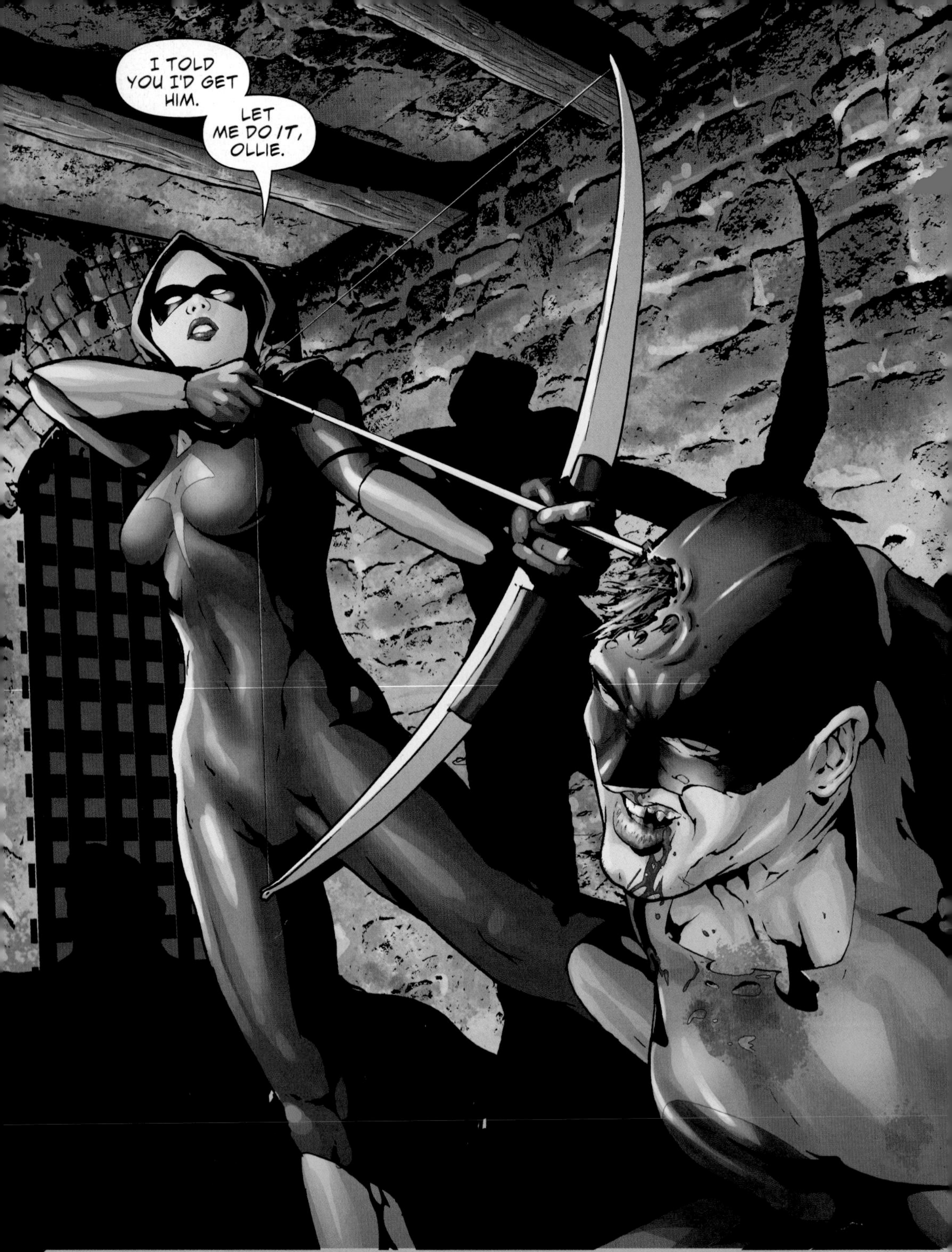
I TOLD YOU I'D GET HIM.
LET ME DO IT, OLLIE.
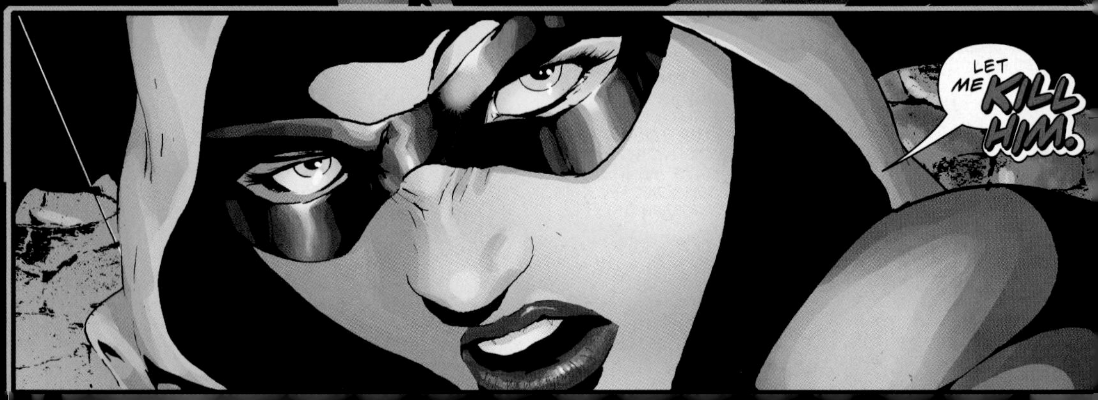
LET ME KILL HIM.

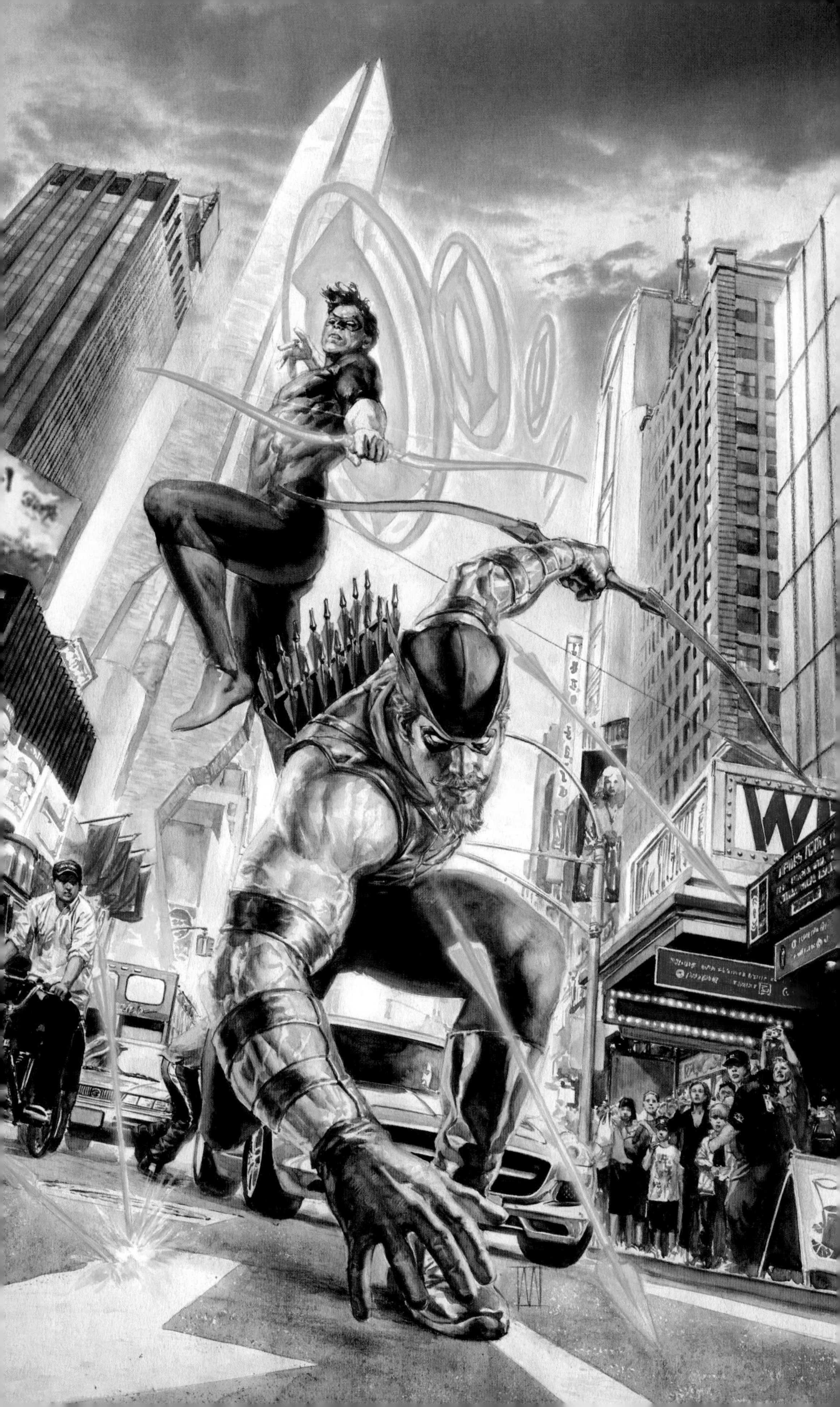

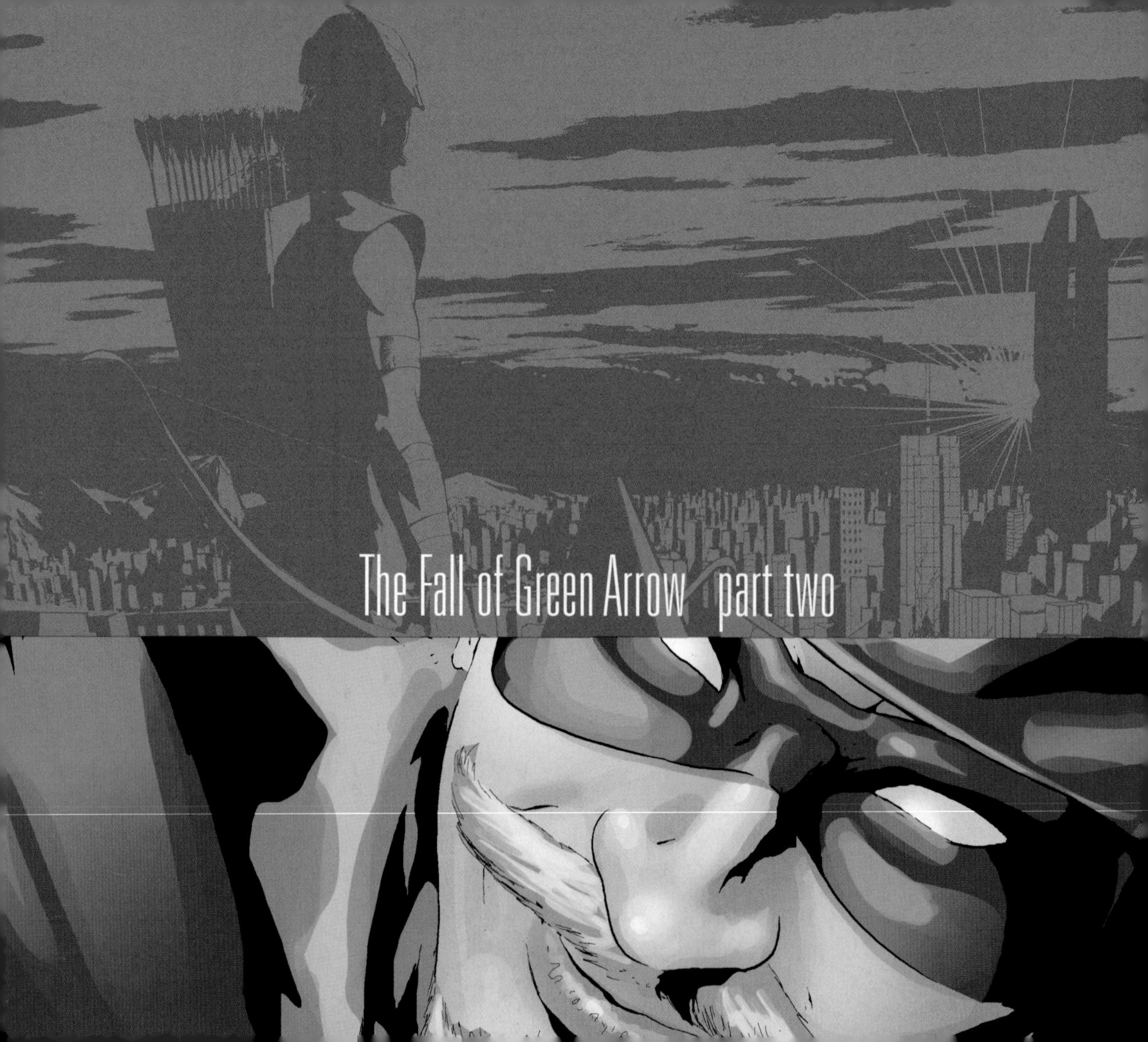
The Fall of Green Arrow part two

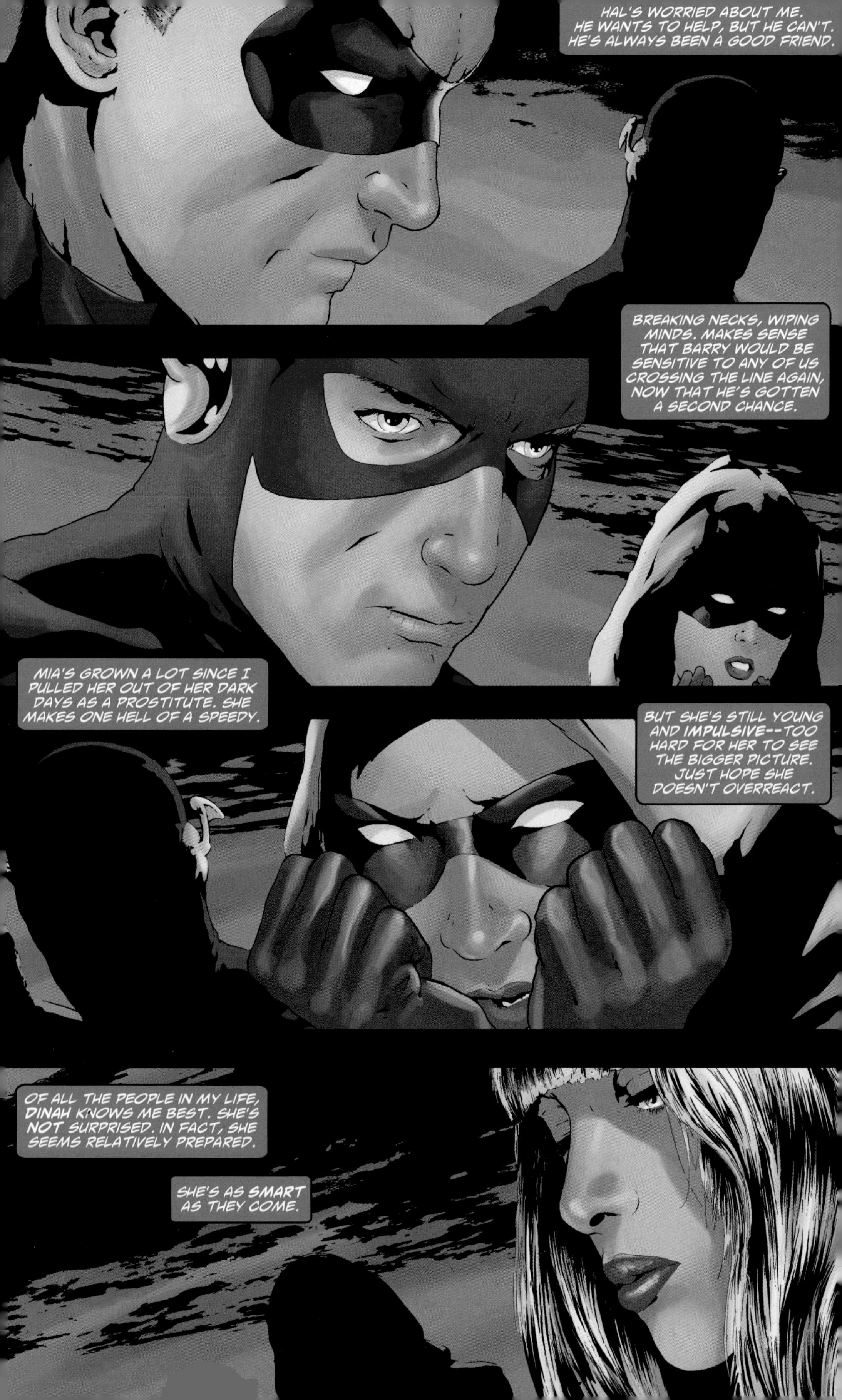
HAL'S WORRIED ABOUT ME. HE WANTS TO HELP, BUT HE CAN'T. HE'S ALWAYS BEEN A GOOD FRIEND.
BREAKING NECKS, WIPING MINDS. MAKES SENSE THAT BARRY WOULD BE SENSITIVE TO ANY OF US CROSSING THE LINE AGAIN, NOW THAT HE'S GOTTEN A SECOND CHANCE.
MIA'S GROWN A LOT SINCE I PULLED HER OUT OF HER DARK DAYS AS A PROSTITUTE. SHE MAKES ONE HELL OF A SPEEDY.
BUT SHE'S STILL YOUNG AND IMPULSIVE--TOO HARD FOR HER TO SEE THE BIGGER PICTURE. JUST HOPE SHE DOESN'T OVERREACT.
OF ALL THE PEOPLE IN MY LIFE, DINAH KNOWS ME BEST. SHE'S NOT SURPRISED. IN FACT, SHE SEEMS RELATIVELY PREPARED.
SHE'S AS SMART AS THEY COME.

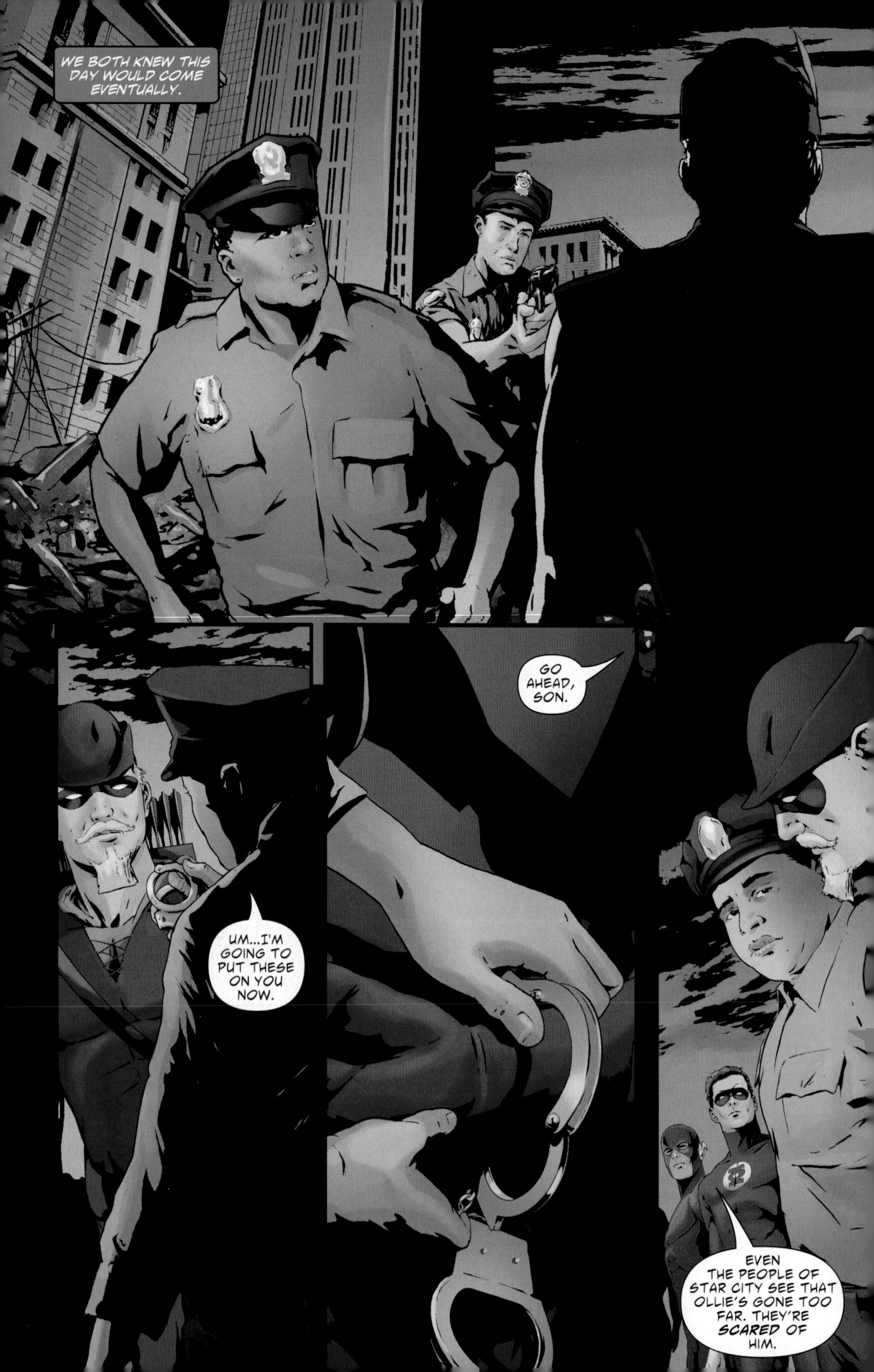
WE BOTH KNEW THIS DAY WOULD COME EVENTUALLY.
GO AHEAD, SON.
UM...I'M GOING TO PUT THESE ON YOU NOW.
EVEN THE PEOPLE OF STAR CITY SEE THAT OLLIE'S GONE TOO FAR. THEY'RE *SCARED* OF HIM.

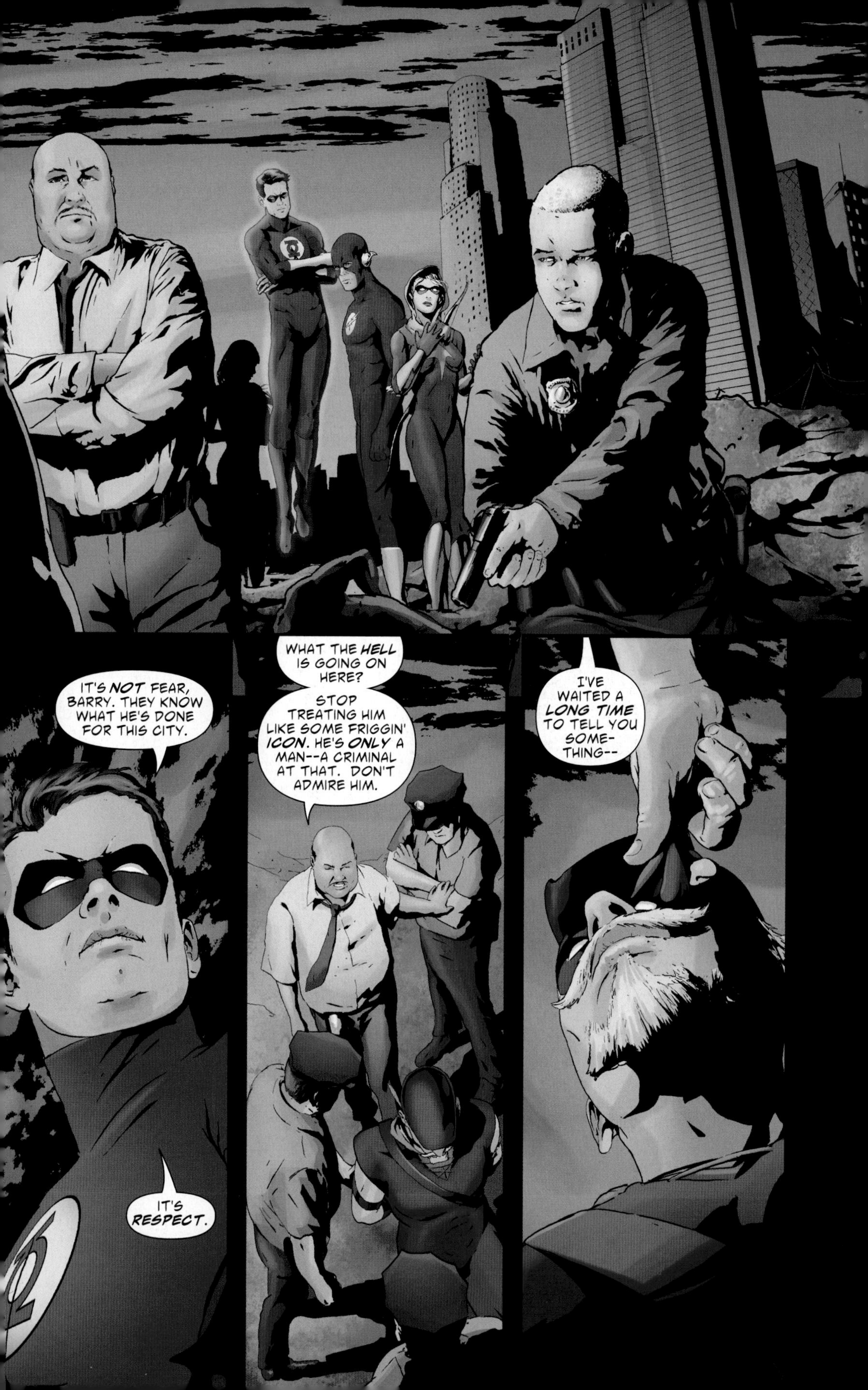
IT'S NOT FEAR, BARRY. THEY KNOW WHAT HE'S DONE FOR THIS CITY.
IT'S RESPECT.
WHAT THE HELL IS GOING ON HERE?
STOP TREATING HIM LIKE SOME FRIGGIN' ICON. HE'S ONLY A MAN--A CRIMINAL AT THAT. DON'T ADMIRE HIM.
I'VE WAITED A LONG TIME TO TELL YOU SOME-THING--

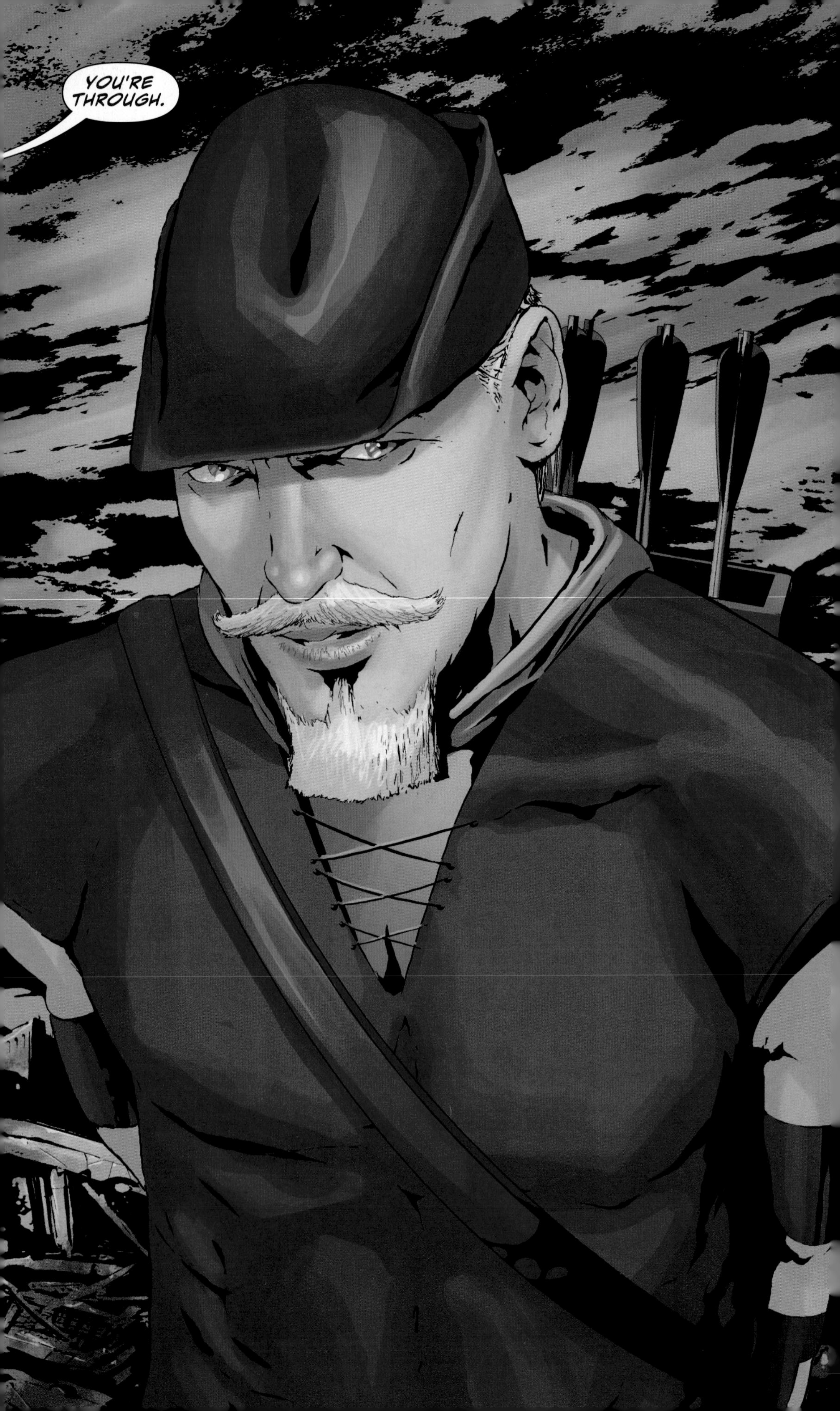
YOU'RE THROUGH.

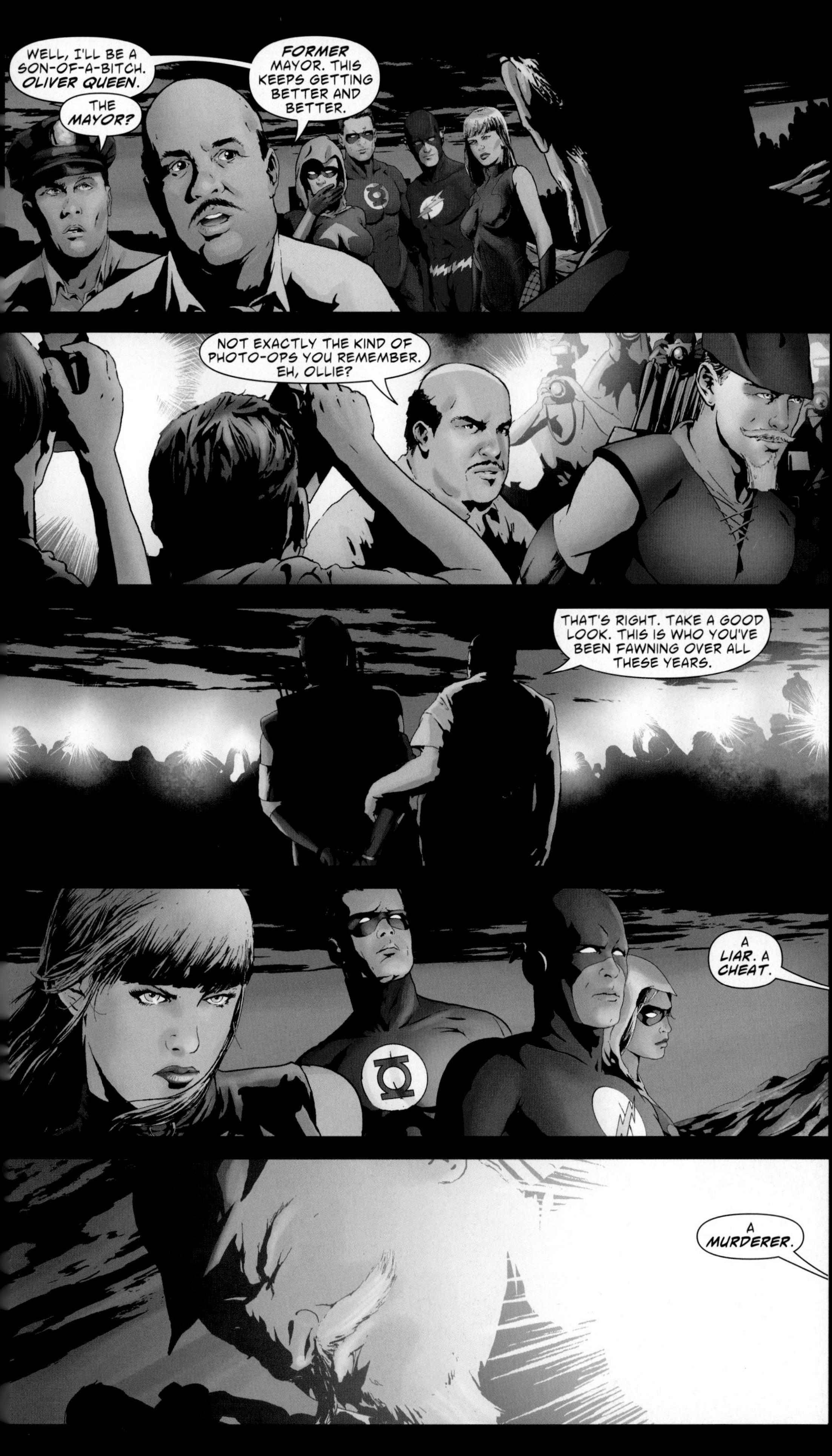
WELL, I'LL BE A SON-OF-A-BITCH. OLIVER QUEEN.
THE MAYOR?
FORMER MAYOR. THIS KEEPS GETTING BETTER AND BETTER.
NOT EXACTLY THE KIND OF PHOTO-OPS YOU REMEMBER. EH, OLLIE?
THAT'S RIGHT. TAKE A GOOD LOOK. THIS IS WHO YOU'VE BEEN FAWNING OVER ALL THESE YEARS.
A LIAR. A CHEAT.
A MURDERER.

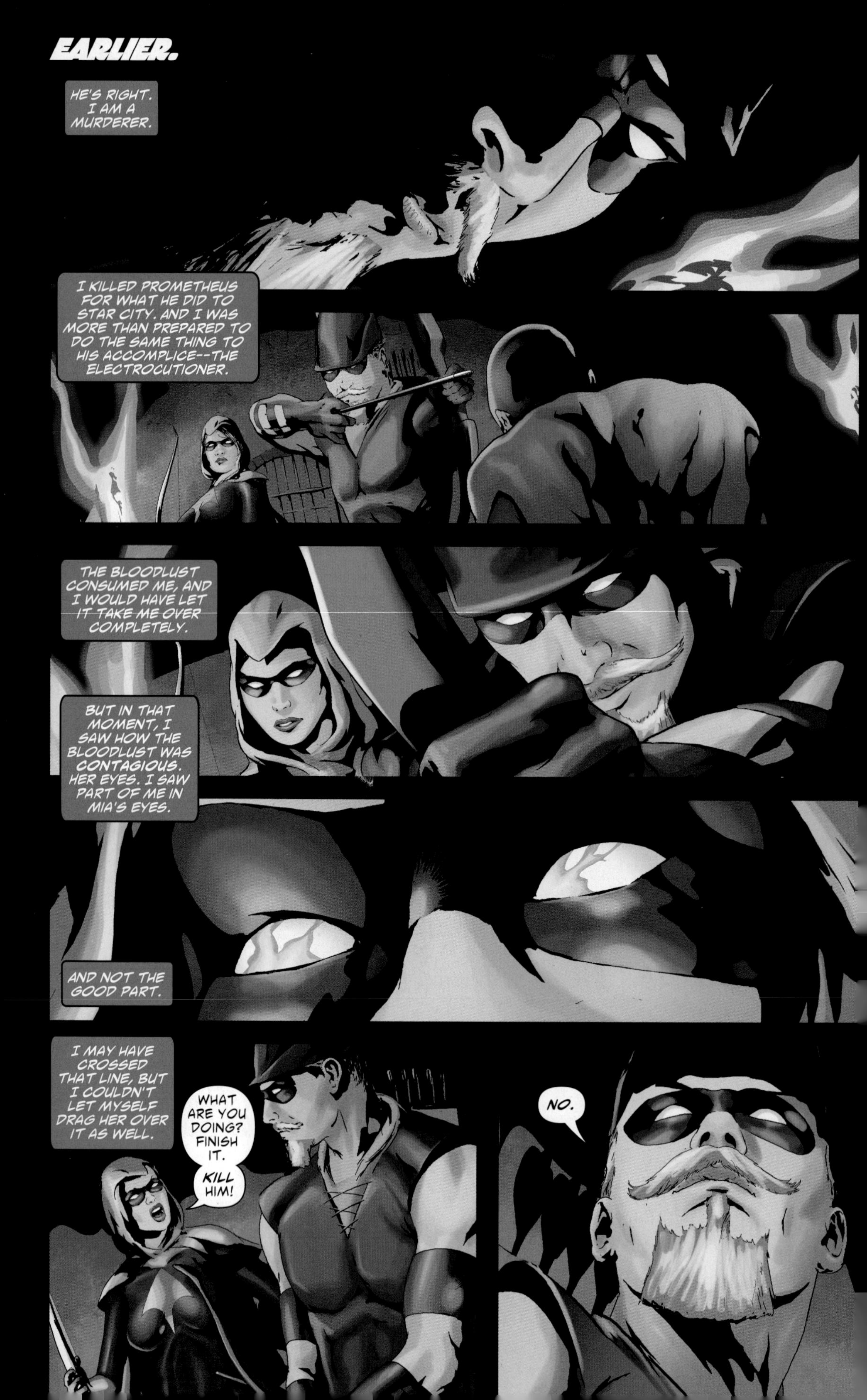
EARLIER.
HE'S RIGHT. I AM A MURDERER.
I KILLED PROMETHEUS FOR WHAT HE DID TO STAR CITY. AND I WAS MORE THAN PREPARED TO DO THE SAME THING TO HIS ACCOMPLICE--THE ELECTROCUTIONER.
THE BLOODLUST CONSUMED ME, AND I WOULD HAVE LET IT TAKE ME OVER COMPLETELY.
BUT IN THAT MOMENT, I SAW HOW THE BLOODLUST WAS CONTAGIOUS. HER EYES. I SAW PART OF ME IN MIA'S EYES.
AND NOT THE GOOD PART.
I MAY HAVE CROSSED THAT LINE, BUT I COULDN'T LET MYSELF DRAG HER OVER IT AS WELL.
WHAT ARE YOU DOING? FINISH IT.
KILL HIM!
NO.

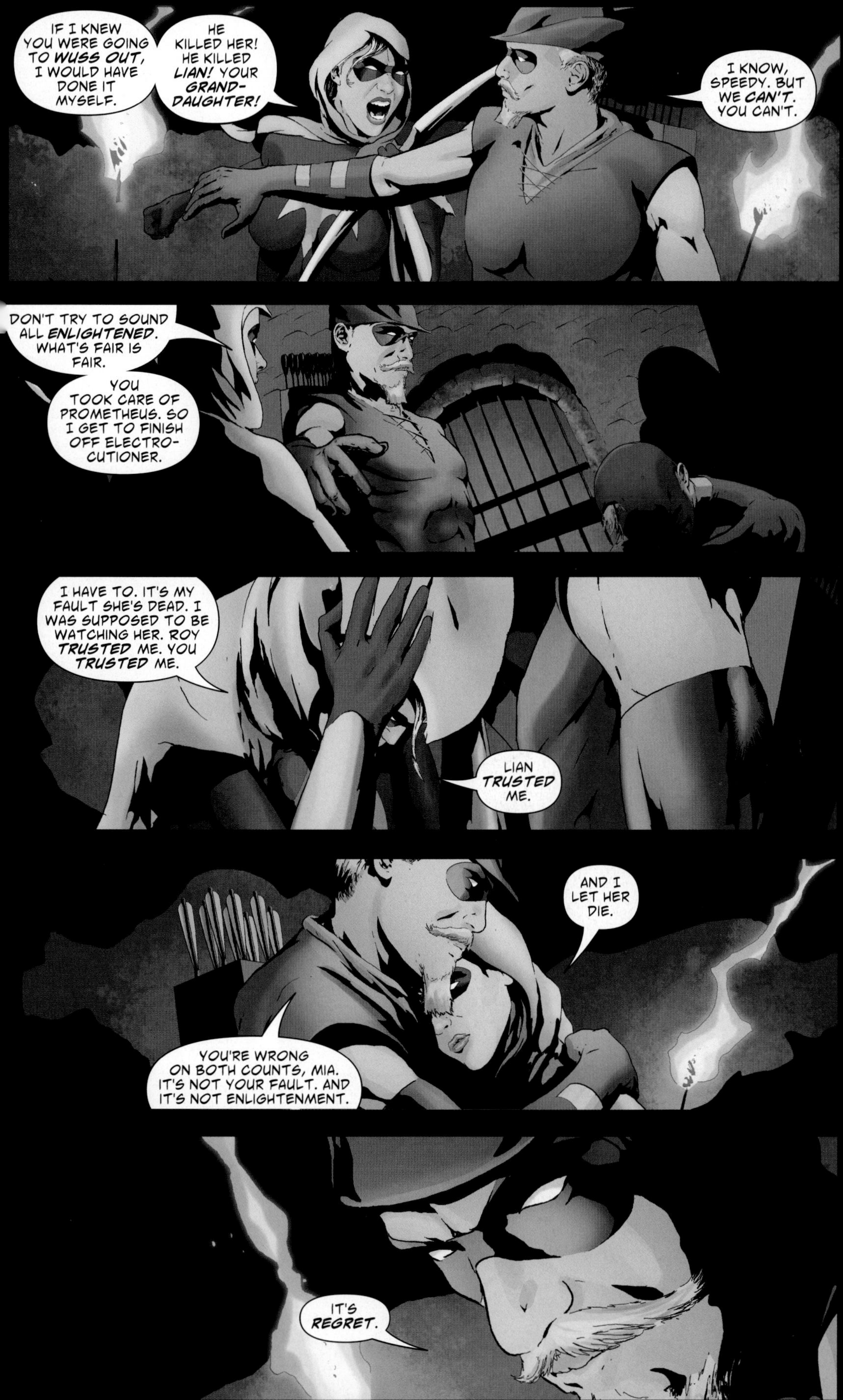

IF I KNEW YOU WERE GOING TO WUSS OUT, I WOULD HAVE DONE IT MYSELF.
HE KILLED HER! HE KILLED LIAN! YOUR GRAND-DAUGHTER!
I KNOW, SPEEDY. BUT WE CAN'T. YOU CAN'T.
DON'T TRY TO SOUND ALL ENLIGHTENED. WHAT'S FAIR IS FAIR.
YOU TOOK CARE OF PROMETHEUS. SO I GET TO FINISH OFF ELECTRO-CUTIONER.
I HAVE TO. IT'S MY FAULT SHE'S DEAD. I WAS SUPPOSED TO BE WATCHING HER. ROY TRUSTED ME. YOU TRUSTED ME.
LIAN TRUSTED ME.
AND I LET HER DIE.
YOU'RE WRONG ON BOTH COUNTS, MIA. IT'S NOT YOUR FAULT. AND IT'S NOT ENLIGHTENMENT.
IT'S REGRET.

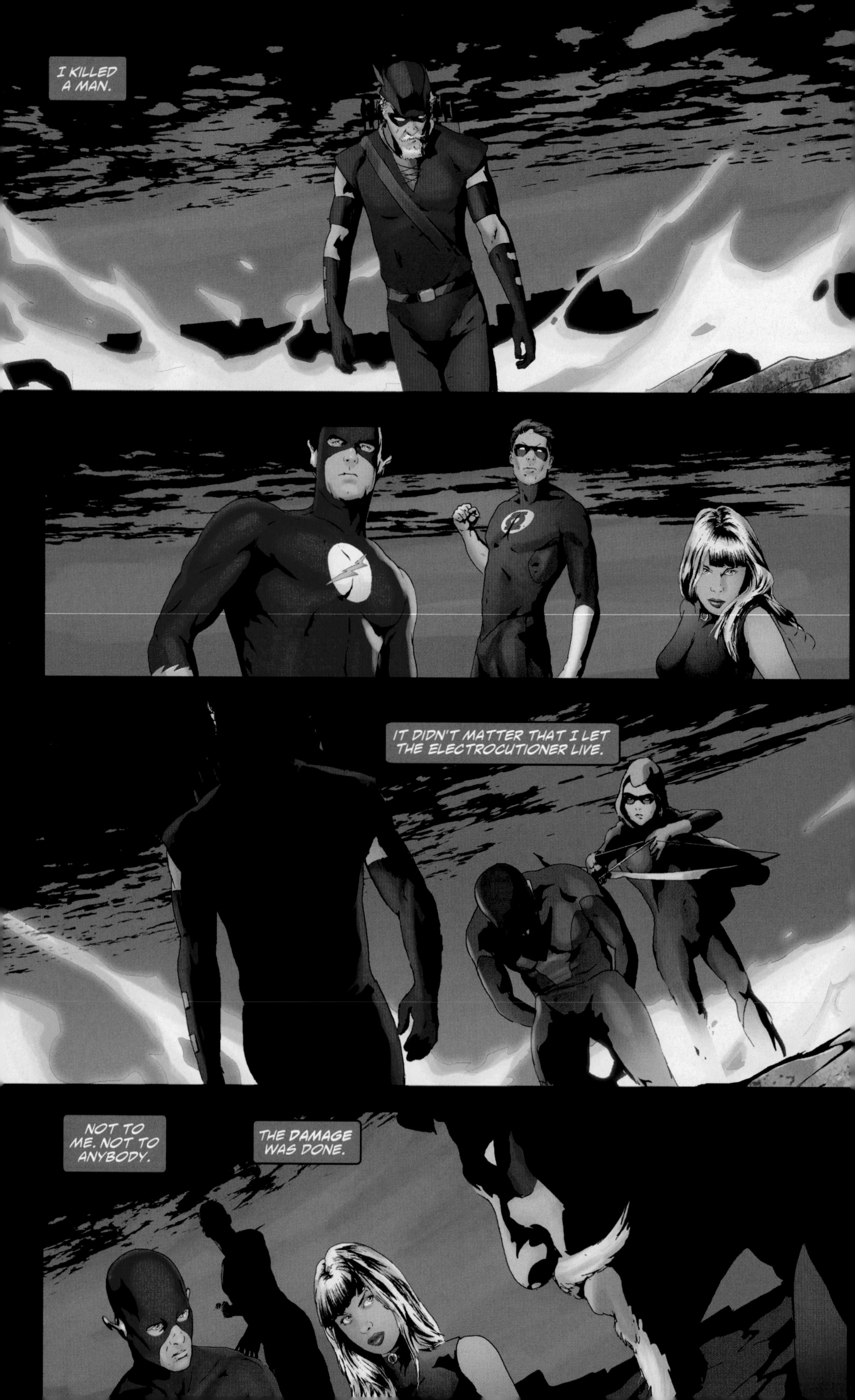
I KILLED A MAN.
IT DIDN'T MATTER THAT I LET THE ELECTROCUTIONER LIVE.
NOT TO ME. NOT TO ANYBODY.
THE DAMAGE WAS DONE.

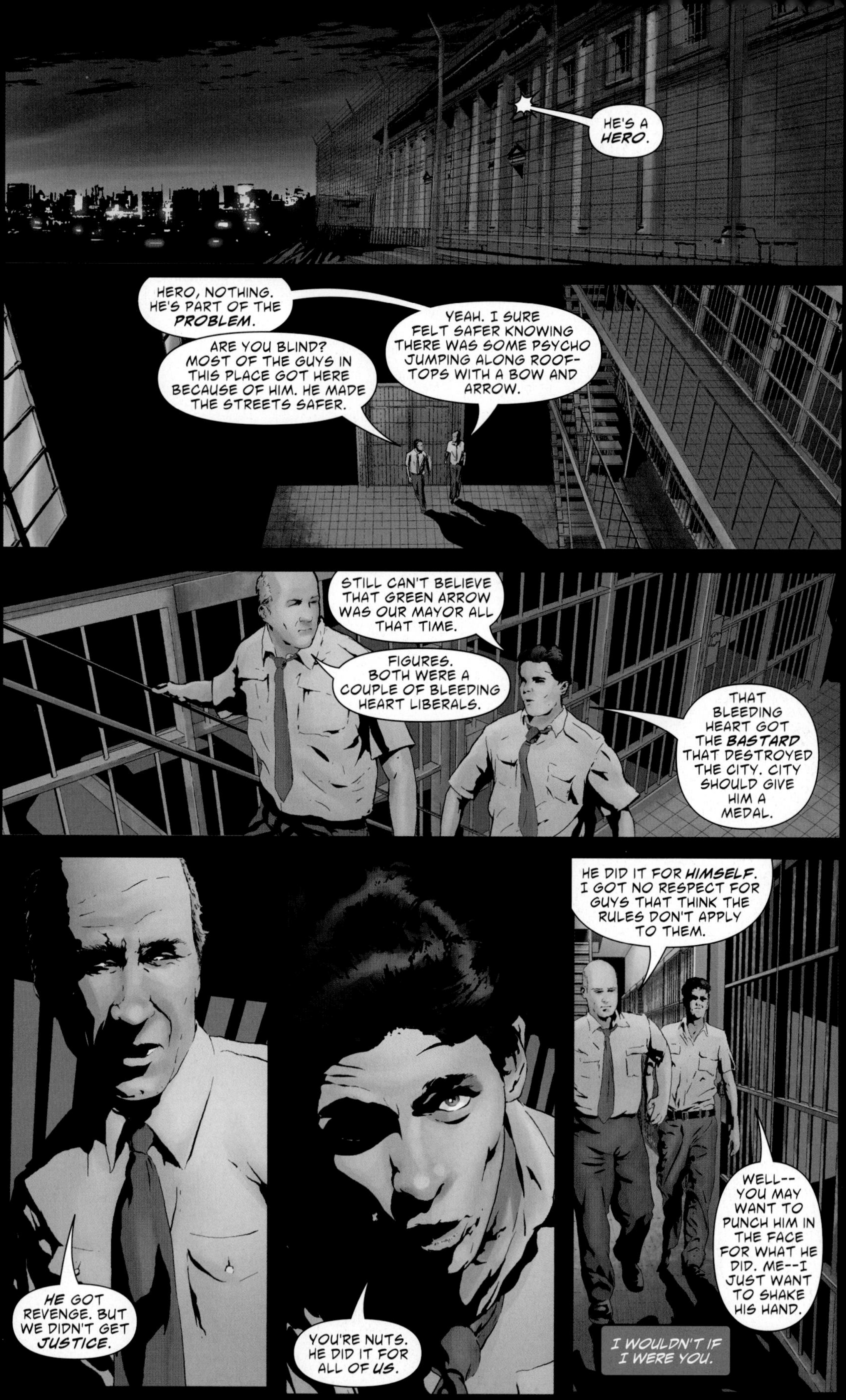
HE'S A HERO.
HERO, NOTHING. HE'S PART OF THE PROBLEM.
ARE YOU BLIND? MOST OF THE GUYS IN THIS PLACE GOT HERE BECAUSE OF HIM. HE MADE THE STREETS SAFER.
YEAH. I SURE FELT SAFER KNOWING THERE WAS SOME PSYCHO JUMPING ALONG ROOF-TOPS WITH A BOW AND ARROW.
STILL CAN'T BELIEVE THAT GREEN ARROW WAS OUR MAYOR ALL THAT TIME.
FIGURES. BOTH WERE A COUPLE OF BLEEDING HEART LIBERALS.
THAT BLEEDING HEART GOT THE BASTARD THAT DESTROYED THE CITY. CITY SHOULD GIVE HIM A MEDAL.
HE GOT REVENGE. BUT WE DIDN'T GET JUSTICE.
YOU'RE NUTS. HE DID IT FOR ALL OF US.
HE DID IT FOR HIMSELF. I GOT NO RESPECT FOR GUYS THAT THINK THE RULES DON'T APPLY TO THEM.
WELL-- YOU MAY WANT TO PUNCH HIM IN THE FACE FOR WHAT HE DID. ME--I JUST WANT TO SHAKE HIS HAND.
I WOULDN'T IF I WERE YOU.

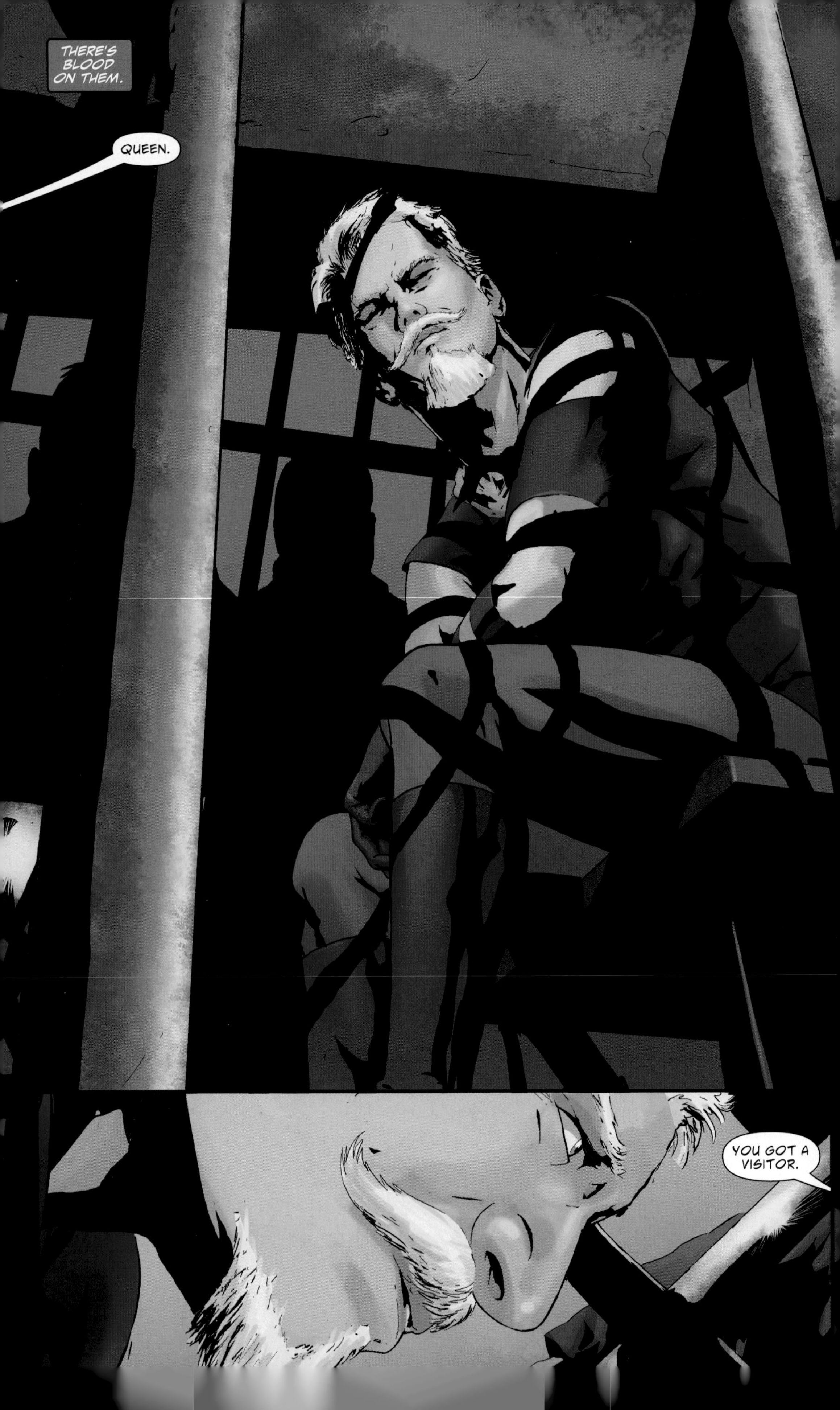
THERE'S BLOOD ON THEM.
QUEEN.
YOU GOT A VISITOR.

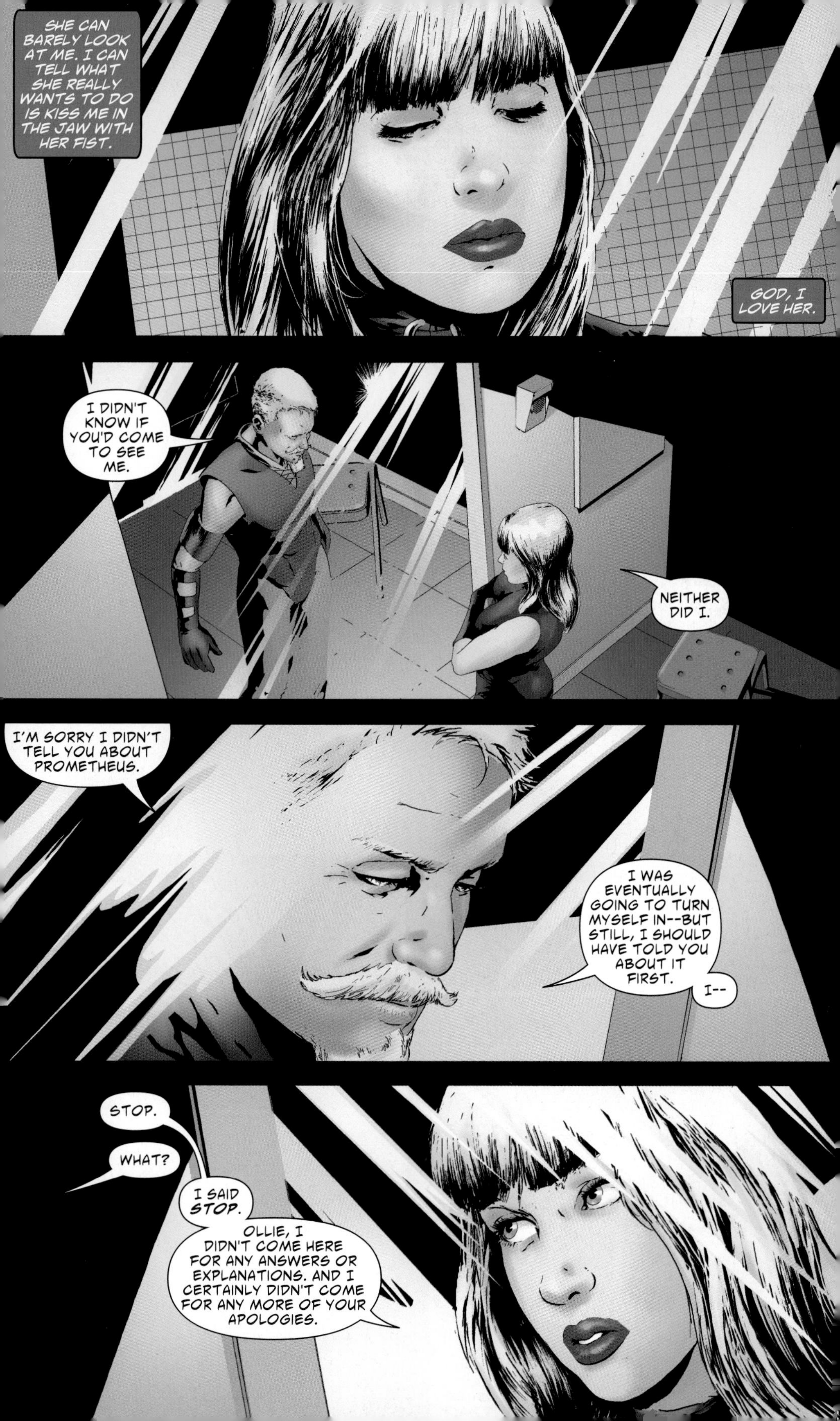
SHE CAN BARELY LOOK AT ME. I CAN TELL WHAT SHE REALLY WANTS TO DO IS KISS ME IN THE JAW WITH HER FIST.
GOD, I LOVE HER.
I DIDN'T KNOW IF YOU'D COME TO SEE ME.
NEITHER DID I.
I'M SORRY I DIDN'T TELL YOU ABOUT PROMETHEUS.
I WAS EVENTUALLY GOING TO TURN MYSELF IN--BUT STILL, I SHOULD HAVE TOLD YOU ABOUT IT FIRST.
I--
STOP.
WHAT?
I SAID *STOP*.
OLLIE, I DIDN'T COME HERE FOR ANY ANSWERS OR EXPLANATIONS. AND I CERTAINLY DIDN'T COME FOR ANY MORE OF YOUR APOLOGIES.

YOU'VE ALWAYS FOUND A WAY TO PUT THINGS BETWEEN US. NOW, THIS GLASS IS MAKING IT LITERALLY TRUE.

WHAT ARE YOU TALKING ABOUT?

I'M TALKING ABOUT YOU, OLLIE. THE WAY YOU ALWAYS MANAGED TO FIND SOME WAY TO MESS IT ALL UP.

THAT'S CRAZY.

GOES BACK TO OUR DAYS IN SEATTLE. WE WERE PERFECTLY HAPPY--SO YOU STARTED TALKING ABOUT GETTING MARRIED AND HAVING A FAMILY.

YOU LET ME FEEL GUILTY FOR NOT WANTING TO HAVE CHILDREN. THEN SHAMED FOR NOT BEING ABLE TO.

BUT THE TRUTH IS--YOU NEVER WANTED TO BE A FATHER. YOU RAN OUT ON CONNOR THE DAY HE WAS BORN. WHEN THAT WHORE OF AN ASSASSIN SHADO TOLD YOU ABOUT YOUR OTHER SON, ROBERT, YOU DIDN'T SEEM INTERESTED THERE EITHER.

FACE IT, OLLIE. LYING ABOUT THIS WAS JUST ANOTHER WEDGE TO DRIVE ME AWAY.

IT WASN'T LIKE THAT, DINAH. I...I KILLED SOMEBODY. DON'T YOU REALIZE THAT? I MURDERED PROMETHEUS. I CROSSED A LINE, AND I CAN NEVER TAKE IT BACK.

PLEASE. YOU CROSSED THAT LINE A LONG TIME AGO, OLLIE. IT'S OLD HAT.

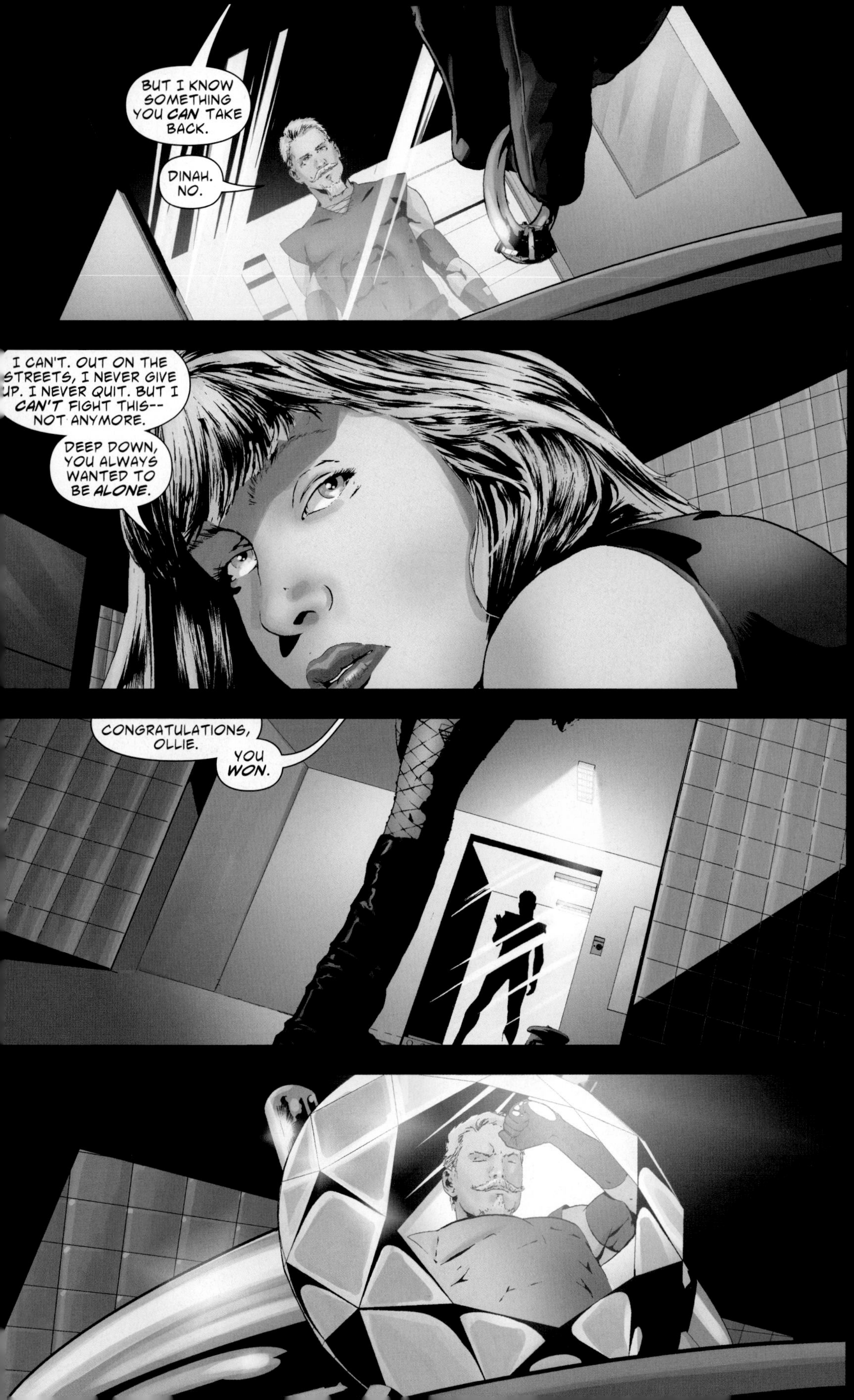
BUT I KNOW SOMETHING YOU CAN TAKE BACK.
DINAH. NO.
I CAN'T. OUT ON THE STREETS, I NEVER GIVE UP. I NEVER QUIT. BUT I CAN'T FIGHT THIS-- NOT ANYMORE.
DEEP DOWN, YOU ALWAYS WANTED TO BE ALONE.
CONGRATULATIONS, OLLIE.
YOU WON.

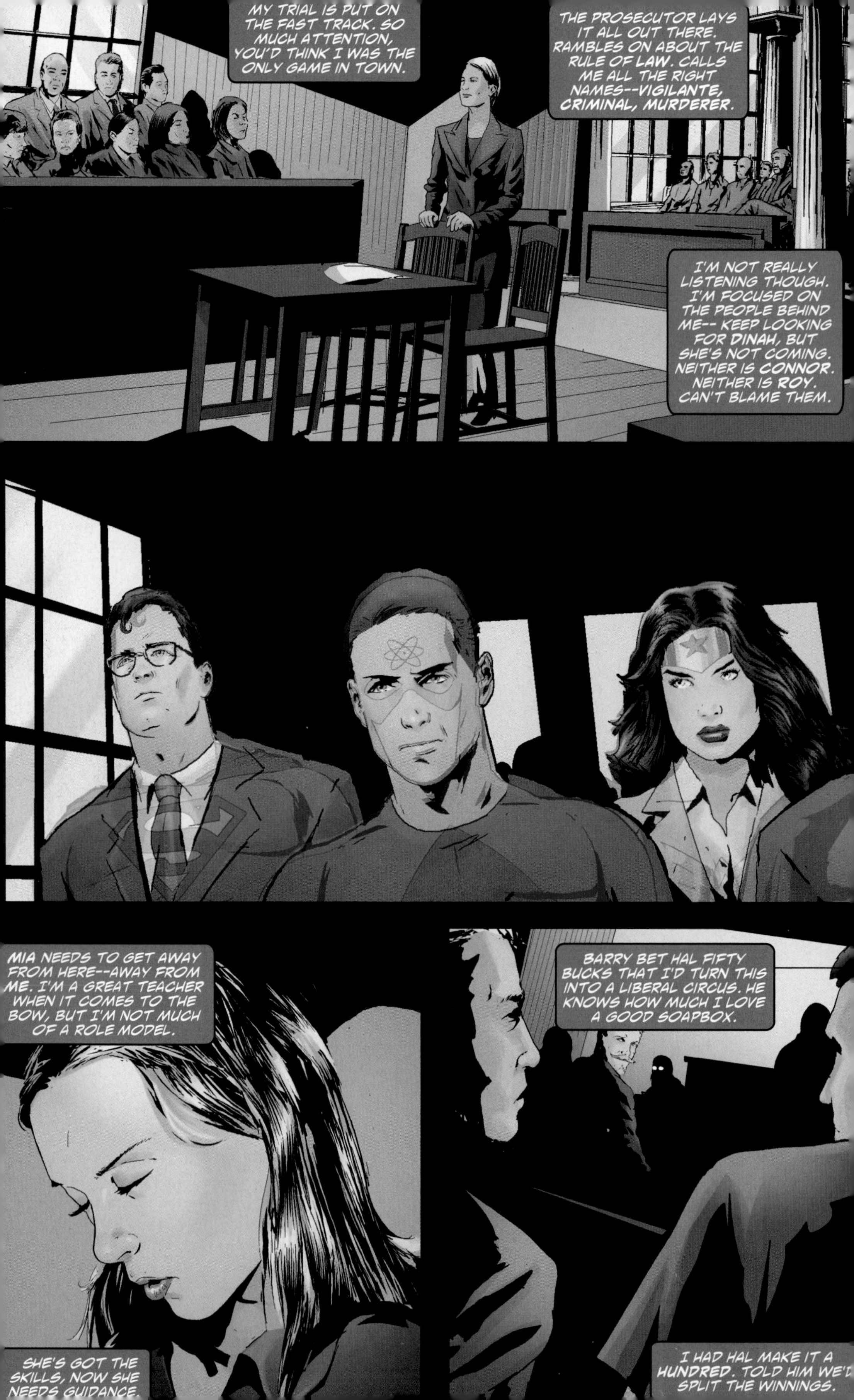
MY TRIAL IS PUT ON THE FAST TRACK. SO MUCH ATTENTION, YOU'D THINK I WAS THE ONLY GAME IN TOWN.
THE PROSECUTOR LAYS IT ALL OUT THERE. RAMBLES ON ABOUT THE RULE OF LAW. CALLS ME ALL THE RIGHT NAMES--VIGILANTE, CRIMINAL, MURDERER.
I'M NOT REALLY LISTENING THOUGH. I'M FOCUSED ON THE PEOPLE BEHIND ME-- KEEP LOOKING FOR DINAH, BUT SHE'S NOT COMING. NEITHER IS CONNOR. NEITHER IS ROY. CAN'T BLAME THEM.
MIA NEEDS TO GET AWAY FROM HERE--AWAY FROM ME. I'M A GREAT TEACHER WHEN IT COMES TO THE BOW, BUT I'M NOT MUCH OF A ROLE MODEL.
SHE'S GOT THE SKILLS, NOW SHE NEEDS GUIDANCE.
BARRY BET HAL FIFTY BUCKS THAT I'D TURN THIS INTO A LIBERAL CIRCUS. HE KNOWS HOW MUCH I LOVE A GOOD SOAPBOX.
I HAD HAL MAKE IT A HUNDRED. TOLD HIM WE'D SPLIT THE WINNINGS.

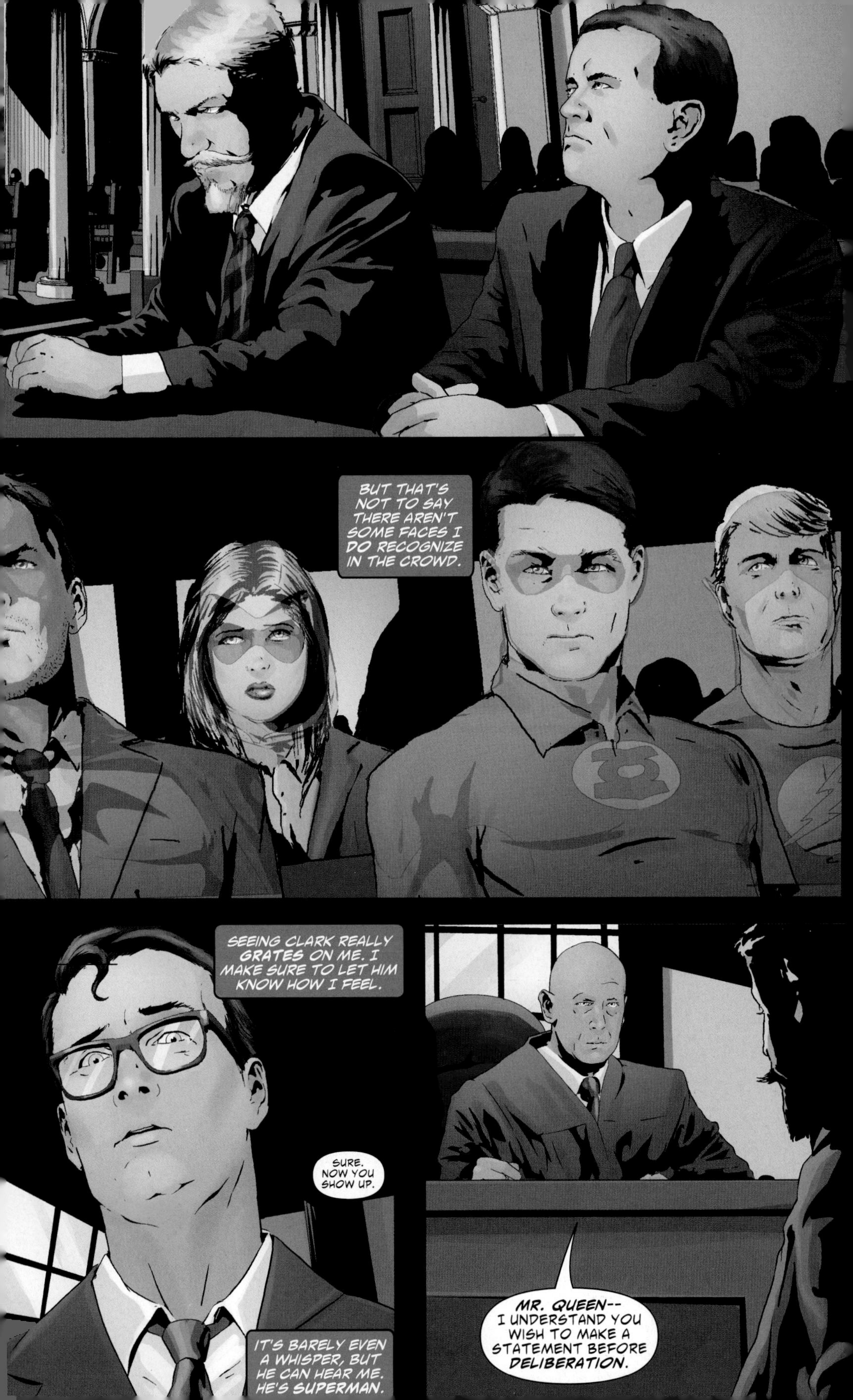
BUT THAT'S NOT TO SAY THERE AREN'T SOME FACES I DO RECOGNIZE IN THE CROWD.
SEEING CLARK REALLY GRATES ON ME. I MAKE SURE TO LET HIM KNOW HOW I FEEL.
SURE. NOW YOU SHOW UP.
IT'S BARELY EVEN A WHISPER, BUT HE CAN HEAR ME. HE'S SUPERMAN.
MR. QUEEN-- I UNDERSTAND YOU WISH TO MAKE A STATEMENT BEFORE DELIBERATION.

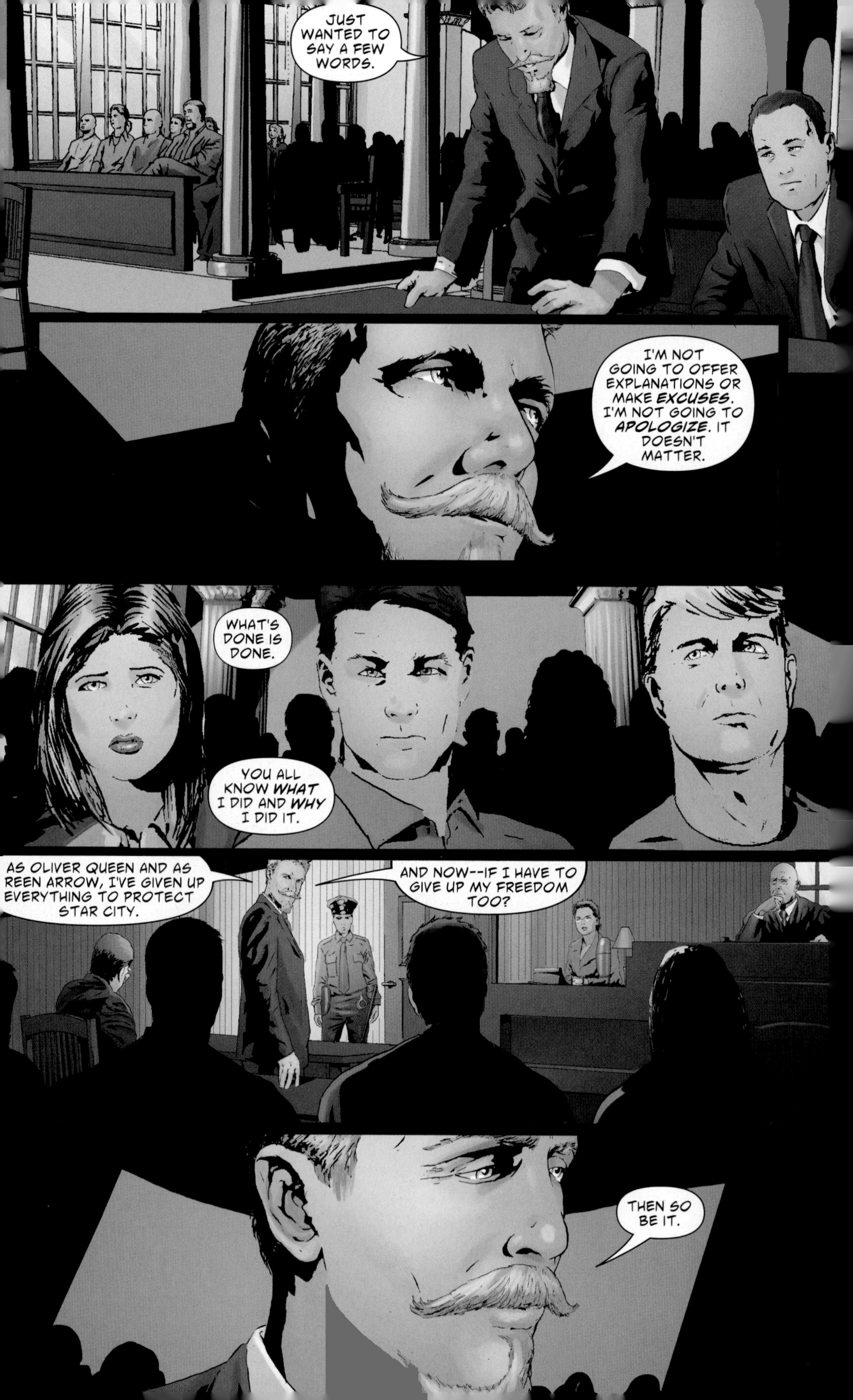
JUST WANTED TO SAY A FEW WORDS.
I'M NOT GOING TO OFFER EXPLANATIONS OR MAKE EXCUSES. I'M NOT GOING TO APOLOGIZE. IT DOESN'T MATTER.
WHAT'S DONE IS DONE.
YOU ALL KNOW WHAT I DID AND WHY I DID IT.
AS OLIVER QUEEN AND AS REEN ARROW, I'VE GIVEN UP EVERYTHING TO PROTECT STAR CITY.
AND NOW--IF I HAVE TO GIVE UP MY FREEDOM TOO?
THEN SO BE IT.

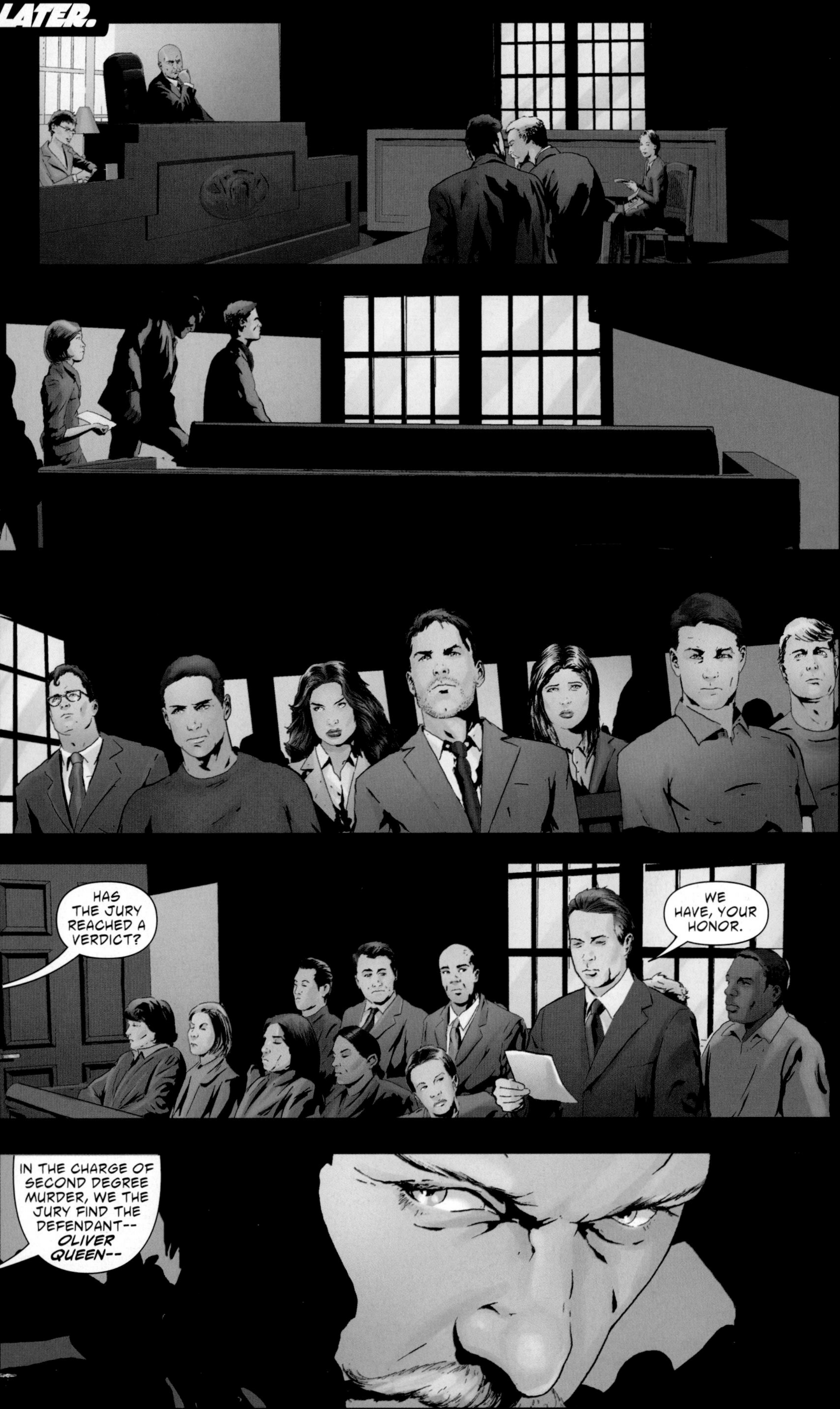
LATER.
HAS THE JURY REACHED A VERDICT?
WE HAVE, YOUR HONOR.
IN THE CHARGE OF SECOND DEGREE MURDER, WE THE JURY FIND THE DEFENDANT-- OLIVER QUEEN--

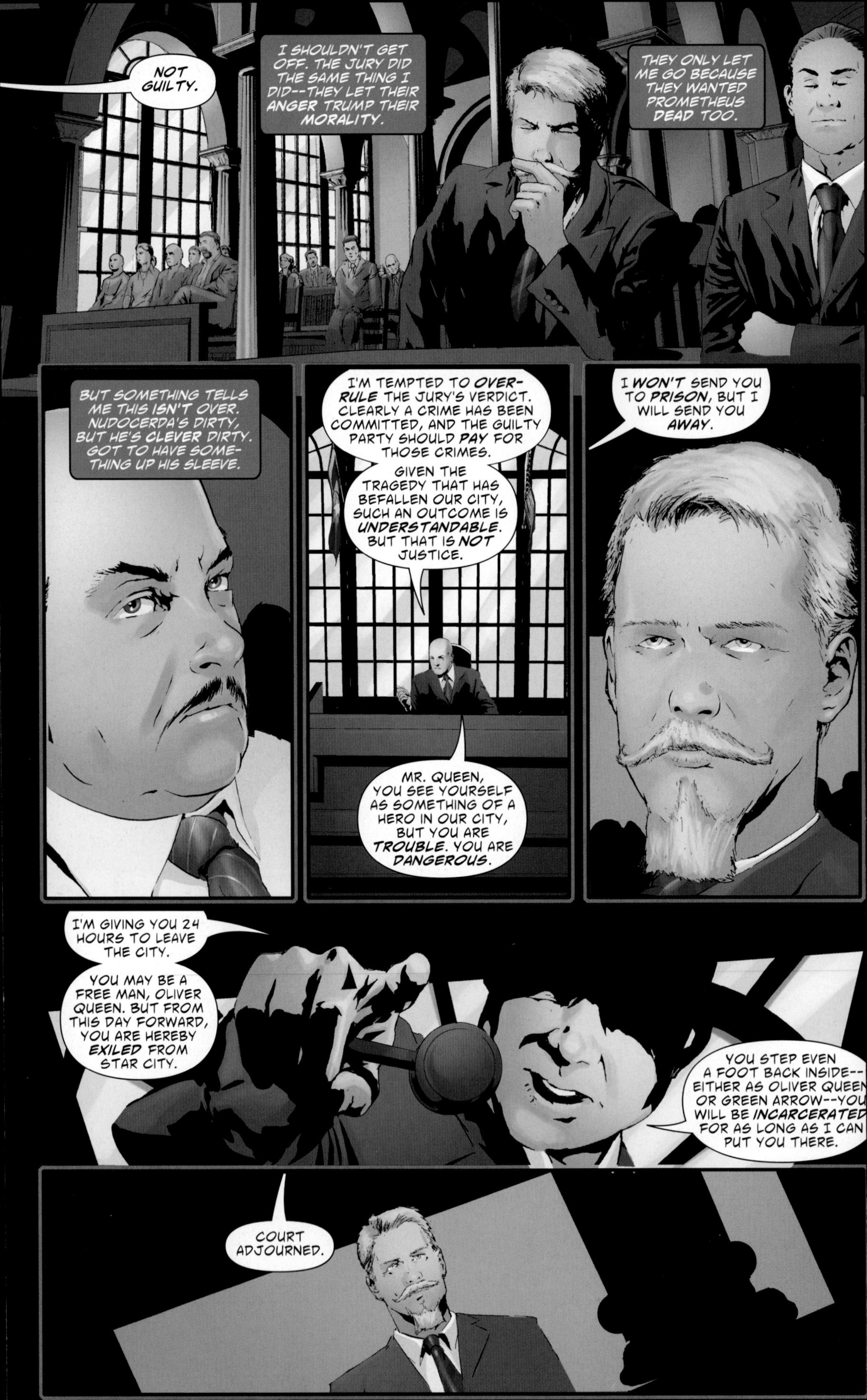
NOT GUILTY.
I SHOULDN'T GET OFF. THE JURY DID THE SAME THING I DID--THEY LET THEIR ANGER TRUMP THEIR MORALITY.
THEY ONLY LET ME GO BECAUSE THEY WANTED PROMETHEUS DEAD TOO.
BUT SOMETHING TELLS ME THIS ISN'T OVER. NUDOCERDA'S DIRTY, BUT HE'S CLEVER DIRTY. GOT TO HAVE SOMETHING UP HIS SLEEVE.
I'M TEMPTED TO OVERRULE THE JURY'S VERDICT. CLEARLY A CRIME HAS BEEN COMMITTED, AND THE GUILTY PARTY SHOULD PAY FOR THOSE CRIMES.
GIVEN THE TRAGEDY THAT HAS BEFALLEN OUR CITY, SUCH AN OUTCOME IS UNDERSTANDABLE. BUT THAT IS NOT JUSTICE.
MR. QUEEN, YOU SEE YOURSELF AS SOMETHING OF A HERO IN OUR CITY, BUT YOU ARE TROUBLE. YOU ARE DANGEROUS.
I WON'T SEND YOU TO PRISON, BUT I WILL SEND YOU AWAY.
I'M GIVING YOU 24 HOURS TO LEAVE THE CITY.
YOU MAY BE A FREE MAN, OLIVER QUEEN. BUT FROM THIS DAY FORWARD, YOU ARE HEREBY EXILED FROM STAR CITY.
YOU STEP EVEN A FOOT BACK INSIDE--EITHER AS OLIVER QUEEN OR GREEN ARROW--YOU WILL BE INCARCERATED FOR AS LONG AS I CAN PUT YOU THERE.
COURT ADJOURNED.

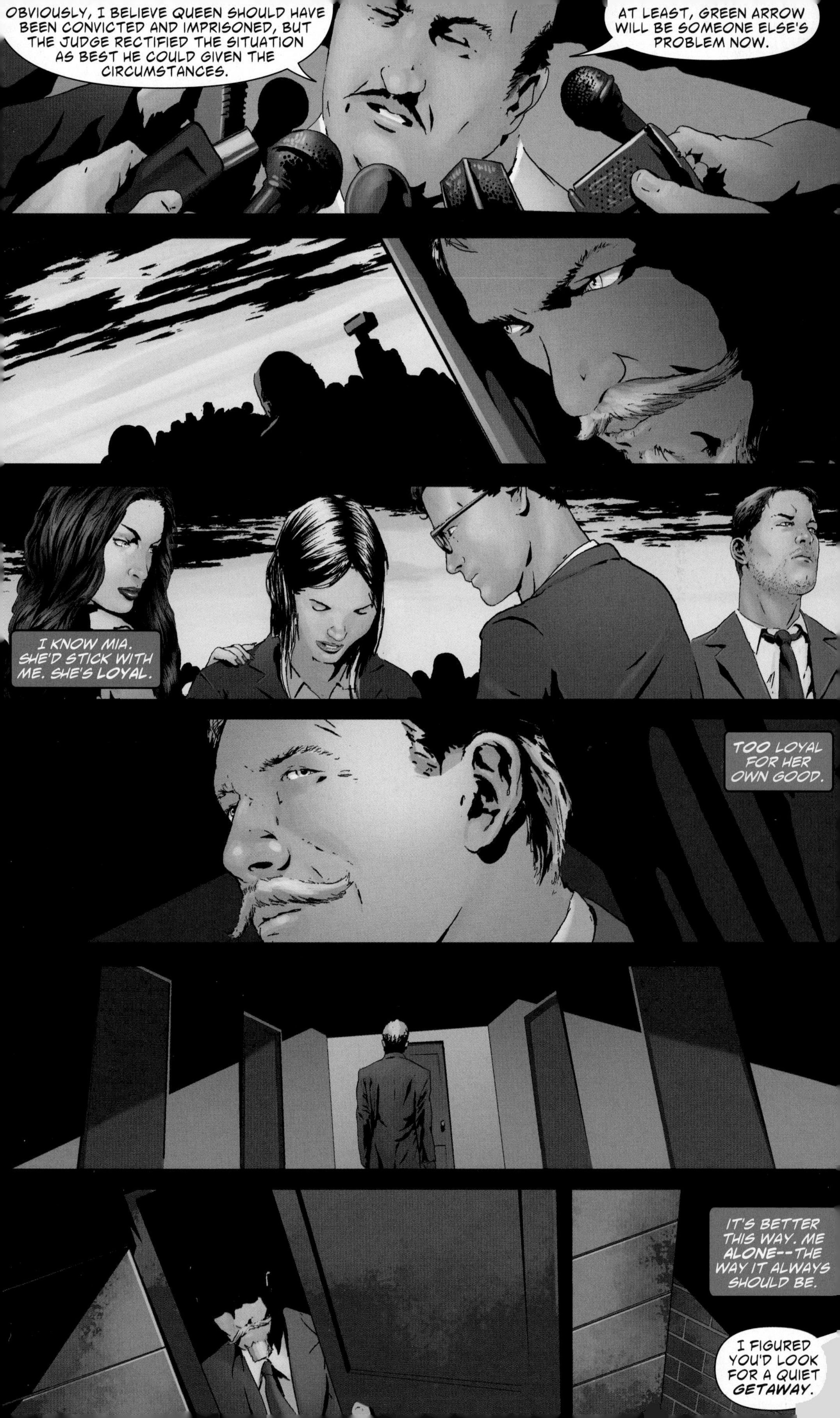
OBVIOUSLY, I BELIEVE QUEEN SHOULD HAVE BEEN CONVICTED AND IMPRISONED, BUT THE JUDGE RECTIFIED THE SITUATION AS BEST HE COULD GIVEN THE CIRCUMSTANCES.
AT LEAST, GREEN ARROW WILL BE SOMEONE ELSE'S PROBLEM NOW.
I KNOW MIA. SHE'D STICK WITH ME. SHE'S LOYAL.
TOO LOYAL FOR HER OWN GOOD.
IT'S BETTER THIS WAY. ME ALONE--THE WAY IT ALWAYS SHOULD BE.
I FIGURED YOU'D LOOK FOR A QUIET GETAWAY.

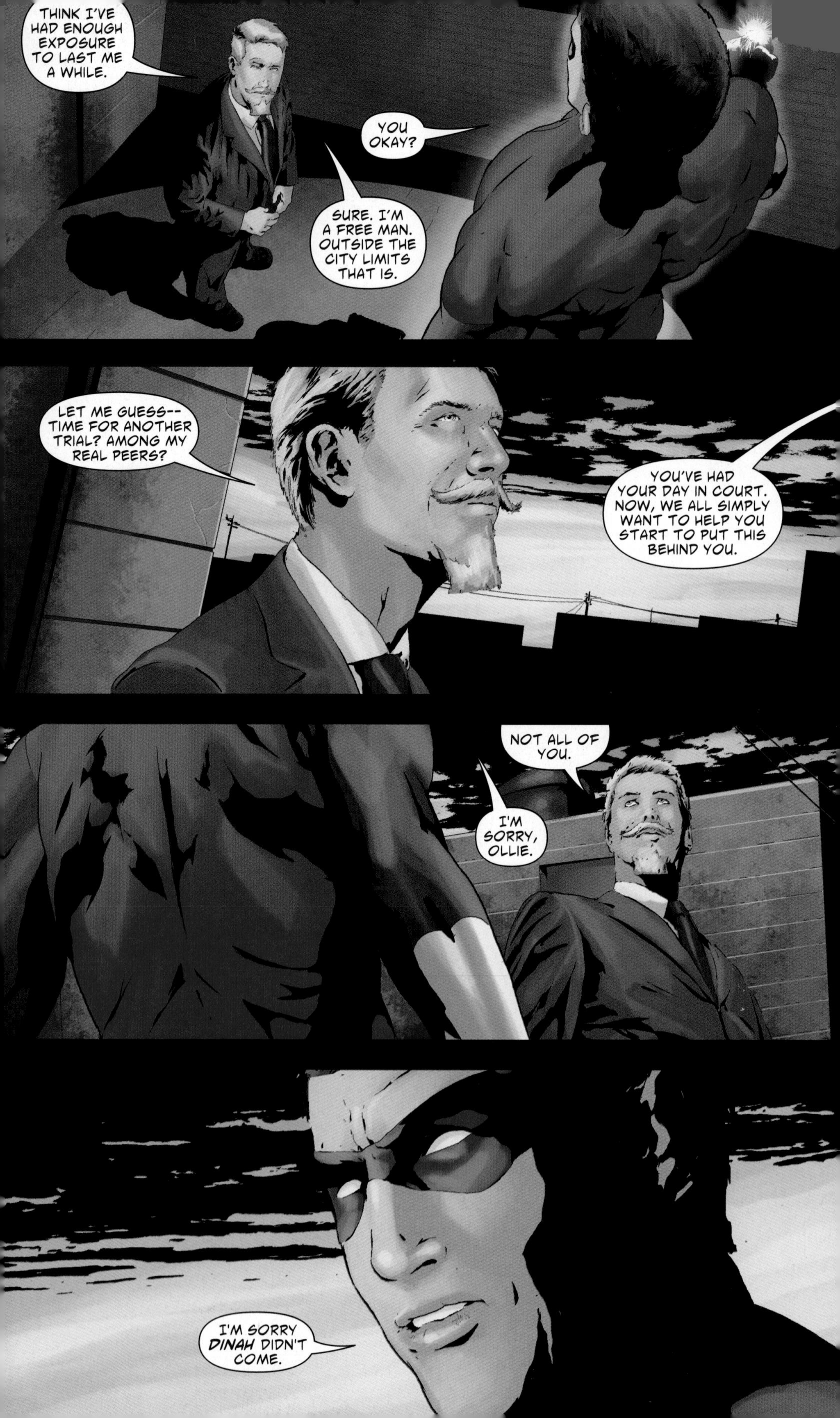
THINK I'VE HAD ENOUGH EXPOSURE TO LAST ME A WHILE.
YOU OKAY?
SURE. I'M A FREE MAN. OUTSIDE THE CITY LIMITS THAT IS.
LET ME GUESS-- TIME FOR ANOTHER TRIAL? AMONG MY REAL PEERS?
YOU'VE HAD YOUR DAY IN COURT. NOW, WE ALL SIMPLY WANT TO HELP YOU START TO PUT THIS BEHIND YOU.
NOT ALL OF YOU.
I'M SORRY, OLLIE.
I'M SORRY *DINAH* DIDN'T COME.

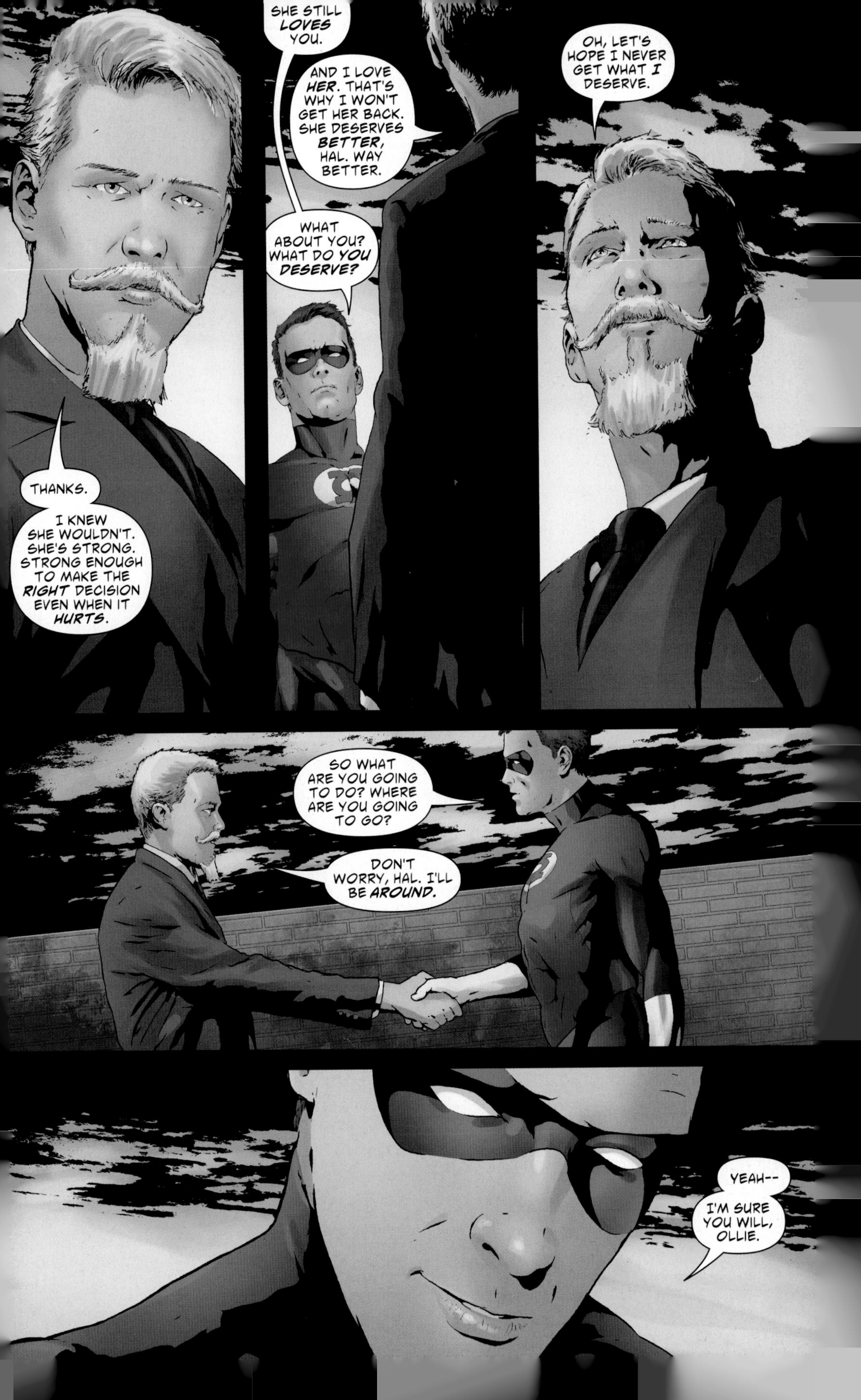
SHE STILL LOVES YOU.
AND I LOVE HER. THAT'S WHY I WON'T GET HER BACK. SHE DESERVES BETTER, HAL. WAY BETTER.
WHAT ABOUT YOU? WHAT DO YOU DESERVE?
OH, LET'S HOPE I NEVER GET WHAT I DESERVE.
THANKS.
I KNEW SHE WOULDN'T. SHE'S STRONG. STRONG ENOUGH TO MAKE THE RIGHT DECISION EVEN WHEN IT HURTS.
SO WHAT ARE YOU GOING TO DO? WHERE ARE YOU GOING TO GO?
DON'T WORRY, HAL. I'LL BE AROUND.
YEAH--
I'M SURE YOU WILL, OLLIE.

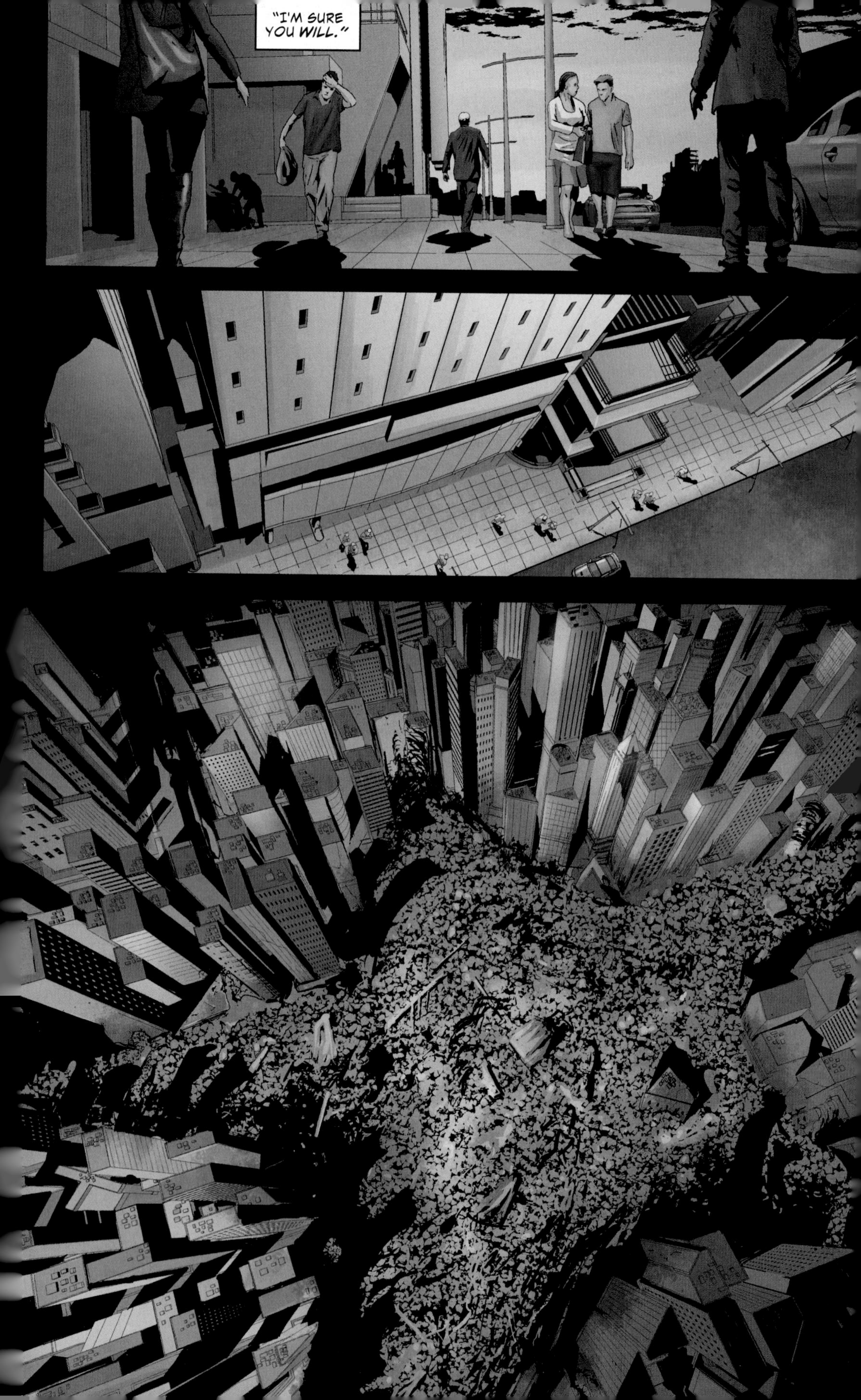
"I'M SURE YOU WILL."

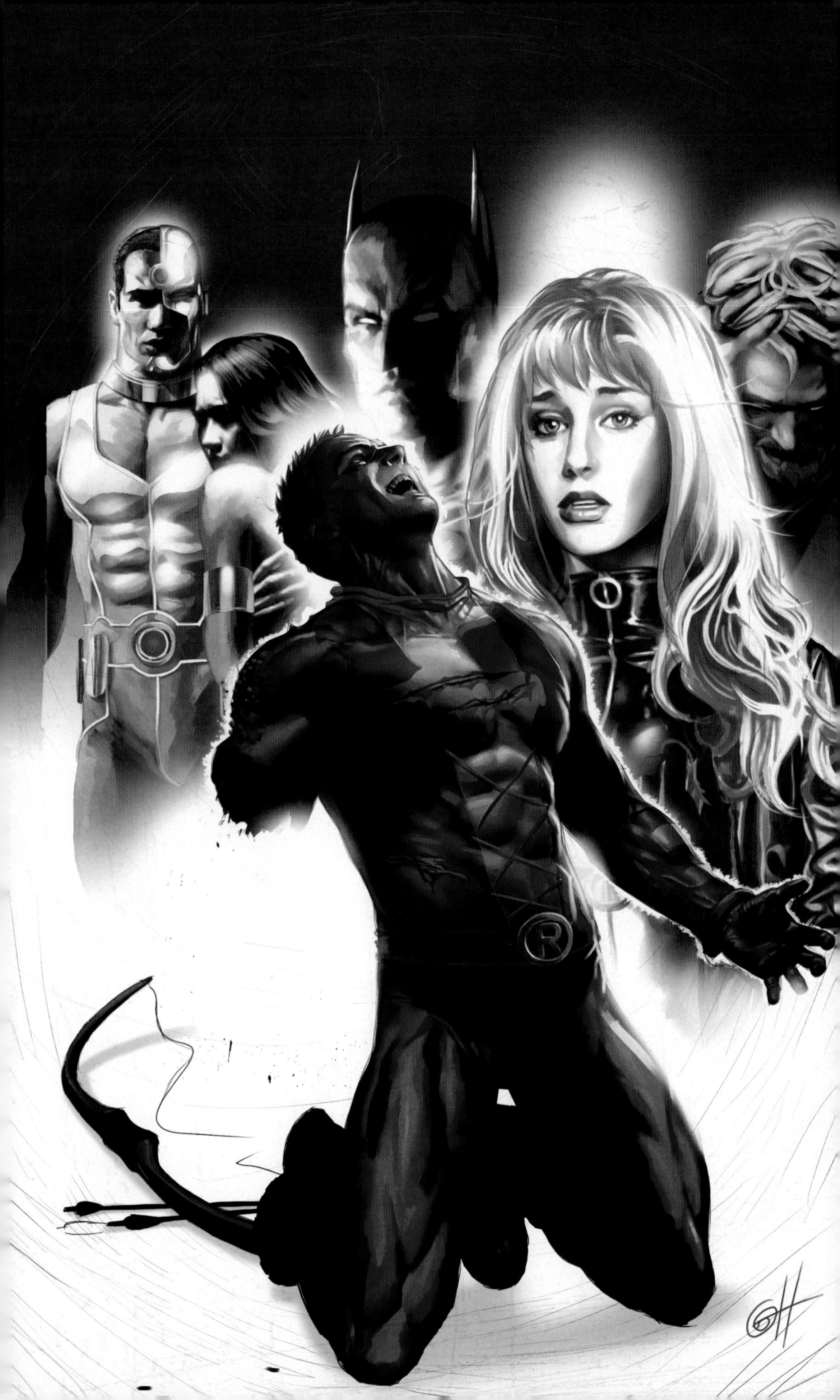

The Rise of Arsenal part one: A Father's Loss

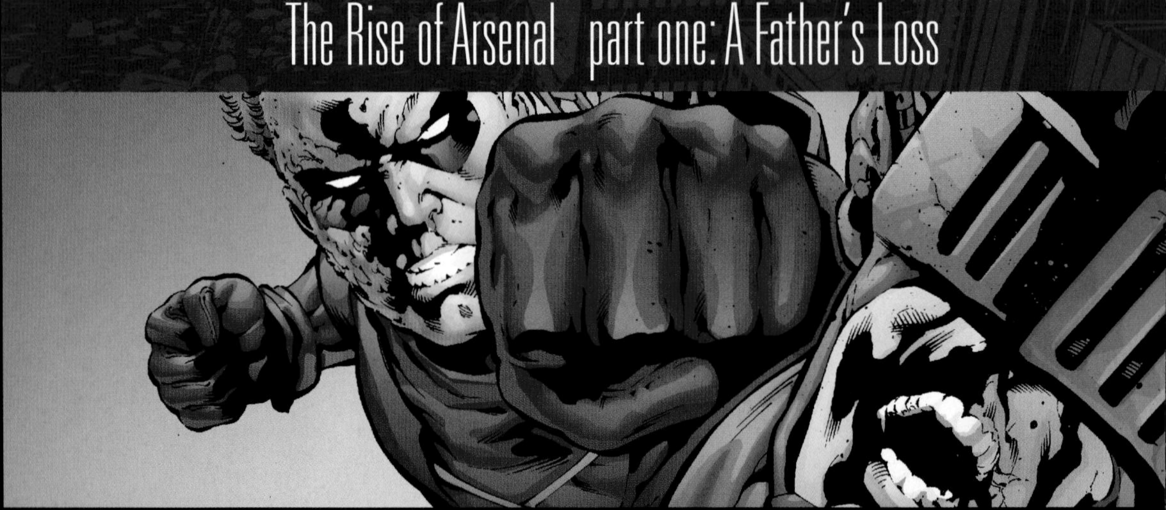

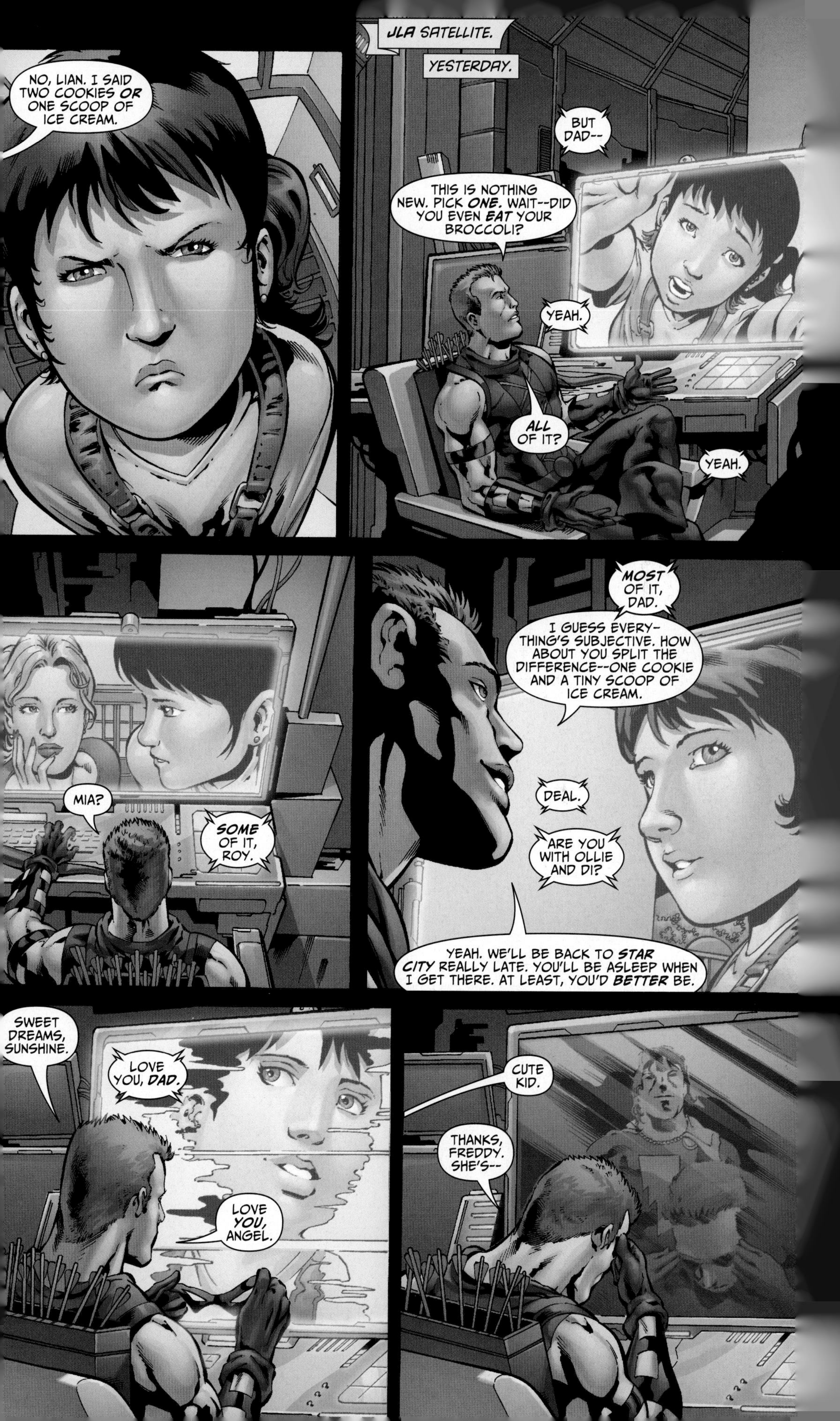
NO, LIAN. I SAID TWO COOKIES OR ONE SCOOP OF ICE CREAM.
JLA SATELLITE.
YESTERDAY.
BUT DAD--
THIS IS NOTHING NEW. PICK ONE. WAIT--DID YOU EVEN EAT YOUR BROCCOLI?
YEAH.
ALL OF IT?
YEAH.
MIA?
SOME OF IT, ROY.
MOST OF IT, DAD.
I GUESS EVERY-THING'S SUBJECTIVE. HOW ABOUT YOU SPLIT THE DIFFERENCE--ONE COOKIE AND A TINY SCOOP OF ICE CREAM.
DEAL.
ARE YOU WITH OLLIE AND DI?
YEAH. WE'LL BE BACK TO STAR CITY REALLY LATE. YOU'LL BE ASLEEP WHEN I GET THERE. AT LEAST, YOU'D BETTER BE.
SWEET DREAMS, SUNSHINE.
LOVE YOU, DAD.
LOVE YOU, ANGEL.
CUTE KID.
THANKS, FREDDY. SHE'S--

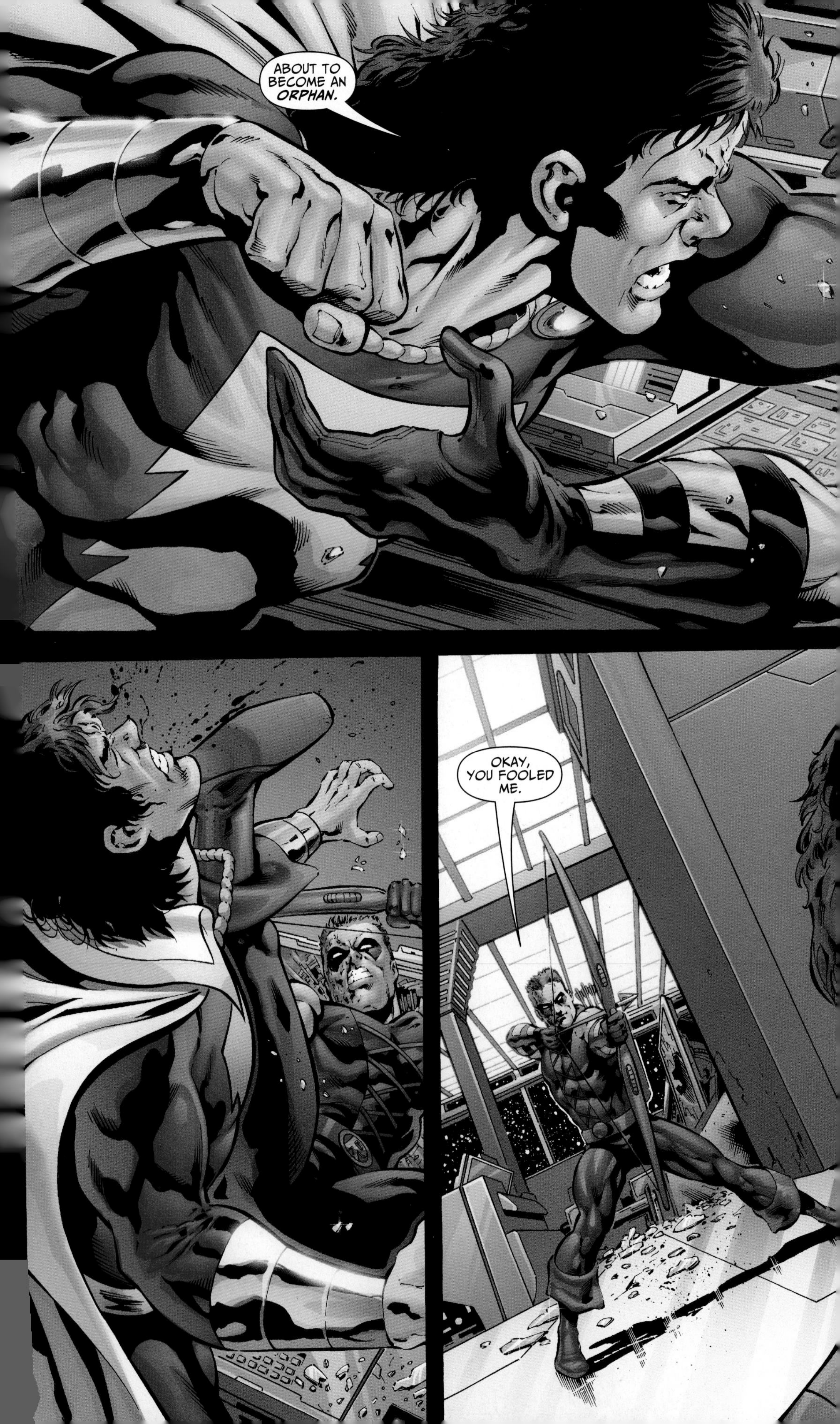
ABOUT TO BECOME AN ORPHAN.
OKAY, YOU FOOLED ME.

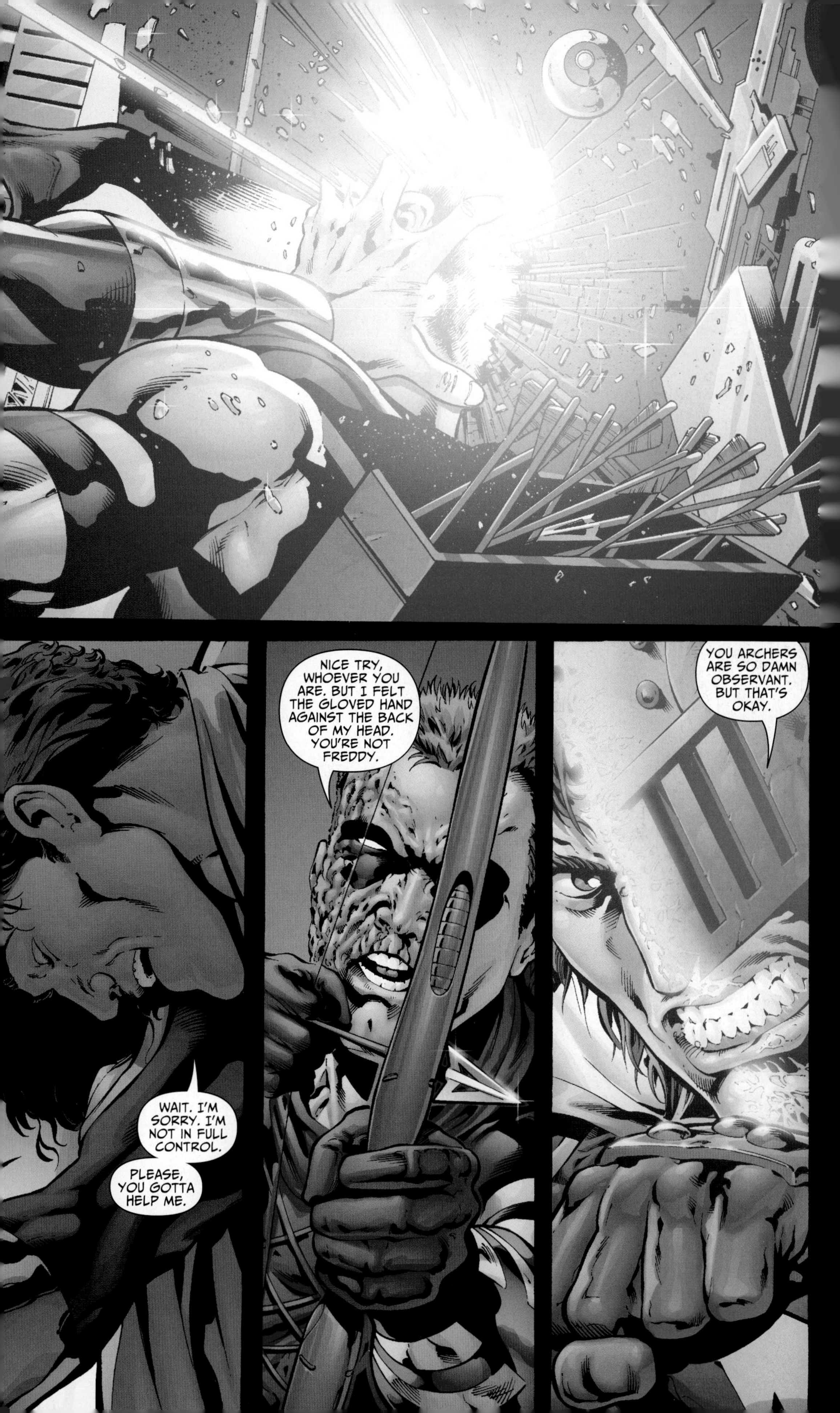
WAIT. I'M SORRY. I'M NOT IN FULL CONTROL.
PLEASE, YOU GOTTA HELP ME.
NICE TRY, WHOEVER YOU ARE. BUT I FELT THE GLOVED HAND AGAINST THE BACK OF MY HEAD. YOU'RE NOT FREDDY.
YOU ARCHERS ARE SO DAMN OBSERVANT. BUT THAT'S OKAY.

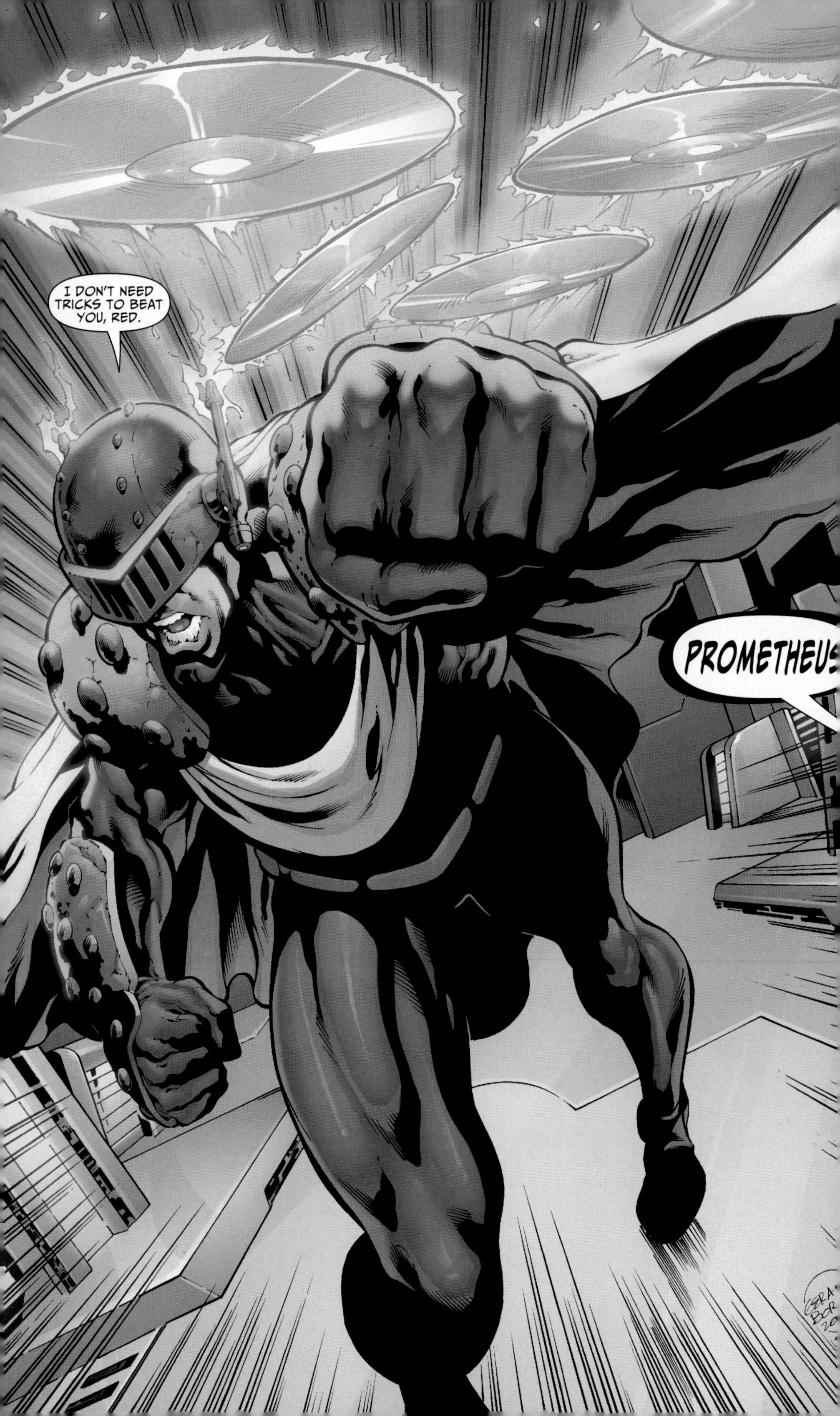
I DON'T NEED TRICKS TO BEAT YOU, RED.
PROMETHEU

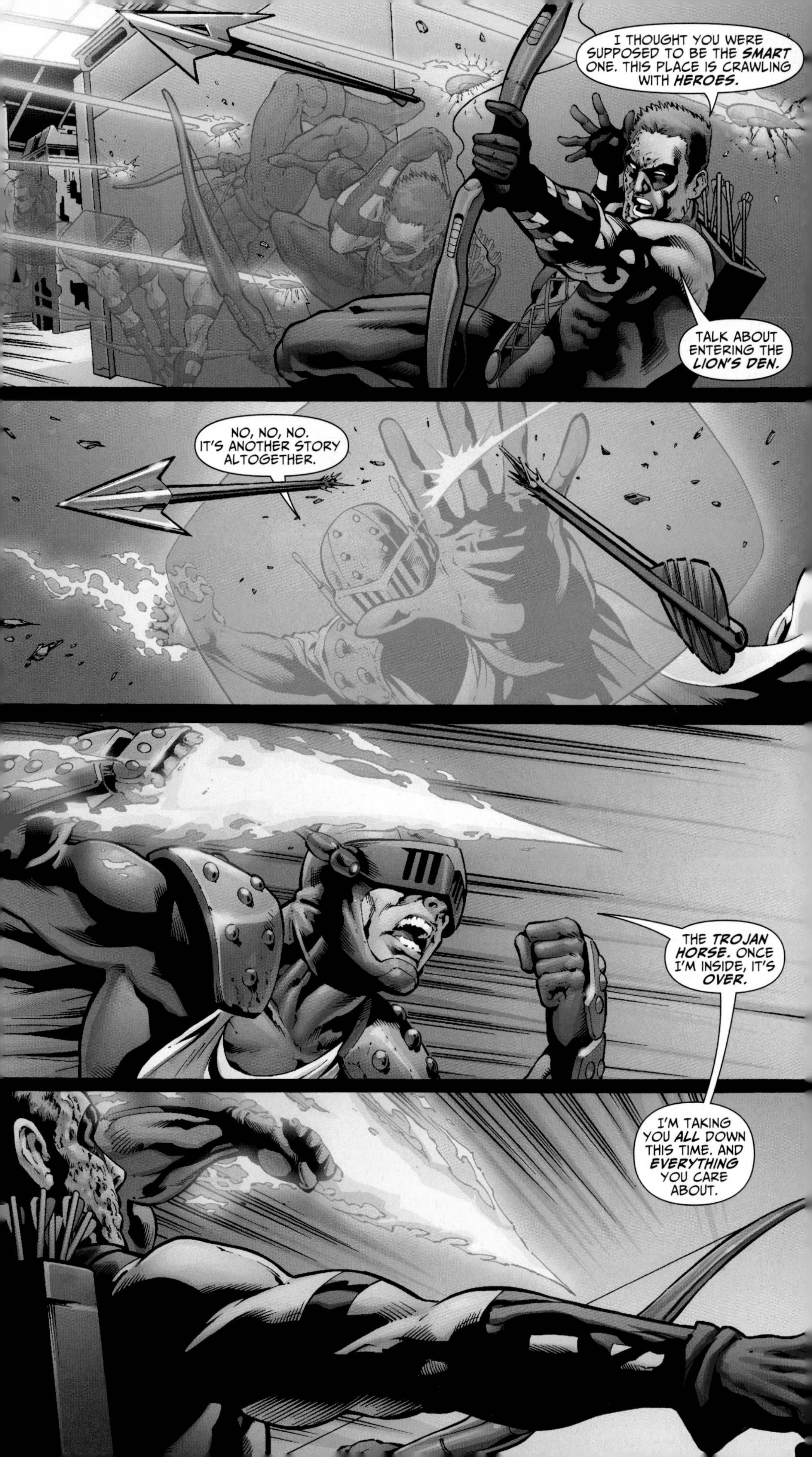
I THOUGHT YOU WERE SUPPOSED TO BE THE SMART ONE. THIS PLACE IS CRAWLING WITH HEROES.
TALK ABOUT ENTERING THE LION'S DEN.
NO, NO, NO. IT'S ANOTHER STORY ALTOGETHER.
THE TROJAN HORSE. ONCE I'M INSIDE, IT'S OVER.
I'M TAKING YOU ALL DOWN THIS TIME. AND EVERYTHING YOU CARE ABOUT.

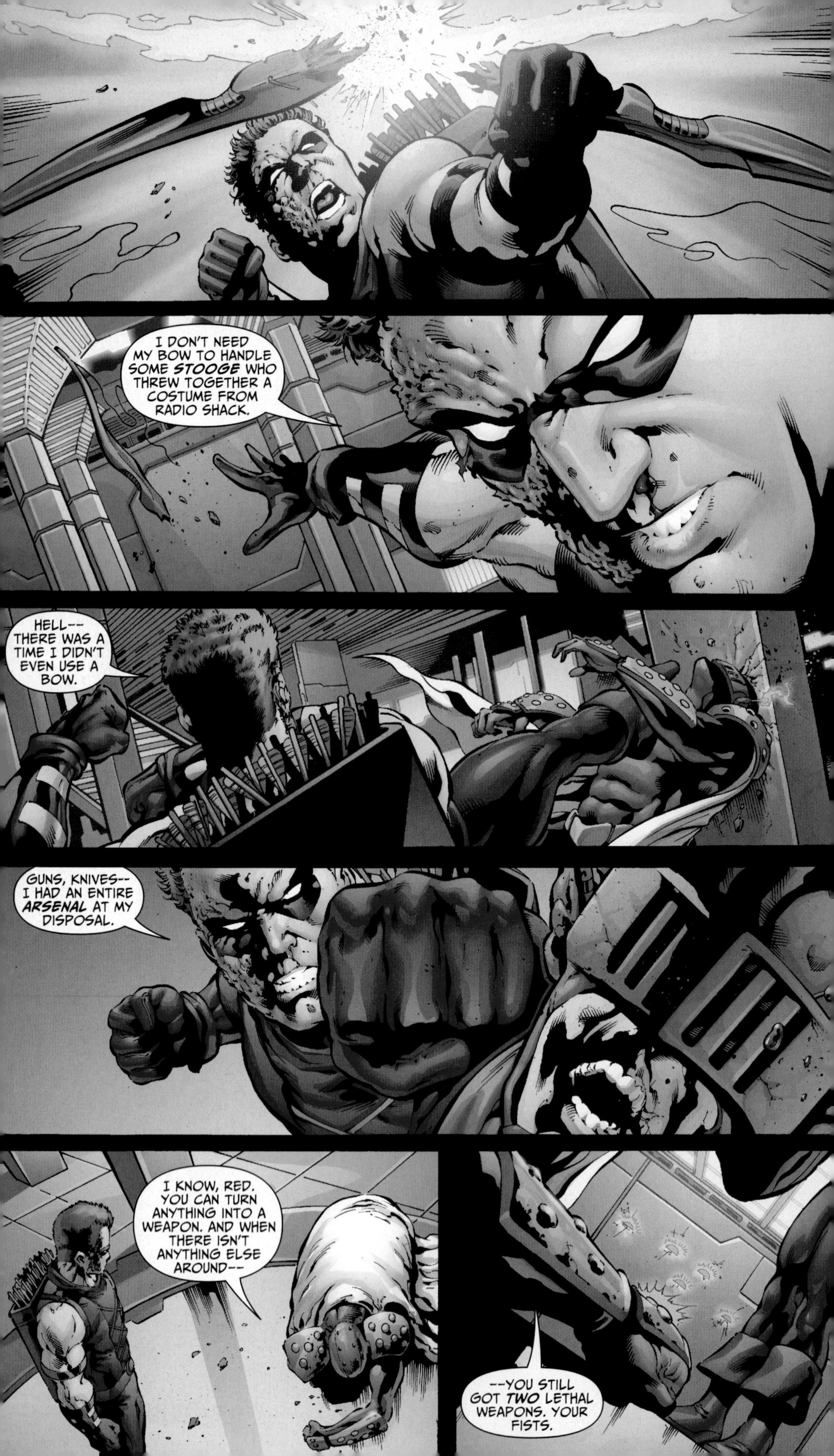
I DON'T NEED MY BOW TO HANDLE SOME STOOGE WHO THREW TOGETHER A COSTUME FROM RADIO SHACK.
HELL-- THERE WAS A TIME I DIDN'T EVEN USE A BOW.
GUNS, KNIVES-- I HAD AN ENTIRE ARSENAL AT MY DISPOSAL.
I KNOW, RED. YOU CAN TURN ANYTHING INTO A WEAPON. AND WHEN THERE ISN'T ANYTHING ELSE AROUND--
--YOU STILL GOT TWO LETHAL WEAPONS. YOUR FISTS.

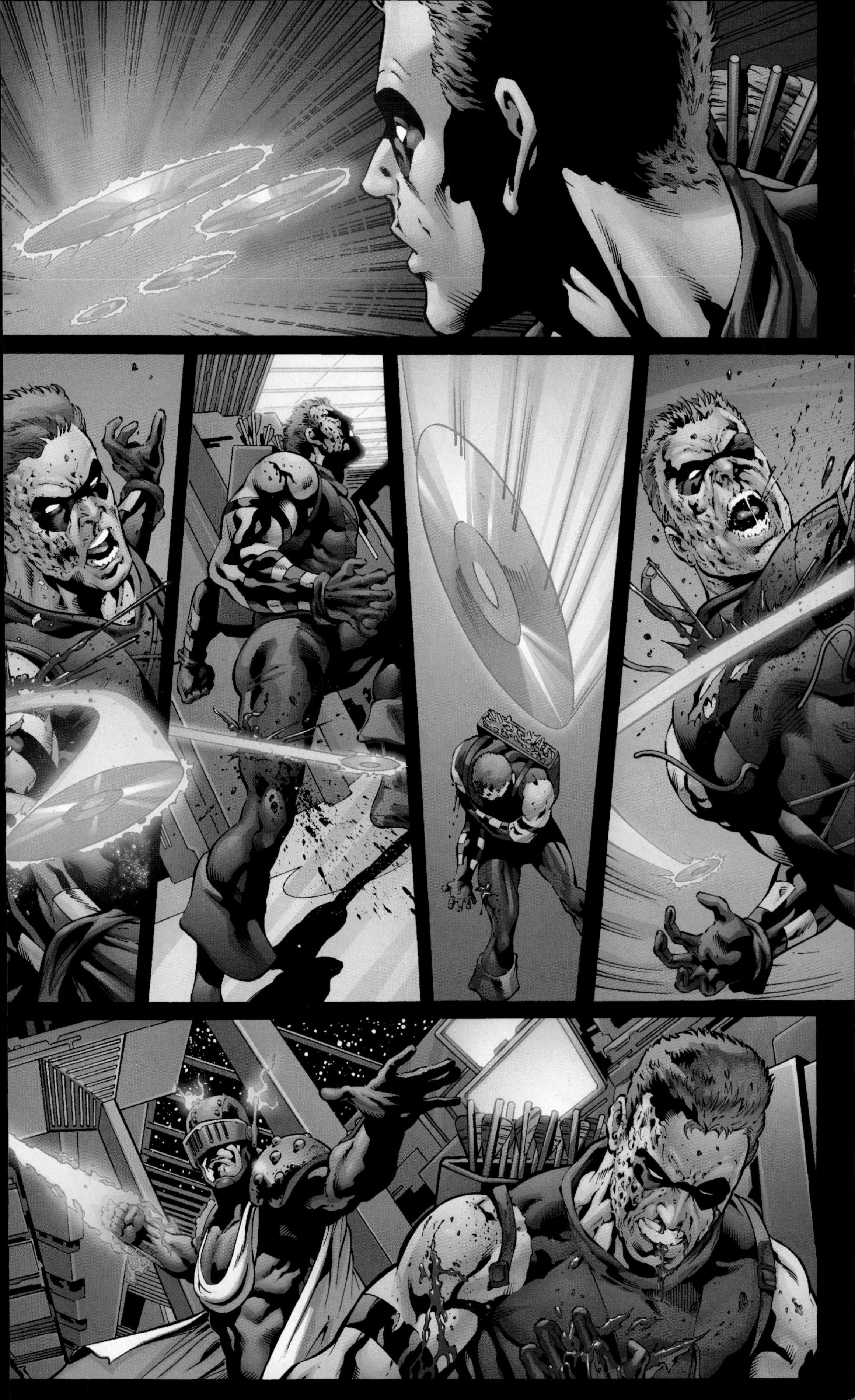

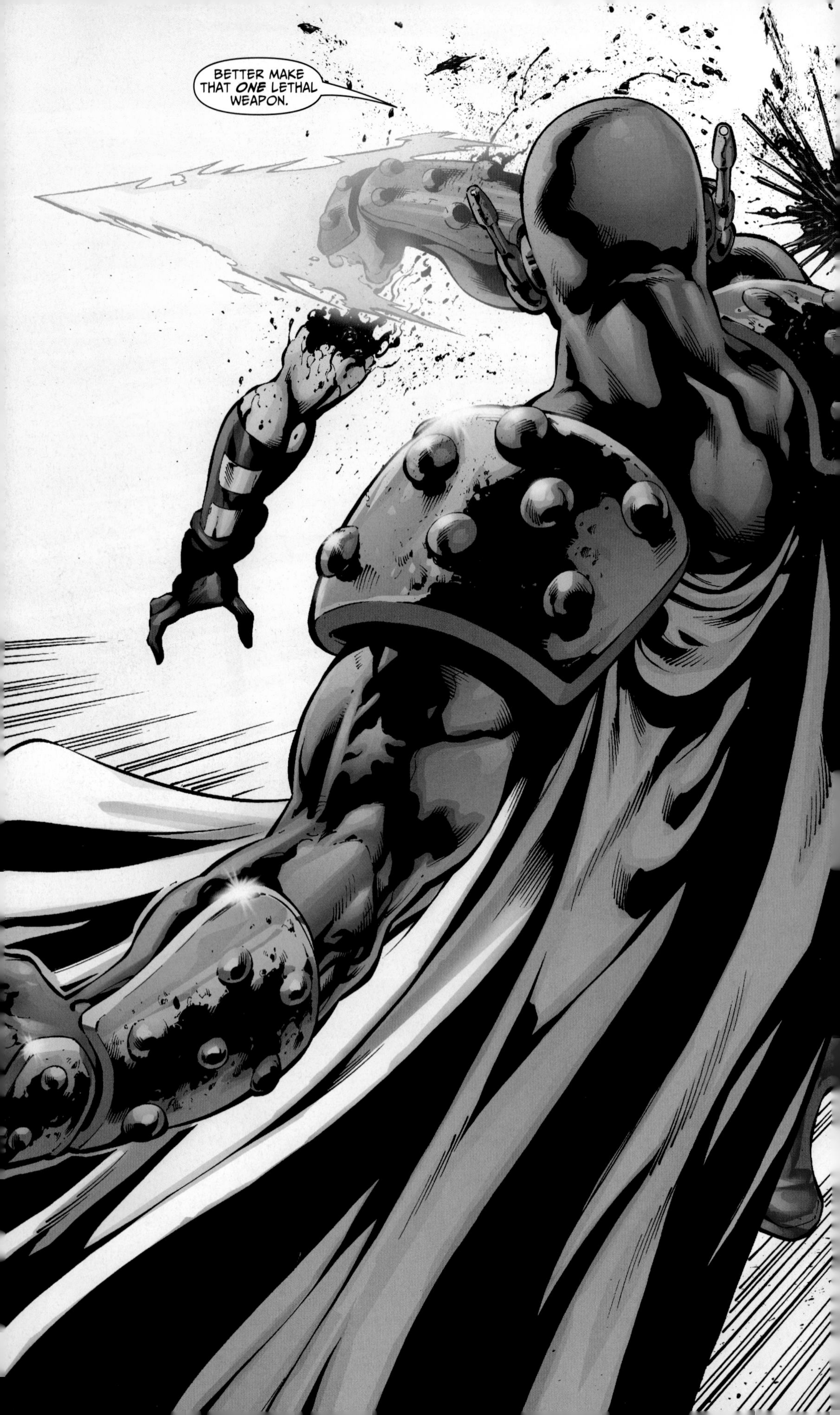
BETTER MAKE THAT *ONE* LETHAL WEAPON.

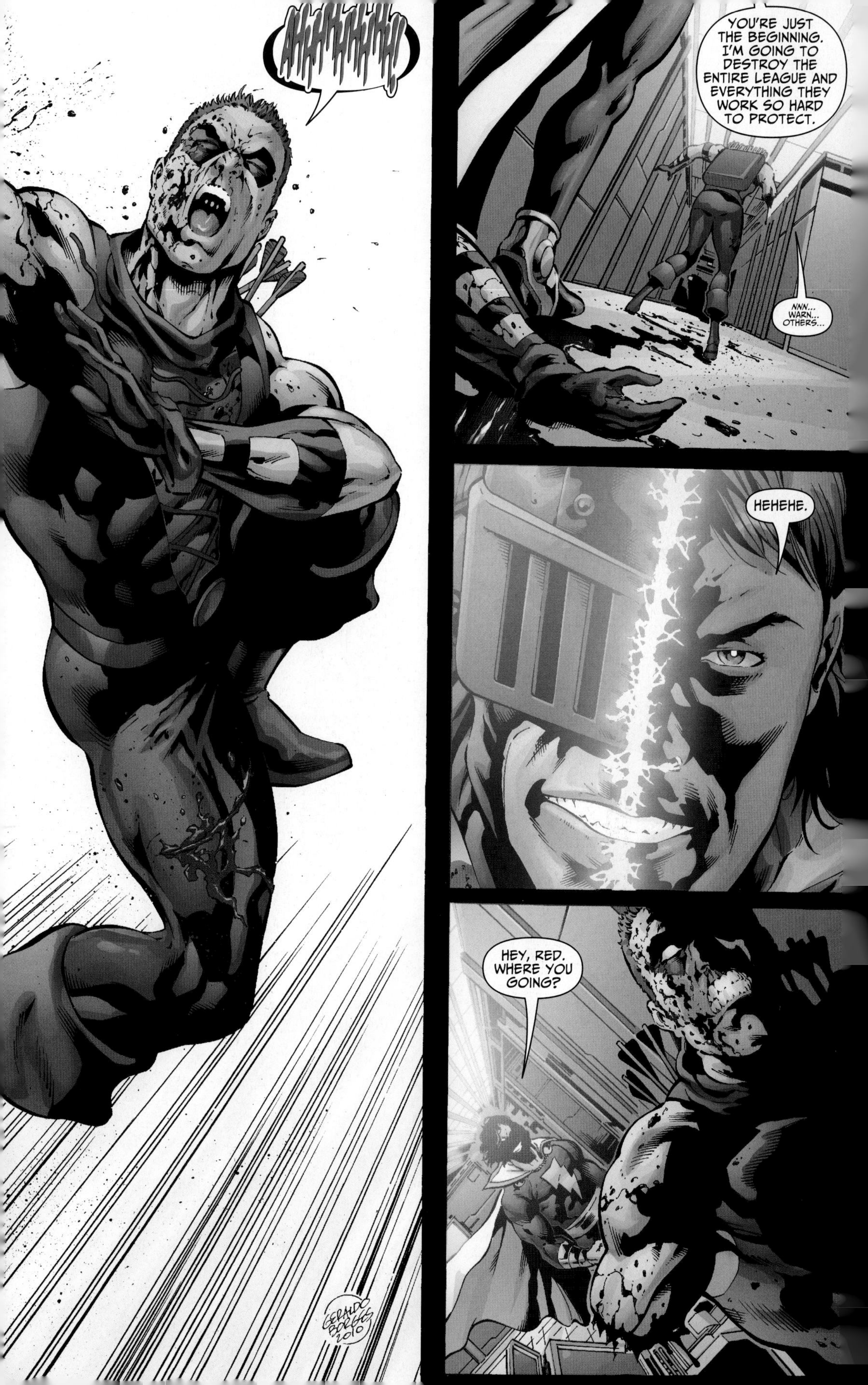
AHHHHHHHH!!
YOU'RE JUST THE BEGINNING. I'M GOING TO DESTROY THE ENTIRE LEAGUE AND EVERYTHING THEY WORK SO HARD TO PROTECT.
NNN... WARN... OTHERS...
HEHEHE.
HEY, RED. WHERE YOU GOING?
GERALDO BORGES 2010

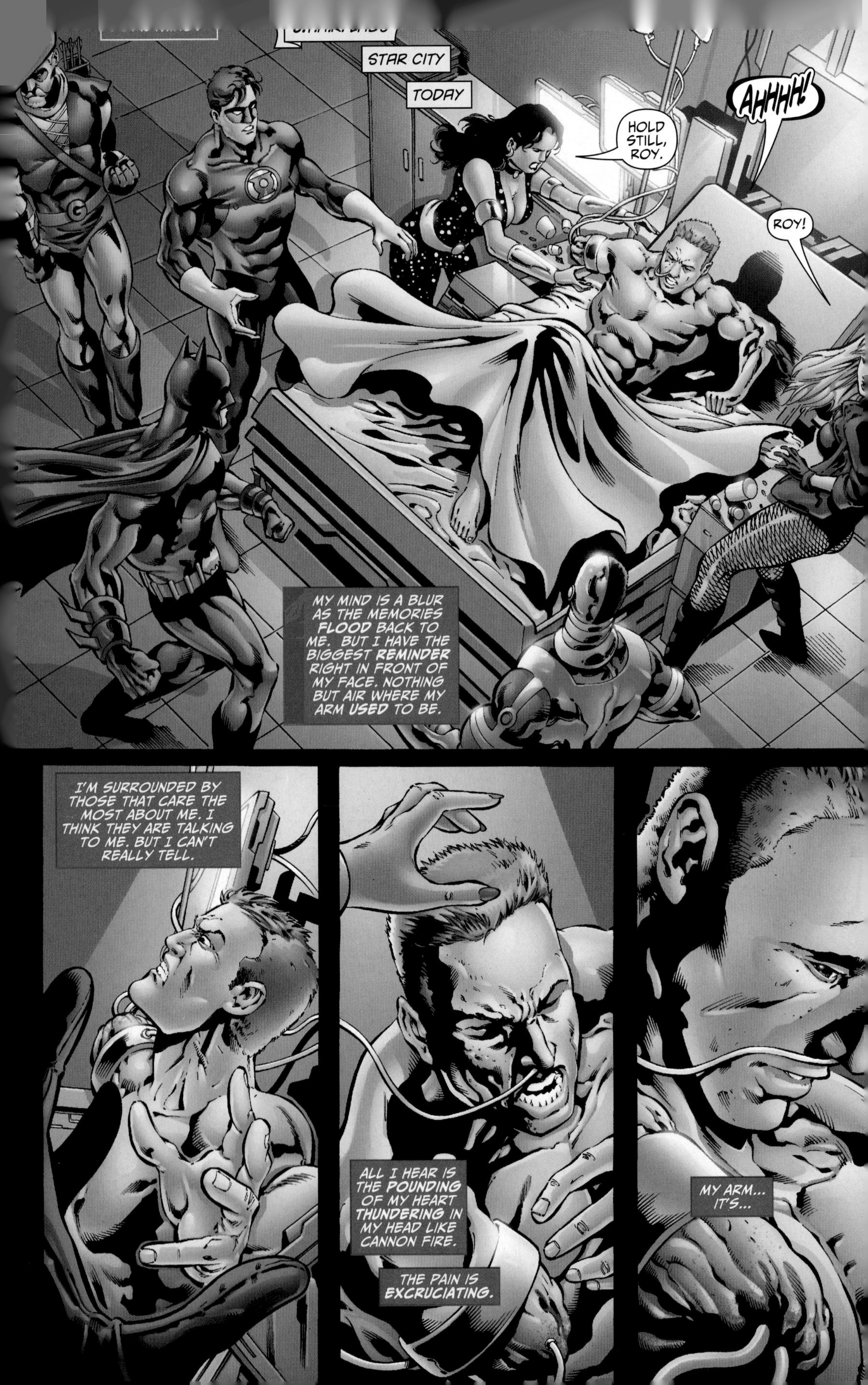
STAR CITY
TODAY
HOLD STILL, ROY.
AHHHH!
ROY!
MY MIND IS A BLUR AS THE MEMORIES FLOOD BACK TO ME. BUT I HAVE THE BIGGEST REMINDER RIGHT IN FRONT OF MY FACE. NOTHING BUT AIR WHERE MY ARM USED TO BE.
I'M SURROUNDED BY THOSE THAT CARE THE MOST ABOUT ME. I THINK THEY ARE TALKING TO ME. BUT I CAN'T REALLY TELL.
ALL I HEAR IS THE POUNDING OF MY HEART THUNDERING IN MY HEAD LIKE CANNON FIRE.
THE PAIN IS EXCRUCIATING.
MY ARM... IT'S...

IT'S REALLY GONE.

TELL ME YOU *GOT* HIM?

I'M SORRY, ROY. PROMETHEUS GOT THE DROP ON ALL OF US. BROKE INTO THE SATELLITE DISGUISED AS CAPTAIN MARVEL. MADE HIS MOVE FROM THERE.

A COORDINATED ATTACK ON *DOZENS* OF CITIES. WE STOPPED HIM, BUT NOT BEFORE *STAR CITY* TOOK *HEAVY* DAMAGE.

NOT YET. BUT WE'LL FIND HIM. *BARRY* AND *WALLY* ARE OUT LOOKING FOR HIM, RIGHT NOW.

I KNOW IT'S HARD, ROY. BUT YOU HAVE TO STAY CALM. YOUR BODY'S BEEN THROUGH A TERRIBLE TRAUMA. YOU NEED TO SAVE YOUR STRENGTH.

THERE'S SOME-THING YOU'RE NOT TELLING ME.

HOW BAD WAS THE DAMAGE TO STAR CITY?

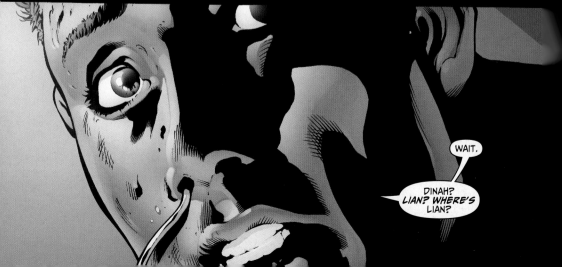

WAIT.

DINAH? *LIAN? WHERE'S* LIAN?

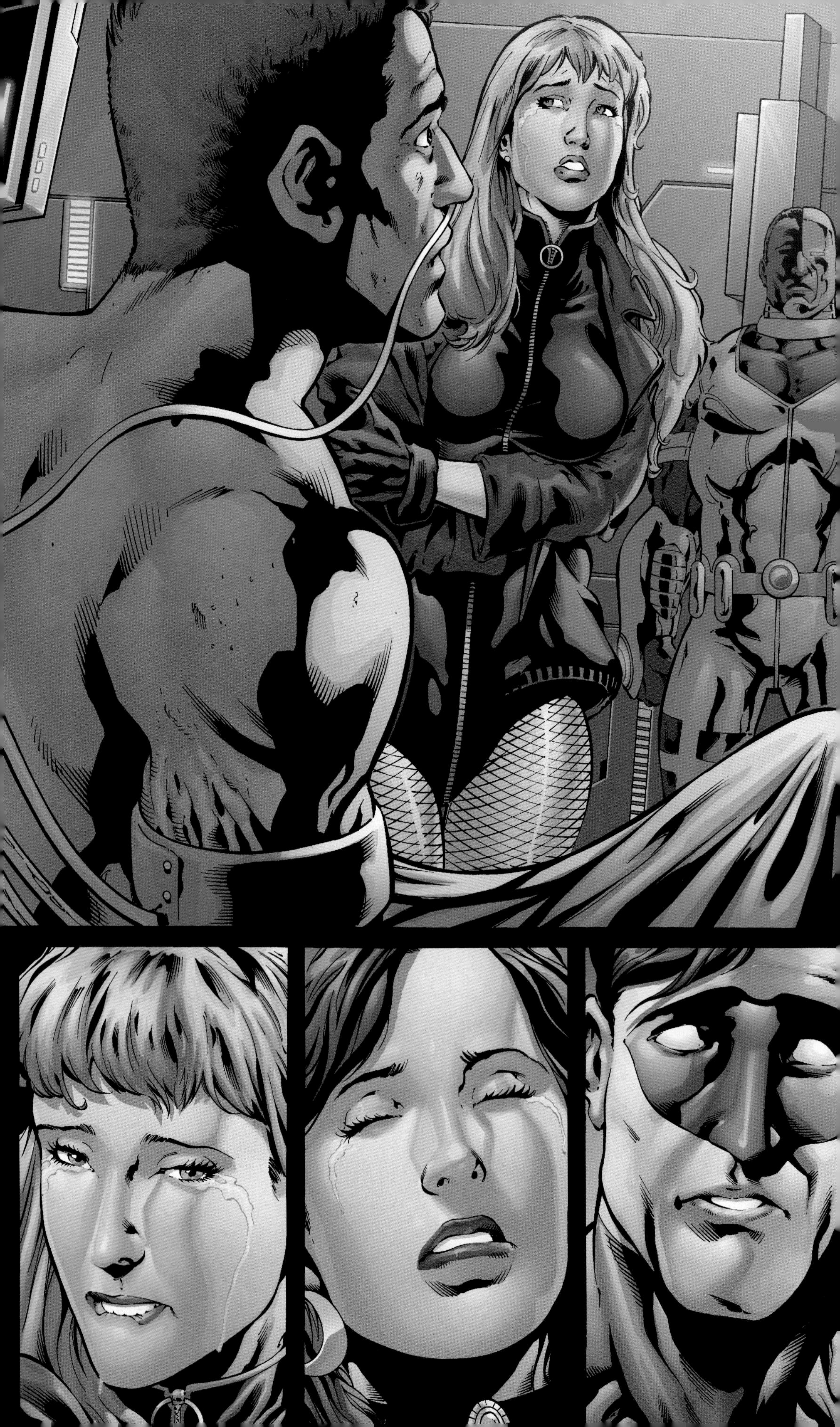

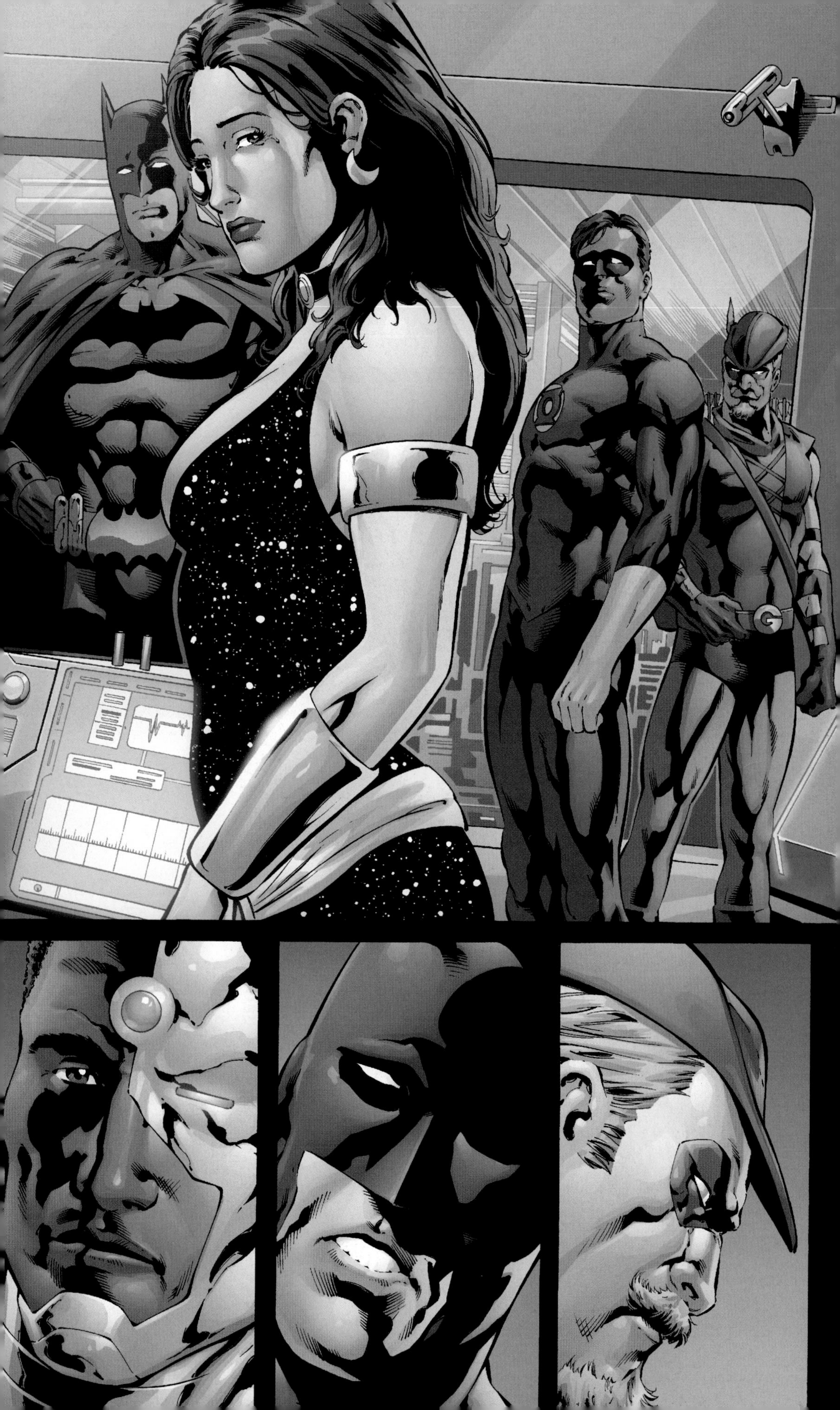

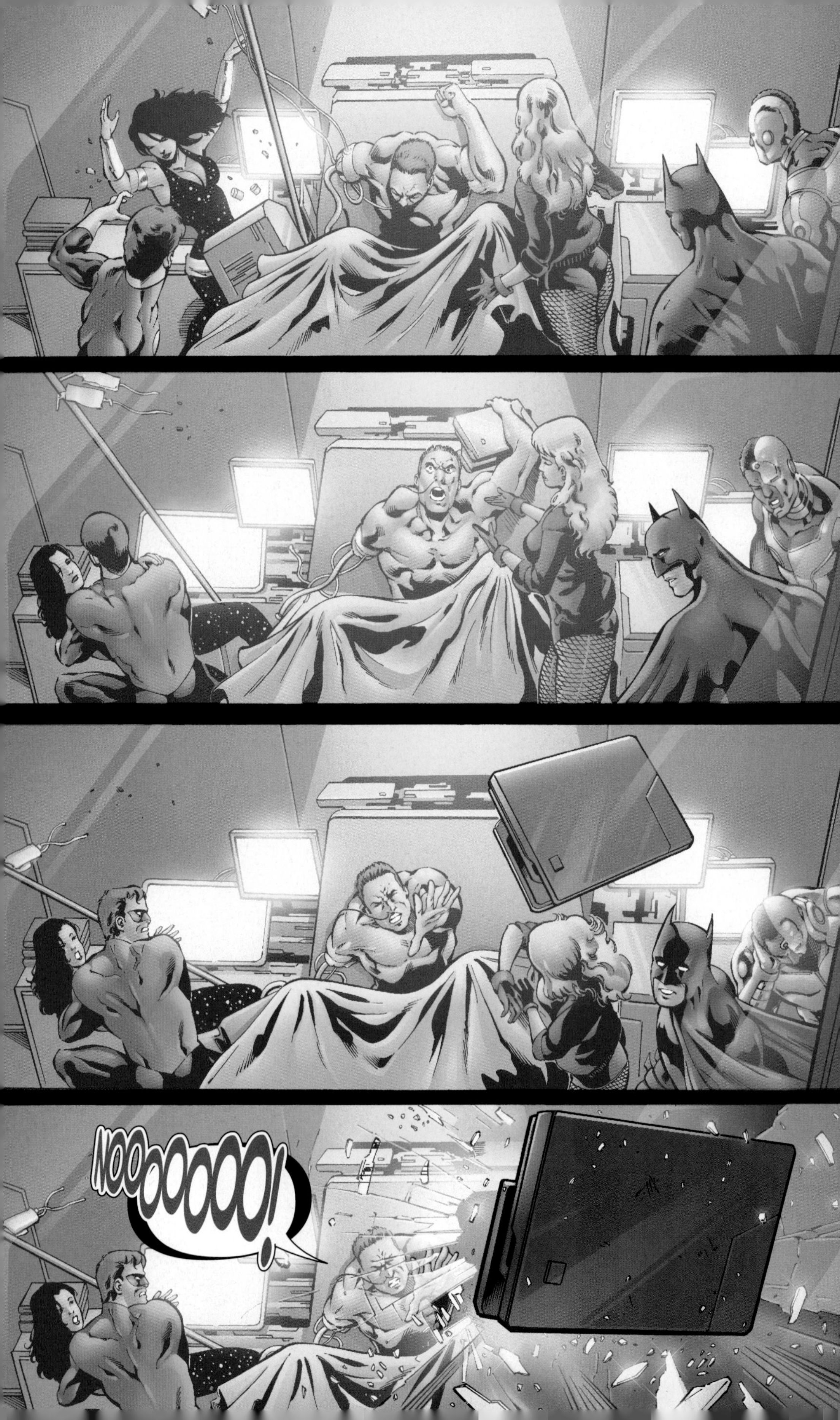
NOOOOOOO!

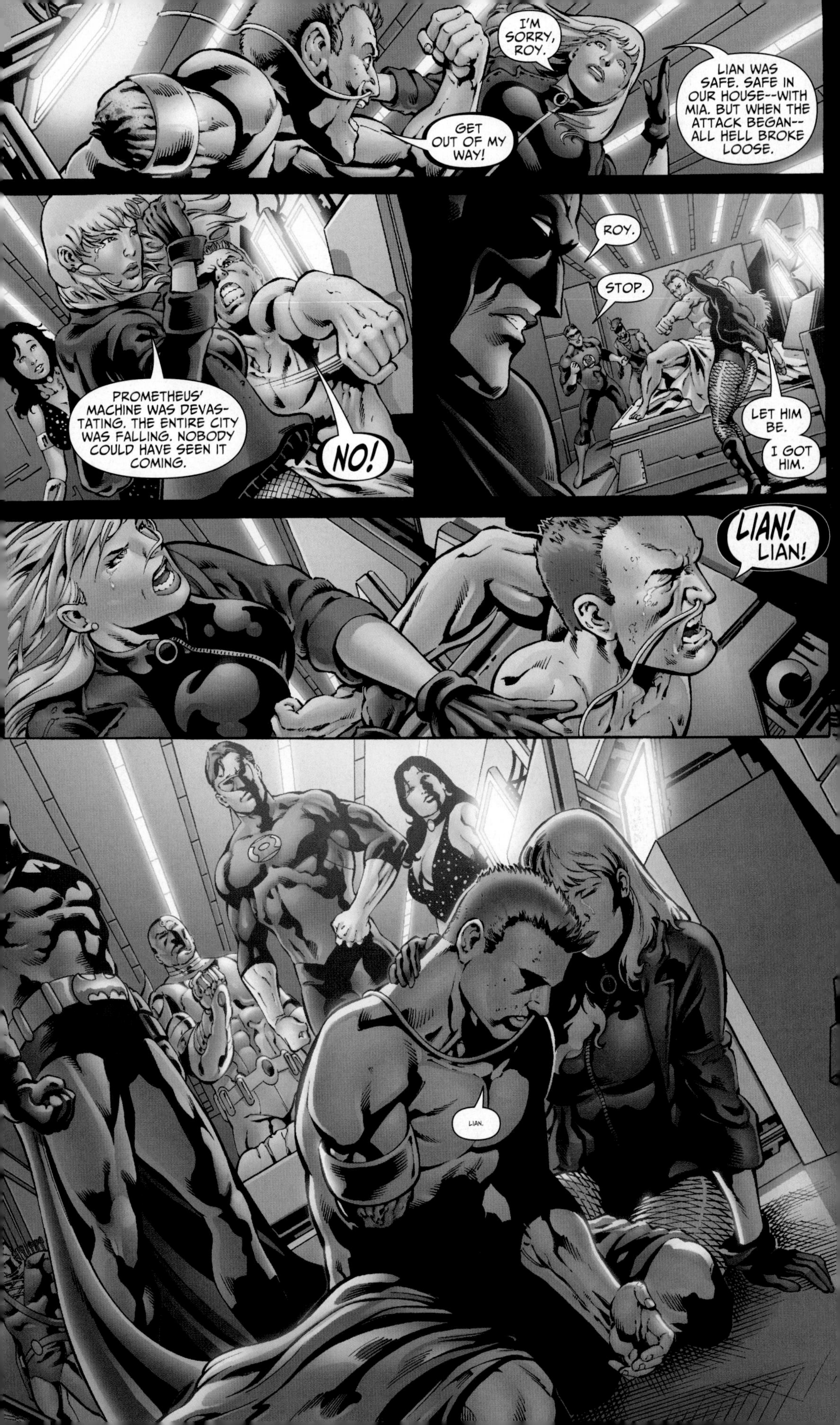
I'M SORRY, ROY.
GET OUT OF MY WAY!
LIAN WAS SAFE. SAFE IN OUR HOUSE--WITH MIA. BUT WHEN THE ATTACK BEGAN--ALL HELL BROKE LOOSE.
PROMETHEUS' MACHINE WAS DEVASTATING. THE ENTIRE CITY WAS FALLING. NOBODY COULD HAVE SEEN IT COMING.
NO!
ROY.
STOP.
LET HIM BE.
I GOT HIM.
LIAN! LIAN!
LIAN.

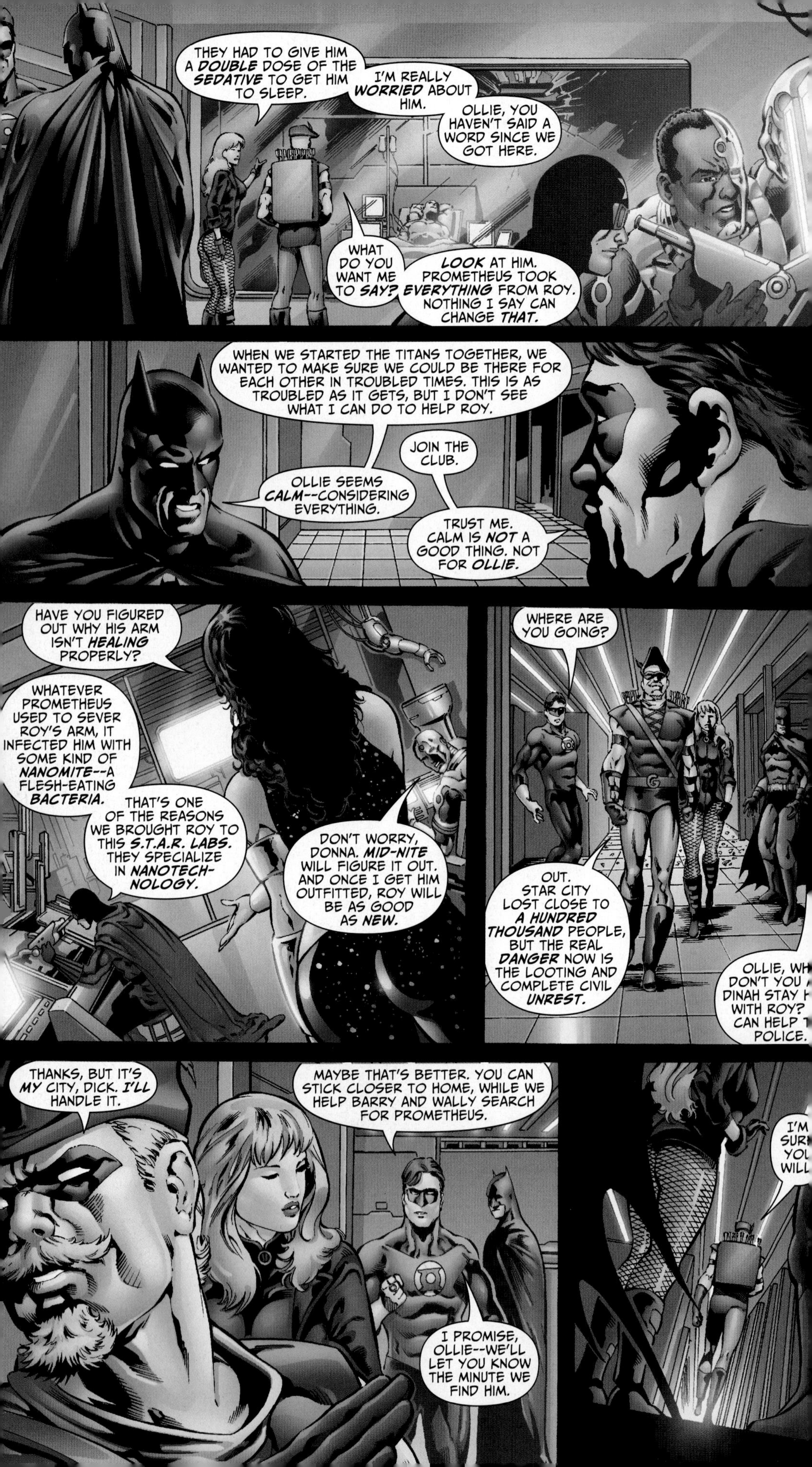
THEY HAD TO GIVE HIM A DOUBLE DOSE OF THE SEDATIVE TO GET HIM TO SLEEP.
I'M REALLY WORRIED ABOUT HIM.
OLLIE, YOU HAVEN'T SAID A WORD SINCE WE GOT HERE.
WHAT DO YOU WANT ME TO SAY?
LOOK AT HIM. PROMETHEUS TOOK EVERYTHING FROM ROY. NOTHING I SAY CAN CHANGE THAT.
WHEN WE STARTED THE TITANS TOGETHER, WE WANTED TO MAKE SURE WE COULD BE THERE FOR EACH OTHER IN TROUBLED TIMES. THIS IS AS TROUBLED AS IT GETS, BUT I DON'T SEE WHAT I CAN DO TO HELP ROY.
OLLIE SEEMS CALM--CONSIDERING EVERYTHING.
JOIN THE CLUB.
TRUST ME. CALM IS NOT A GOOD THING. NOT FOR OLLIE.
HAVE YOU FIGURED OUT WHY HIS ARM ISN'T HEALING PROPERLY?
WHATEVER PROMETHEUS USED TO SEVER ROY'S ARM, IT INFECTED HIM WITH SOME KIND OF NANOMITE--A FLESH-EATING BACTERIA.
THAT'S ONE OF THE REASONS WE BROUGHT ROY TO THIS S.T.A.R. LABS. THEY SPECIALIZE IN NANOTECH-NOLOGY.
DON'T WORRY, DONNA. MID-NITE WILL FIGURE IT OUT. AND ONCE I GET HIM OUTFITTED, ROY WILL BE AS GOOD AS NEW.
WHERE ARE YOU GOING?
OUT. STAR CITY LOST CLOSE TO A HUNDRED THOUSAND PEOPLE, BUT THE REAL DANGER NOW IS THE LOOTING AND COMPLETE CIVIL UNREST.
OLLIE, WH DON'T YOU DINAH STAY H WITH ROY? CAN HELP T POLICE.
THANKS, BUT IT'S MY CITY, DICK. I'LL HANDLE IT.
MAYBE THAT'S BETTER. YOU CAN STICK CLOSER TO HOME, WHILE WE HELP BARRY AND WALLY SEARCH FOR PROMETHEUS.
I PROMISE, OLLIE--WE'LL LET YOU KNOW THE MINUTE WE FIND HIM.
I'M SUR YOU WILL

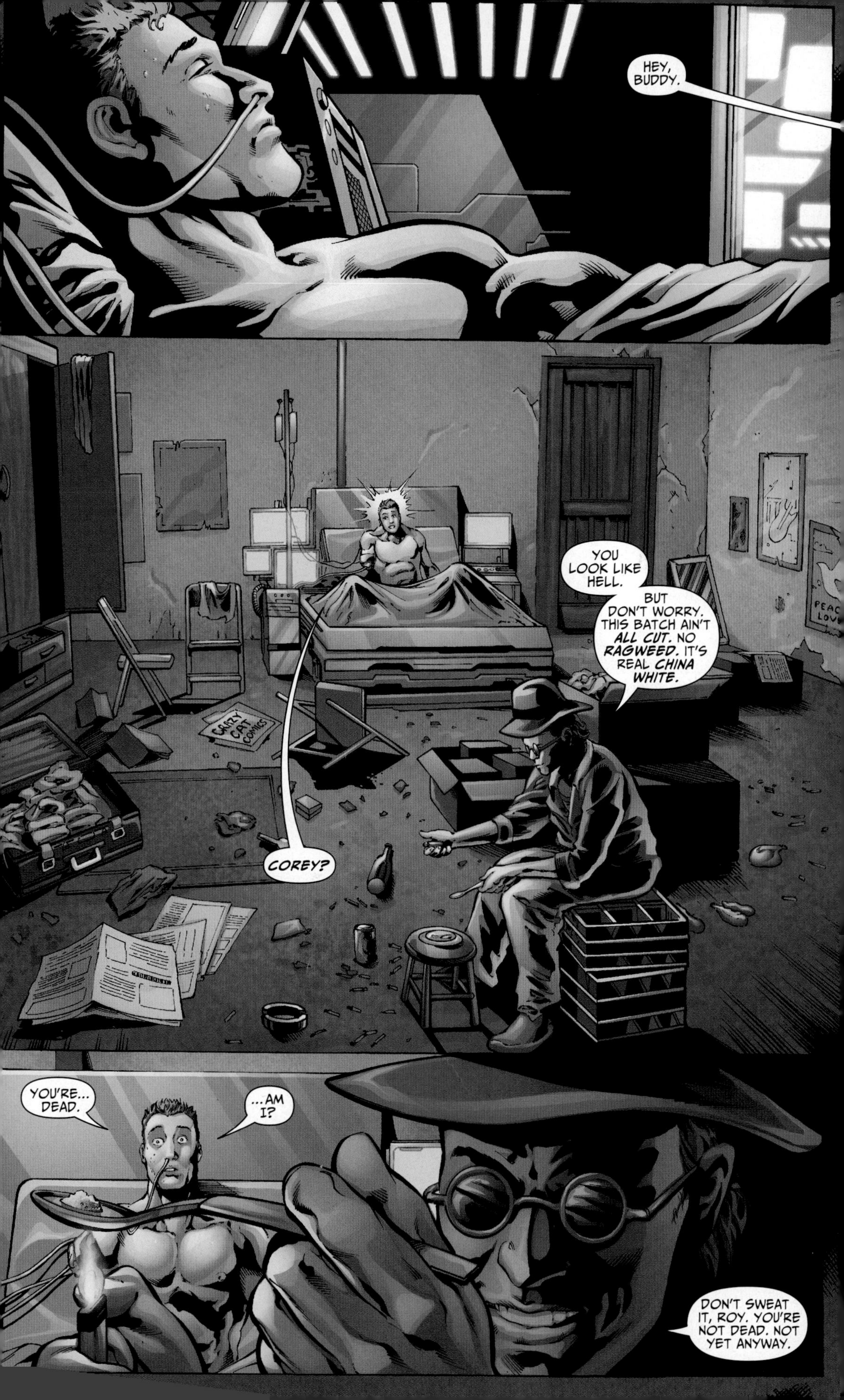

HEY, BUDDY.
YOU LOOK LIKE HELL.
BUT DON'T WORRY. THIS BATCH AIN'T ALL CUT. NO RAGWEED. IT'S REAL CHINA WHITE.
COREY?
CRAZY CAT COMICS
YOU'RE... DEAD.
...AM I?
DON'T SWEAT IT, ROY. YOU'RE NOT DEAD. NOT YET ANYWAY.

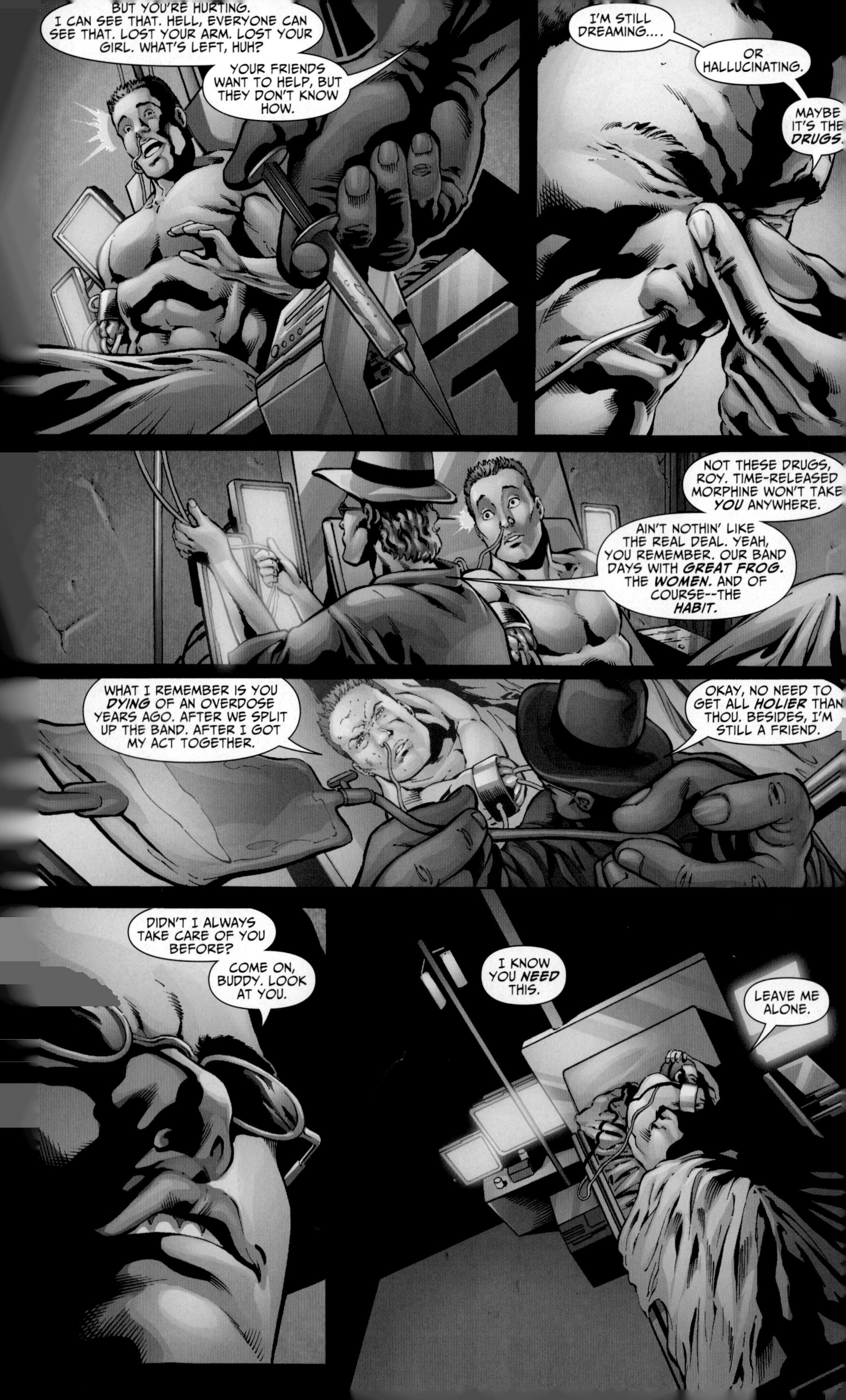
BUT YOU'RE HURTING. I CAN SEE THAT. HELL, EVERYONE CAN SEE THAT. LOST YOUR ARM. LOST YOUR GIRL. WHAT'S LEFT, HUH?
YOUR FRIENDS WANT TO HELP, BUT THEY DON'T KNOW HOW.
I'M STILL DREAMING....
OR HALLUCINATING.
MAYBE IT'S THE DRUGS.
NOT THESE DRUGS, ROY. TIME-RELEASED MORPHINE WON'T TAKE YOU ANYWHERE.
AIN'T NOTHIN' LIKE THE REAL DEAL. YEAH, YOU REMEMBER. OUR BAND DAYS WITH GREAT FROG. THE WOMEN. AND OF COURSE--THE HABIT.
WHAT I REMEMBER IS YOU DYING OF AN OVERDOSE YEARS AGO. AFTER WE SPLIT UP THE BAND. AFTER I GOT MY ACT TOGETHER.
OKAY, NO NEED TO GET ALL HOLIER THAN THOU. BESIDES, I'M STILL A FRIEND.
DIDN'T I ALWAYS TAKE CARE OF YOU BEFORE?
COME ON, BUDDY. LOOK AT YOU.
I KNOW YOU NEED THIS.
LEAVE ME ALONE.

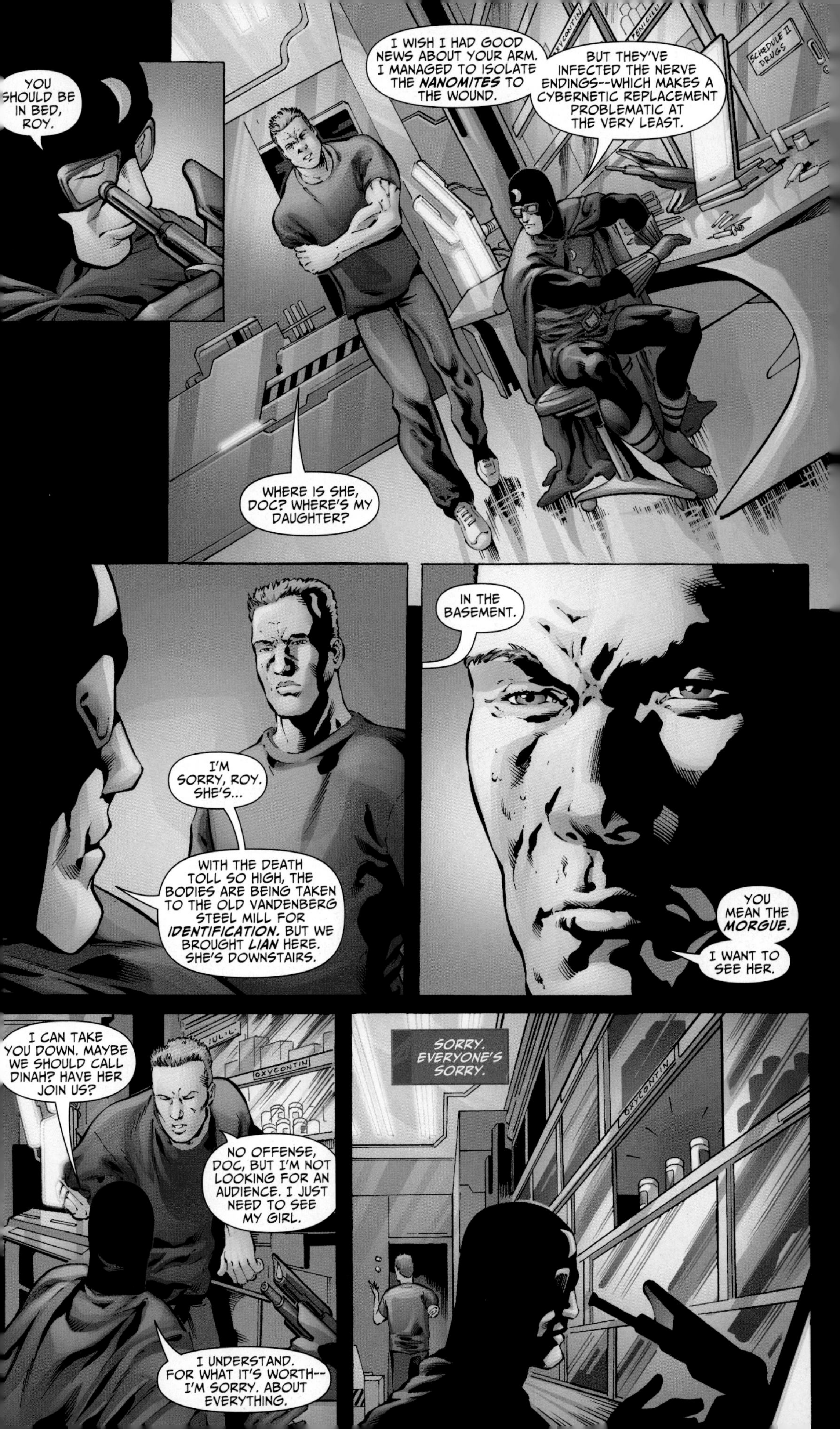
YOU SHOULD BE IN BED, ROY.
I WISH I HAD GOOD NEWS ABOUT YOUR ARM. I MANAGED TO ISOLATE THE NANOMITES TO THE WOUND.
BUT THEY'VE INFECTED THE NERVE ENDINGS--WHICH MAKES A CYBERNETIC REPLACEMENT PROBLEMATIC AT THE VERY LEAST.
SCHEDULE II DRUGS
OXYCONTIN
PENICILLIN
WHERE IS SHE, DOC? WHERE'S MY DAUGHTER?
I'M SORRY, ROY. SHE'S...
WITH THE DEATH TOLL SO HIGH, THE BODIES ARE BEING TAKEN TO THE OLD VANDENBERG STEEL MILL FOR IDENTIFICATION. BUT WE BROUGHT LIAN HERE. SHE'S DOWNSTAIRS.
IN THE BASEMENT.
YOU MEAN THE MORGUE.
I WANT TO SEE HER.
I CAN TAKE YOU DOWN. MAYBE WE SHOULD CALL DINAH? HAVE HER JOIN US?
OXYCONTIN
NO OFFENSE, DOC, BUT I'M NOT LOOKING FOR AN AUDIENCE. I JUST NEED TO SEE MY GIRL.
I UNDERSTAND. FOR WHAT IT'S WORTH--I'M SORRY. ABOUT EVERYTHING.
SORRY. EVERYONE'S SORRY.
OXYCONTIN

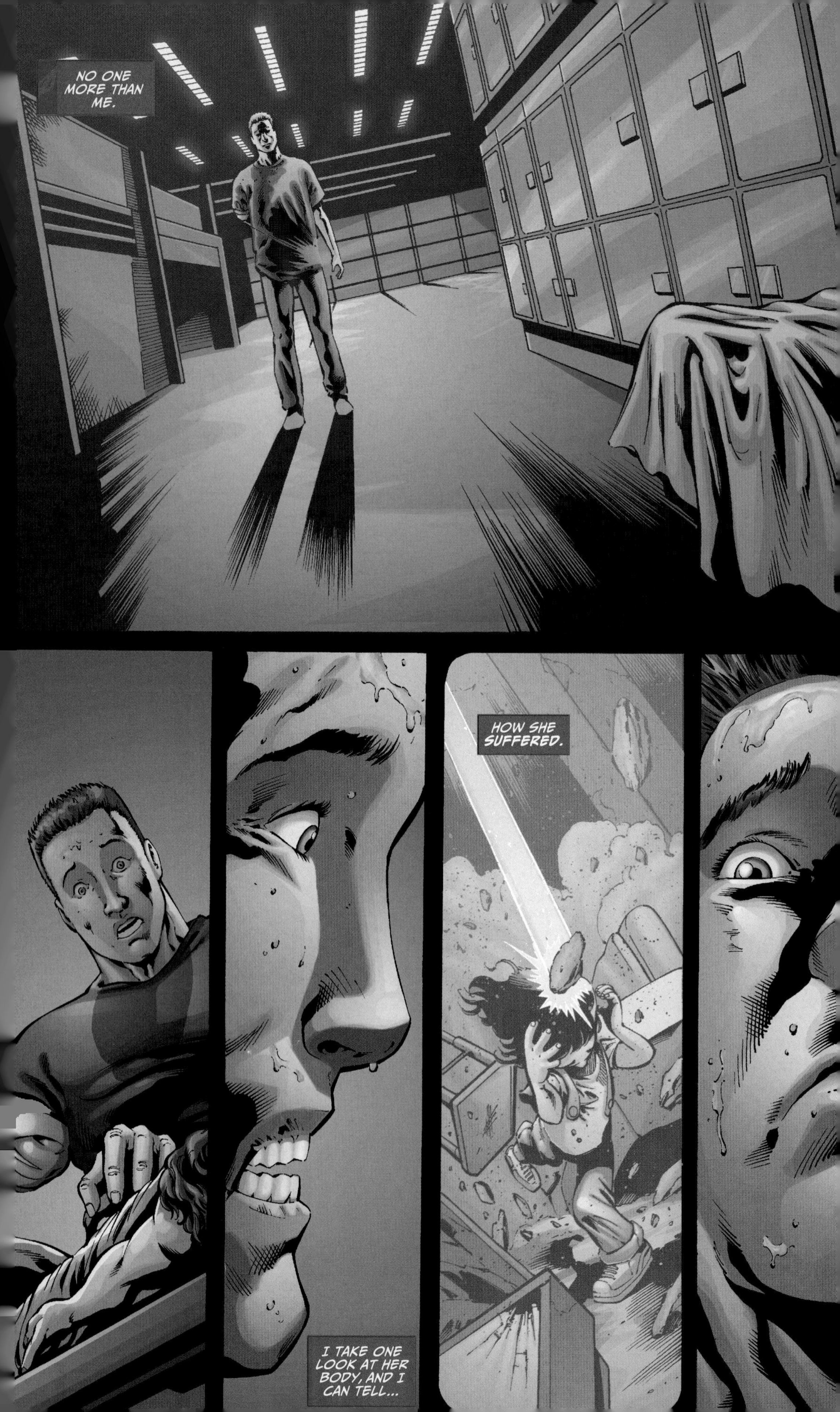
NO ONE MORE THAN ME.
I TAKE ONE LOOK AT HER BODY, AND I CAN TELL...
HOW SHE SUFFERED.

HOW SHE STRUGGLED.

AND HOW SHE FOUGHT.

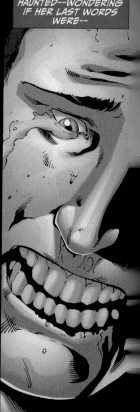

BUT FOR THE REST OF MY LIFE, I'LL BE HAUNTED--WONDERING IF HER LAST WORDS WERE--

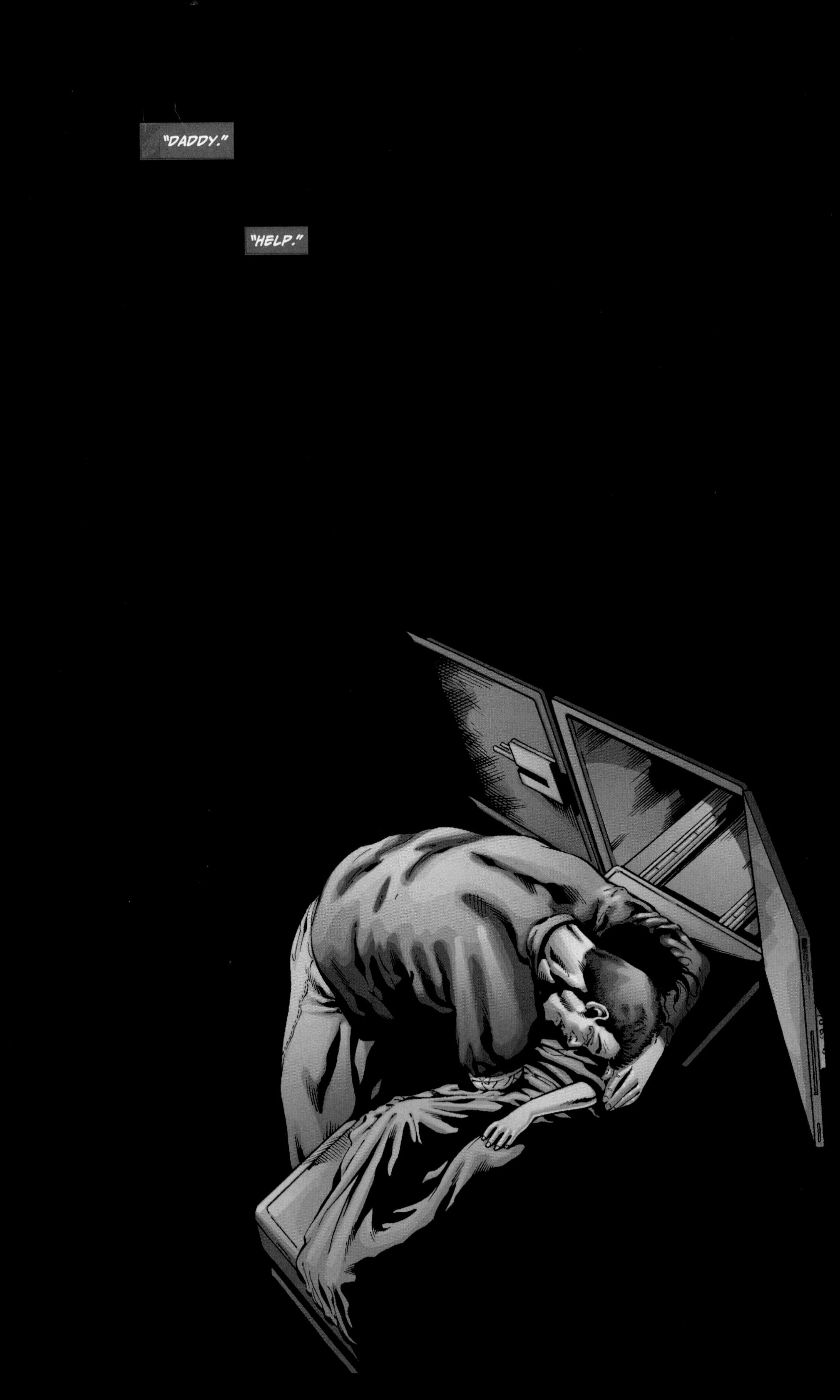
"DADDY."
"HELP."

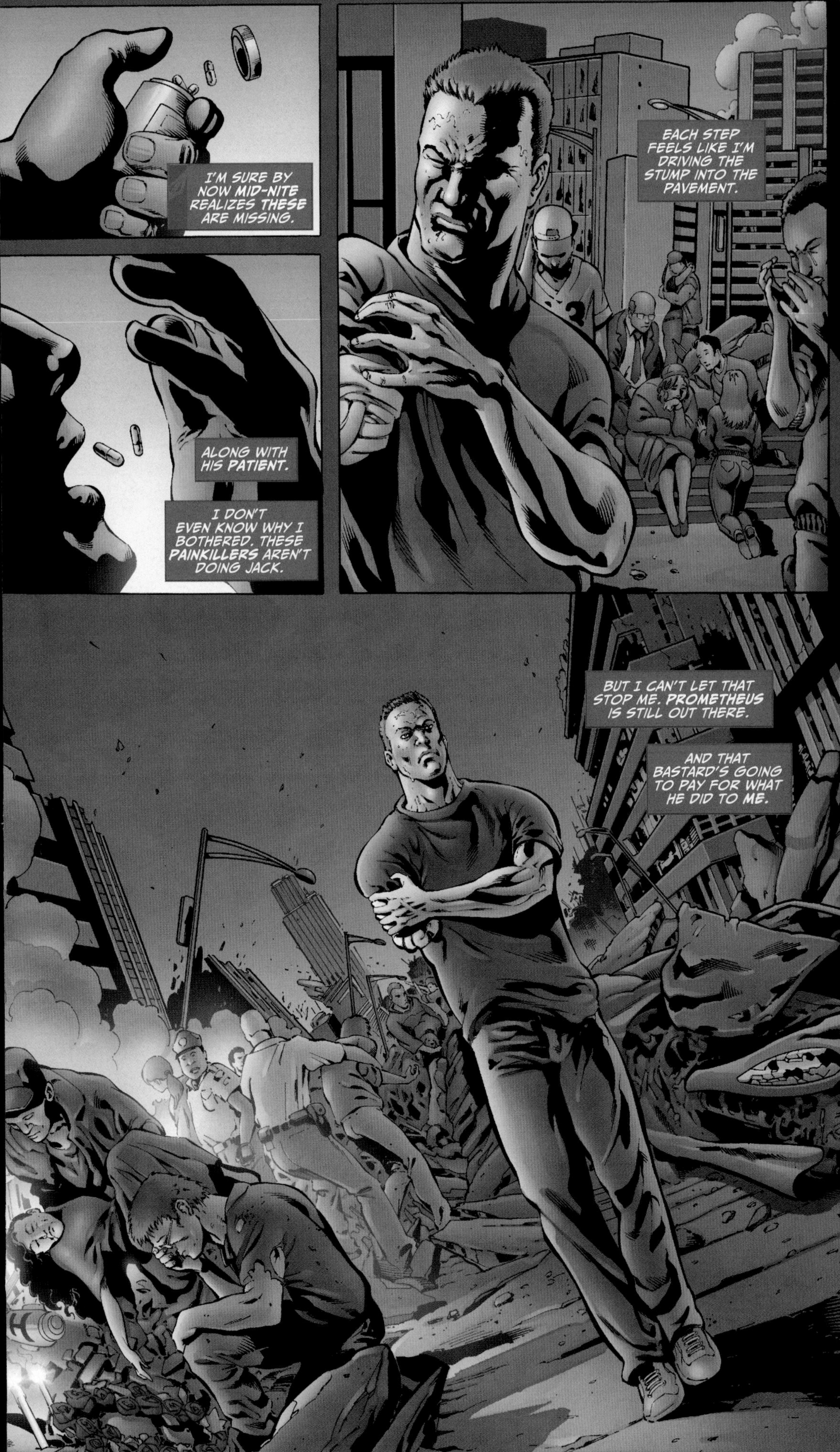
I'M SURE BY NOW MID-NITE REALIZES THESE ARE MISSING.
ALONG WITH HIS PATIENT.
I DON'T EVEN KNOW WHY I BOTHERED. THESE PAINKILLERS AREN'T DOING JACK.
EACH STEP FEELS LIKE I'M DRIVING THE STUMP INTO THE PAVEMENT.
BUT I CAN'T LET THAT STOP ME. PROMETHEUS IS STILL OUT THERE.
AND THAT BASTARD'S GOING TO PAY FOR WHAT HE DID TO ME.

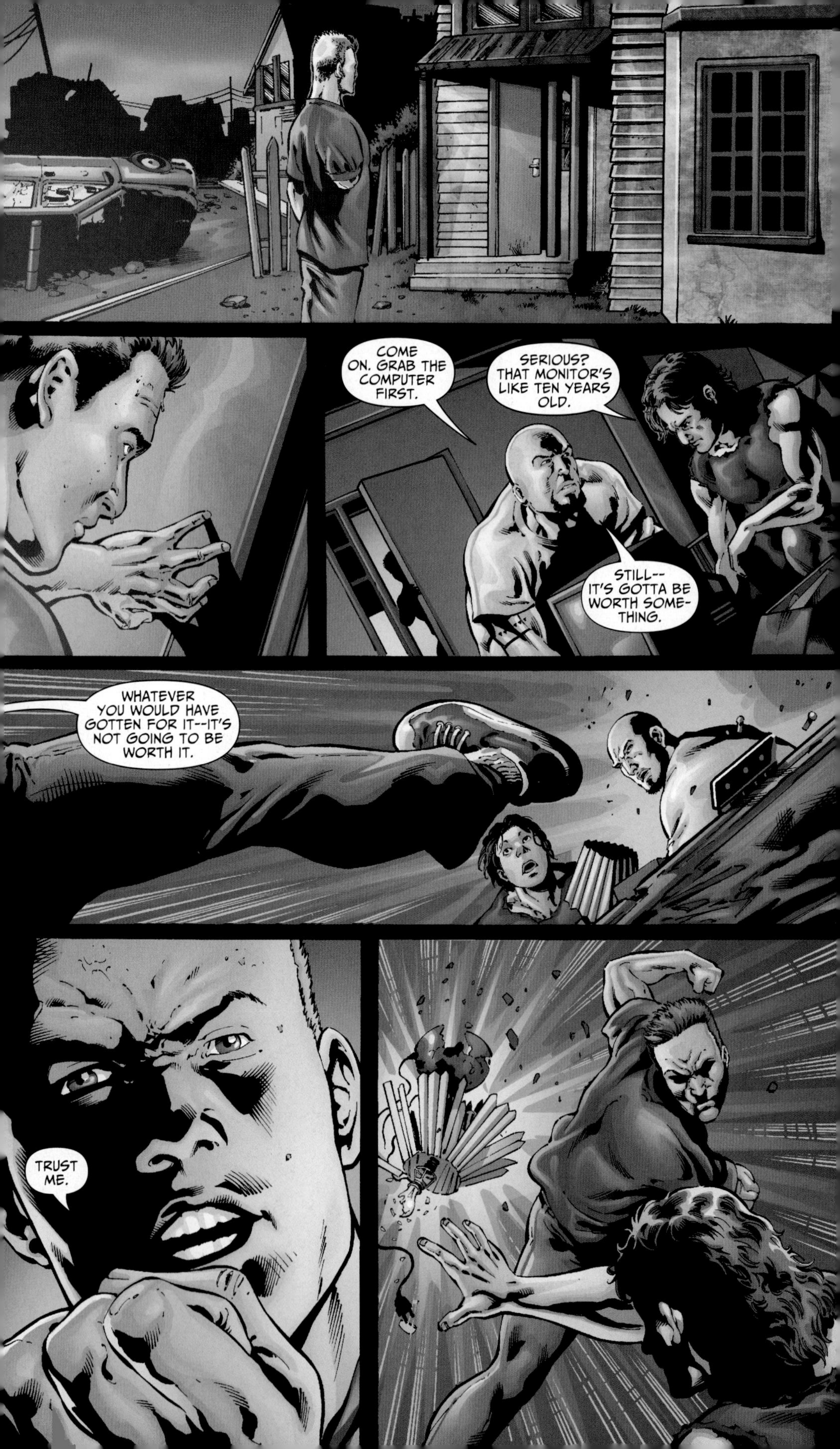
COME ON. GRAB THE COMPUTER FIRST.
SERIOUS? THAT MONITOR'S LIKE TEN YEARS OLD.
STILL-- IT'S GOTTA BE WORTH SOME-THING.
WHATEVER YOU WOULD HAVE GOTTEN FOR IT--IT'S NOT GOING TO BE WORTH IT.
TRUST ME.

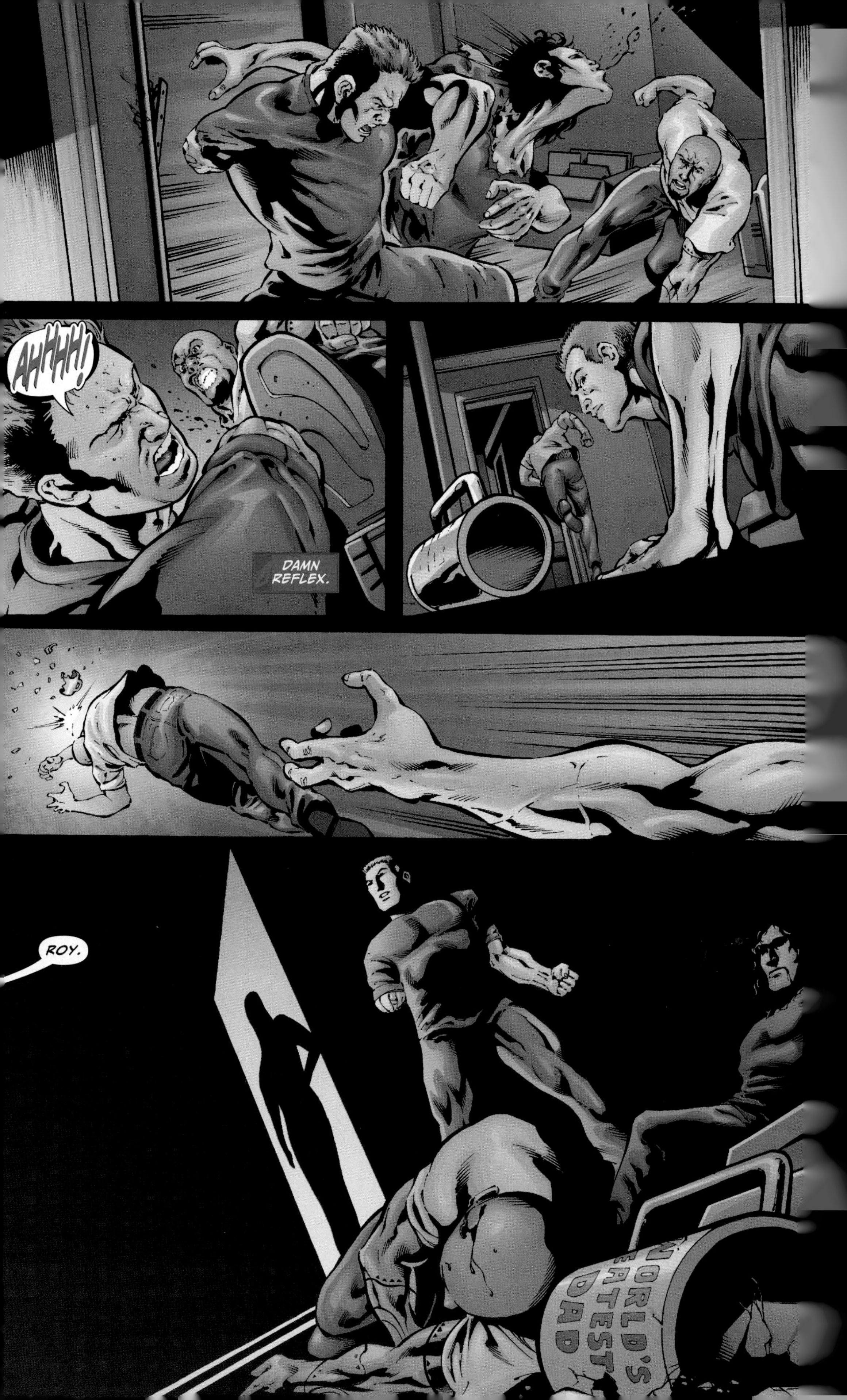
AHHHH!
DAMN REFLEX.
ROY.
WORLD'S GREATEST DAD

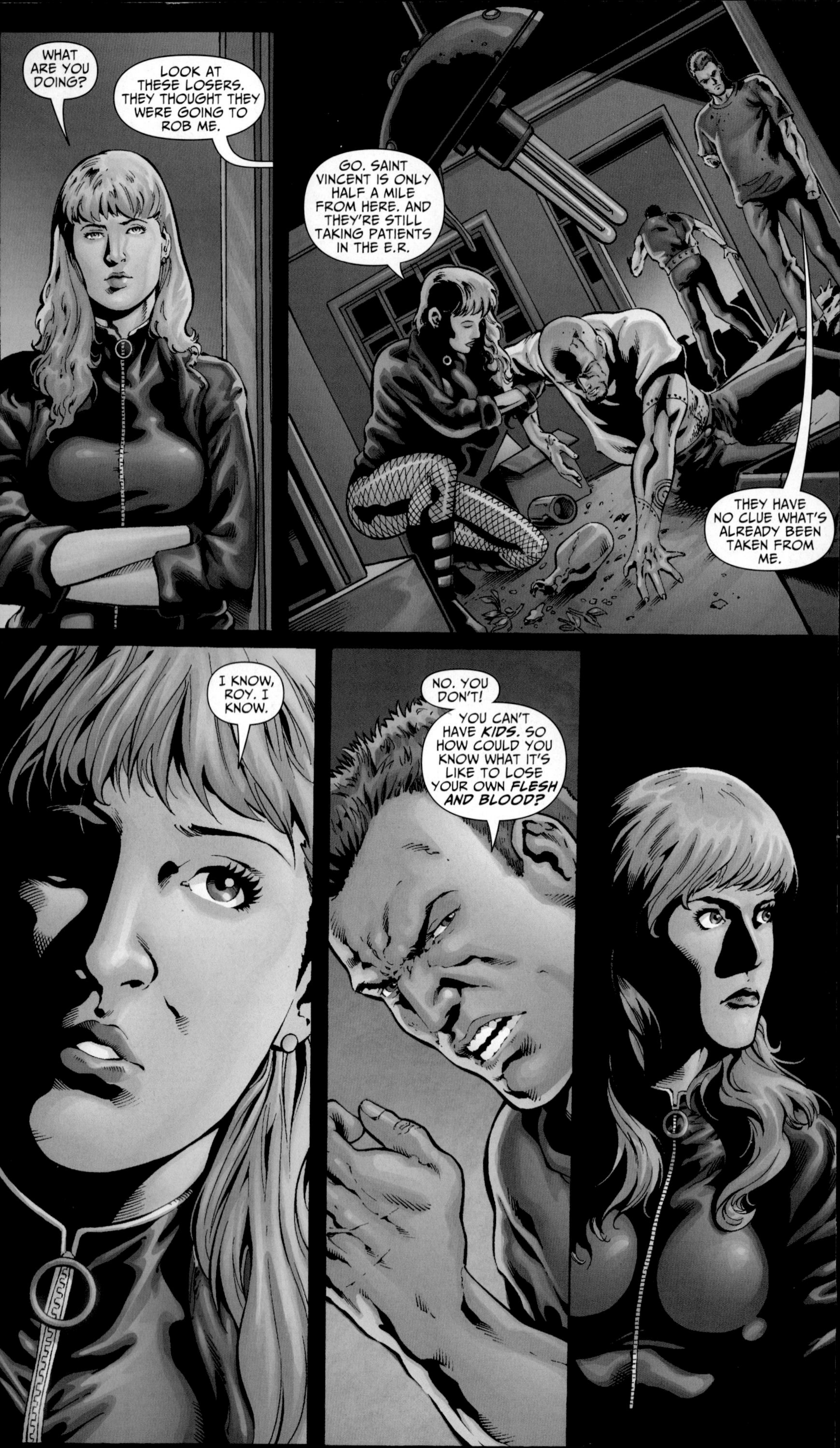
WHAT ARE YOU DOING?
LOOK AT THESE LOSERS. THEY THOUGHT THEY WERE GOING TO ROB ME.
GO. SAINT VINCENT IS ONLY HALF A MILE FROM HERE. AND THEY'RE STILL TAKING PATIENTS IN THE E.R.
THEY HAVE NO CLUE WHAT'S ALREADY BEEN TAKEN FROM ME.
I KNOW, ROY. I KNOW.
NO. YOU DON'T!
YOU CAN'T HAVE **KIDS.** SO HOW COULD YOU KNOW WHAT IT'S LIKE TO LOSE YOUR OWN **FLESH AND BLOOD?**

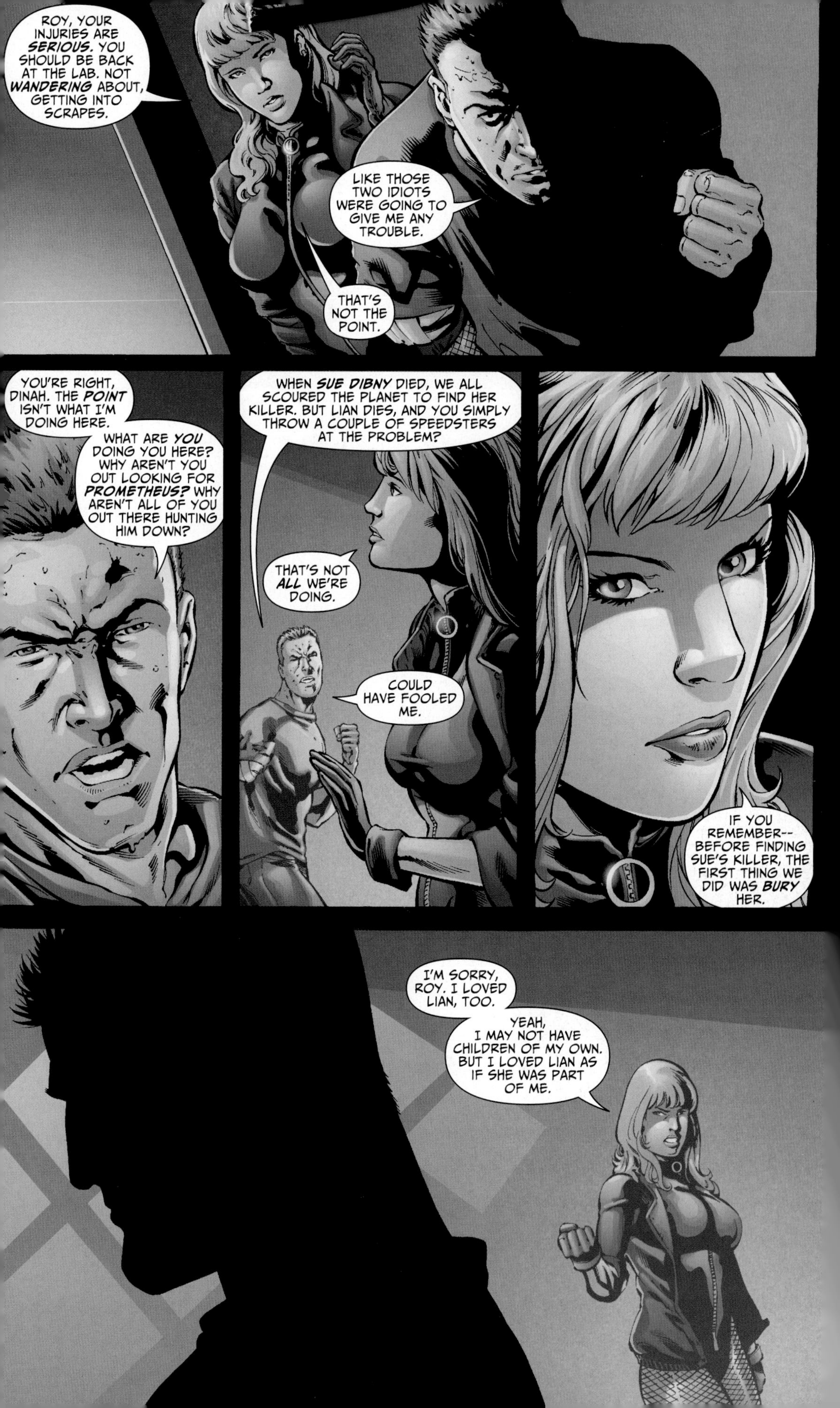
ROY, YOUR INJURIES ARE SERIOUS. YOU SHOULD BE BACK AT THE LAB. NOT WANDERING ABOUT, GETTING INTO SCRAPES.
LIKE THOSE TWO IDIOTS WERE GOING TO GIVE ME ANY TROUBLE.
THAT'S NOT THE POINT.
YOU'RE RIGHT, DINAH. THE POINT ISN'T WHAT I'M DOING HERE.
WHAT ARE YOU DOING YOU HERE? WHY AREN'T YOU OUT LOOKING FOR PROMETHEUS? WHY AREN'T ALL OF YOU OUT THERE HUNTING HIM DOWN?
WHEN SUE DIBNY DIED, WE ALL SCOURED THE PLANET TO FIND HER KILLER. BUT LIAN DIES, AND YOU SIMPLY THROW A COUPLE OF SPEEDSTERS AT THE PROBLEM?
THAT'S NOT ALL WE'RE DOING.
COULD HAVE FOOLED ME.
IF YOU REMEMBER-- BEFORE FINDING SUE'S KILLER, THE FIRST THING WE DID WAS BURY HER.
I'M SORRY, ROY. I LOVED LIAN, TOO.
YEAH, I MAY NOT HAVE CHILDREN OF MY OWN. BUT I LOVED LIAN AS IF SHE WAS PART OF ME.

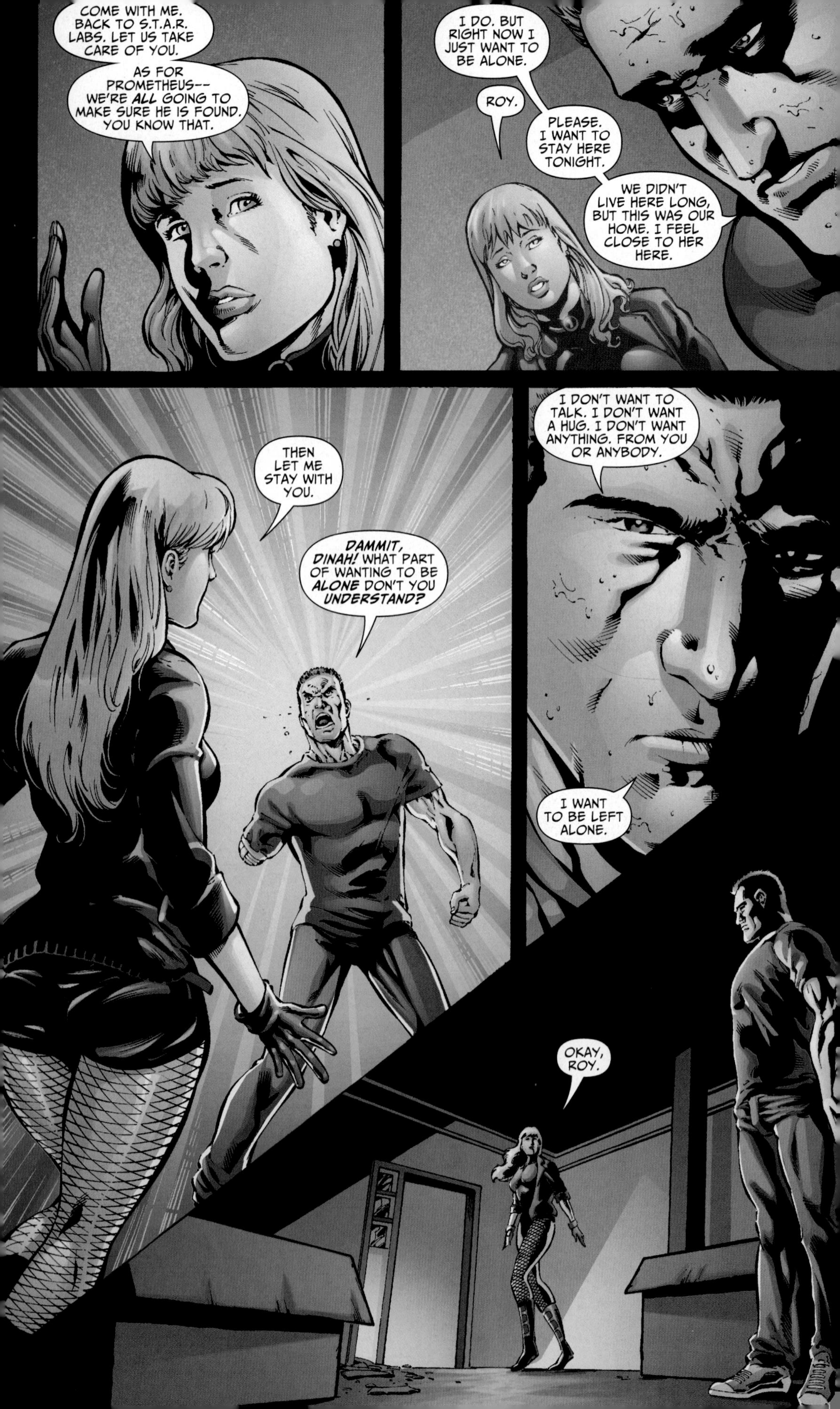

COME WITH ME. BACK TO S.T.A.R. LABS. LET US TAKE CARE OF YOU.
AS FOR PROMETHEUS-- WE'RE ALL GOING TO MAKE SURE HE IS FOUND. YOU KNOW THAT.
I DO. BUT RIGHT NOW I JUST WANT TO BE ALONE.
ROY.
PLEASE. I WANT TO STAY HERE TONIGHT.
WE DIDN'T LIVE HERE LONG, BUT THIS WAS OUR HOME. I FEEL CLOSE TO HER HERE.
THEN LET ME STAY WITH YOU.
DAMMIT, DINAH! WHAT PART OF WANTING TO BE ALONE DON'T YOU UNDERSTAND?
I DON'T WANT TO TALK. I DON'T WANT A HUG. I DON'T WANT ANYTHING. FROM YOU OR ANYBODY.
I WANT TO BE LEFT ALONE.
OKAY, ROY.

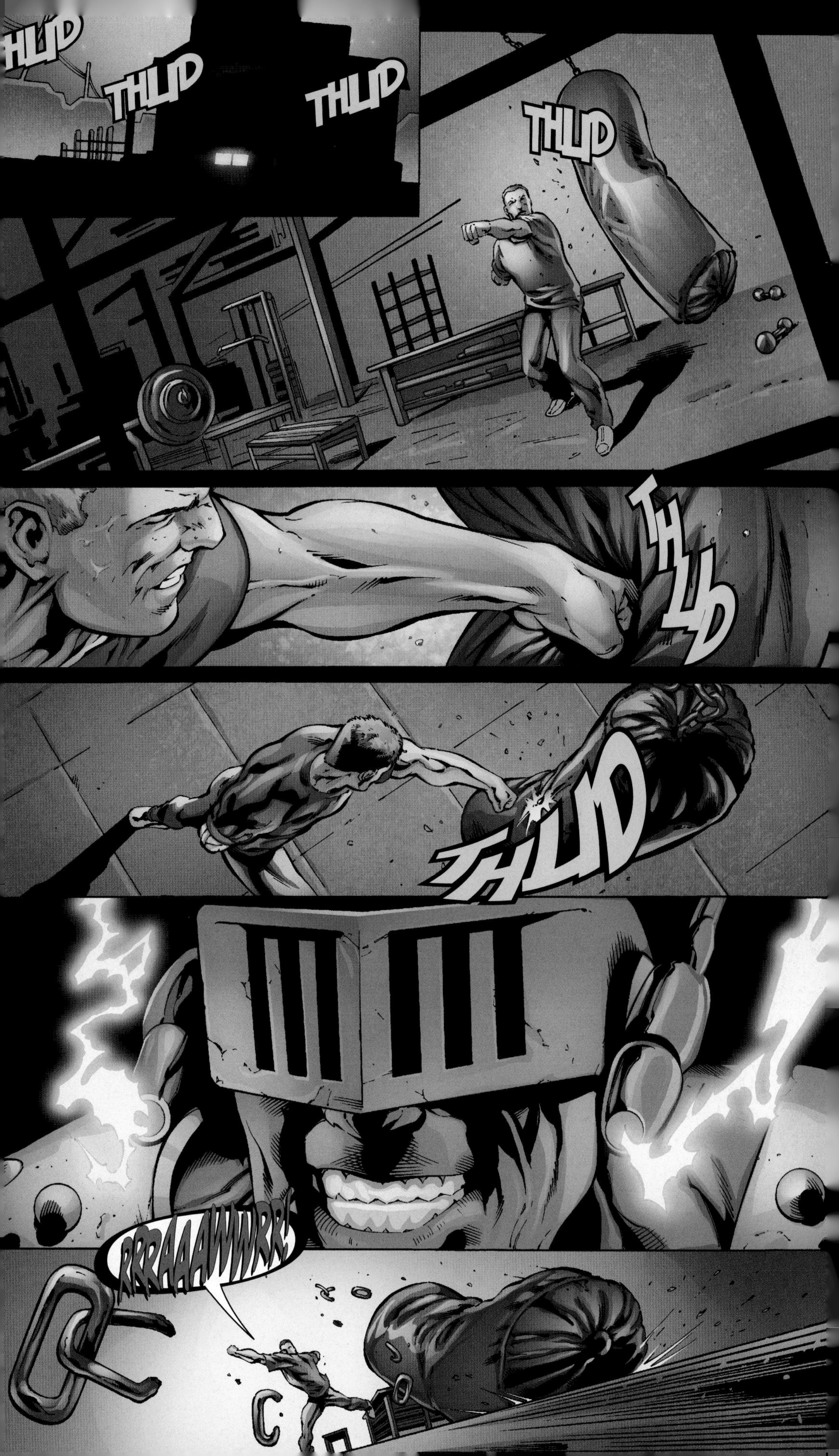
THUD
THUD
THUD
THUD
THUD
THUD
RRRAAAWWRR!

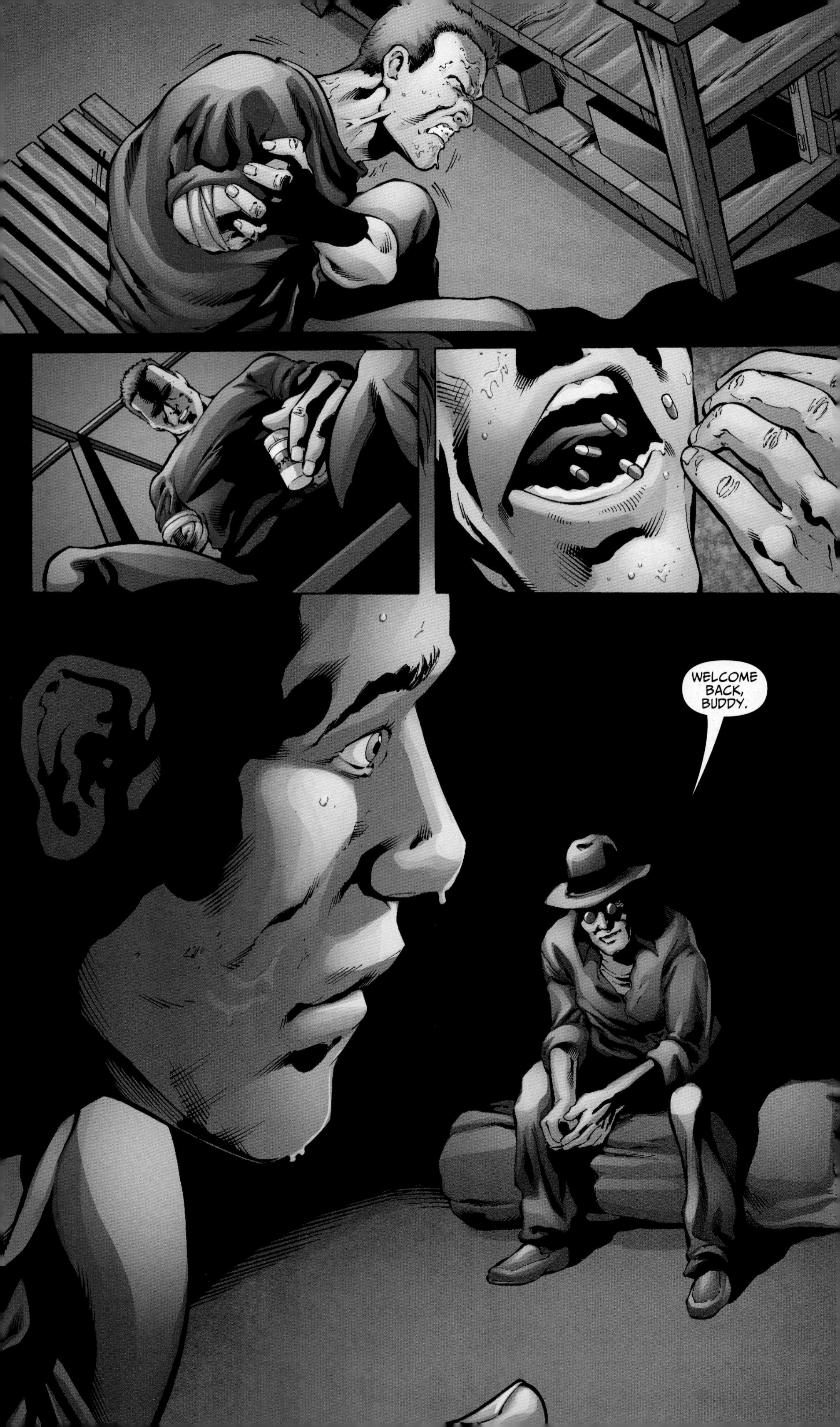
WELCOME BACK, BUDDY.

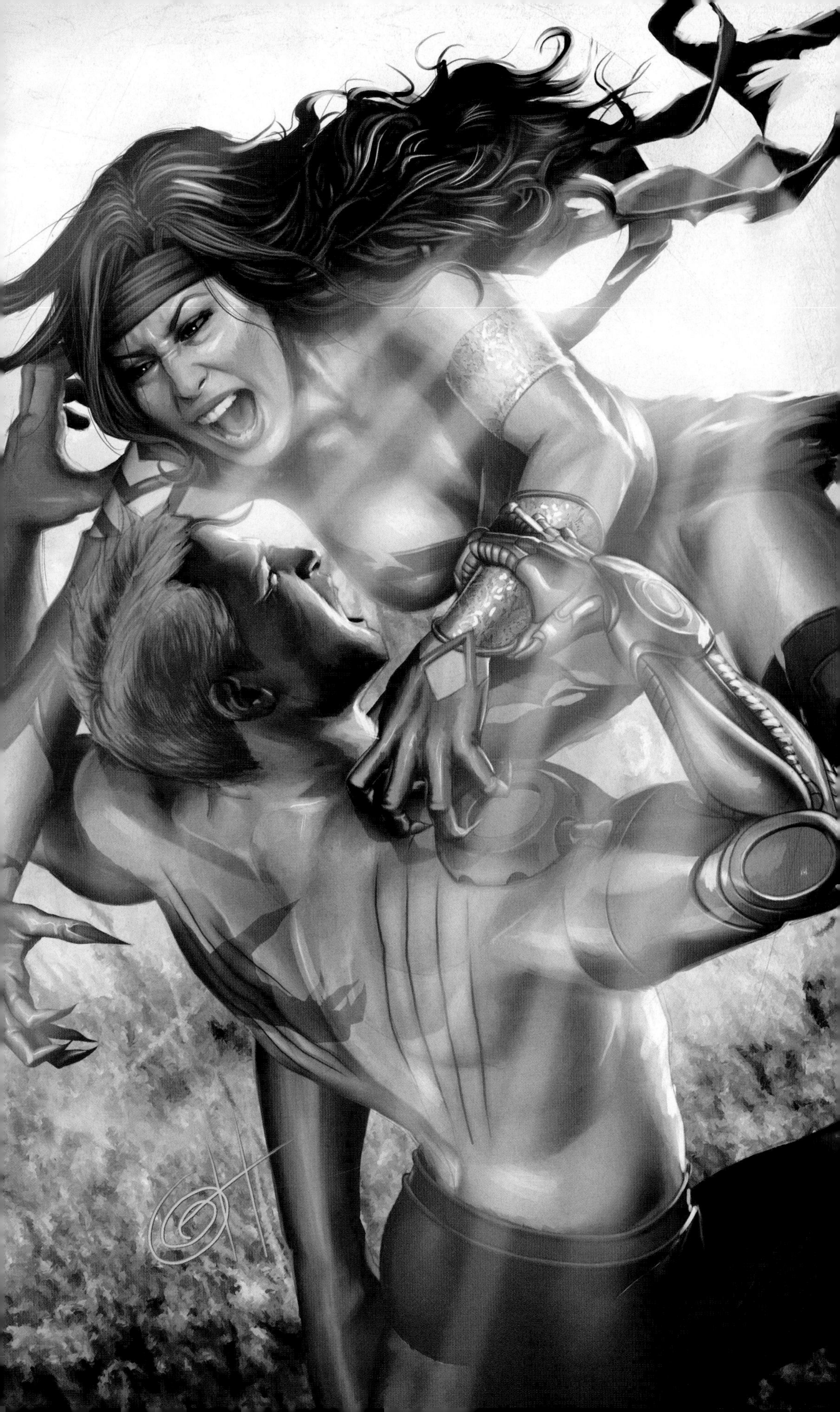

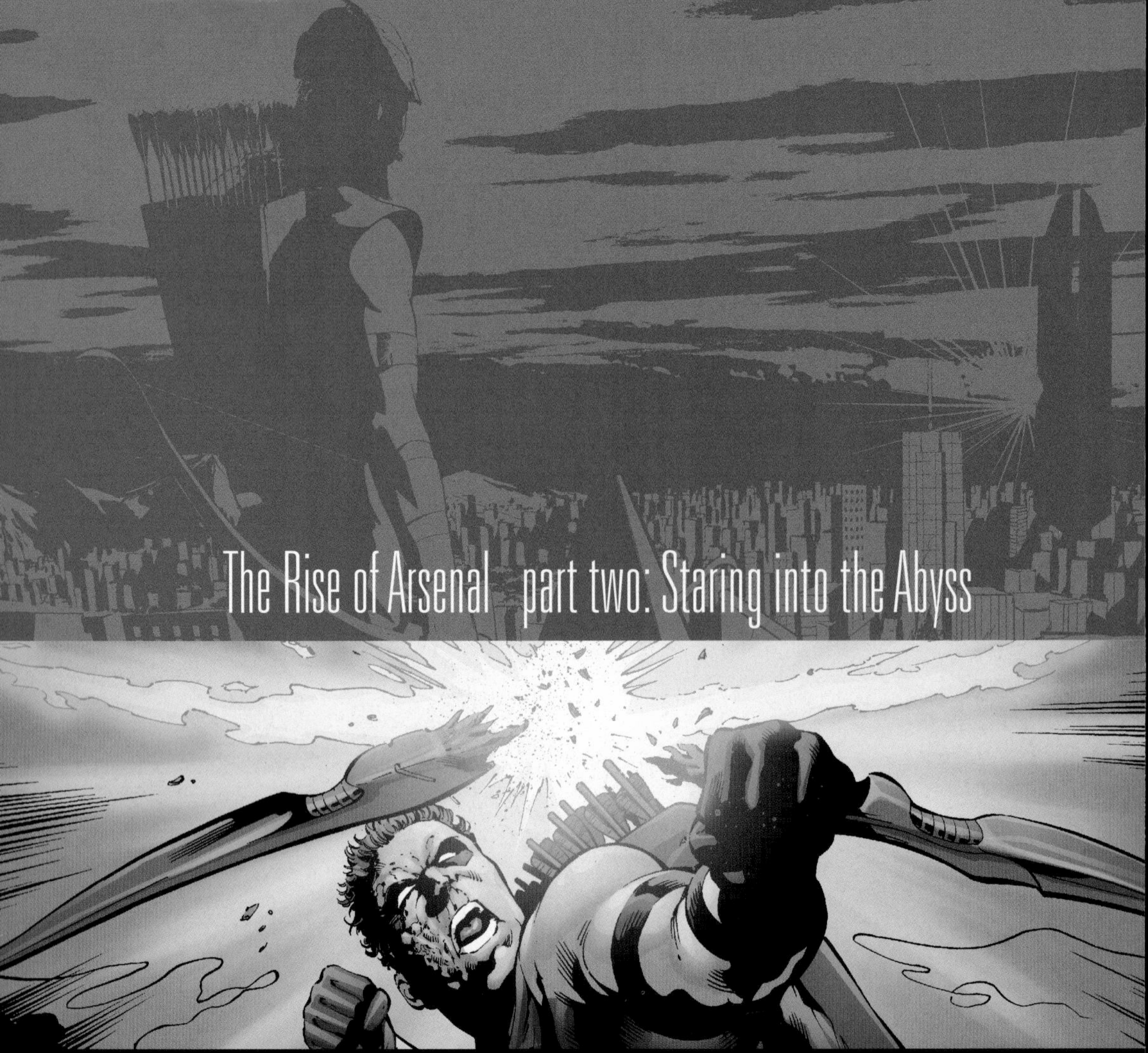

The Rise of Arsenal part two: Staring into the Abyss

Cover by Greg Horn

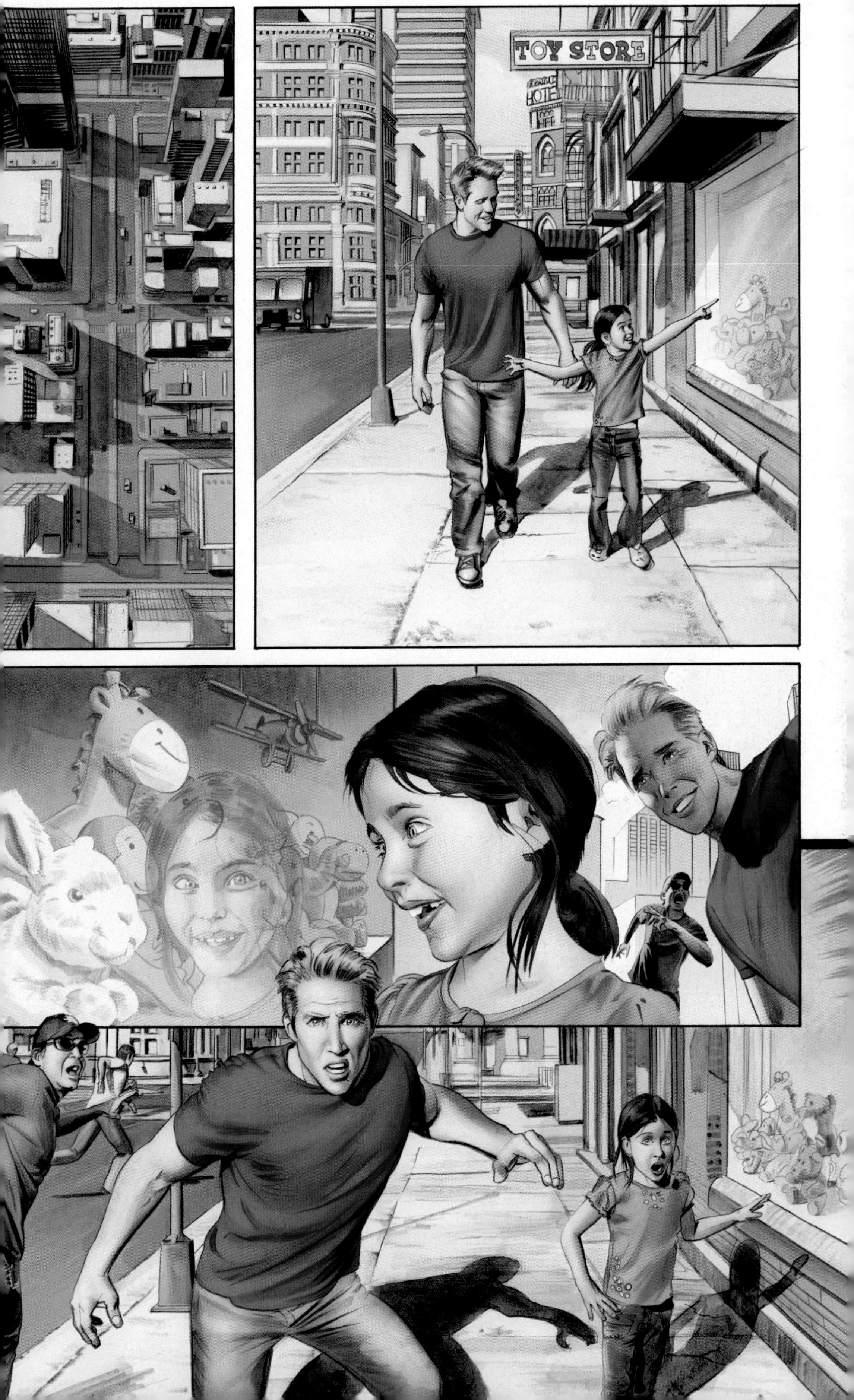
TOY STORE

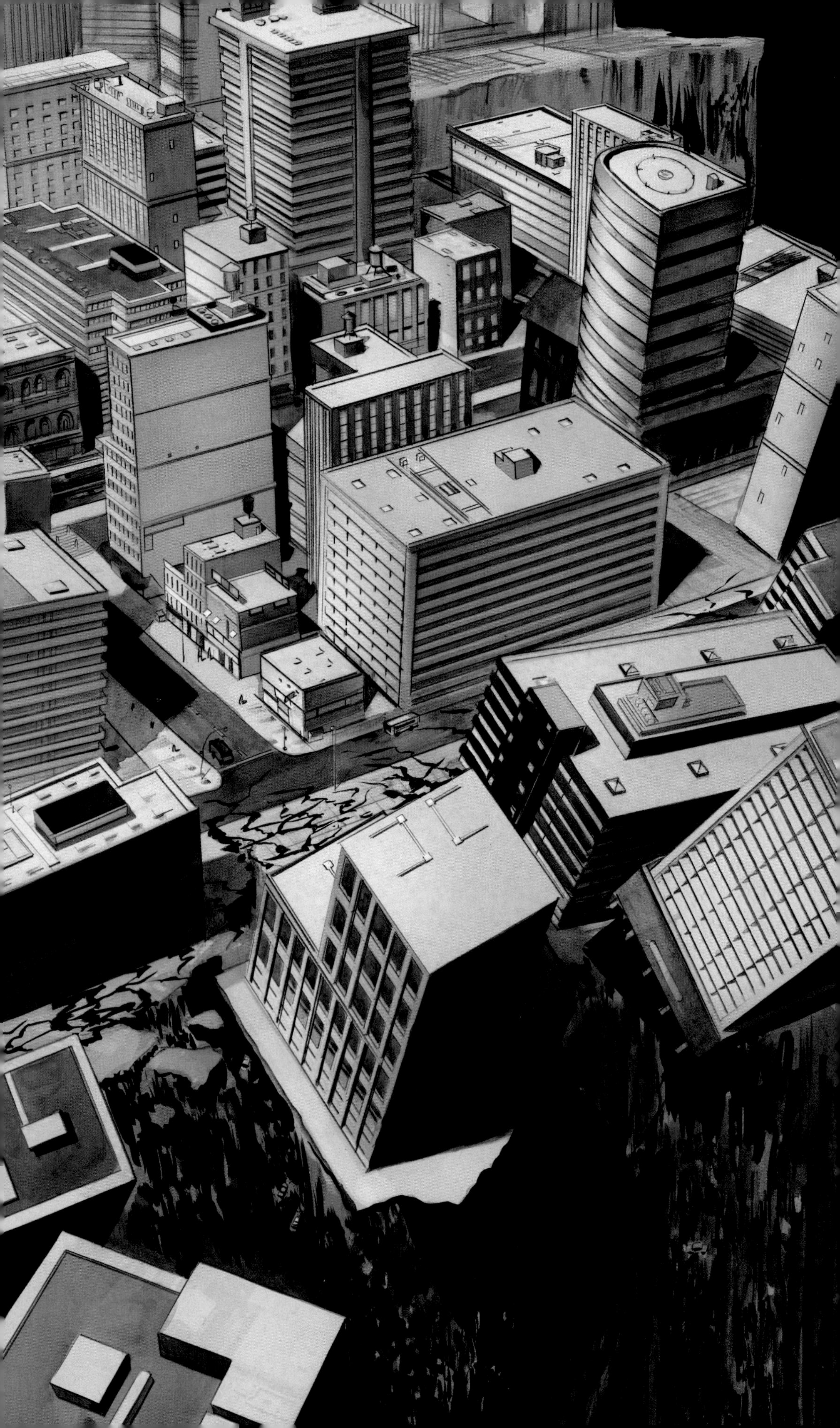

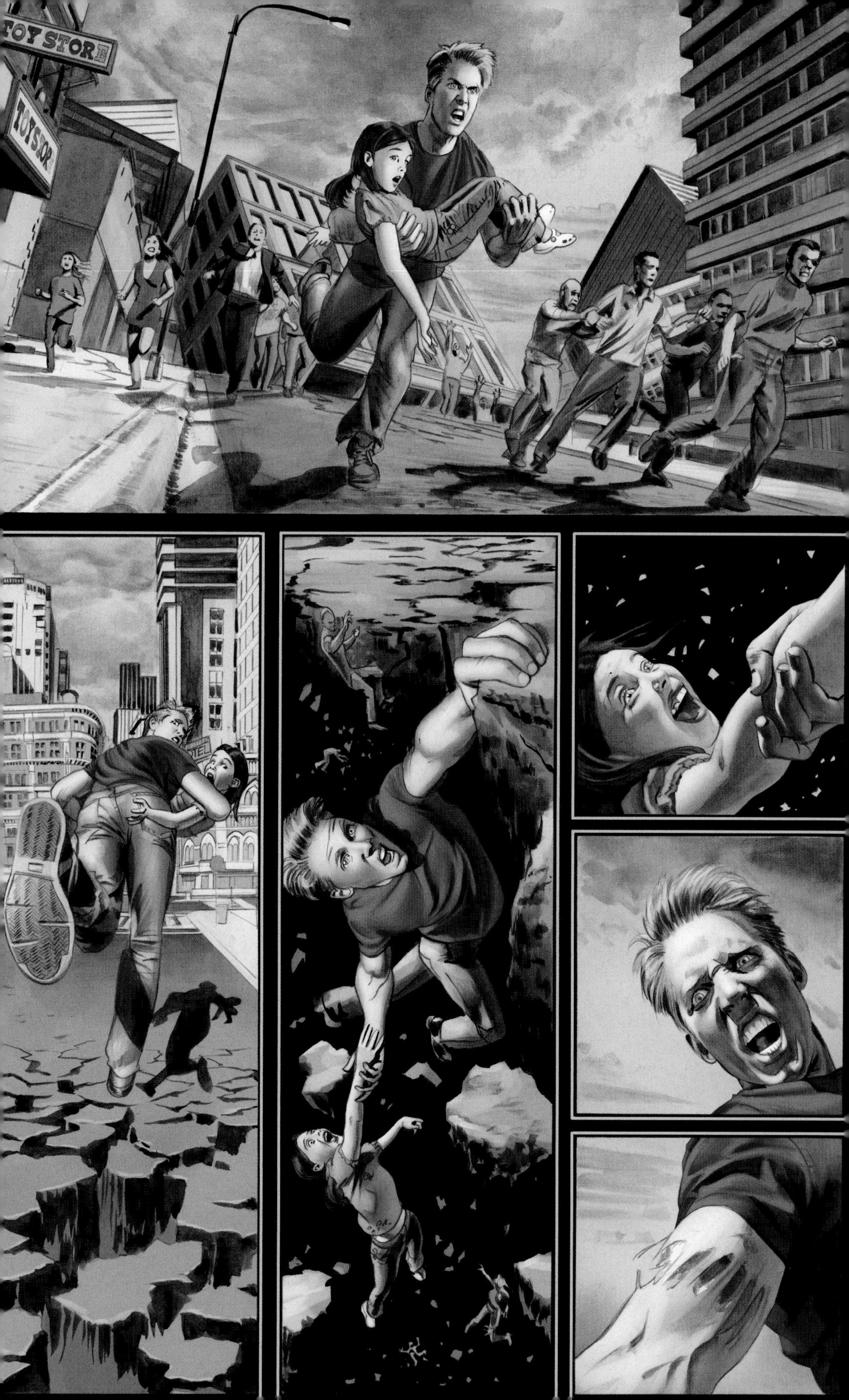
TOY STORE
TOYSTORE

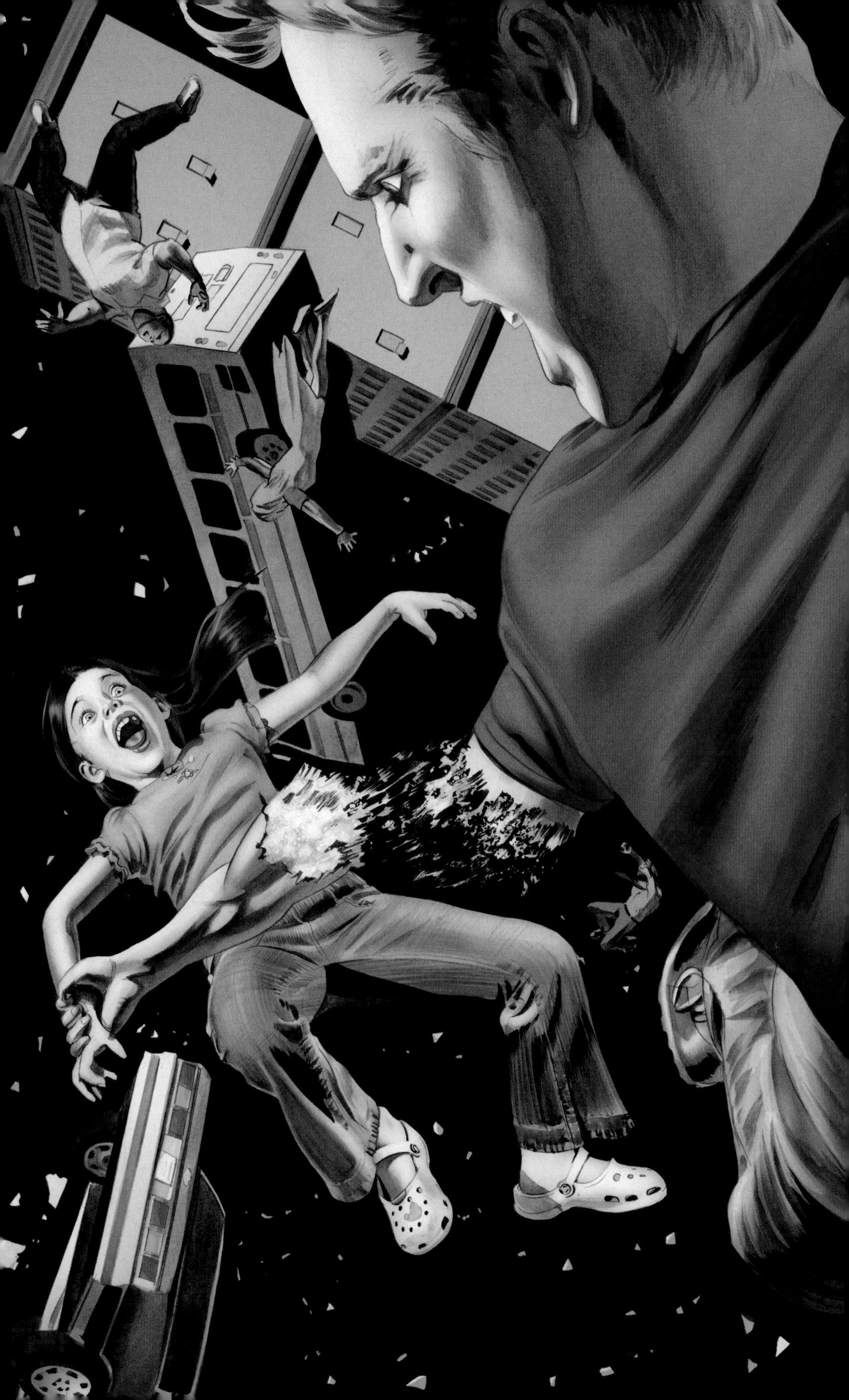

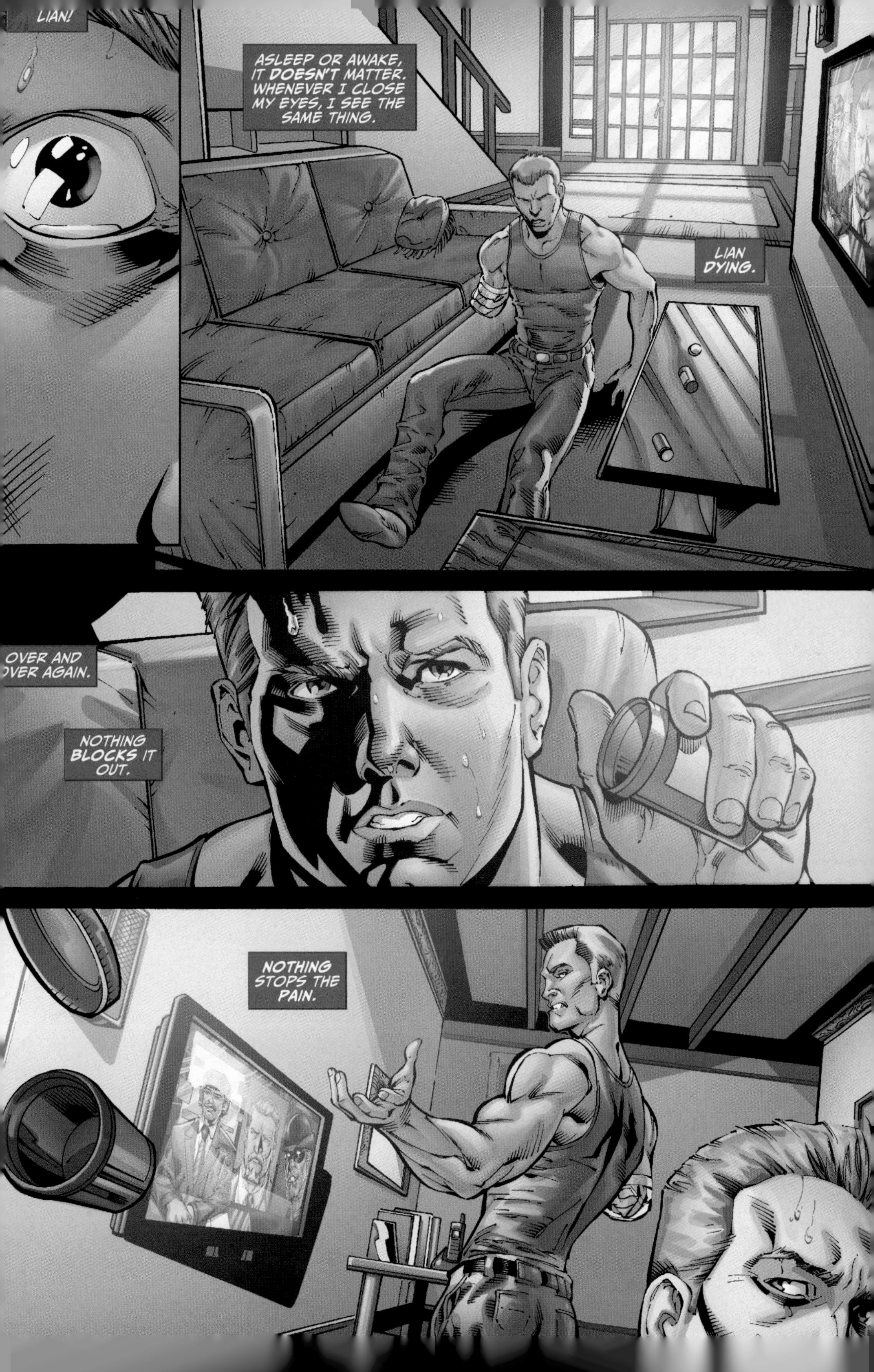
LIAN!
ASLEEP OR AWAKE, IT DOESN'T MATTER. WHENEVER I CLOSE MY EYES, I SEE THE SAME THING.
LIAN DYING.
OVER AND OVER AGAIN.
NOTHING BLOCKS IT OUT.
NOTHING STOPS THE PAIN.

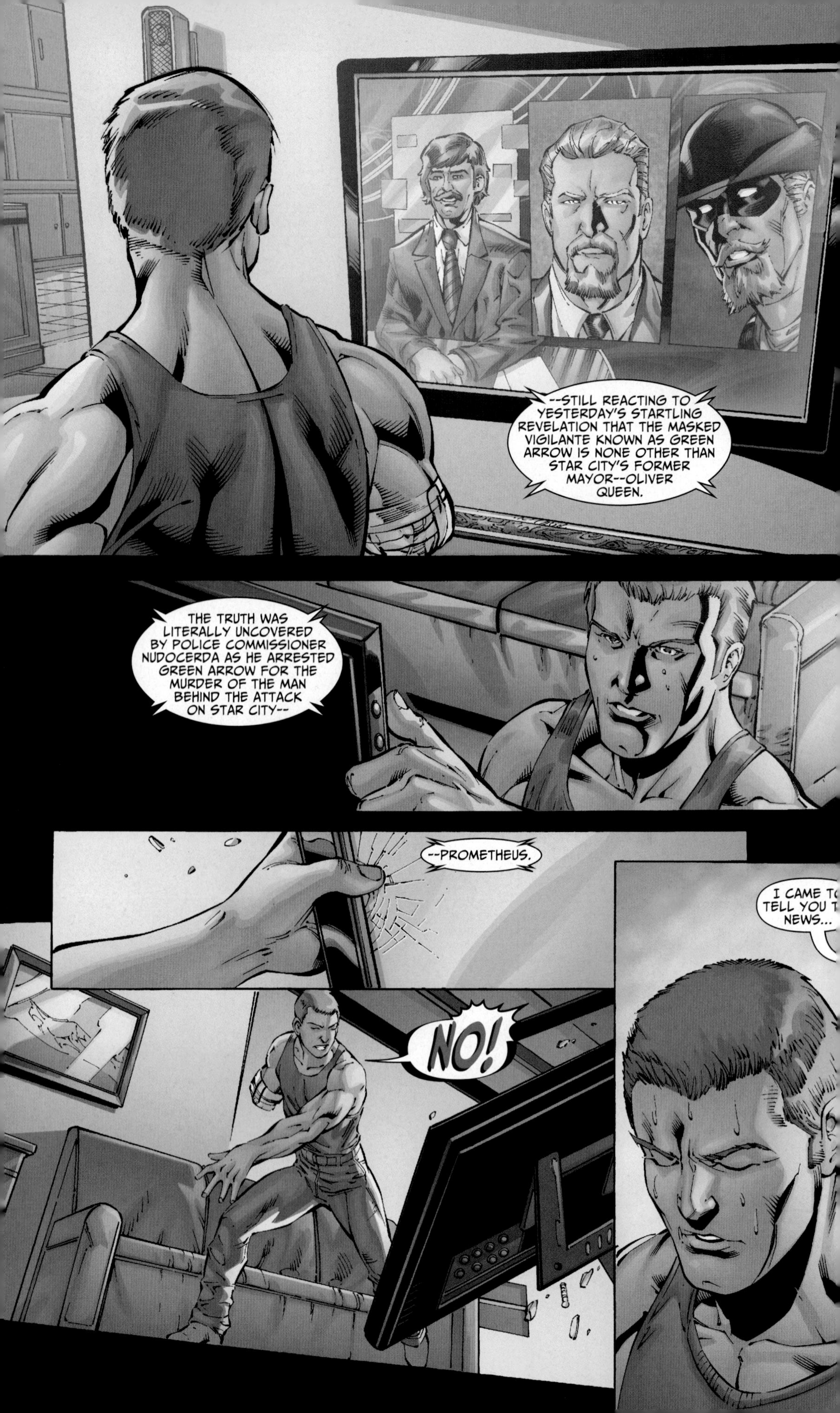
--STILL REACTING TO YESTERDAY'S STARTLING REVELATION THAT THE MASKED VIGILANTE KNOWN AS GREEN ARROW IS NONE OTHER THAN STAR CITY'S FORMER MAYOR--OLIVER QUEEN.
THE TRUTH WAS LITERALLY UNCOVERED BY POLICE COMMISSIONER NUDOCERDA AS HE ARRESTED GREEN ARROW FOR THE MURDER OF THE MAN BEHIND THE ATTACK ON STAR CITY--
--PROMETHEUS.
NO!
I CAME T
TELL YOU T
NEWS...

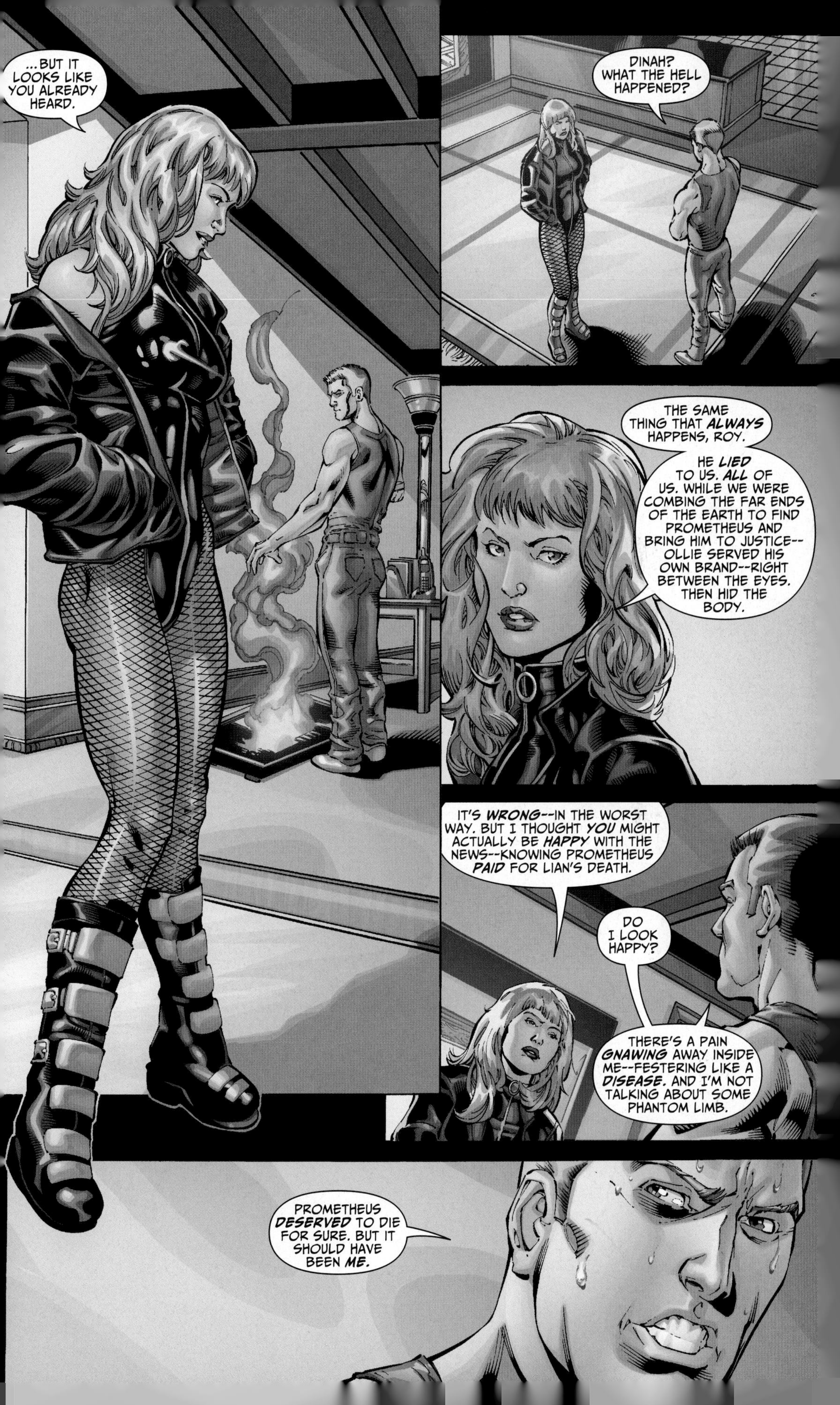
...BUT IT LOOKS LIKE YOU ALREADY HEARD.
DINAH? WHAT THE HELL HAPPENED?
THE SAME THING THAT ALWAYS HAPPENS, ROY.
HE LIED TO US. ALL OF US. WHILE WE WERE COMBING THE FAR ENDS OF THE EARTH TO FIND PROMETHEUS AND BRING HIM TO JUSTICE--OLLIE SERVED HIS OWN BRAND--RIGHT BETWEEN THE EYES. THEN HID THE BODY.
IT'S WRONG--IN THE WORST WAY. BUT I THOUGHT YOU MIGHT ACTUALLY BE HAPPY WITH THE NEWS--KNOWING PROMETHEUS PAID FOR LIAN'S DEATH.
DO I LOOK HAPPY?
THERE'S A PAIN GNAWING AWAY INSIDE ME--FESTERING LIKE A DISEASE. AND I'M NOT TALKING ABOUT SOME PHANTOM LIMB.
PROMETHEUS DESERVED TO DIE FOR SURE. BUT IT SHOULD HAVE BEEN ME.

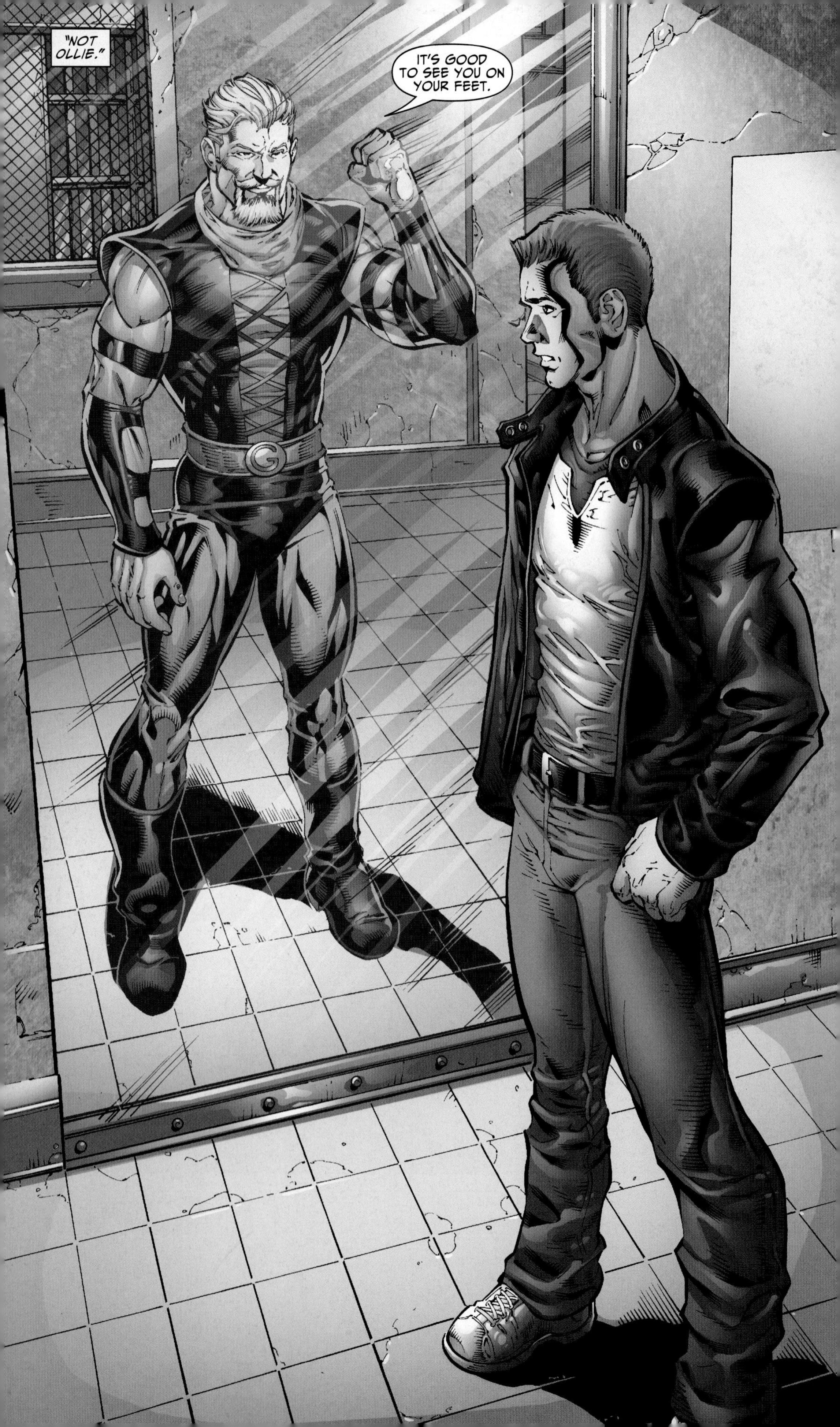
"NOT OLLIE."
IT'S GOOD TO SEE YOU ON YOUR FEET.

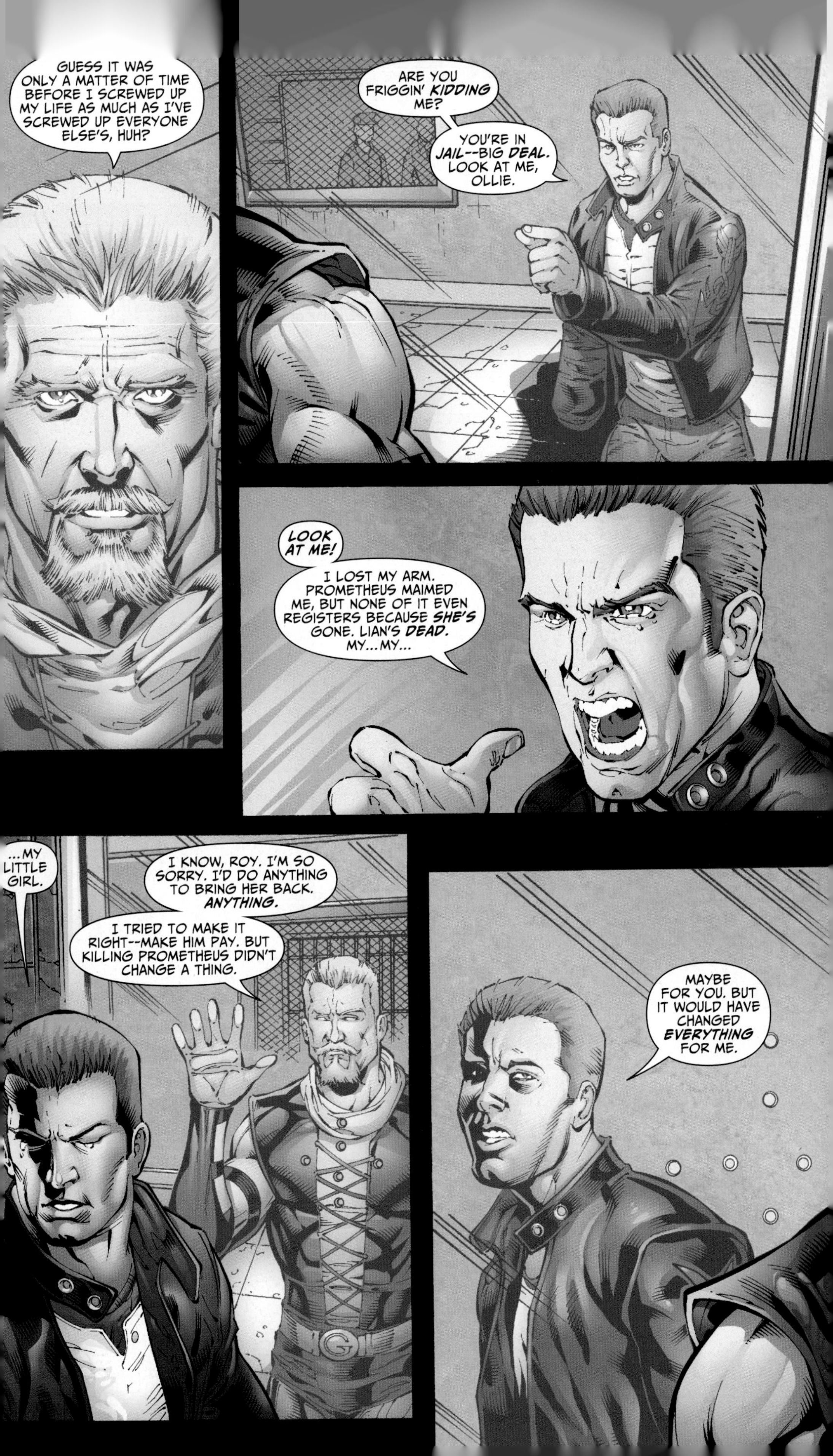
GUESS IT WAS ONLY A MATTER OF TIME BEFORE I SCREWED UP MY LIFE AS MUCH AS I'VE SCREWED UP EVERYONE ELSE'S, HUH?
ARE YOU FRIGGIN' KIDDING ME?
YOU'RE IN JAIL--BIG DEAL. LOOK AT ME, OLLIE.
LOOK AT ME!
I LOST MY ARM. PROMETHEUS MAIMED ME, BUT NONE OF IT EVEN REGISTERS BECAUSE SHE'S GONE. LIAN'S DEAD. MY...MY...
...MY LITTLE GIRL.
I KNOW, ROY. I'M SO SORRY. I'D DO ANYTHING TO BRING HER BACK. ANYTHING.
I TRIED TO MAKE IT RIGHT--MAKE HIM PAY. BUT KILLING PROMETHEUS DIDN'T CHANGE A THING.
MAYBE FOR YOU. BUT IT WOULD HAVE CHANGED EVERYTHING FOR ME.

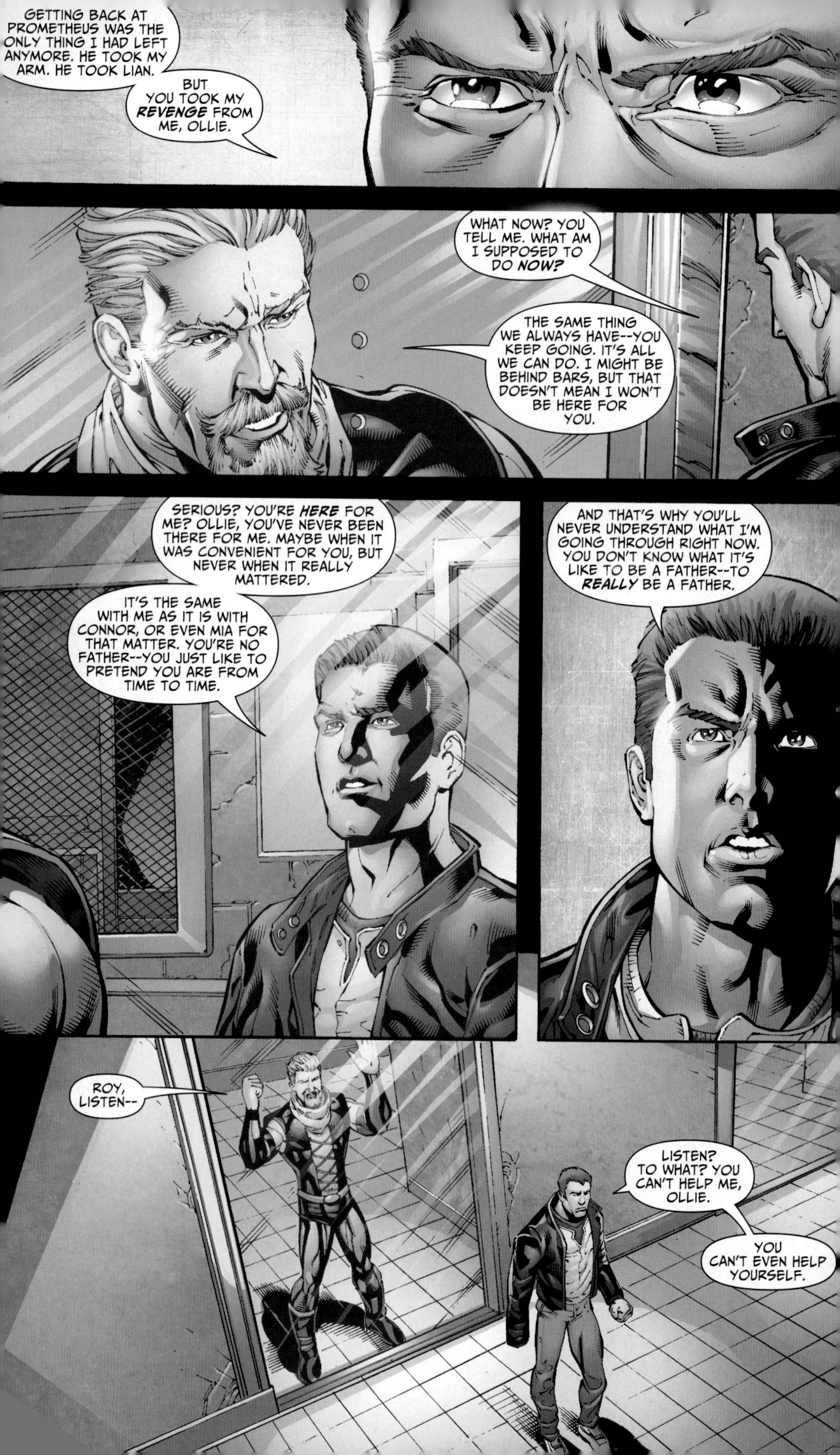
GETTING BACK AT PROMETHEUS WAS THE ONLY THING I HAD LEFT ANYMORE. HE TOOK MY ARM. HE TOOK LIAN.
BUT YOU TOOK MY REVENGE FROM ME, OLLIE.
WHAT NOW? YOU TELL ME. WHAT AM I SUPPOSED TO DO NOW?
THE SAME THING WE ALWAYS HAVE--YOU KEEP GOING. IT'S ALL WE CAN DO. I MIGHT BE BEHIND BARS, BUT THAT DOESN'T MEAN I WON'T BE HERE FOR YOU.
SERIOUS? YOU'RE HERE FOR ME? OLLIE, YOU'VE NEVER BEEN THERE FOR ME. MAYBE WHEN IT WAS CONVENIENT FOR YOU, BUT NEVER WHEN IT REALLY MATTERED.
IT'S THE SAME WITH ME AS IT IS WITH CONNOR, OR EVEN MIA FOR THAT MATTER. YOU'RE NO FATHER--YOU JUST LIKE TO PRETEND YOU ARE FROM TIME TO TIME.
AND THAT'S WHY YOU'LL NEVER UNDERSTAND WHAT I'M GOING THROUGH RIGHT NOW. YOU DON'T KNOW WHAT IT'S LIKE TO BE A FATHER--TO REALLY BE A FATHER.
ROY, LISTEN--
LISTEN? TO WHAT? YOU CAN'T HELP ME, OLLIE.
YOU CAN'T EVEN HELP YOURSELF.

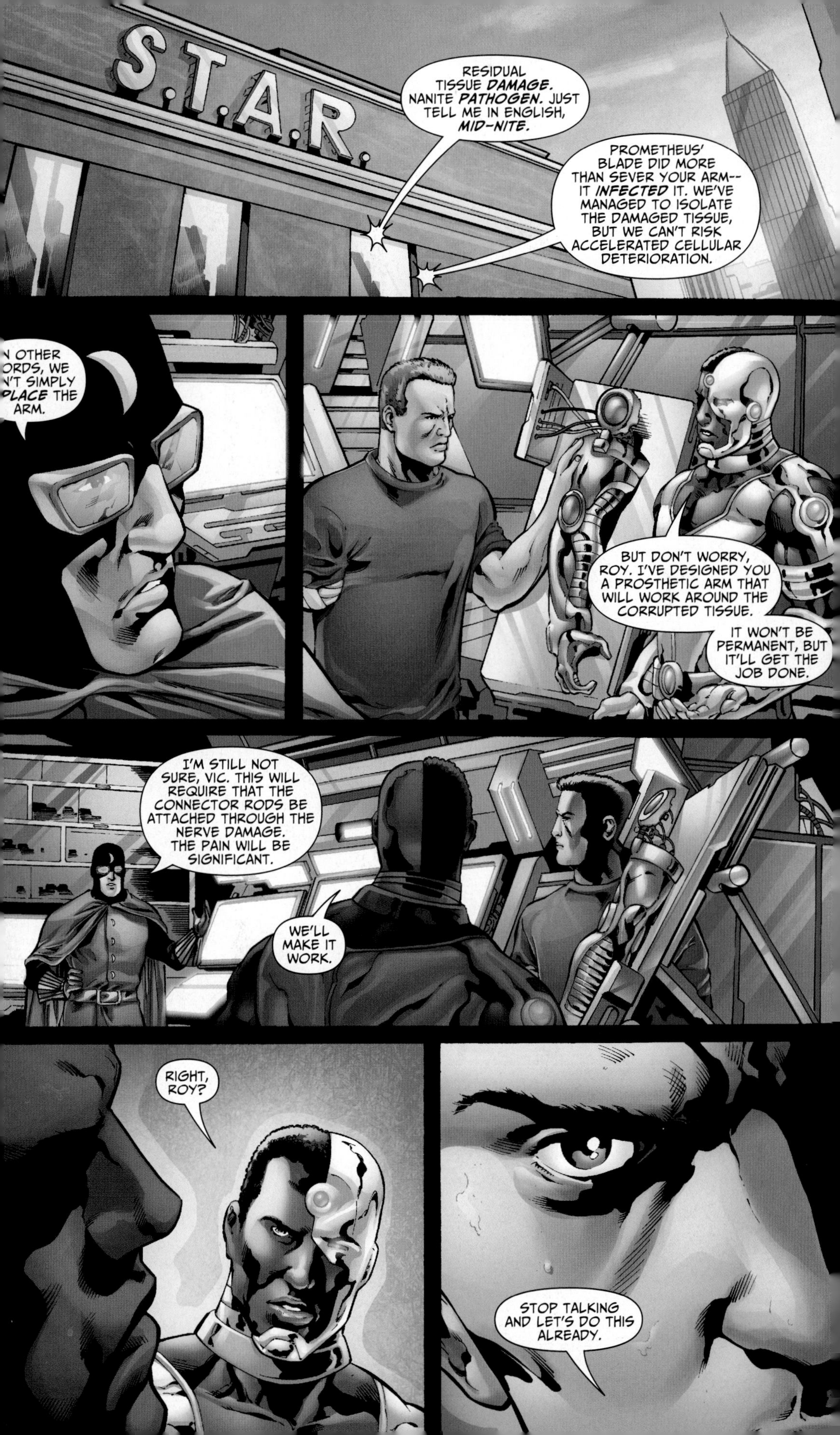
S.T.A.R.
RESIDUAL TISSUE DAMAGE. NANITE PATHOGEN. JUST TELL ME IN ENGLISH, MID-NITE.
PROMETHEUS' BLADE DID MORE THAN SEVER YOUR ARM-- IT INFECTED IT. WE'VE MANAGED TO ISOLATE THE DAMAGED TISSUE, BUT WE CAN'T RISK ACCELERATED CELLULAR DETERIORATION.
N OTHER ORDS, WE N'T SIMPLY PLACE THE ARM.
BUT DON'T WORRY, ROY. I'VE DESIGNED YOU A PROSTHETIC ARM THAT WILL WORK AROUND THE CORRUPTED TISSUE.
IT WON'T BE PERMANENT, BUT IT'LL GET THE JOB DONE.
I'M STILL NOT SURE, VIC. THIS WILL REQUIRE THAT THE CONNECTOR RODS BE ATTACHED THROUGH THE NERVE DAMAGE. THE PAIN WILL BE SIGNIFICANT.
WE'LL MAKE IT WORK.
RIGHT, ROY?
STOP TALKING AND LET'S DO THIS ALREADY.

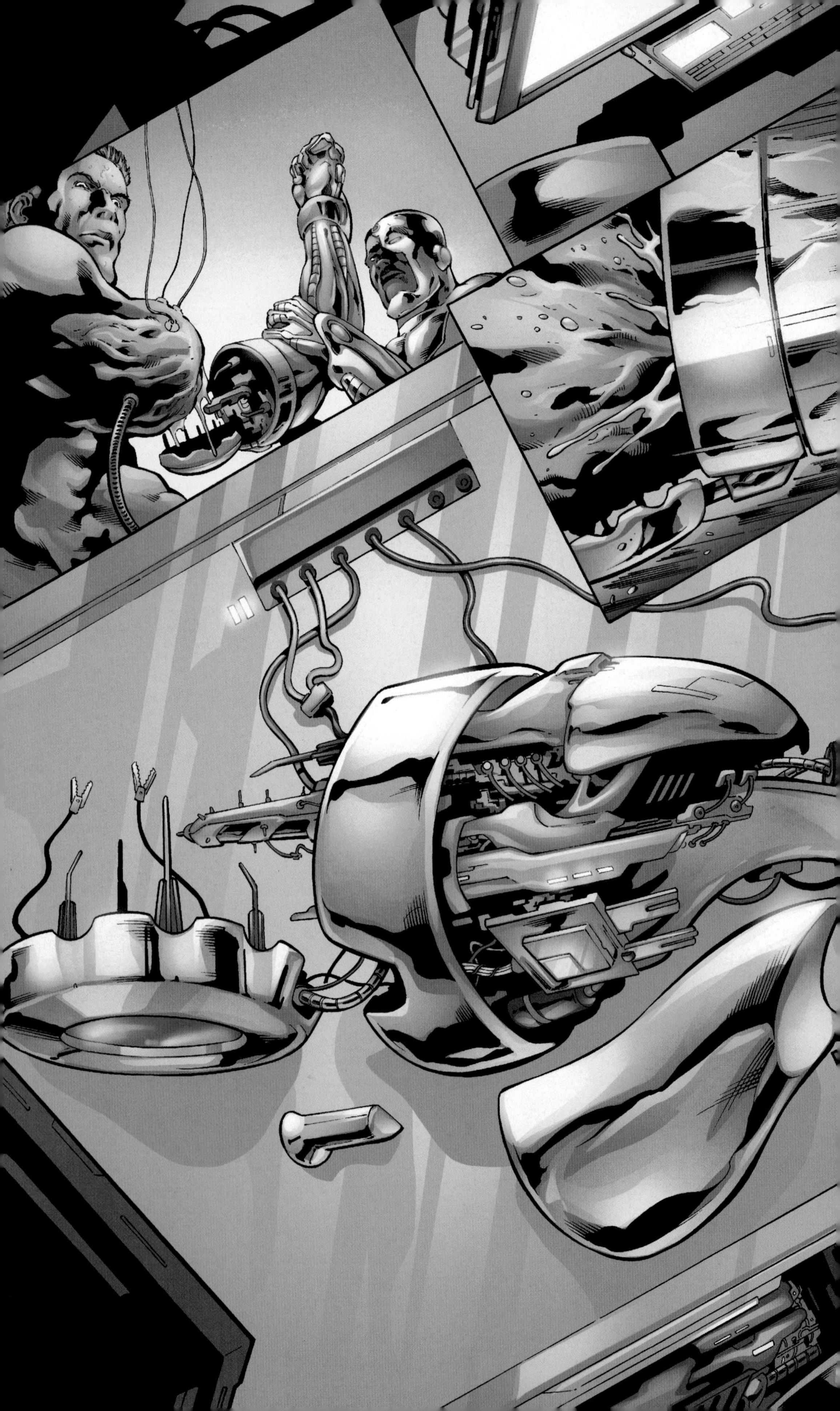

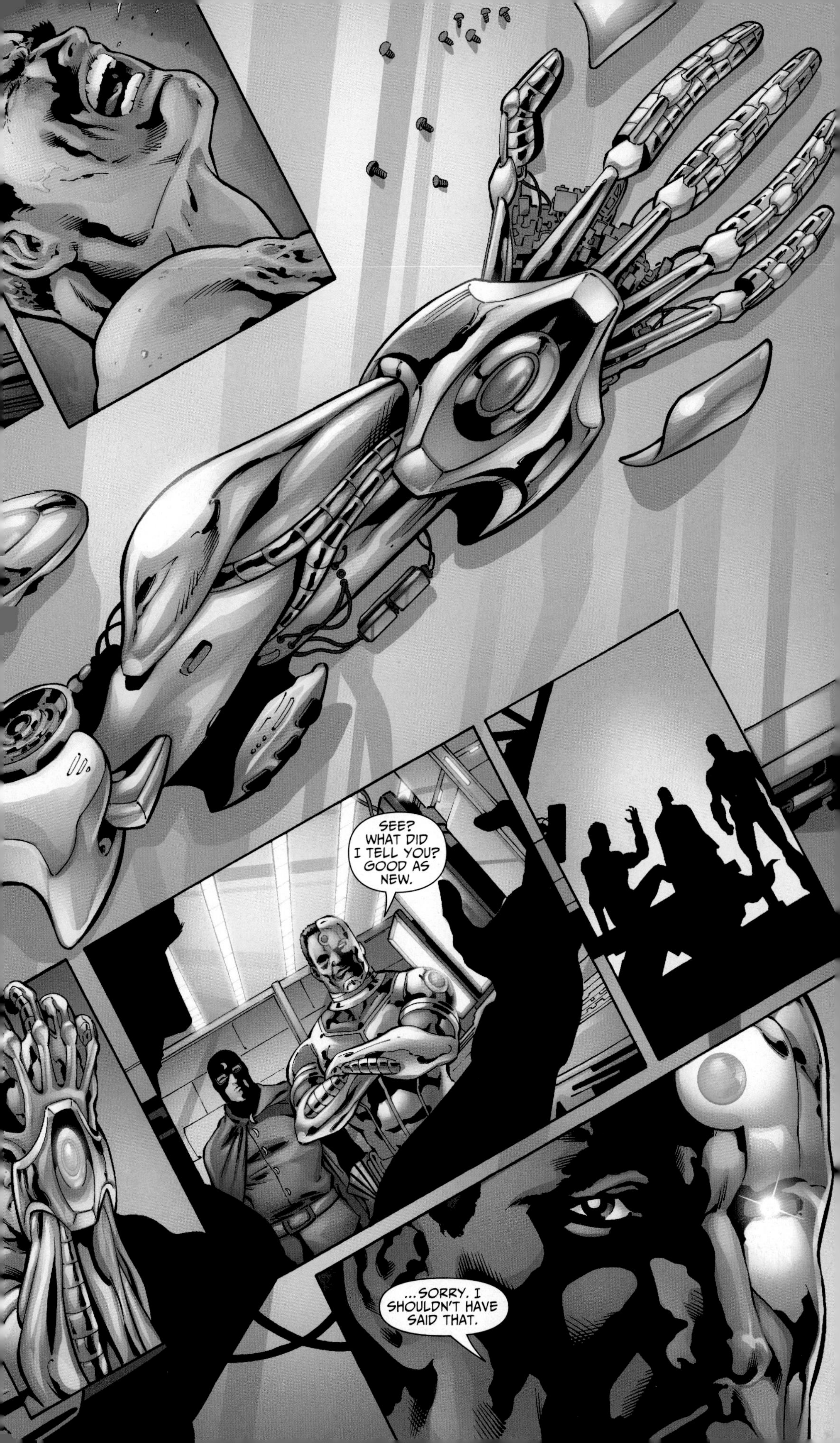
SEE? WHAT DID I TELL YOU? GOOD AS NEW.
...SORRY. I SHOULDN'T HAVE SAID THAT.

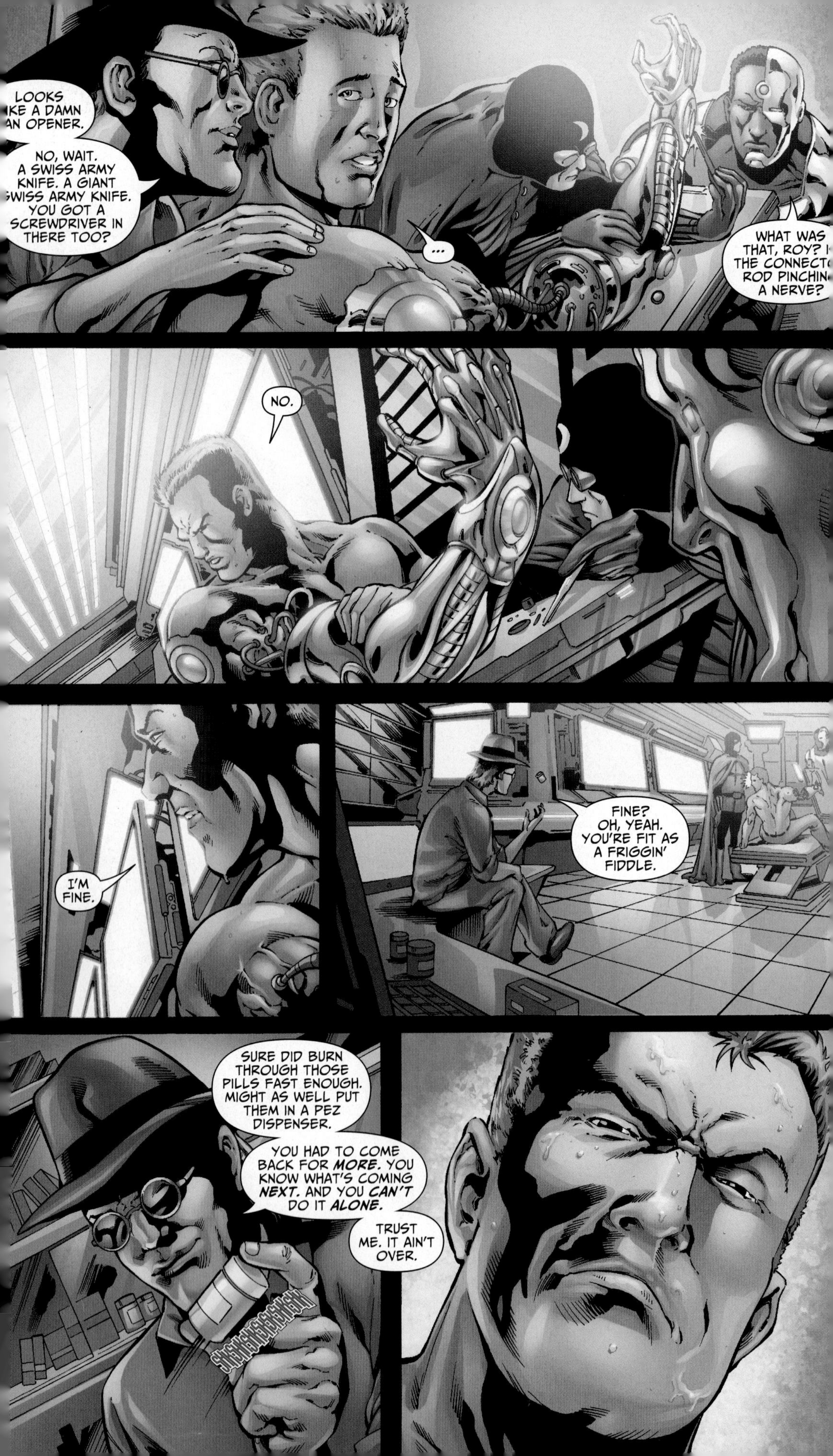
LOOKS LIKE A DAMN CAN OPENER.
NO, WAIT. A SWISS ARMY KNIFE. A GIANT SWISS ARMY KNIFE. YOU GOT A SCREWDRIVER IN THERE TOO?
...
WHAT WAS THAT, ROY? IS THE CONNECTOR ROD PINCHING A NERVE?
NO.
I'M FINE.
FINE? OH, YEAH. YOU'RE FIT AS A FRIGGIN' FIDDLE.
SURE DID BURN THROUGH THOSE PILLS FAST ENOUGH. MIGHT AS WELL PUT THEM IN A PEZ DISPENSER.
YOU HAD TO COME BACK FOR MORE. YOU KNOW WHAT'S COMING NEXT. AND YOU CAN'T DO IT ALONE.
TRUST ME. IT AIN'T OVER.
SHKSHKSHKSHKSHK

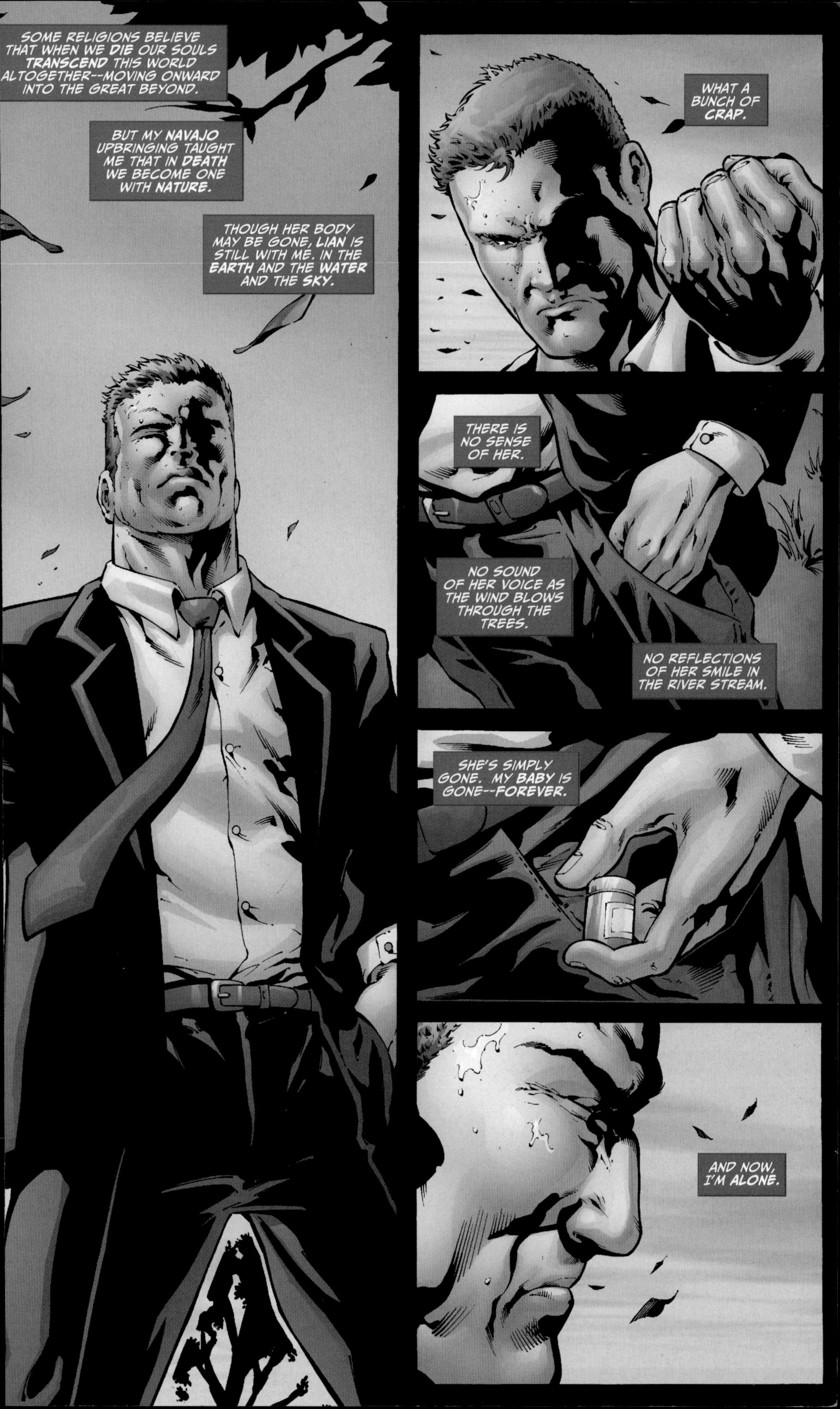

SOME RELIGIONS BELIEVE THAT WHEN WE DIE OUR SOULS TRANSCEND THIS WORLD ALTOGETHER--MOVING ONWARD INTO THE GREAT BEYOND.
BUT MY NAVAJO UPBRINGING TAUGHT ME THAT IN DEATH WE BECOME ONE WITH NATURE.
THOUGH HER BODY MAY BE GONE, LIAN IS STILL WITH ME. IN THE EARTH AND THE WATER AND THE SKY.
WHAT A BUNCH OF CRAP.
THERE IS NO SENSE OF HER.
NO SOUND OF HER VOICE AS THE WIND BLOWS THROUGH THE TREES.
NO REFLECTIONS OF HER SMILE IN THE RIVER STREAM.
SHE'S SIMPLY GONE. MY BABY IS GONE--FOREVER.
AND NOW, I'M ALONE.

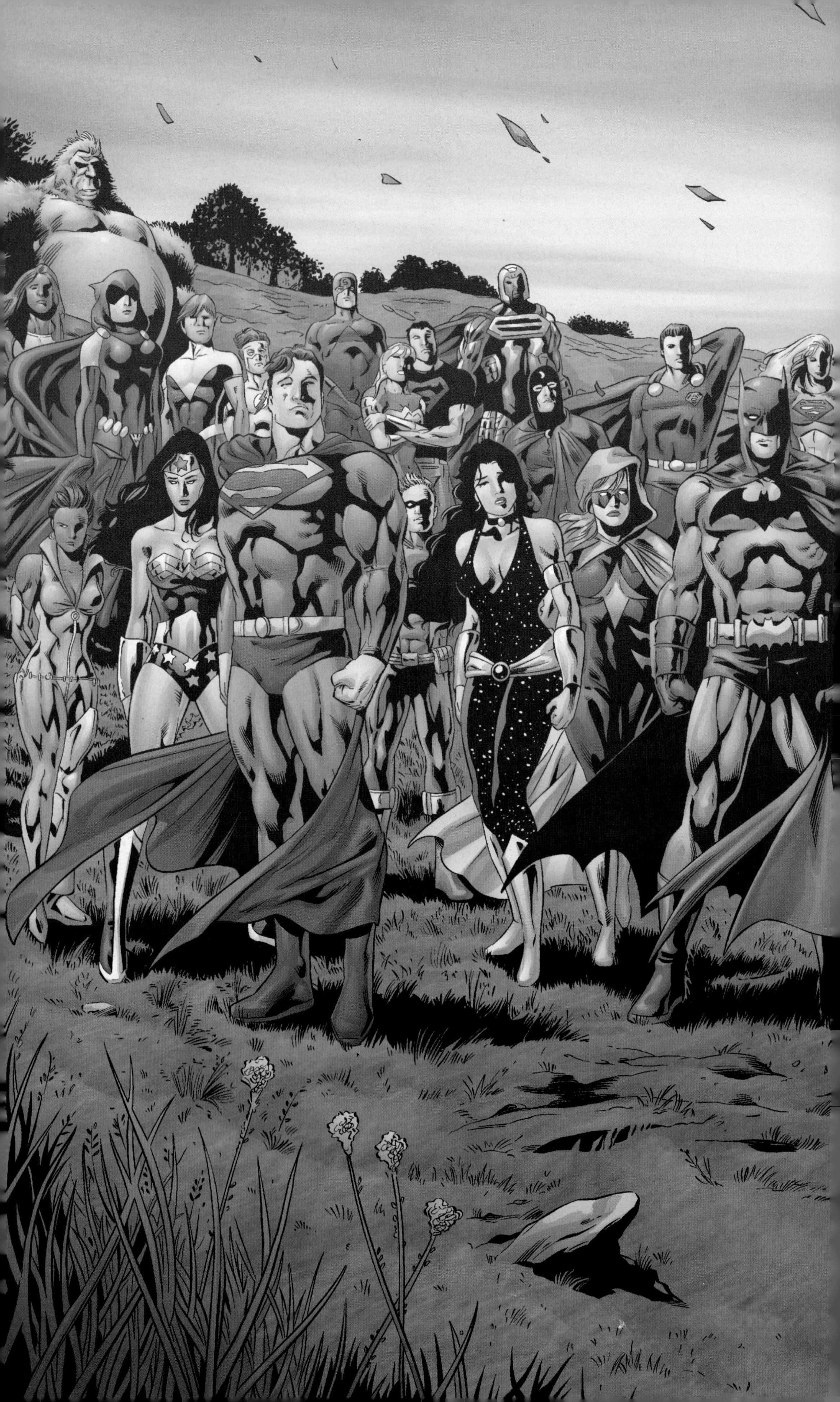

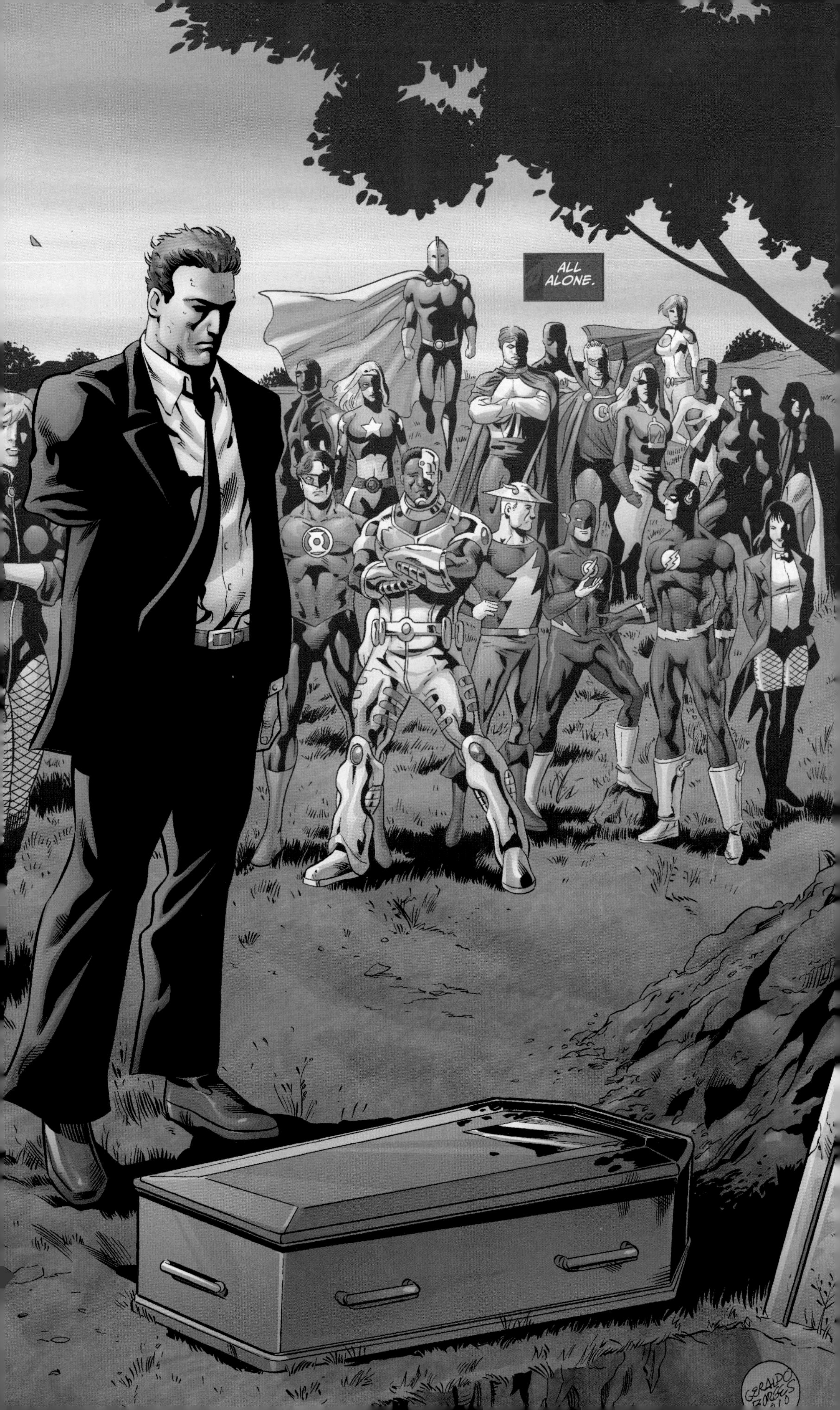
ALL ALONE.
GERALDO BORGES '10

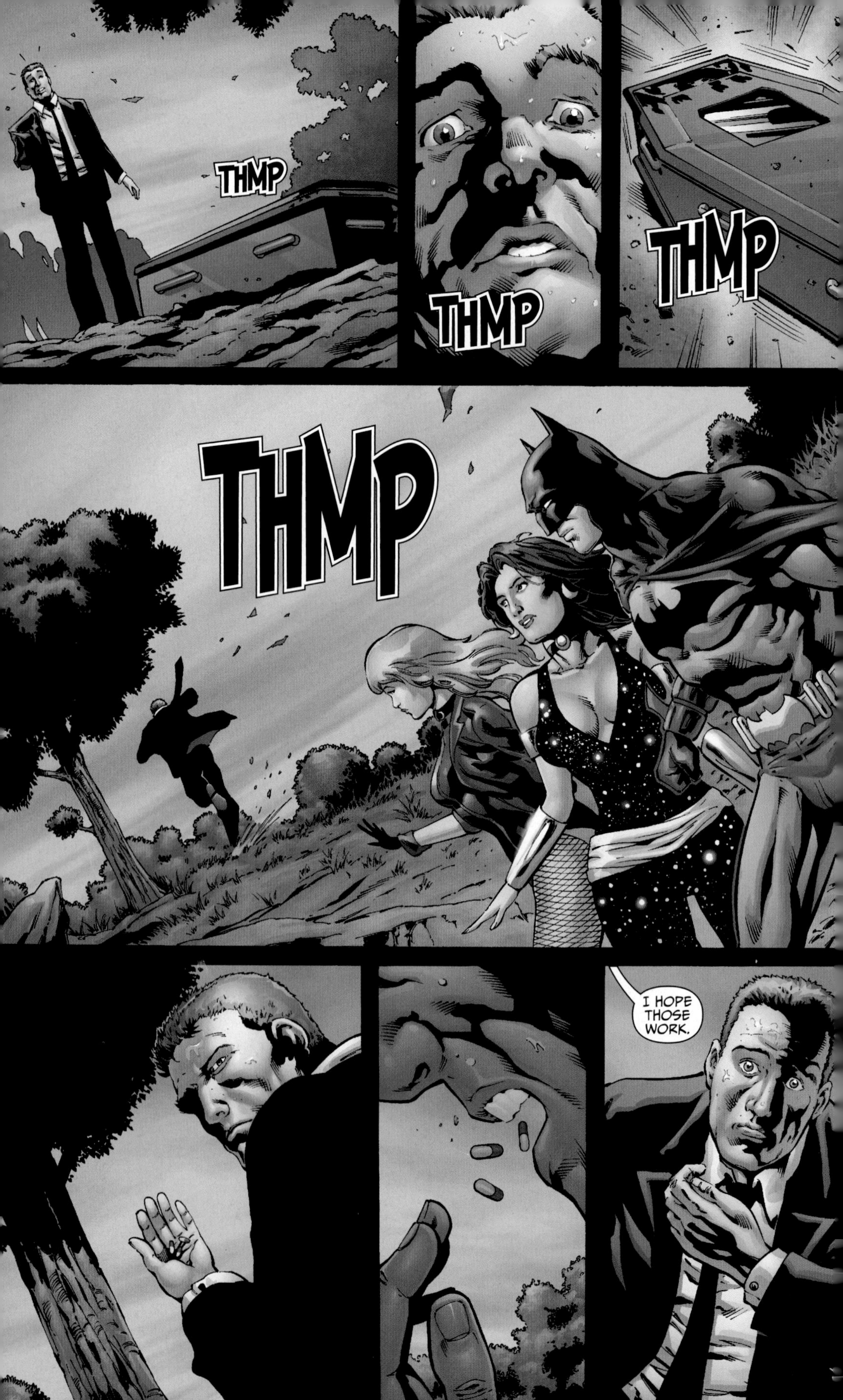
THMP
THMP
THMP
THMP
I HOPE THOSE WORK.

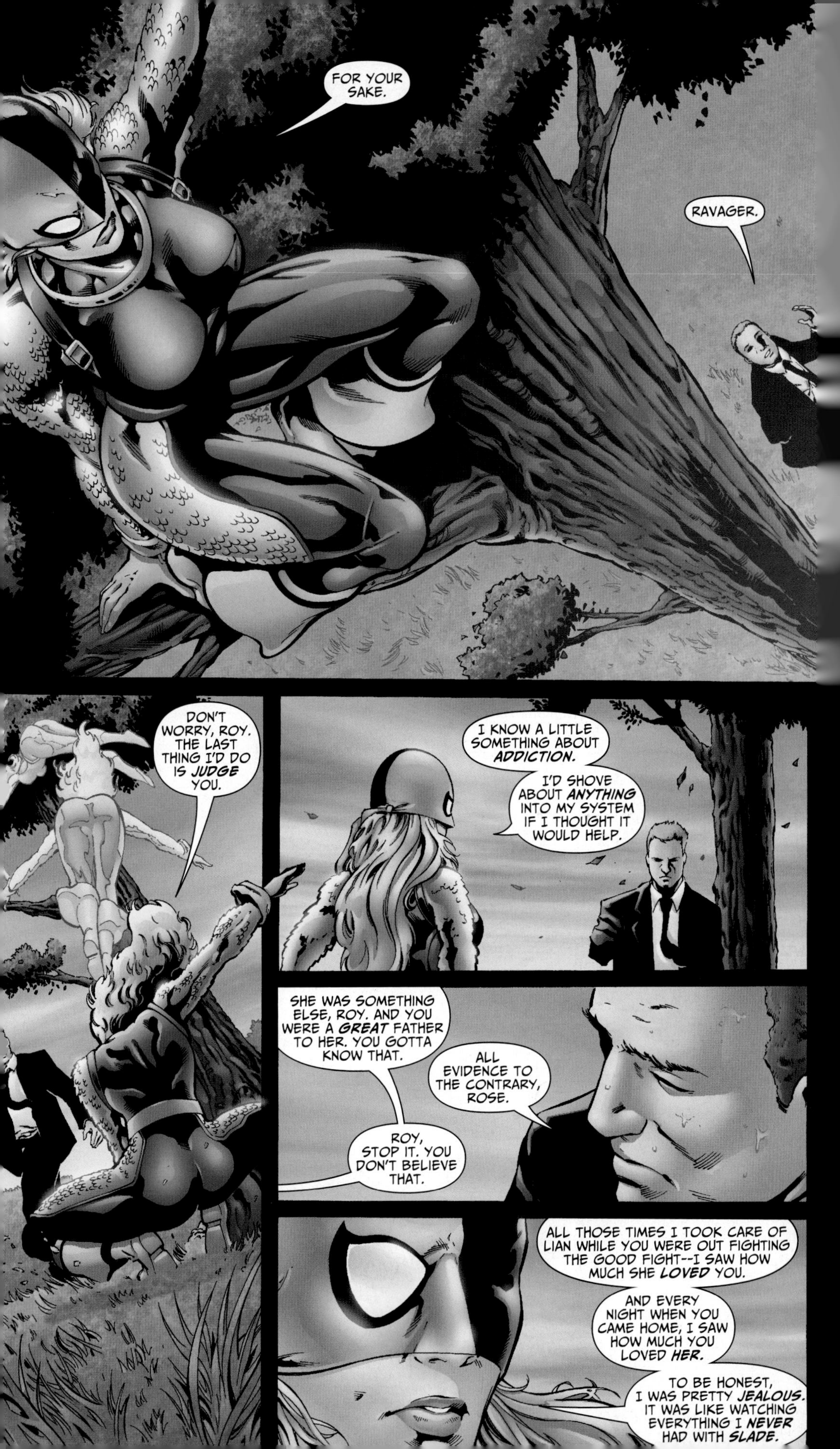
FOR YOUR SAKE.
RAVAGER.
DON'T WORRY, ROY. THE LAST THING I'D DO IS JUDGE YOU.
I KNOW A LITTLE SOMETHING ABOUT ADDICTION.
I'D SHOVE ABOUT ANYTHING INTO MY SYSTEM IF I THOUGHT IT WOULD HELP.
SHE WAS SOMETHING ELSE, ROY. AND YOU WERE A GREAT FATHER TO HER. YOU GOTTA KNOW THAT.
ALL EVIDENCE TO THE CONTRARY, ROSE.
ROY, STOP IT. YOU DON'T BELIEVE THAT.
ALL THOSE TIMES I TOOK CARE OF LIAN WHILE YOU WERE OUT FIGHTING THE GOOD FIGHT--I SAW HOW MUCH SHE LOVED YOU.
AND EVERY NIGHT WHEN YOU CAME HOME, I SAW HOW MUCH YOU LOVED HER.
TO BE HONEST, I WAS PRETTY JEALOUS. IT WAS LIKE WATCHING EVERYTHING I NEVER HAD WITH SLADE.

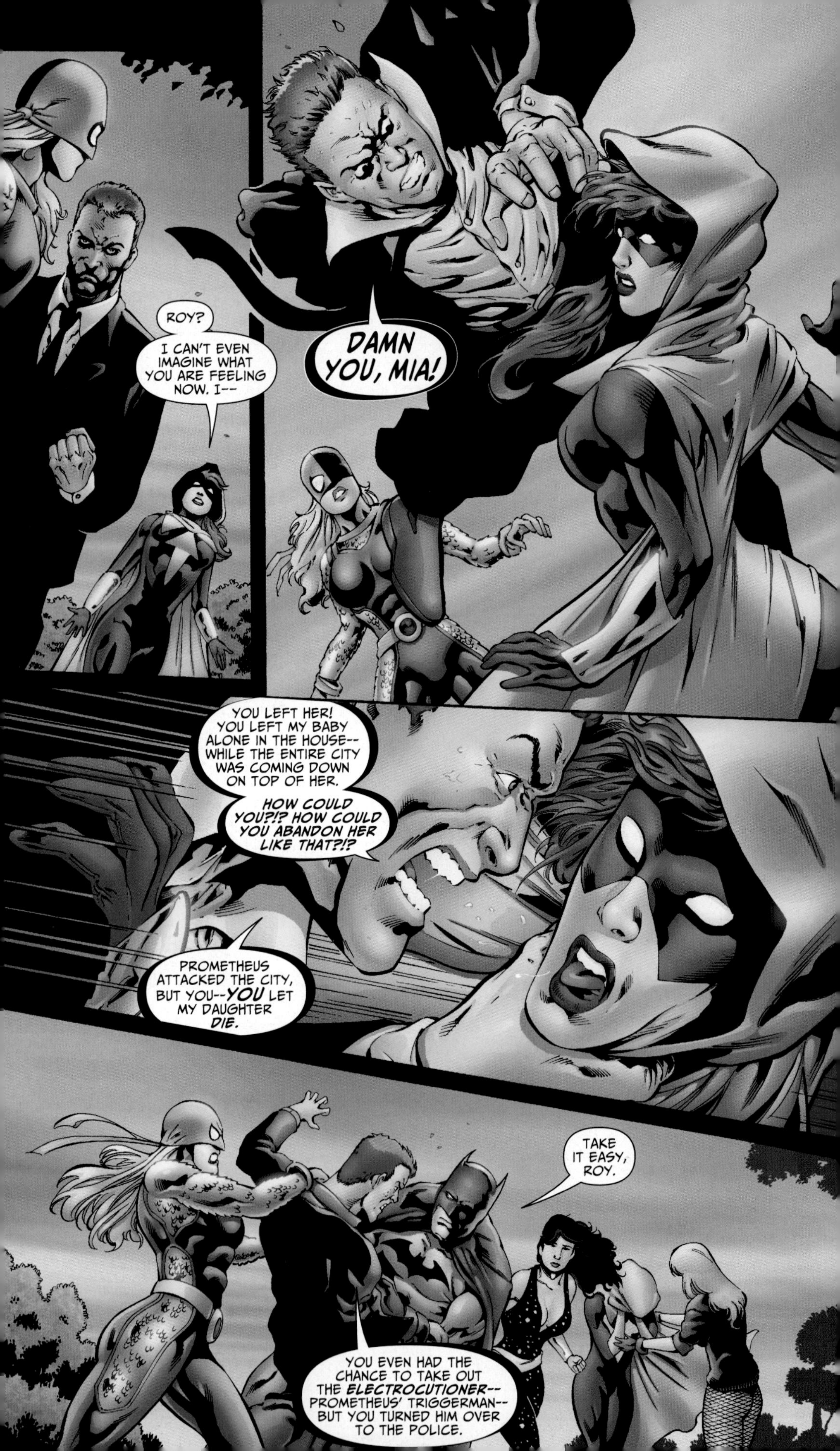
ROY?
I CAN'T EVEN IMAGINE WHAT YOU ARE FEELING NOW. I--
DAMN YOU, MIA!
YOU LEFT HER! YOU LEFT MY BABY ALONE IN THE HOUSE-- WHILE THE ENTIRE CITY WAS COMING DOWN ON TOP OF HER.
HOW COULD YOU?!? HOW COULD YOU ABANDON HER LIKE THAT?!?
PROMETHEUS ATTACKED THE CITY, BUT YOU--YOU LET MY DAUGHTER DIE.
TAKE IT EASY, ROY.
YOU EVEN HAD THE CHANCE TO TAKE OUT THE ELECTROCUTIONER-- PROMETHEUS' TRIGGERMAN-- BUT YOU TURNED HIM OVER TO THE POLICE.

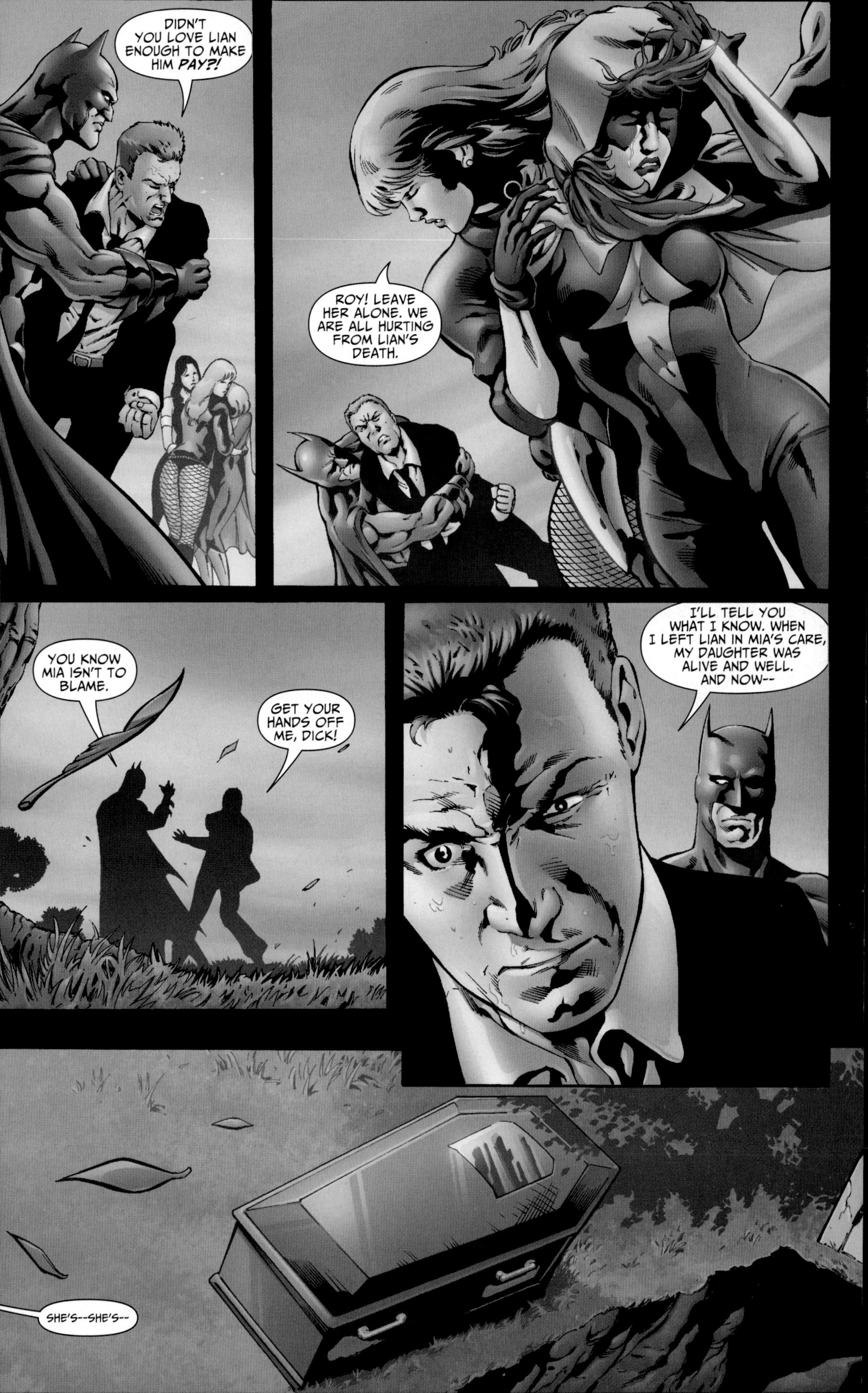
DIDN'T YOU LOVE LIAN ENOUGH TO MAKE HIM PAY?!
ROY! LEAVE HER ALONE. WE ARE ALL HURTING FROM LIAN'S DEATH.
YOU KNOW MIA ISN'T TO BLAME.
GET YOUR HANDS OFF ME, DICK!
I'LL TELL YOU WHAT I KNOW. WHEN I LEFT LIAN IN MIA'S CARE, MY DAUGHTER WAS ALIVE AND WELL. AND NOW--
SHE'S--SHE'S--

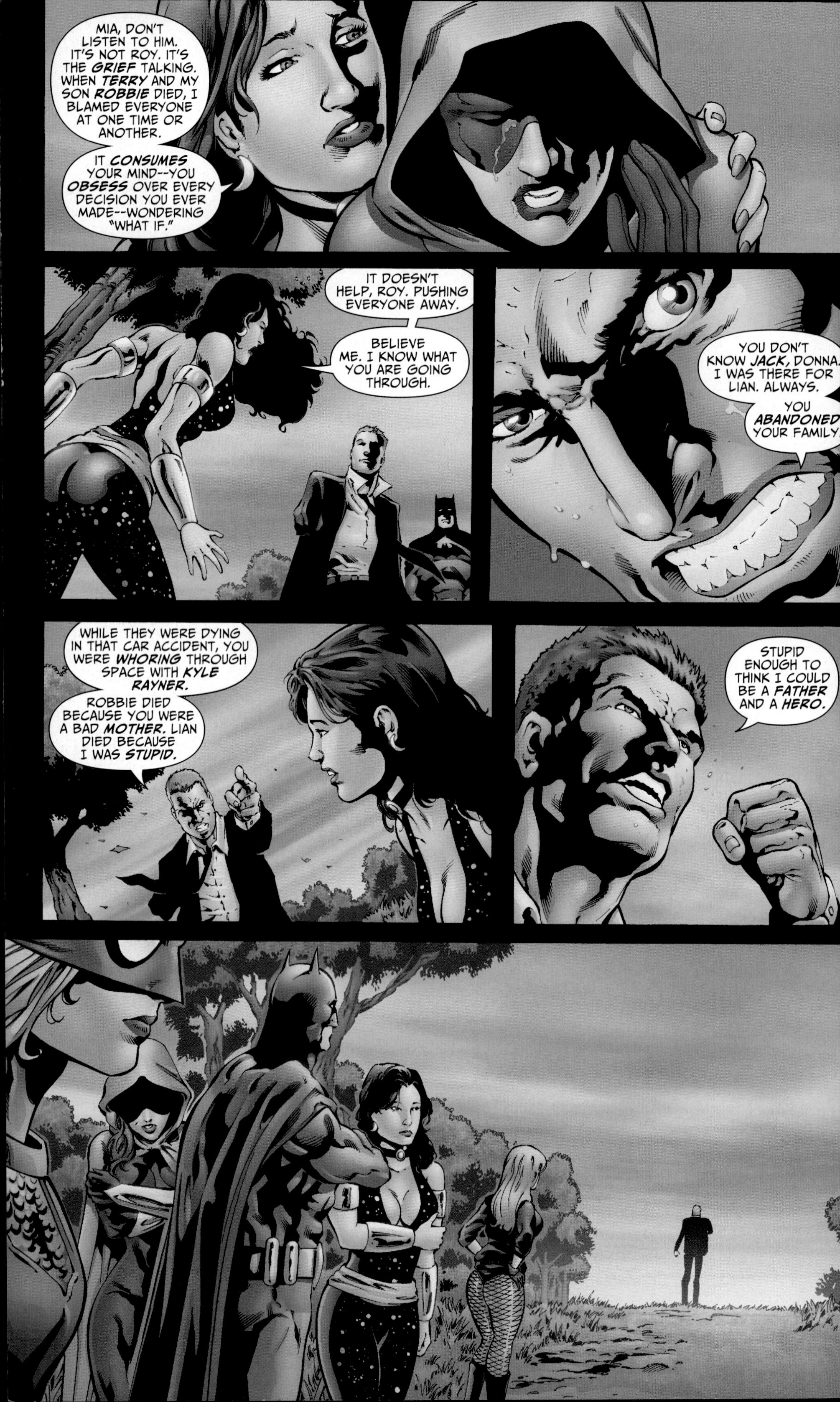
MIA, DON'T LISTEN TO HIM. IT'S NOT ROY. IT'S THE GRIEF TALKING. WHEN TERRY AND MY SON ROBBIE DIED, I BLAMED EVERYONE AT ONE TIME OR ANOTHER.
IT CONSUMES YOUR MIND--YOU OBSESS OVER EVERY DECISION YOU EVER MADE--WONDERING "WHAT IF."
IT DOESN'T HELP, ROY. PUSHING EVERYONE AWAY.
BELIEVE ME. I KNOW WHAT YOU ARE GOING THROUGH.
YOU DON'T KNOW JACK, DONNA. I WAS THERE FOR LIAN. ALWAYS.
YOU ABANDONED YOUR FAMILY.
WHILE THEY WERE DYING IN THAT CAR ACCIDENT, YOU WERE WHORING THROUGH SPACE WITH KYLE RAYNER.
ROBBIE DIED BECAUSE YOU WERE A BAD MOTHER. LIAN DIED BECAUSE I WAS STUPID.
STUPID ENOUGH TO THINK I COULD BE A FATHER AND A HERO.

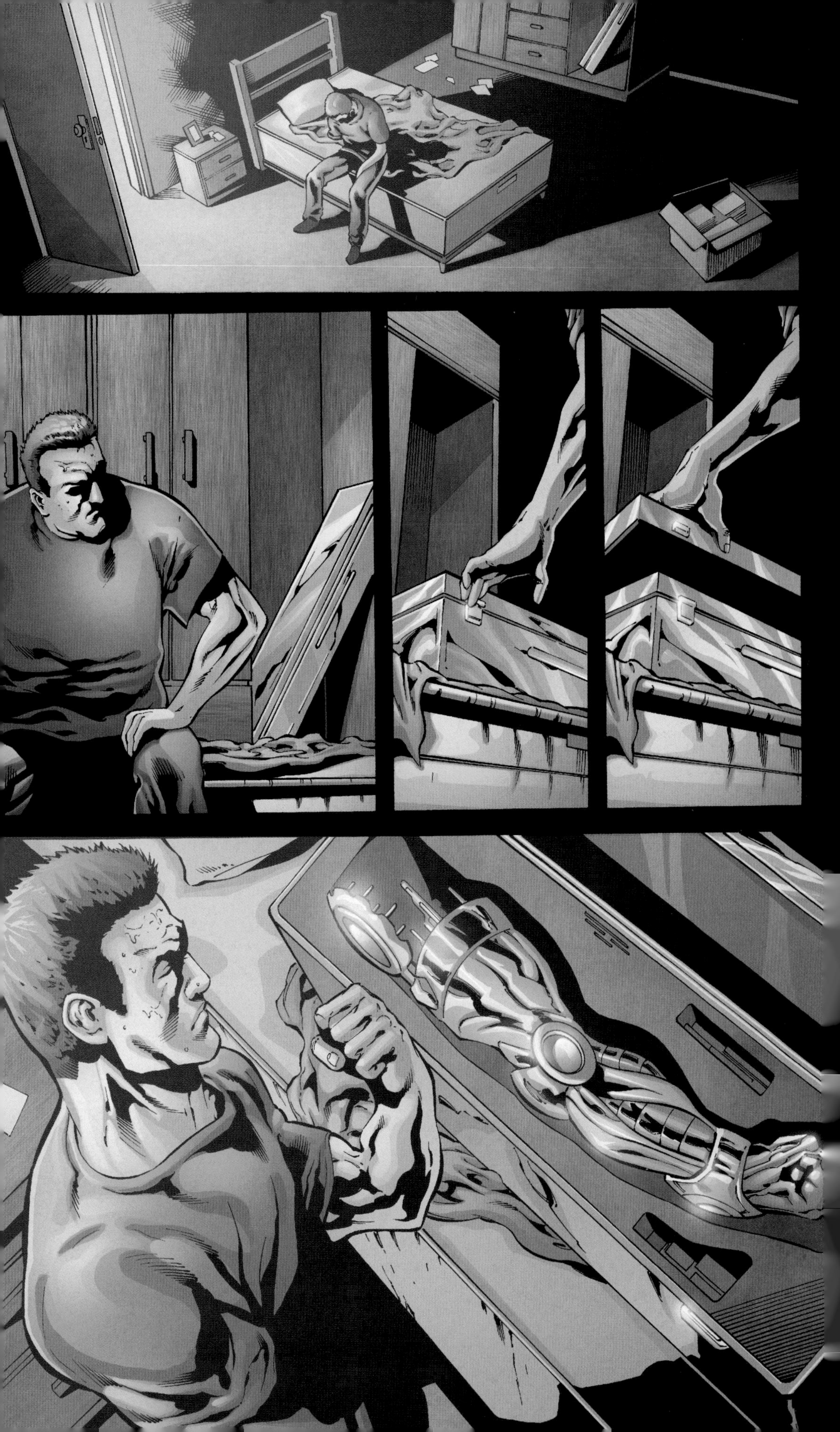

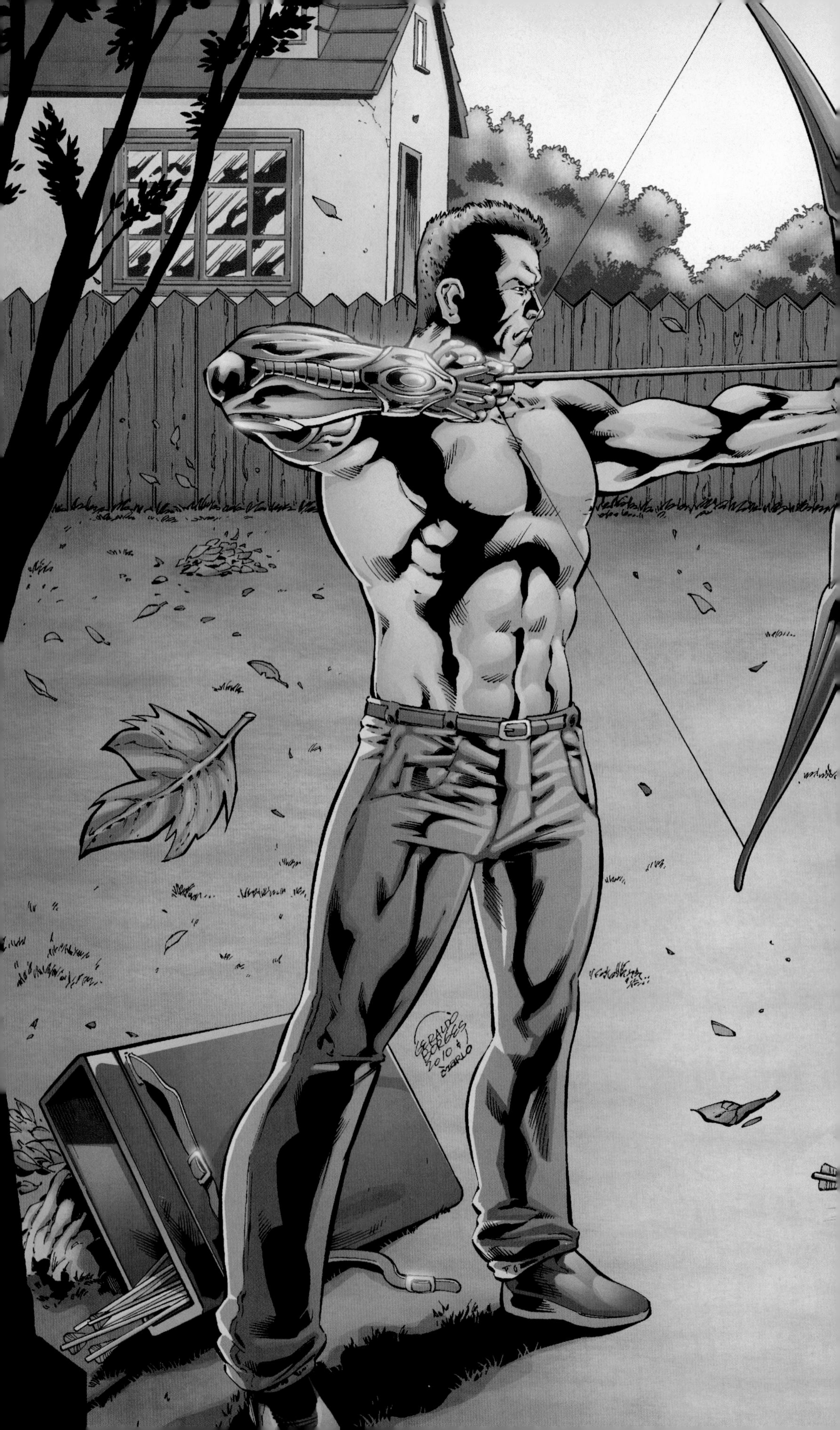

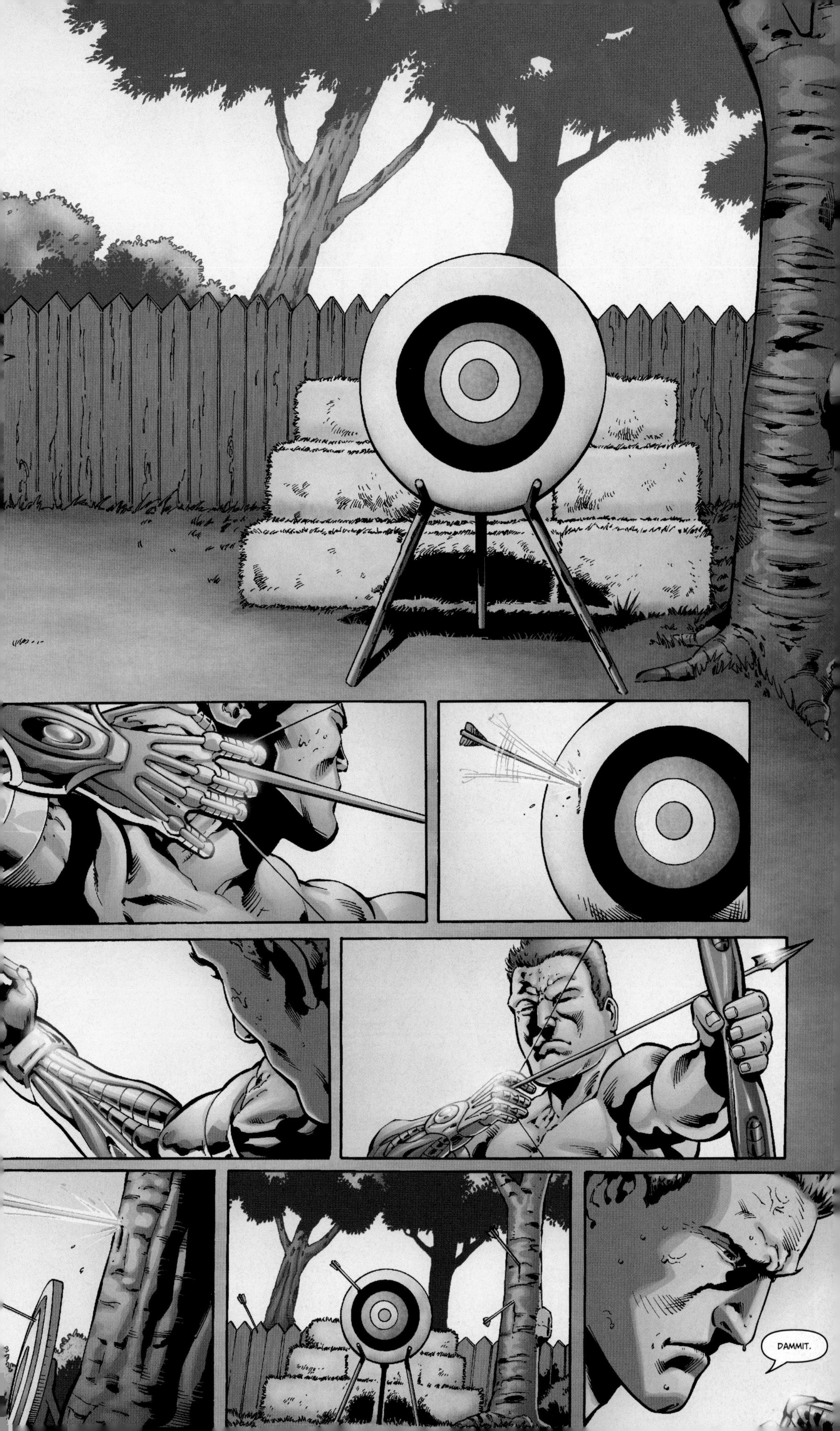
DAMMIT.

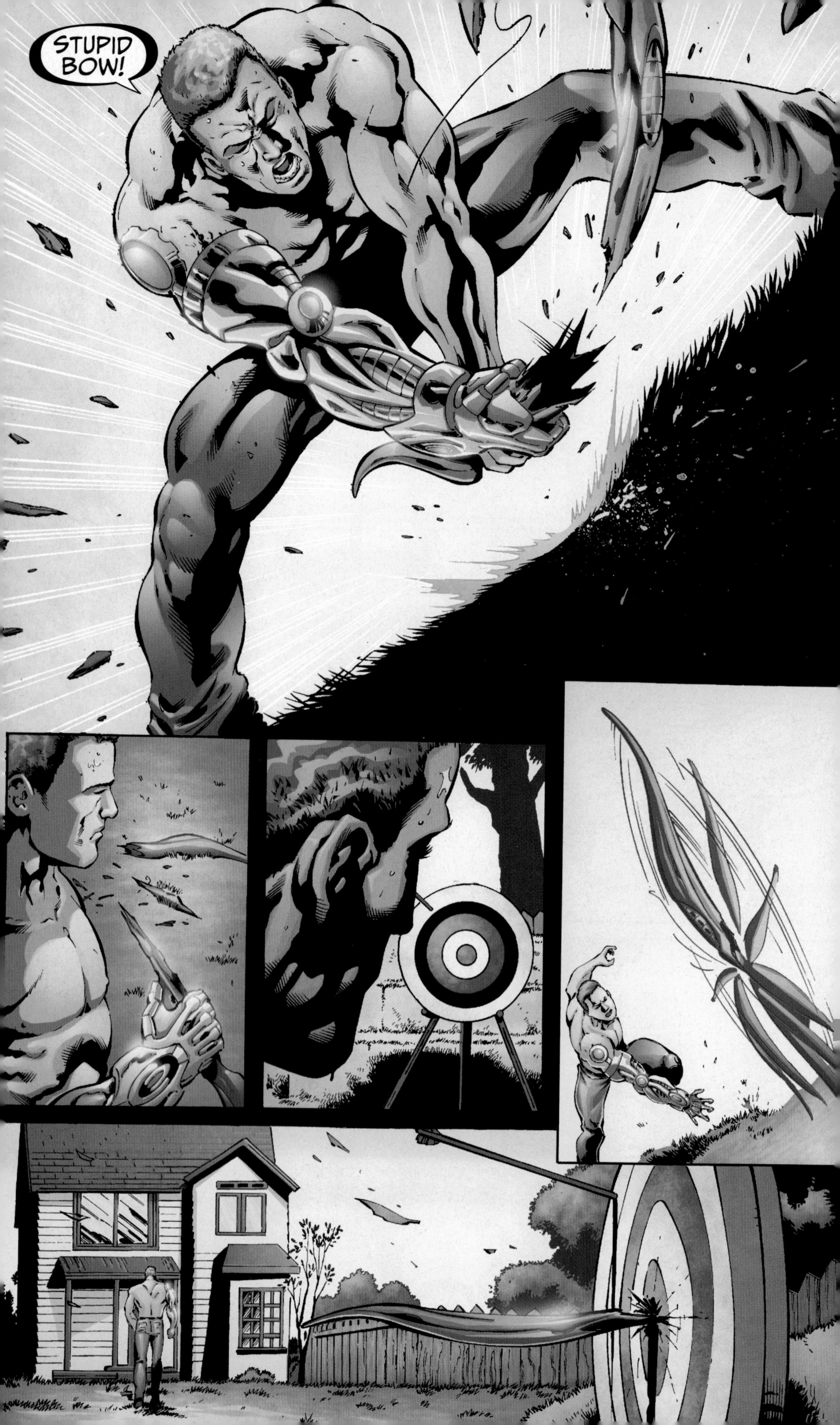
STUPID BOW!

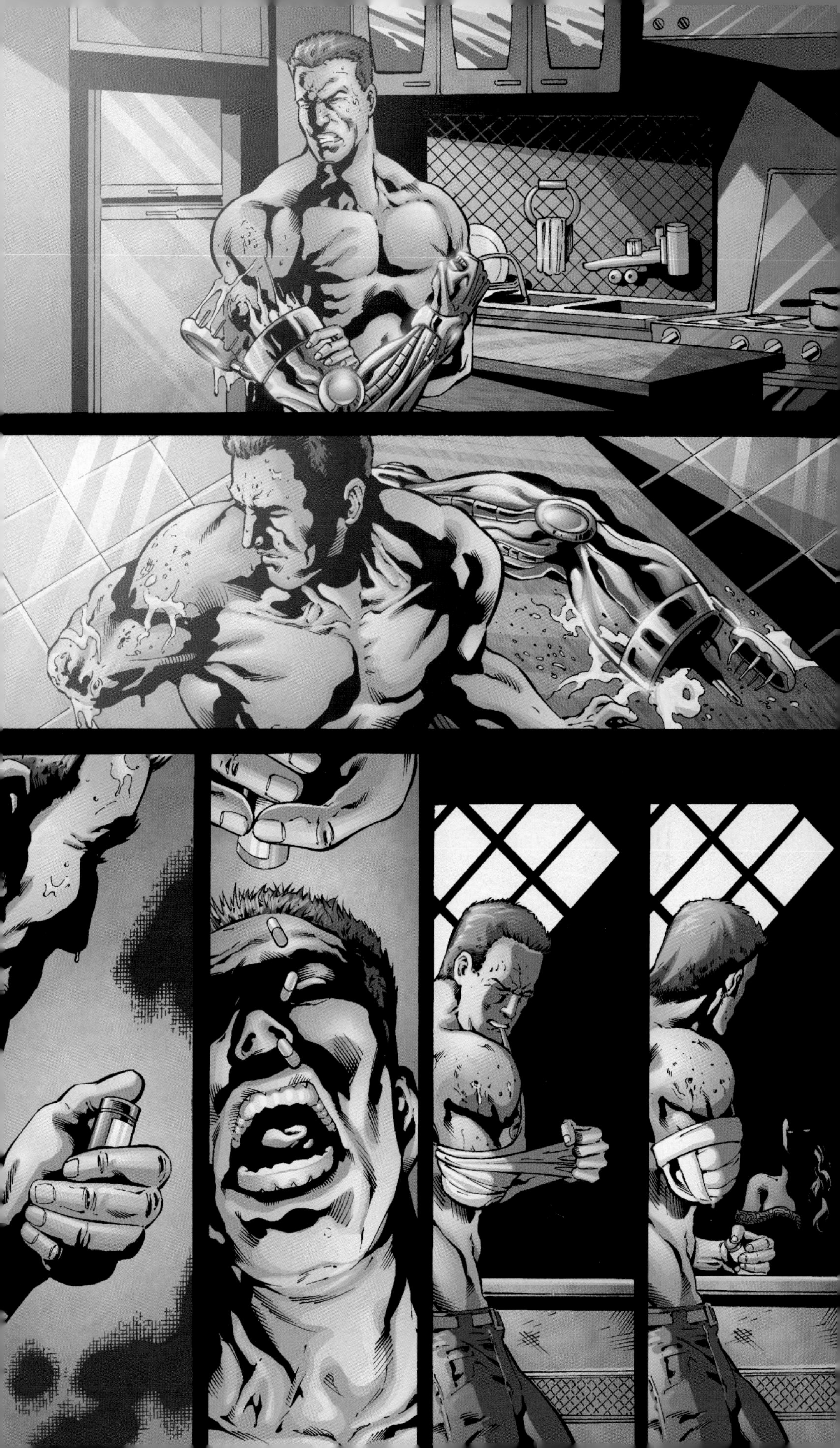

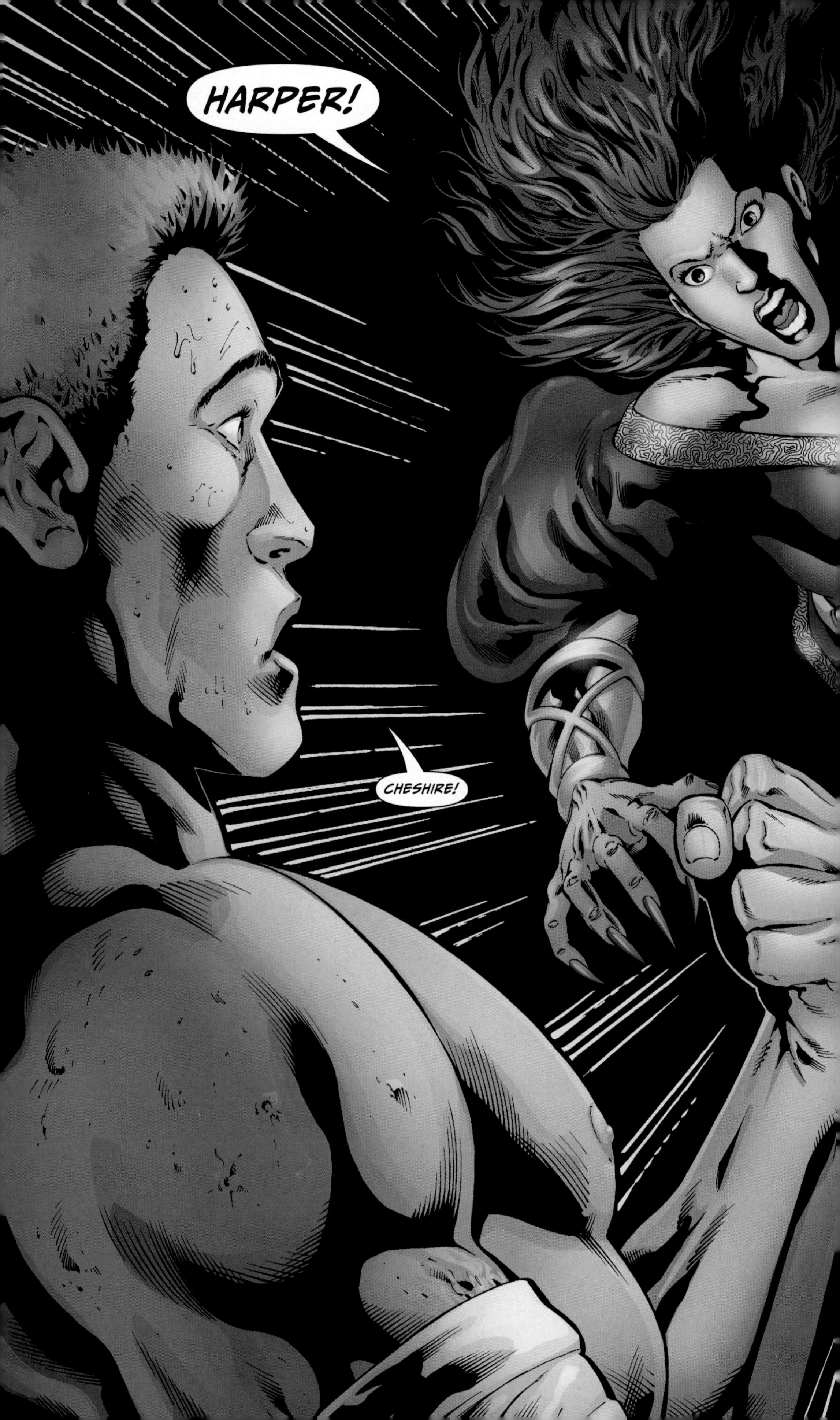
HARPER!
CHESHIRE!

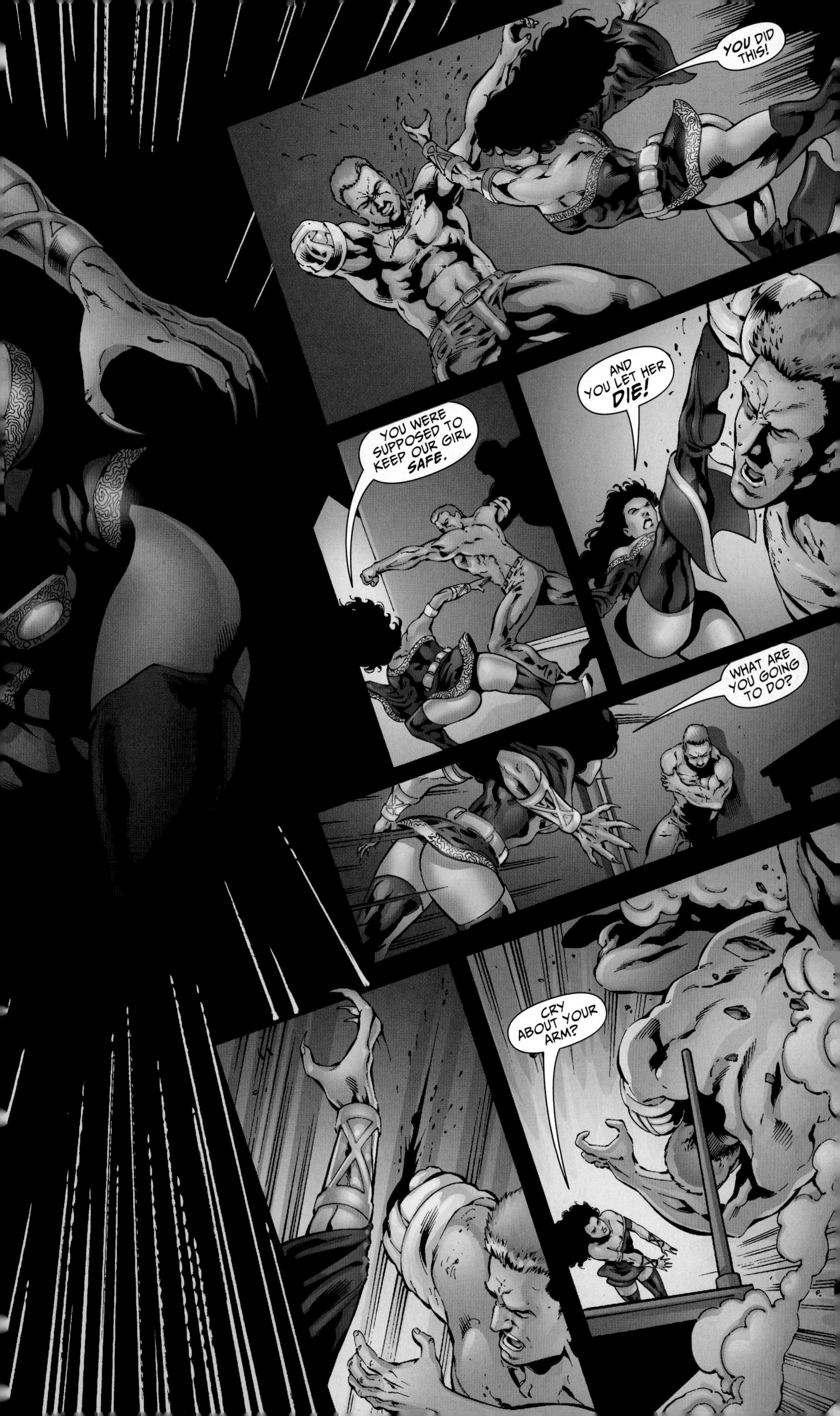
YOU DID THIS!
YOU WERE SUPPOSED TO KEEP OUR GIRL SAFE.
AND YOU LET HER DIE!
WHAT ARE YOU GOING TO DO?
CRY ABOUT YOUR ARM?

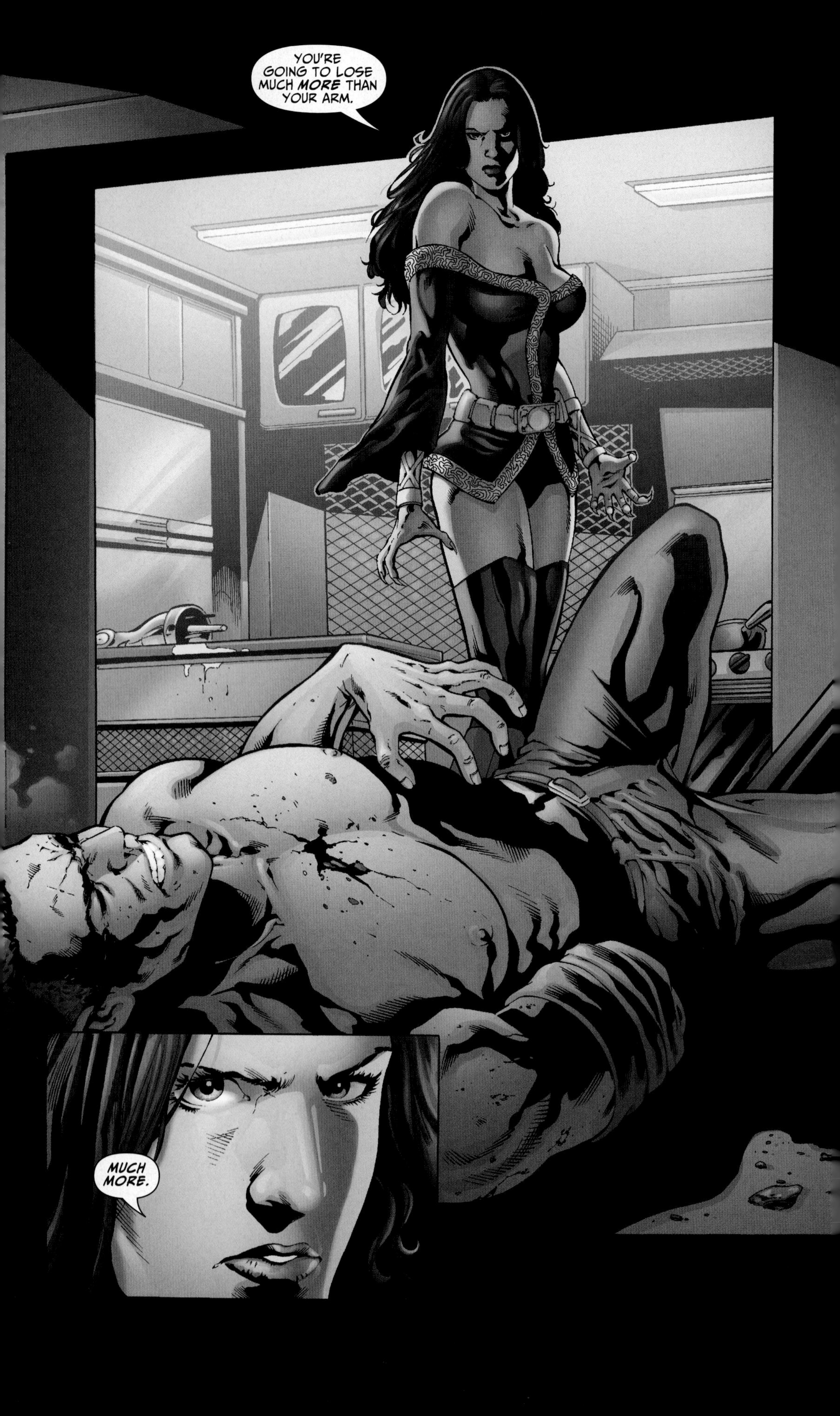
YOU'RE GOING TO LOSE MUCH MORE THAN YOUR ARM.
MUCH MORE.

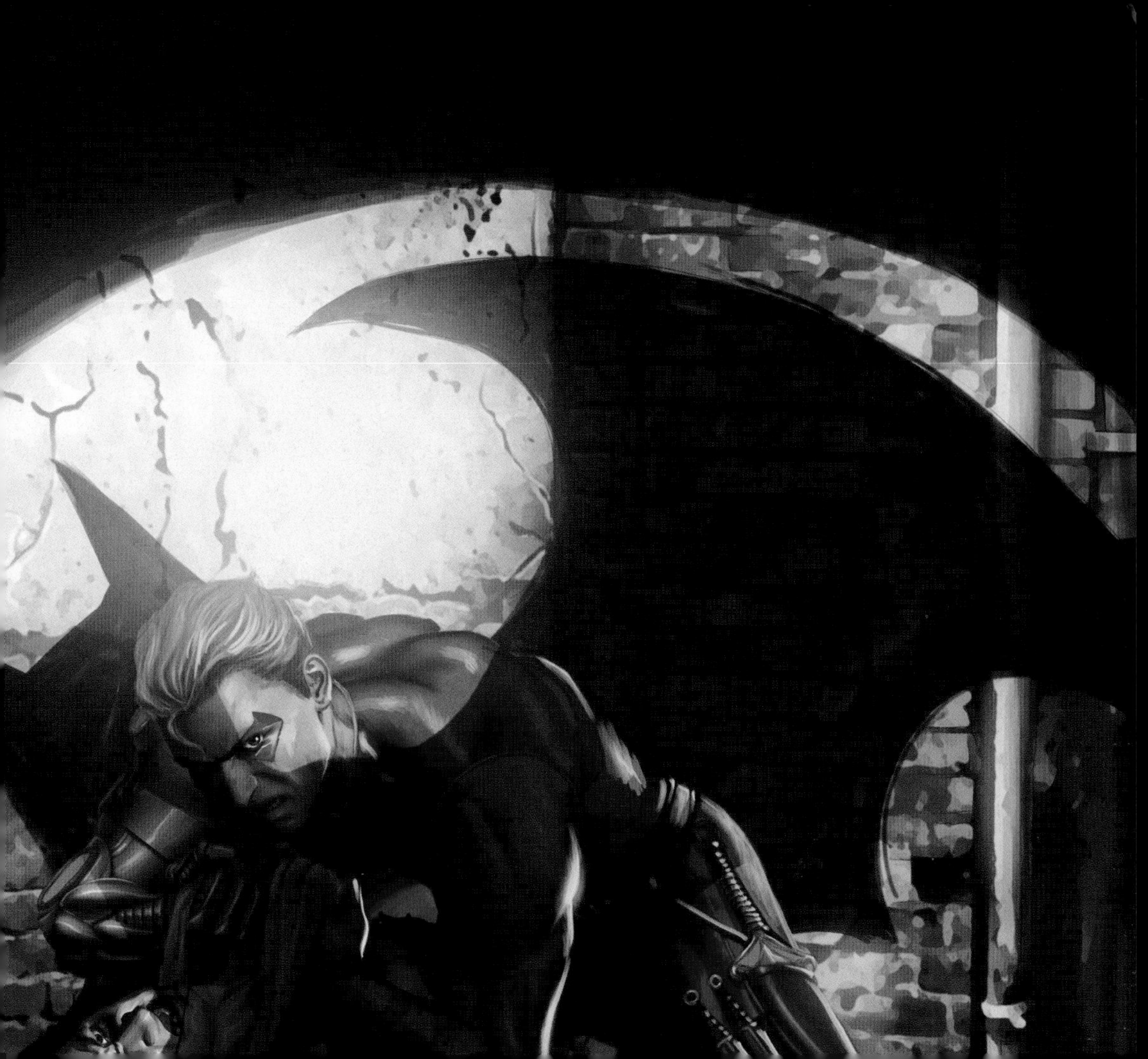

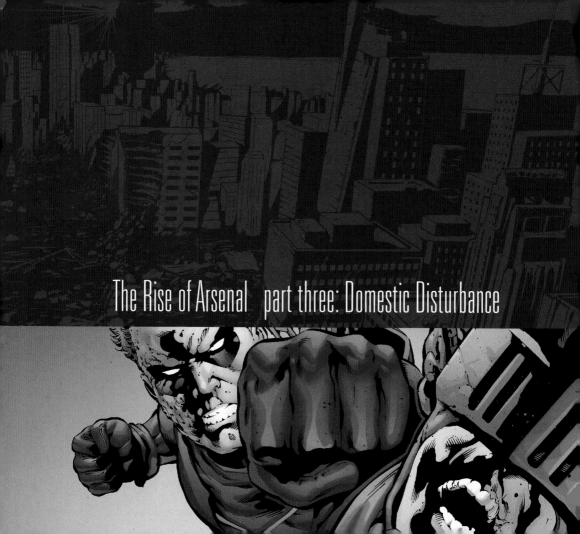

The Rise of Arsenal   part three: Domestic Disturbance

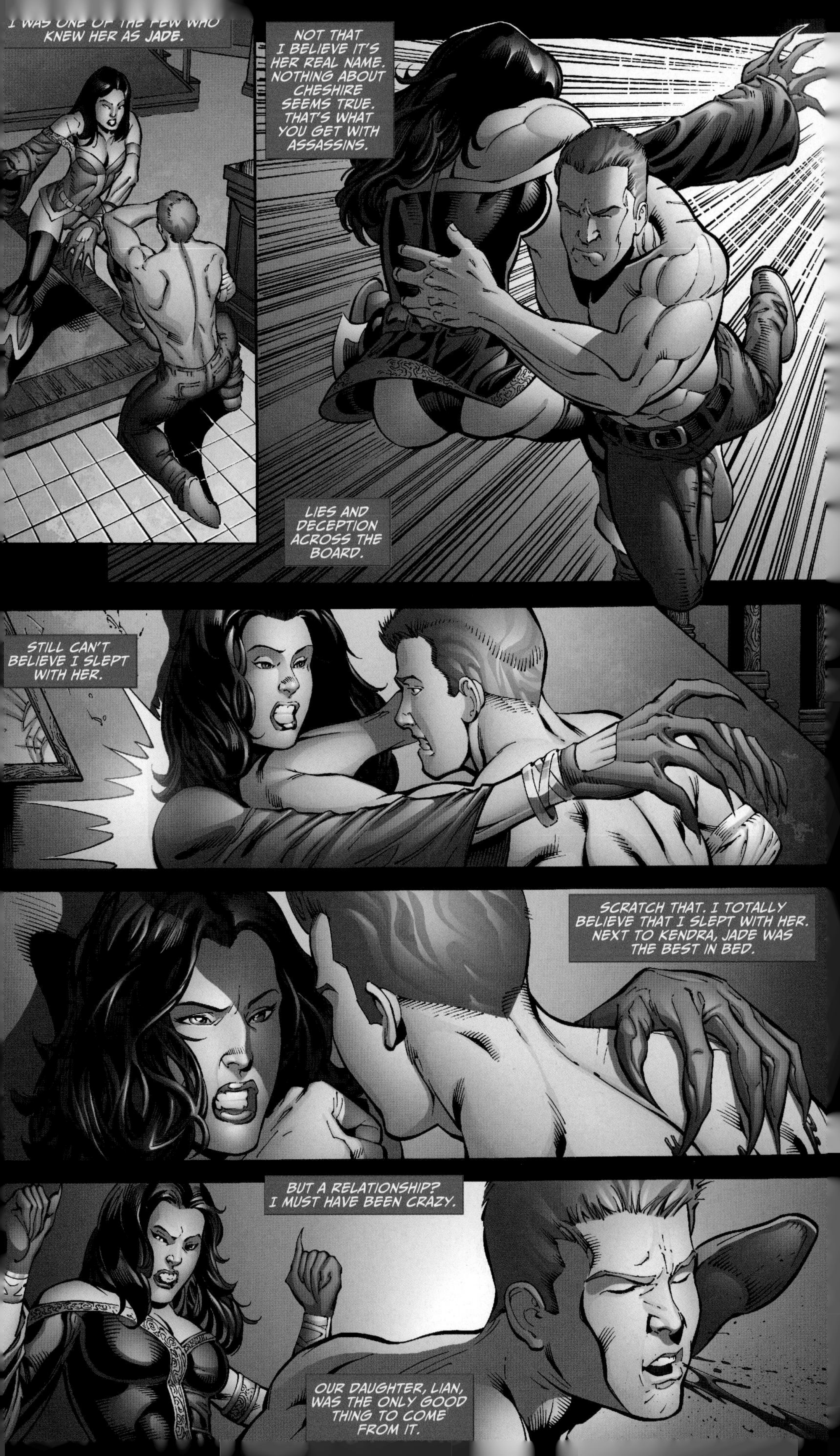
I WAS ONE OF THE FEW WHO KNEW HER AS JADE.
NOT THAT I BELIEVE IT'S HER REAL NAME. NOTHING ABOUT CHESHIRE SEEMS TRUE. THAT'S WHAT YOU GET WITH ASSASSINS.
LIES AND DECEPTION ACROSS THE BOARD.
STILL CAN'T BELIEVE I SLEPT WITH HER.
SCRATCH THAT. I TOTALLY BELIEVE THAT I SLEPT WITH HER. NEXT TO KENDRA, JADE WAS THE BEST IN BED.
BUT A RELATIONSHIP? I MUST HAVE BEEN CRAZY.
OUR DAUGHTER, LIAN, WAS THE ONLY GOOD THING TO COME FROM IT.

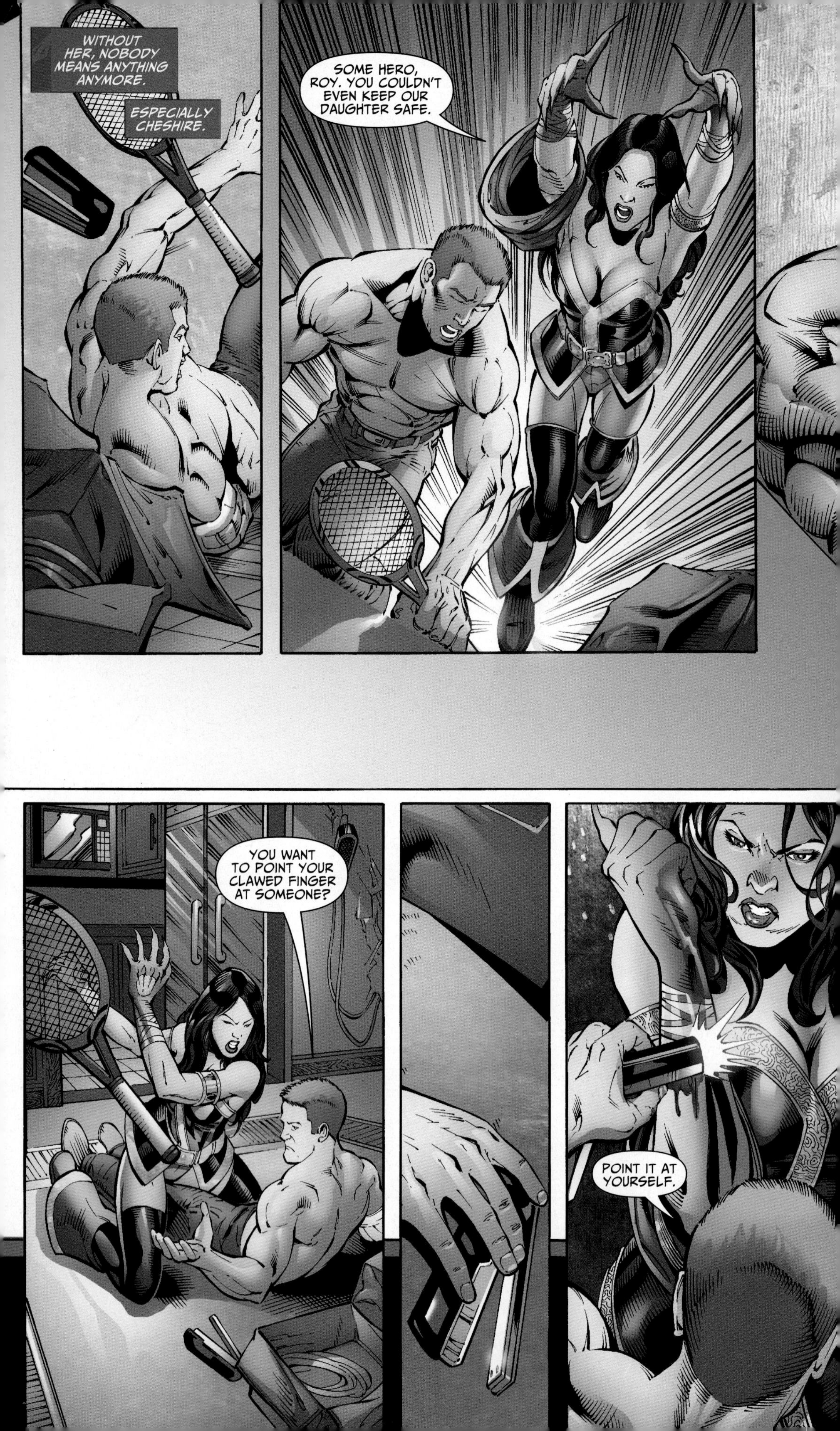
WITHOUT HER, NOBODY MEANS ANYTHING ANYMORE.
ESPECIALLY CHESHIRE.
SOME HERO, ROY. YOU COULDN'T EVEN KEEP OUR DAUGHTER SAFE.
YOU WANT TO POINT YOUR CLAWED FINGER AT SOMEONE?
POINT IT AT YOURSELF.

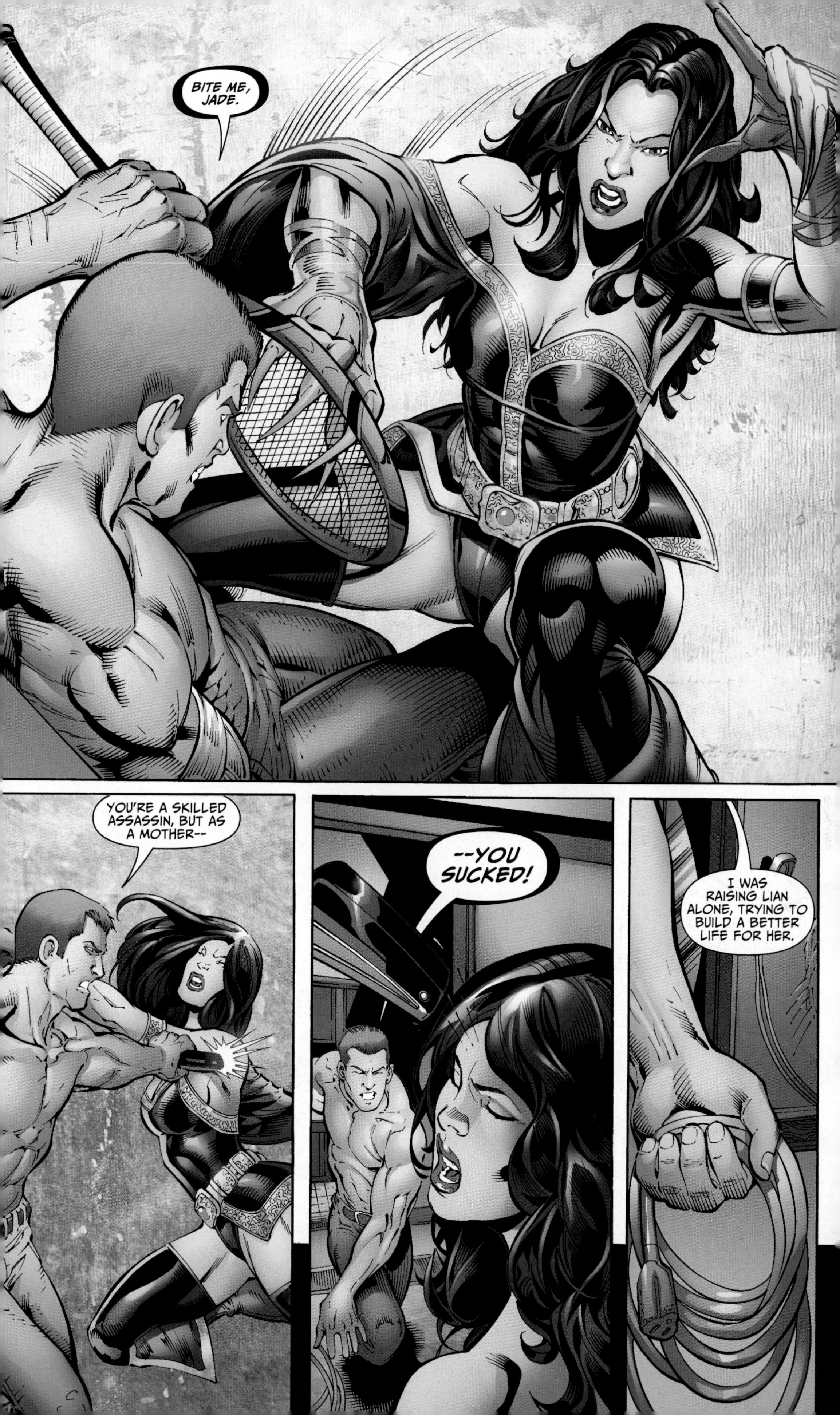
BITE ME, JADE.
YOU'RE A SKILLED ASSASSIN, BUT AS A MOTHER--
--YOU SUCKED!
I WAS RAISING LIAN ALONE, TRYING TO BUILD A BETTER LIFE FOR HER.

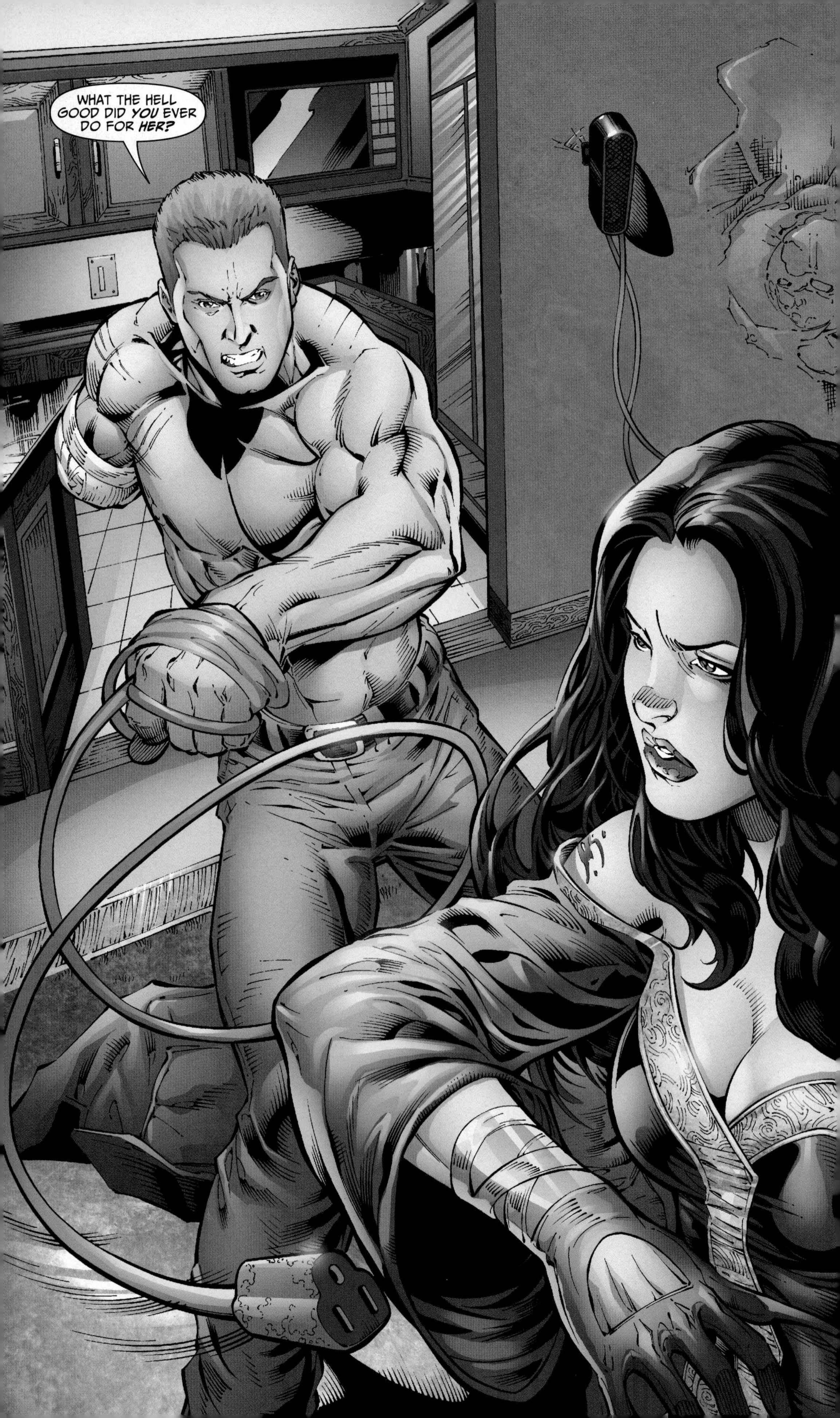
WHAT THE HELL GOOD DID *YOU* EVER DO FOR *HER?*

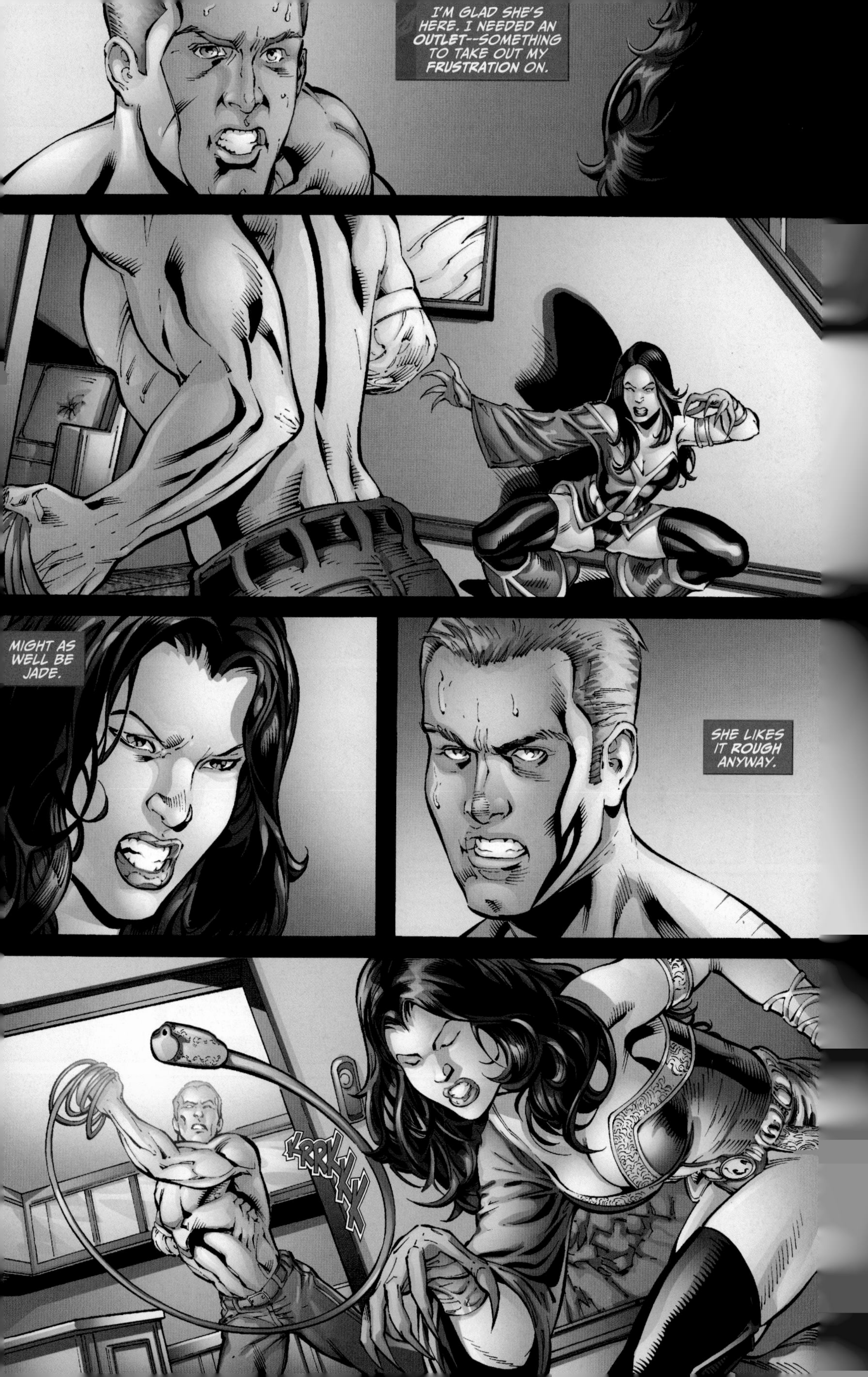
I'M GLAD SHE'S HERE. I NEEDED AN OUTLET--SOMETHING TO TAKE OUT MY FRUSTRATION ON.
MIGHT AS WELL BE JADE.
SHE LIKES IT ROUGH ANYWAY.
KRRKLLK

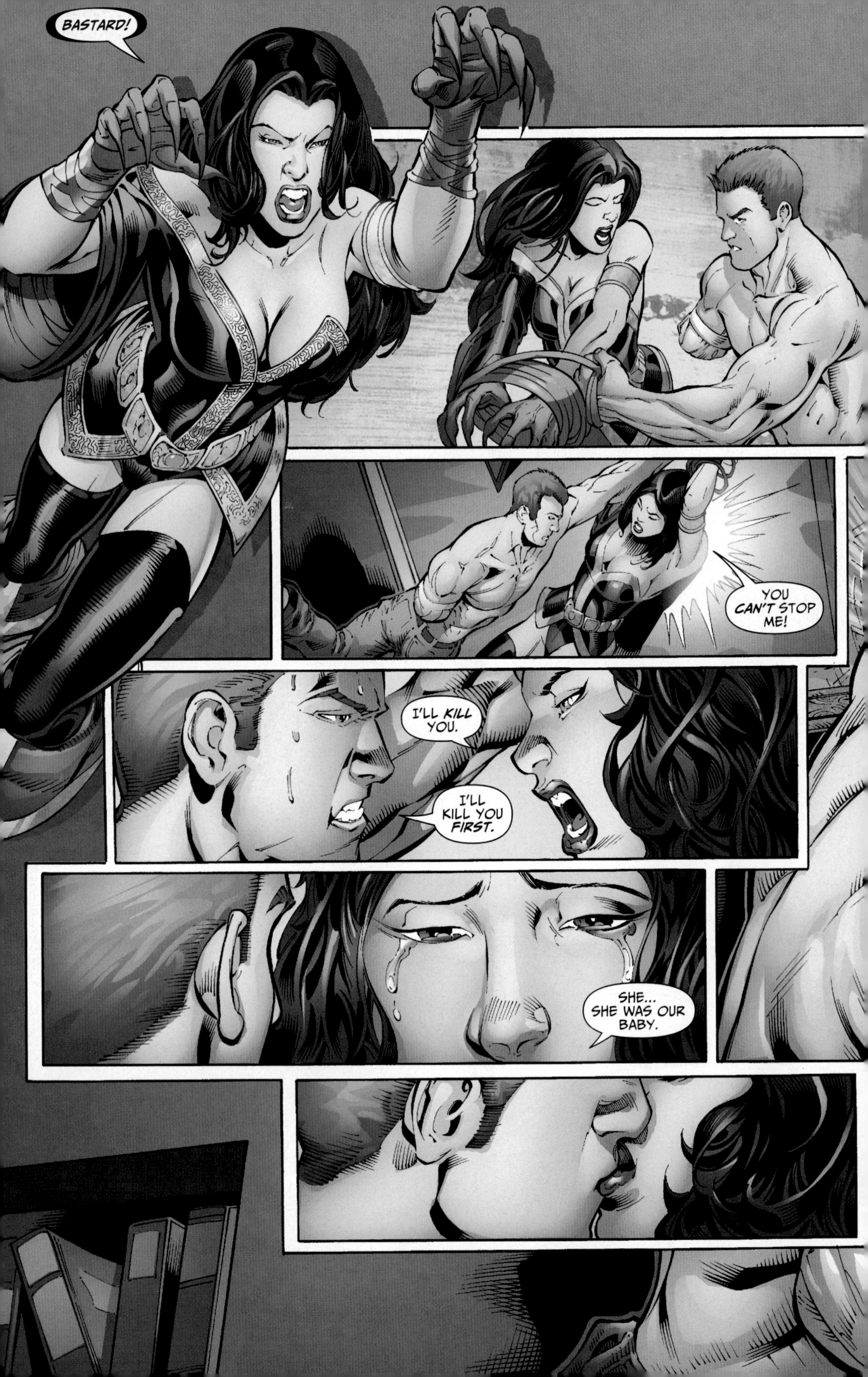
BASTARD!
YOU CAN'T STOP ME!
I'LL KILL YOU.
I'LL KILL YOU FIRST.
SHE... SHE WAS OUR BABY.

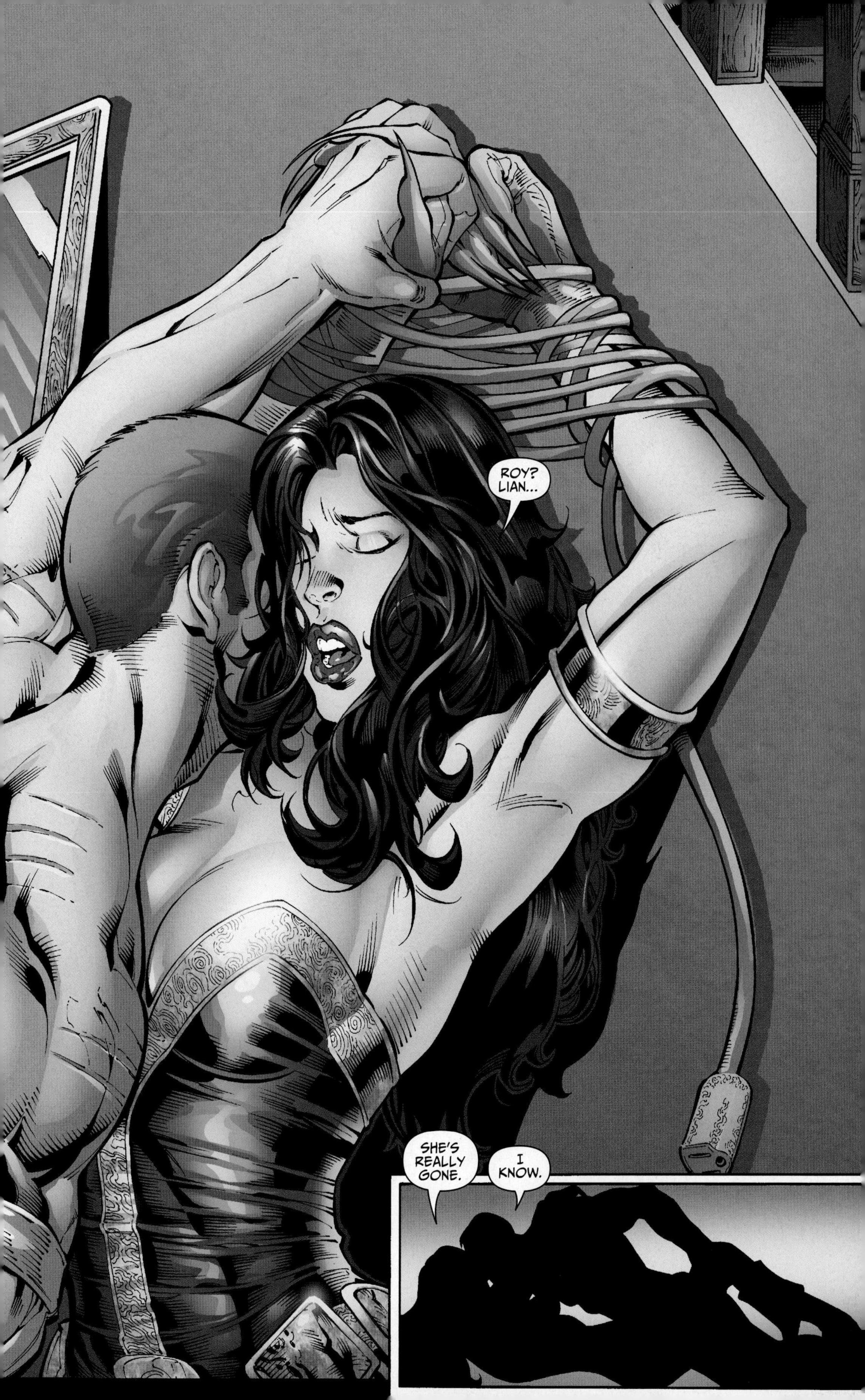
ROY? LIAN...
SHE'S REALLY GONE.
I KNOW.

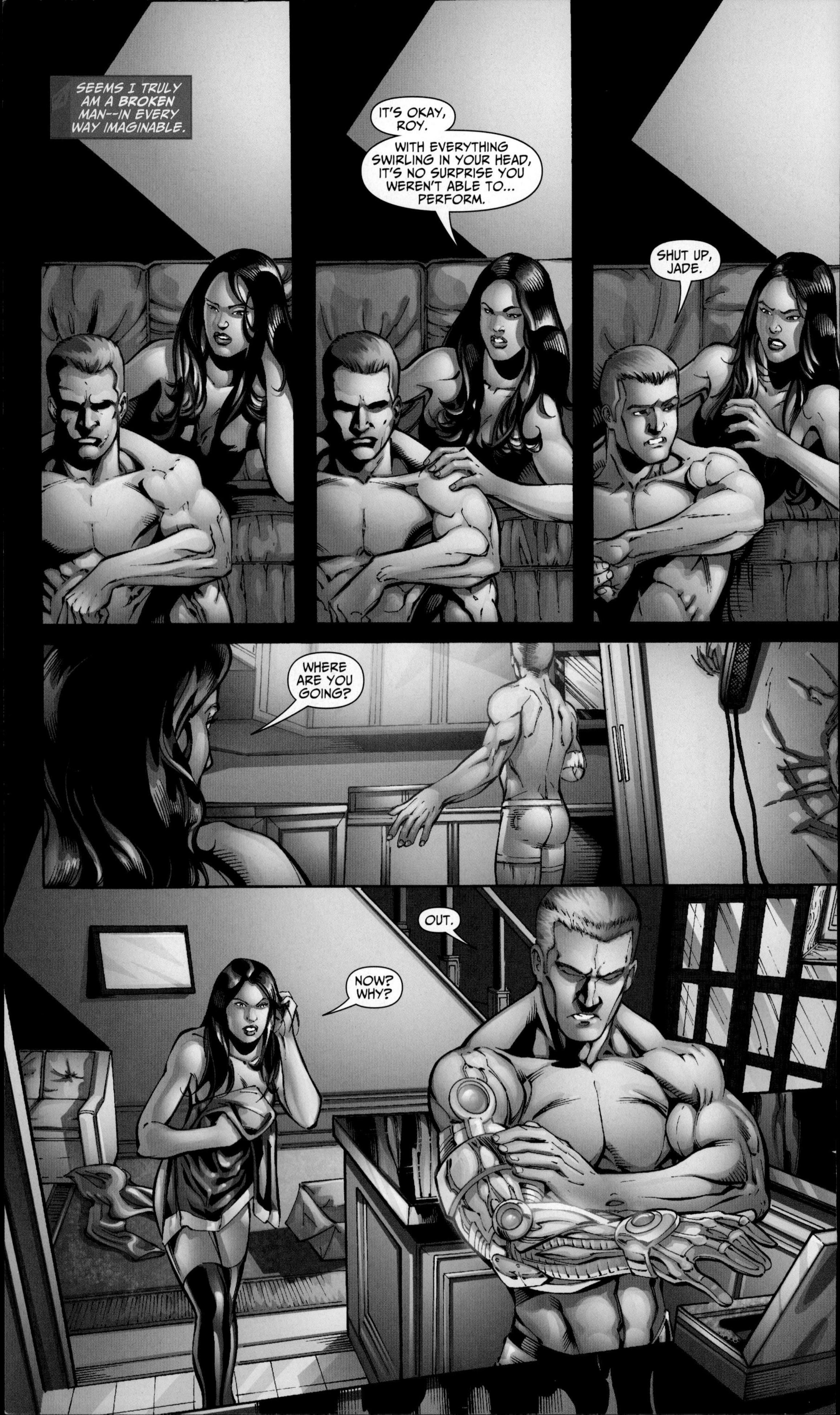

SEEMS I TRULY AM A BROKEN MAN--IN EVERY WAY IMAGINABLE.
IT'S OKAY, ROY.
WITH EVERYTHING SWIRLING IN YOUR HEAD, IT'S NO SURPRISE YOU WEREN'T ABLE TO... PERFORM.
SHUT UP, JADE.
WHERE ARE YOU GOING?
OUT.
NOW? WHY?

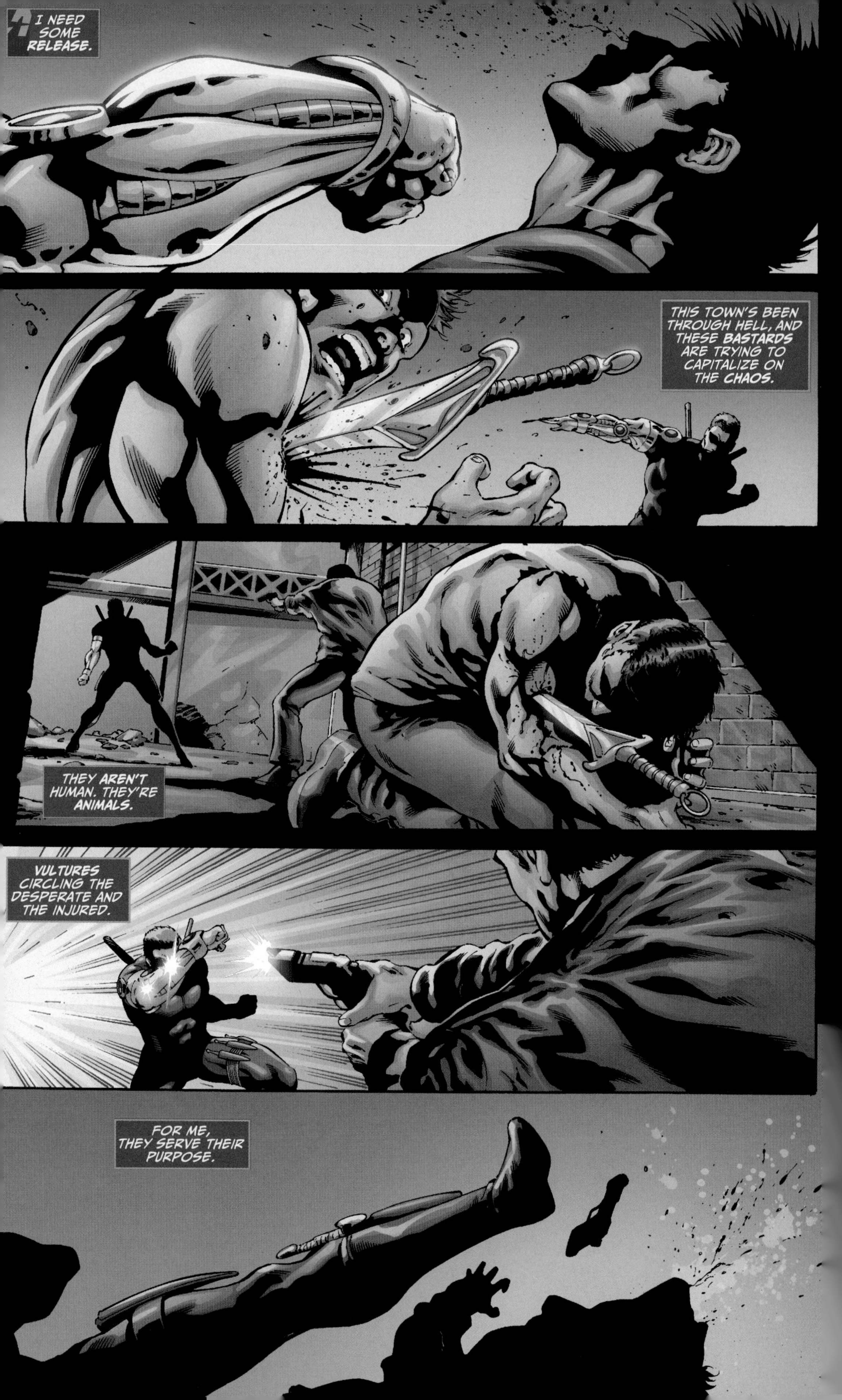
I NEED SOME RELEASE.
THIS TOWN'S BEEN THROUGH HELL, AND THESE BASTARDS ARE TRYING TO CAPITALIZE ON THE CHAOS.
THEY AREN'T HUMAN. THEY'RE ANIMALS.
VULTURES CIRCLING THE DESPERATE AND THE INJURED.
FOR ME, THEY SERVE THEIR PURPOSE.

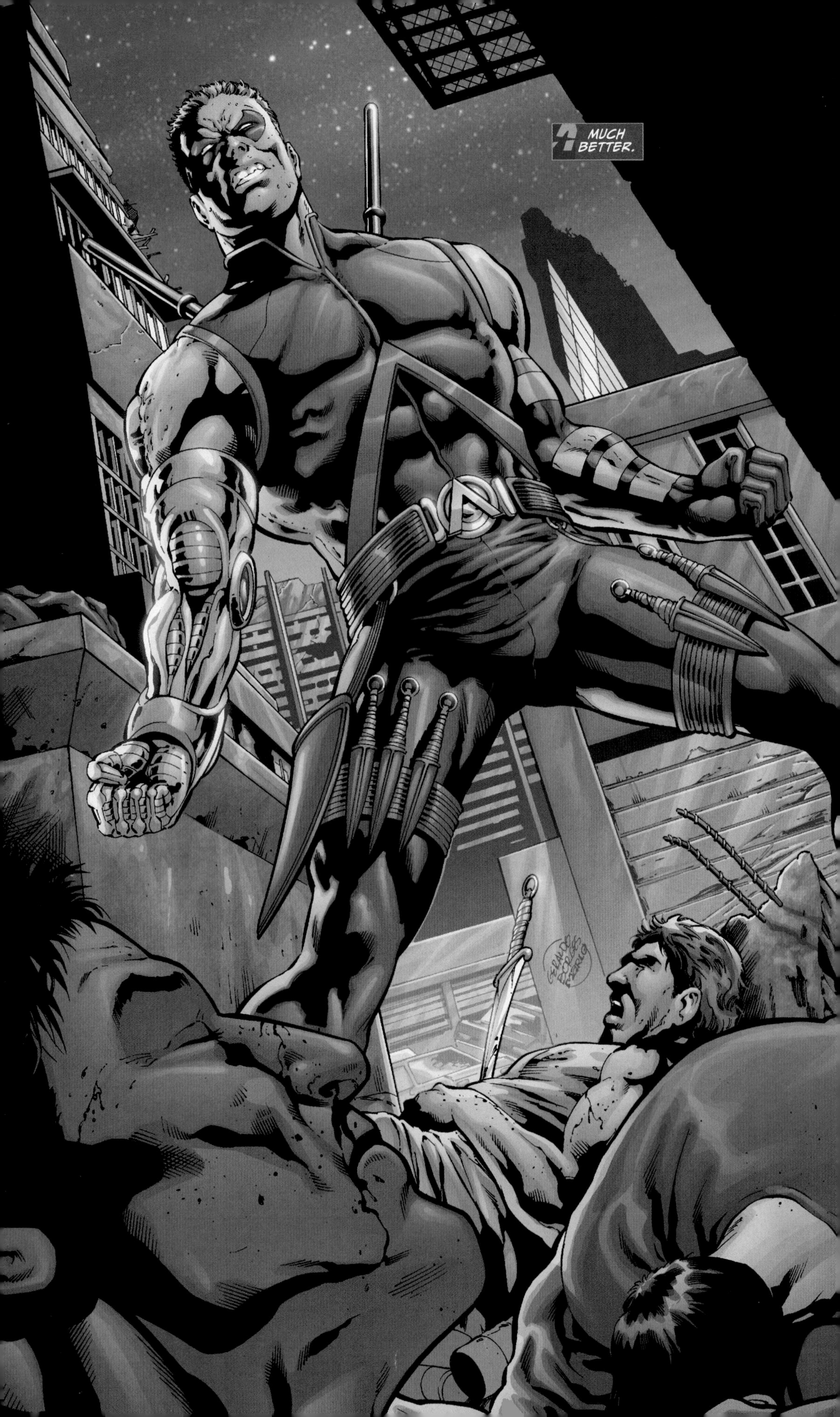
MUCH BETTER.

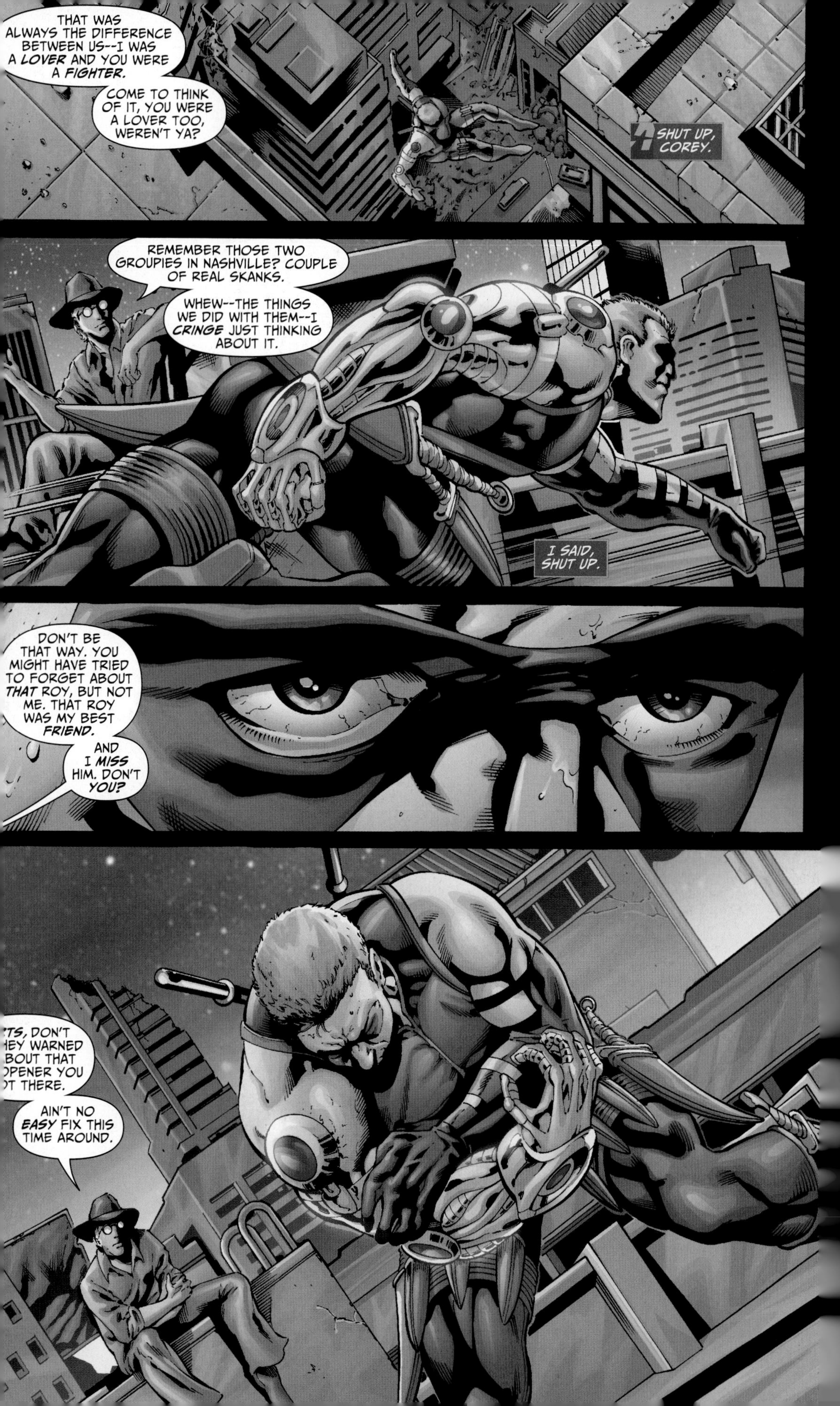
THAT WAS ALWAYS THE DIFFERENCE BETWEEN US--I WAS A LOVER AND YOU WERE A FIGHTER.
COME TO THINK OF IT, YOU WERE A LOVER TOO, WEREN'T YA?
SHUT UP, COREY.
REMEMBER THOSE TWO GROUPIES IN NASHVILLE? COUPLE OF REAL SKANKS.
WHEW--THE THINGS WE DID WITH THEM--I CRINGE JUST THINKING ABOUT IT.
I SAID, SHUT UP.
DON'T BE THAT WAY. YOU MIGHT HAVE TRIED TO FORGET ABOUT THAT ROY, BUT NOT ME. THAT ROY WAS MY BEST FRIEND.
AND I MISS HIM. DON'T YOU?
AIN'T NO EASY FIX THIS TIME AROUND.

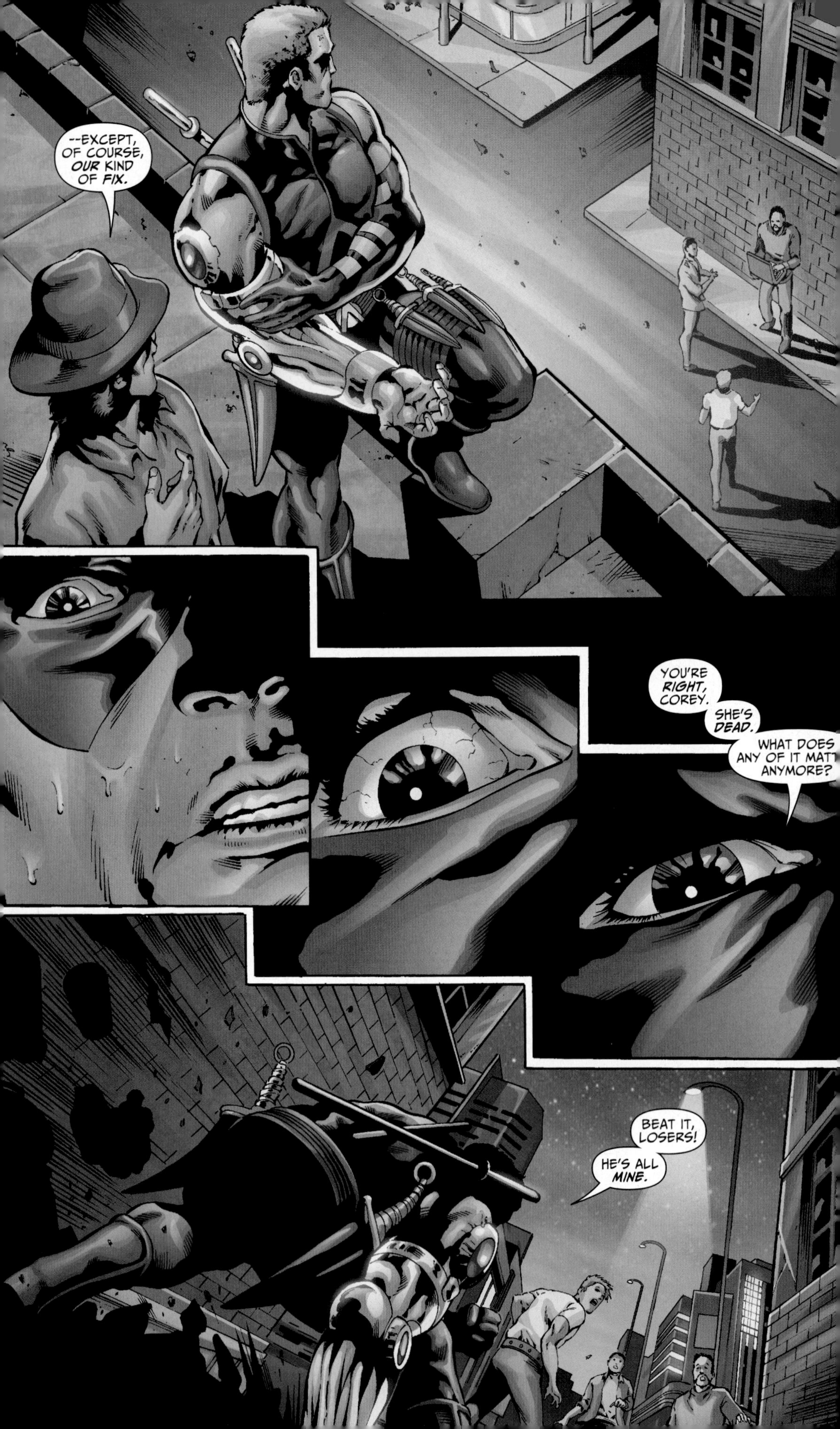
--EXCEPT, OF COURSE, OUR KIND OF FIX.
YOU'RE RIGHT, COREY.
SHE'S DEAD.
WHAT DOES ANY OF IT MATT ANYMORE?
BEAT IT, LOSERS!
HE'S ALL MINE.

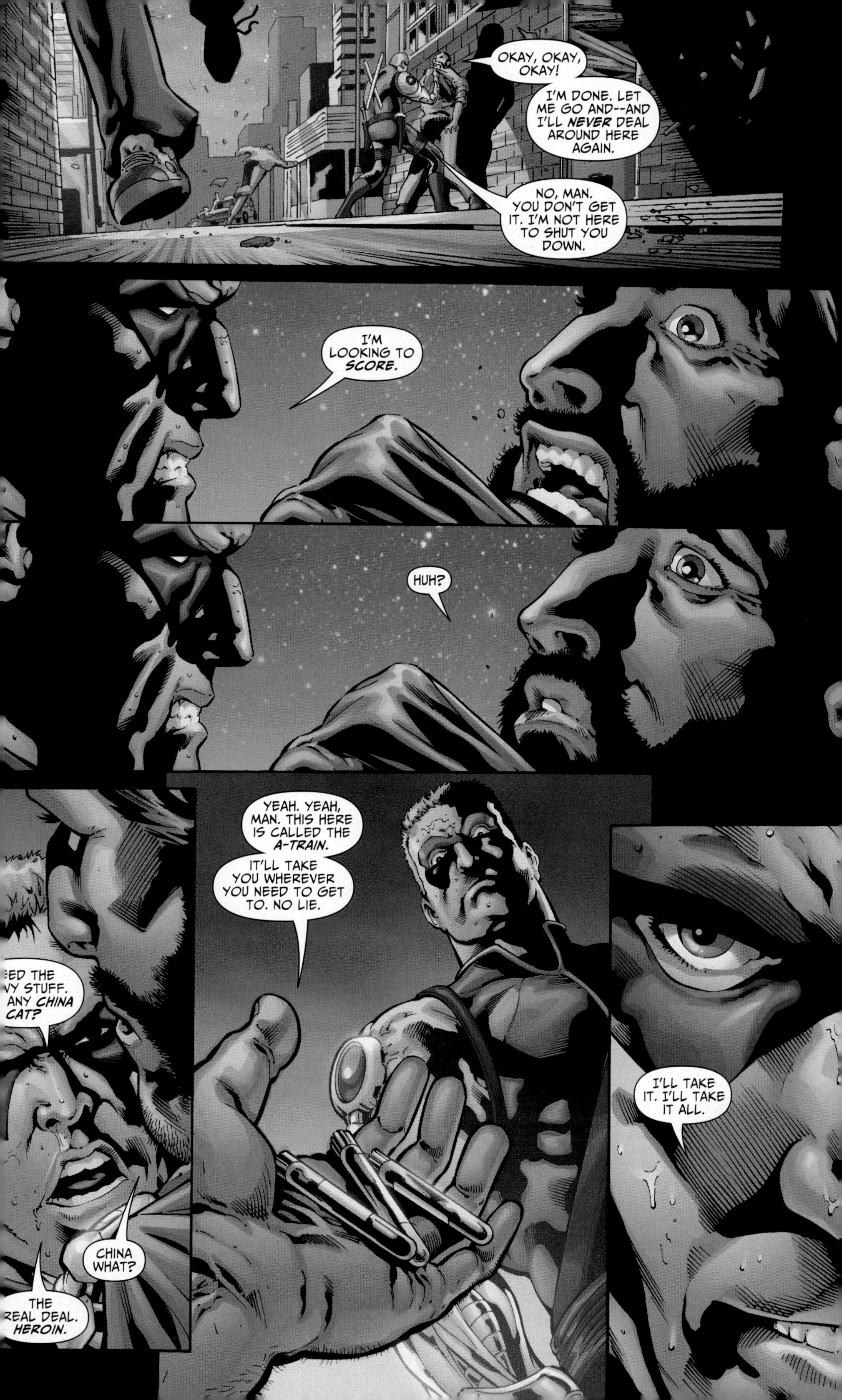
OKAY, OKAY, OKAY!
I'M DONE. LET ME GO AND--AND I'LL NEVER DEAL AROUND HERE AGAIN.
NO, MAN. YOU DON'T GET IT. I'M NOT HERE TO SHUT YOU DOWN.
I'M LOOKING TO SCORE.
HUH?
EED THE VY STUFF. ANY CHINA CAT?
CHINA WHAT?
THE REAL DEAL. HEROIN.
YEAH. YEAH, MAN. THIS HERE IS CALLED THE A-TRAIN.
IT'LL TAKE YOU WHEREVER YOU NEED TO GET TO. NO LIE.
I'LL TAKE IT. I'LL TAKE IT ALL.

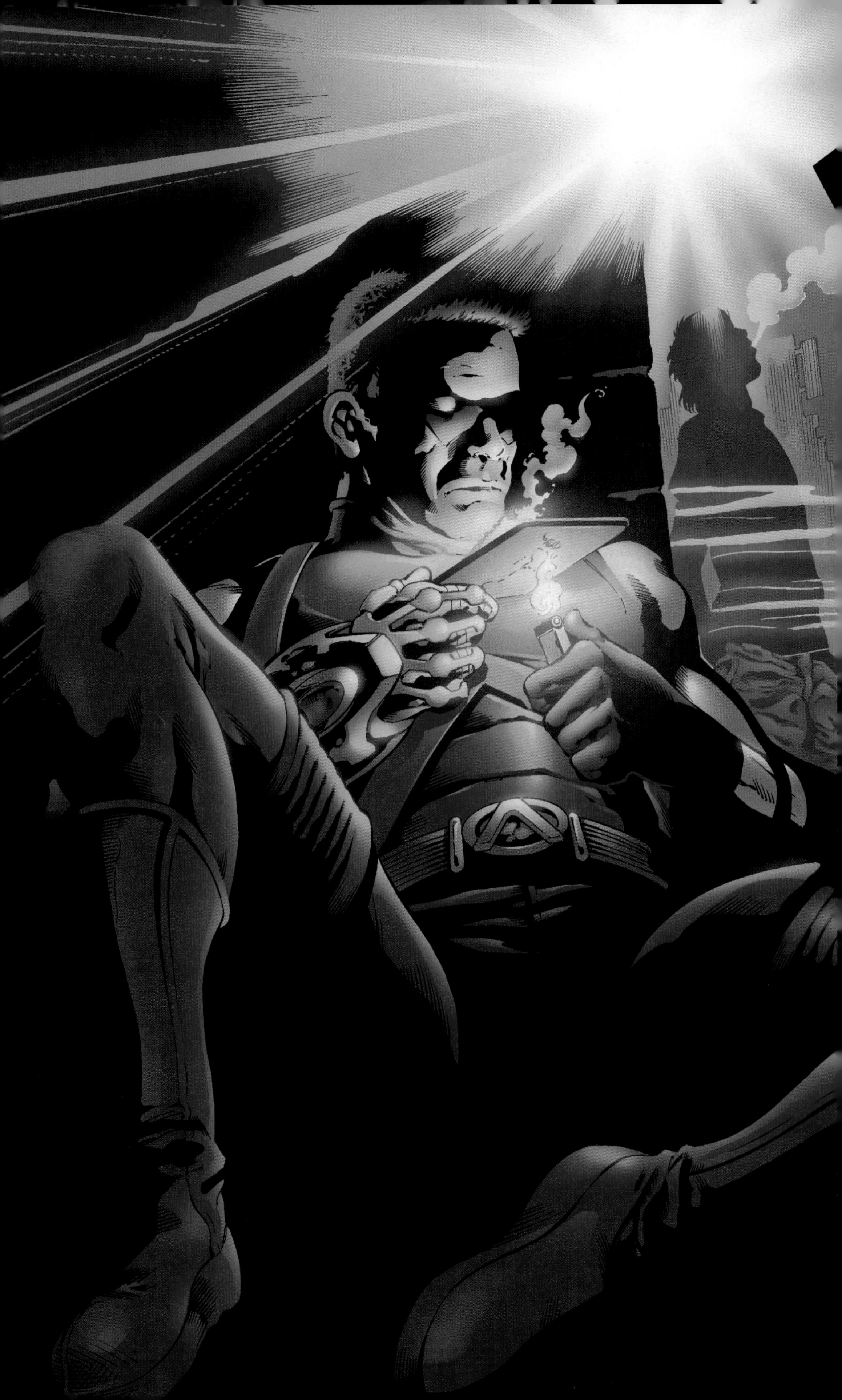

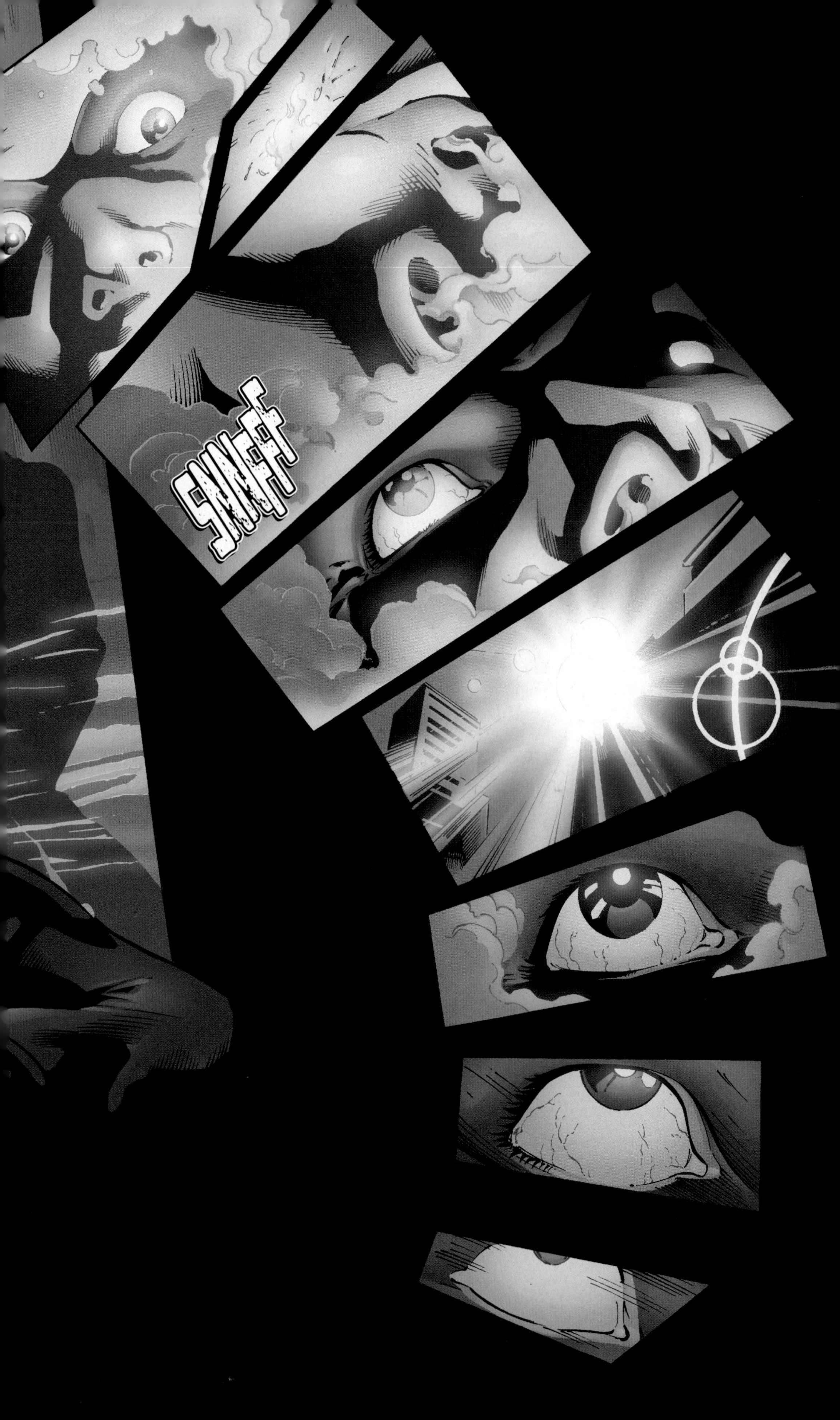
SNIFF

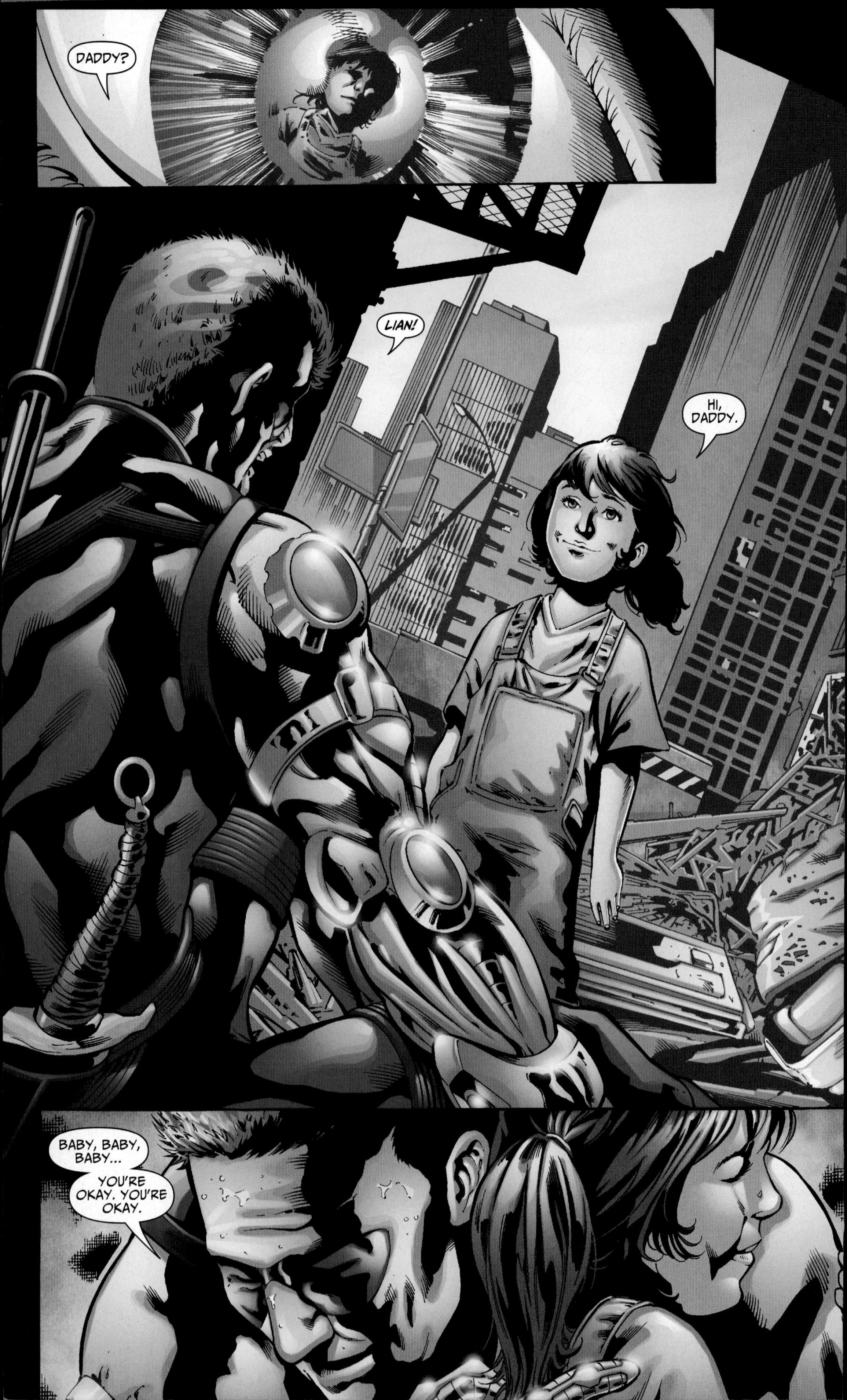
DADDY?
LIAN!
HI, DADDY.
BABY, BABY, BABY...
YOU'RE OKAY. YOU'RE OKAY.

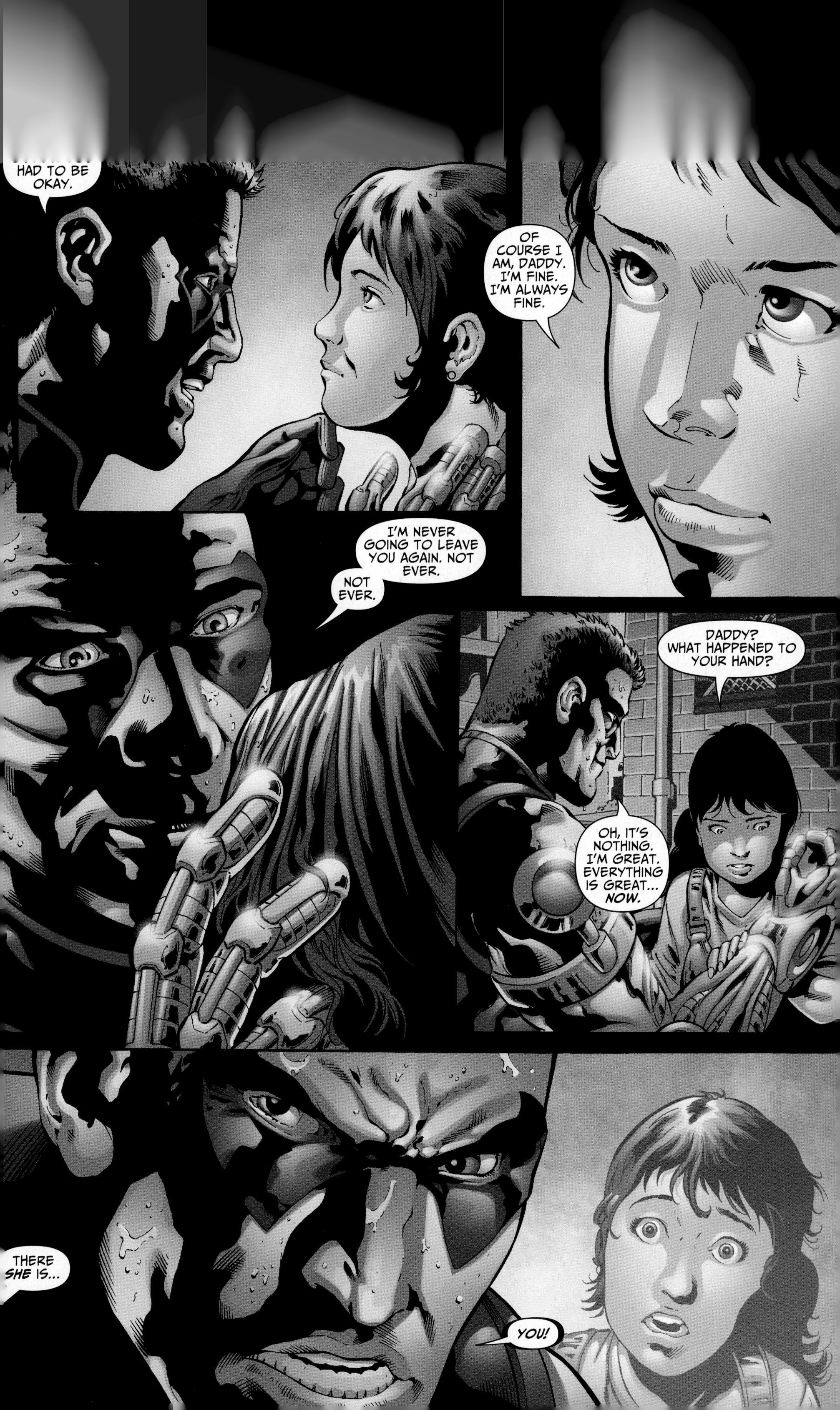

HAD TO BE OKAY.
OF COURSE I AM, DADDY. I'M FINE. I'M ALWAYS FINE.
I'M NEVER GOING TO LEAVE YOU AGAIN. NOT EVER.
NOT EVER.
DADDY? WHAT HAPPENED TO YOUR HAND?
OH, IT'S NOTHING. I'M GREAT. EVERYTHING IS GREAT... NOW.
THERE SHE IS...
YOU!

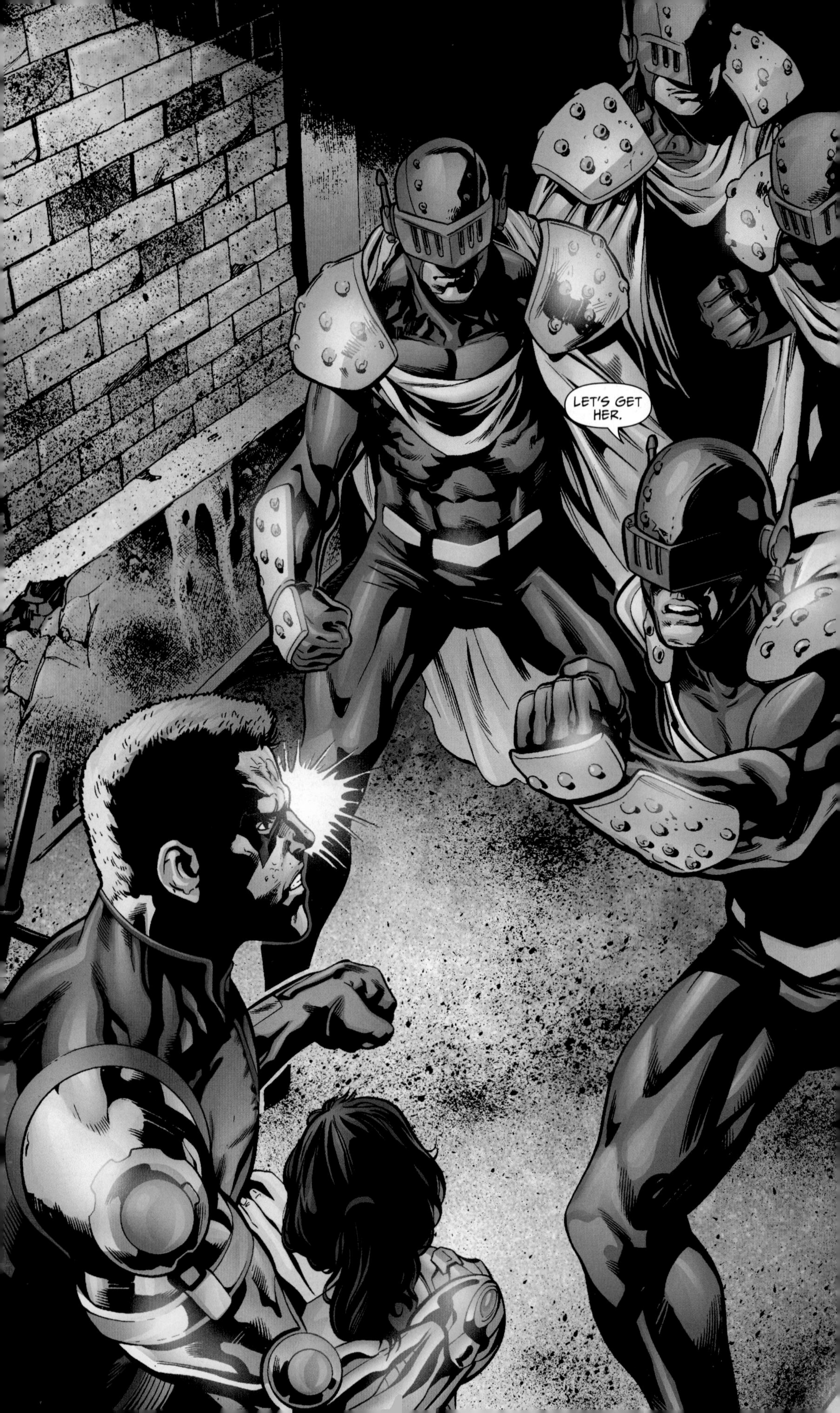
LET'S GET HER.

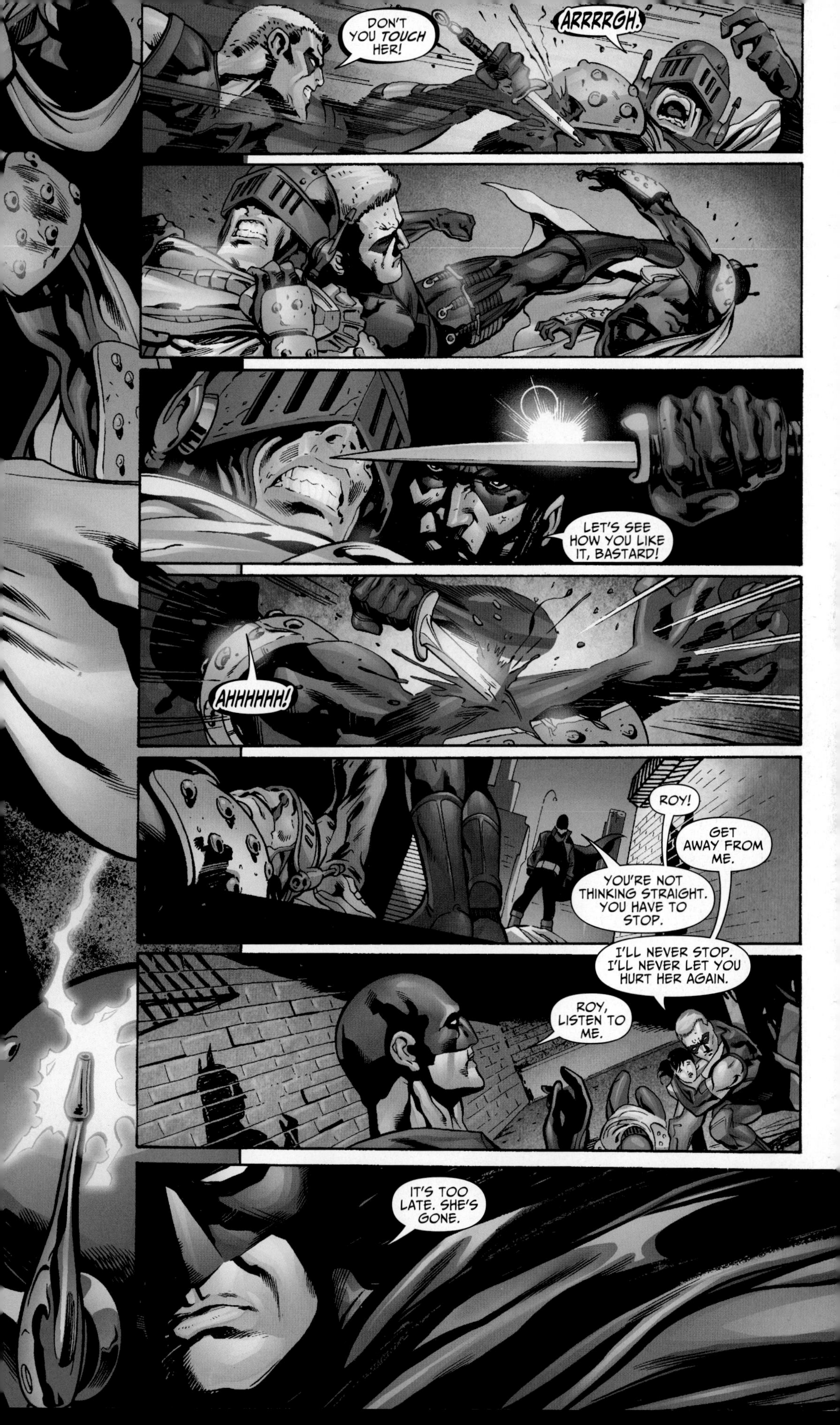
DON'T YOU TOUCH HER!
ARRRRGH!
LET'S SEE HOW YOU LIKE IT, BASTARD!
AHHHHHH!
ROY!
GET AWAY FROM ME.
YOU'RE NOT THINKING STRAIGHT. YOU HAVE TO STOP.
I'LL NEVER STOP. I'LL NEVER LET YOU HURT HER AGAIN.
ROY, LISTEN TO ME.
IT'S TOO LATE. SHE'S GONE.

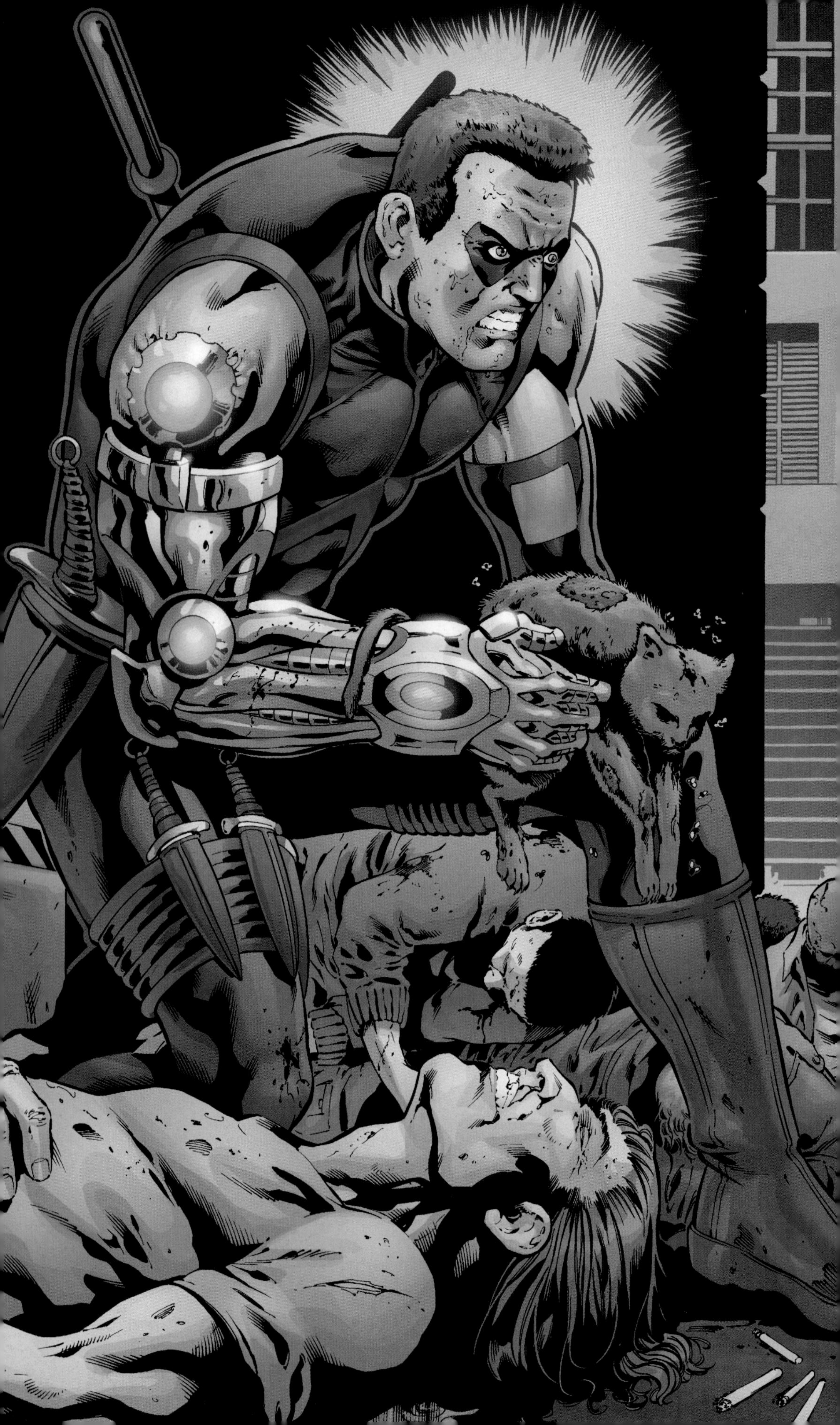

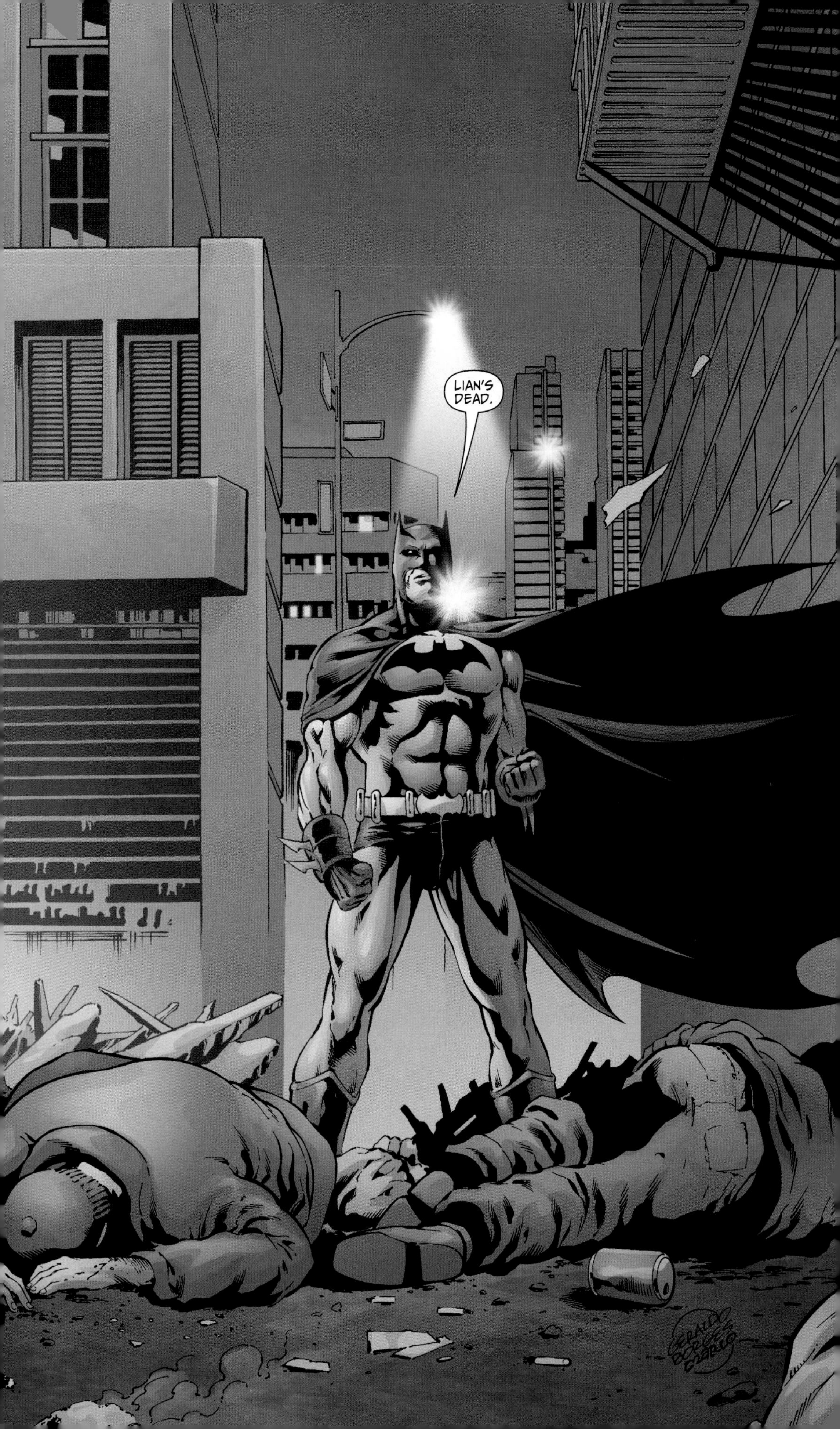
LIAN'S DEAD.

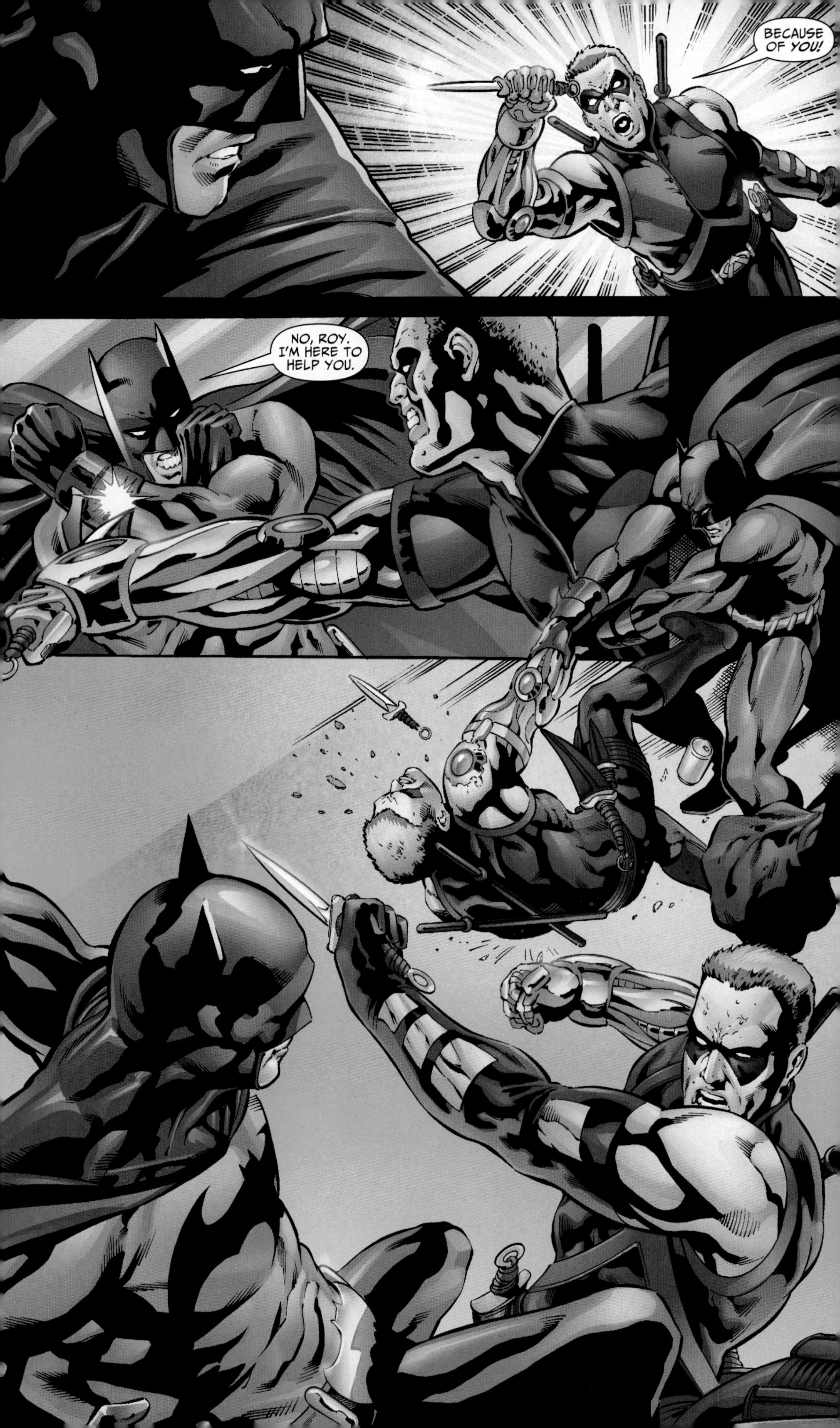
BECAUSE OF YOU!
NO, ROY. I'M HERE TO HELP YOU.

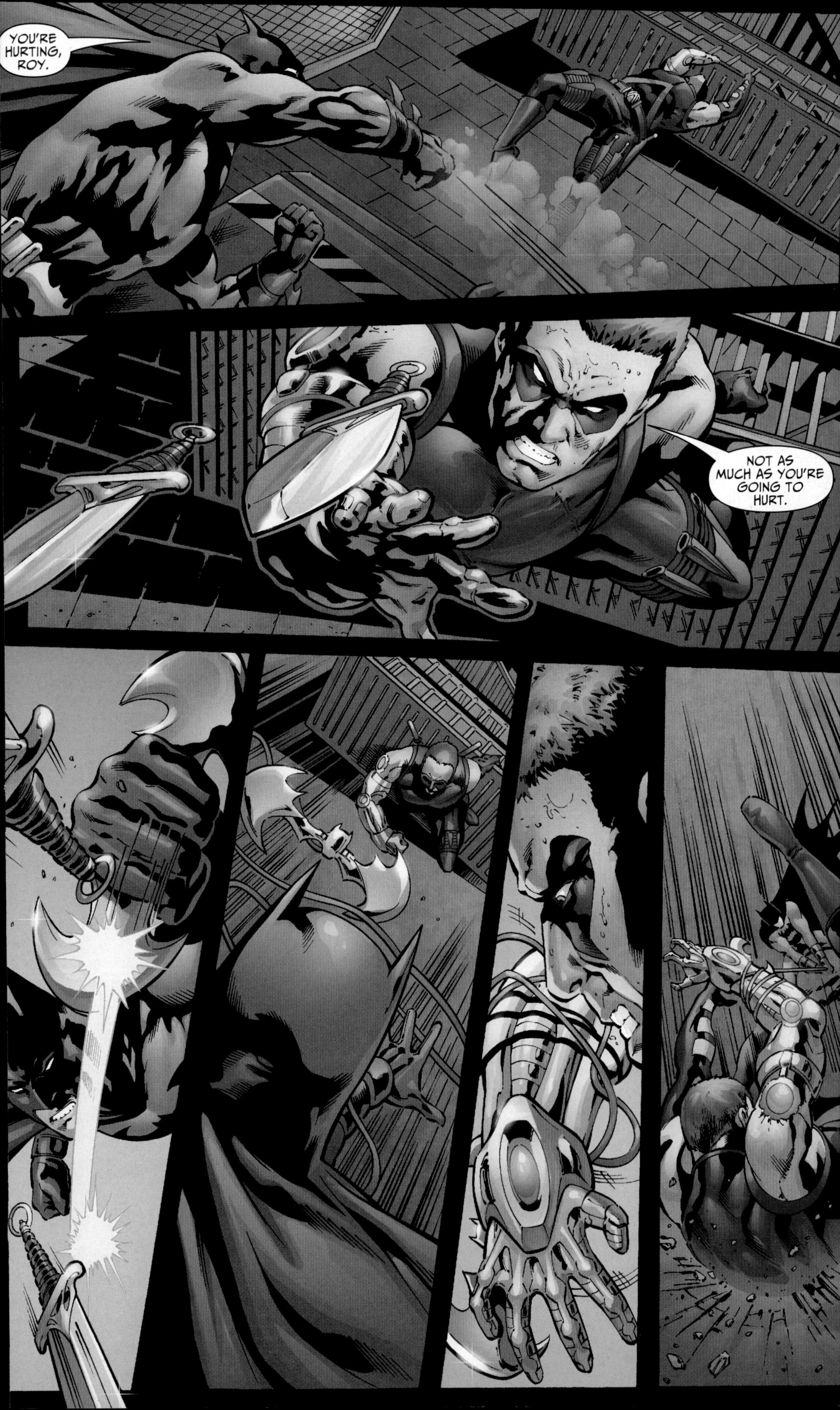
YOU'RE HURTING, ROY.
NOT AS MUCH AS YOU'RE GOING TO HURT.

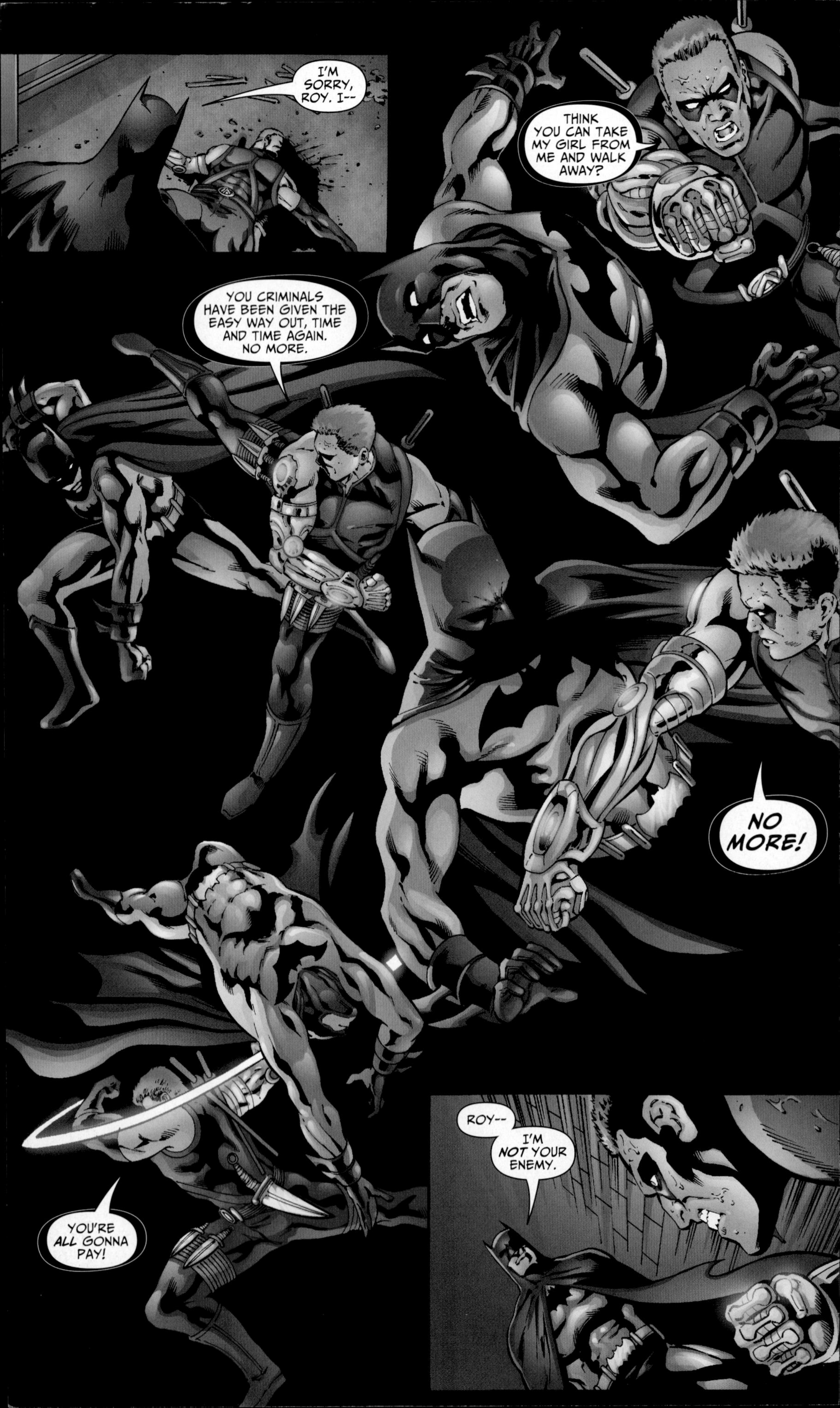

I'M SORRY, ROY. I--
THINK YOU CAN TAKE MY GIRL FROM ME AND WALK AWAY?
YOU CRIMINALS HAVE BEEN GIVEN THE EASY WAY OUT, TIME AND TIME AGAIN. NO MORE.
NO MORE!
YOU'RE ALL GONNA PAY!
ROY--
I'M NOT YOUR ENEMY.

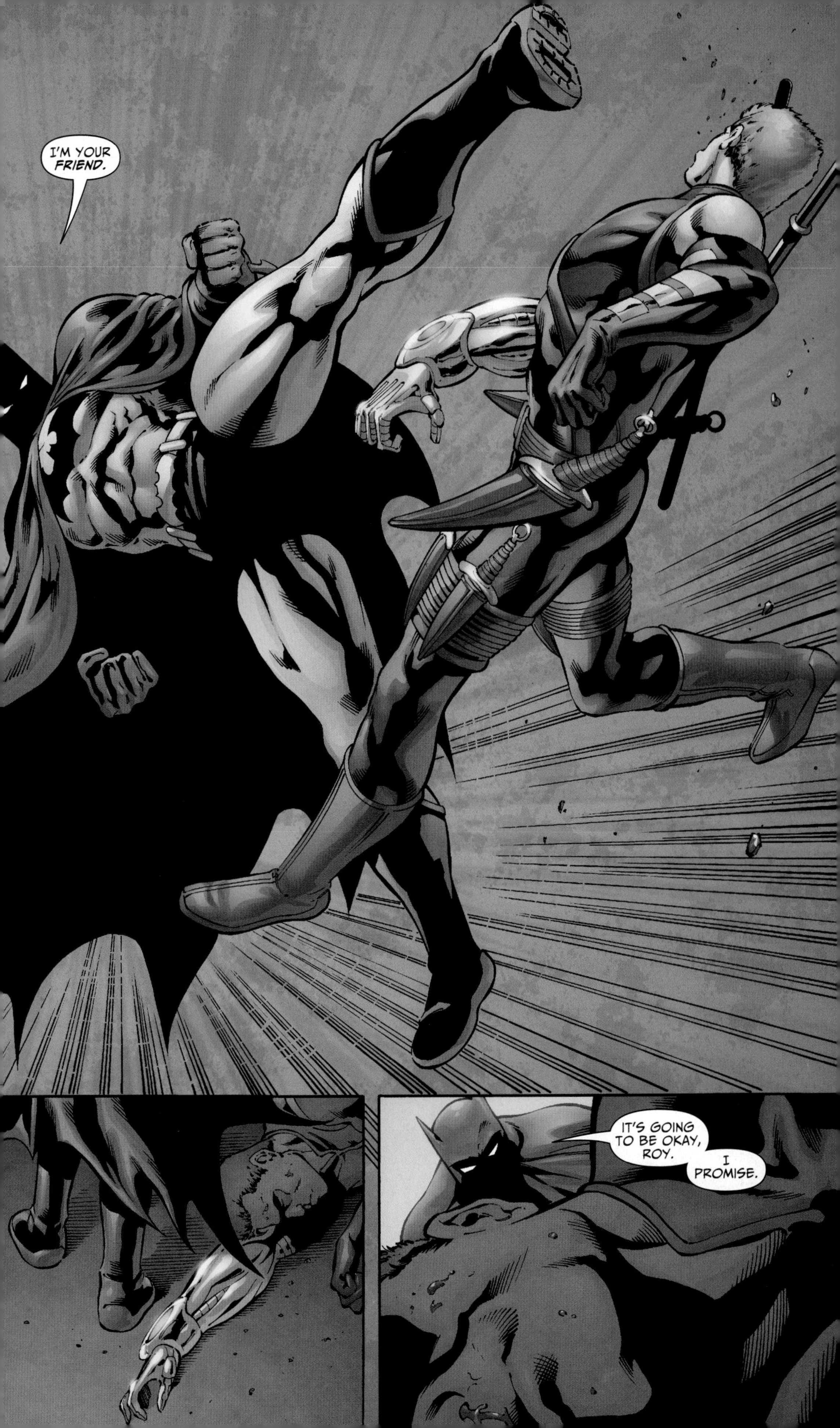
I'M YOUR FRIEND.
IT'S GOING TO BE OKAY, ROY.
I PROMISE.

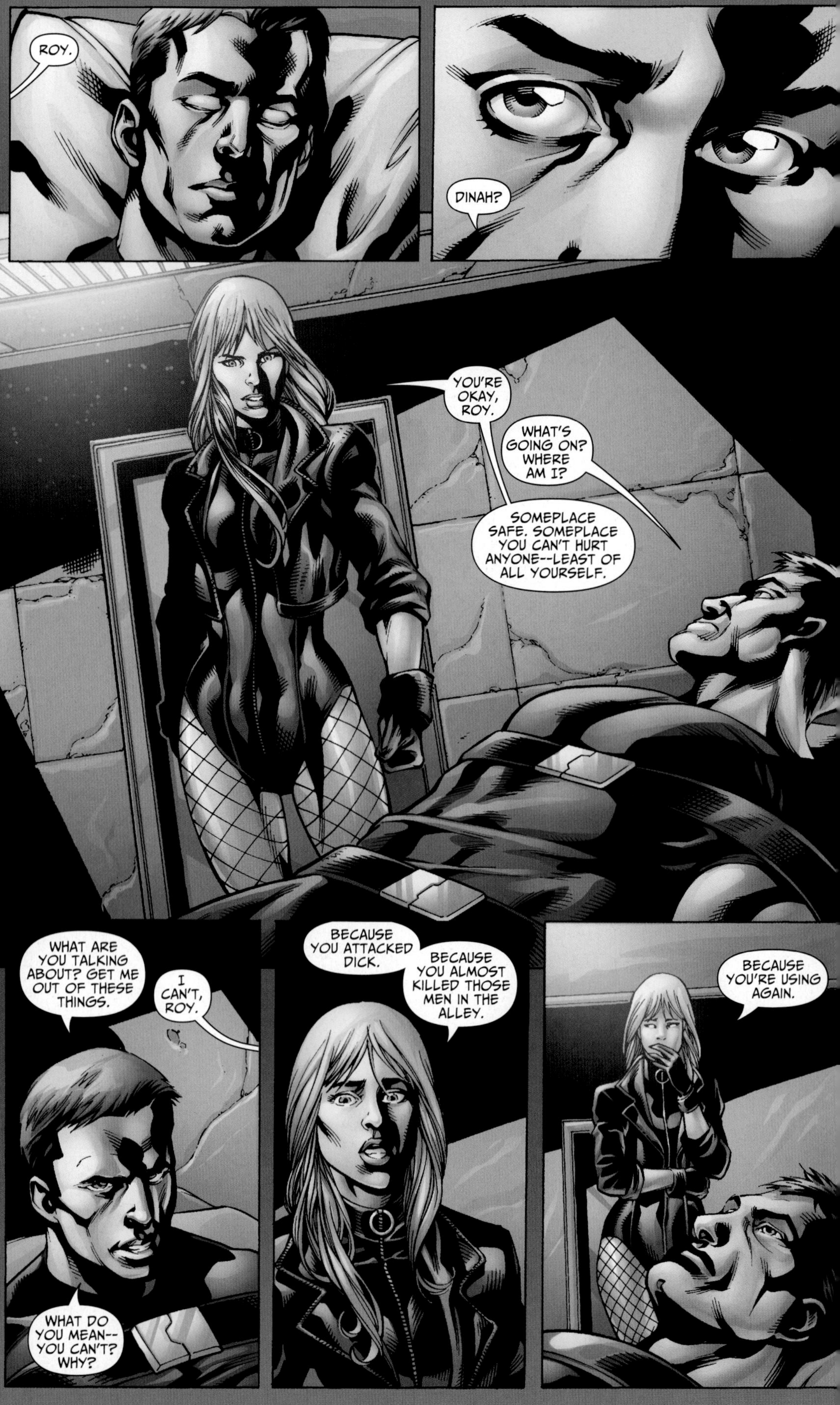
ROY.
DINAH?
YOU'RE OKAY, ROY.
WHAT'S GOING ON? WHERE AM I?
SOMEPLACE SAFE. SOMEPLACE YOU CAN'T HURT ANYONE--LEAST OF ALL YOURSELF.
WHAT ARE YOU TALKING ABOUT? GET ME OUT OF THESE THINGS.
I CAN'T, ROY.
WHAT DO YOU MEAN-- YOU CAN'T? WHY?
BECAUSE YOU ATTACKED DICK.
BECAUSE YOU ALMOST KILLED THOSE MEN IN THE ALLEY.
BECAUSE YOU'RE USING AGAIN.

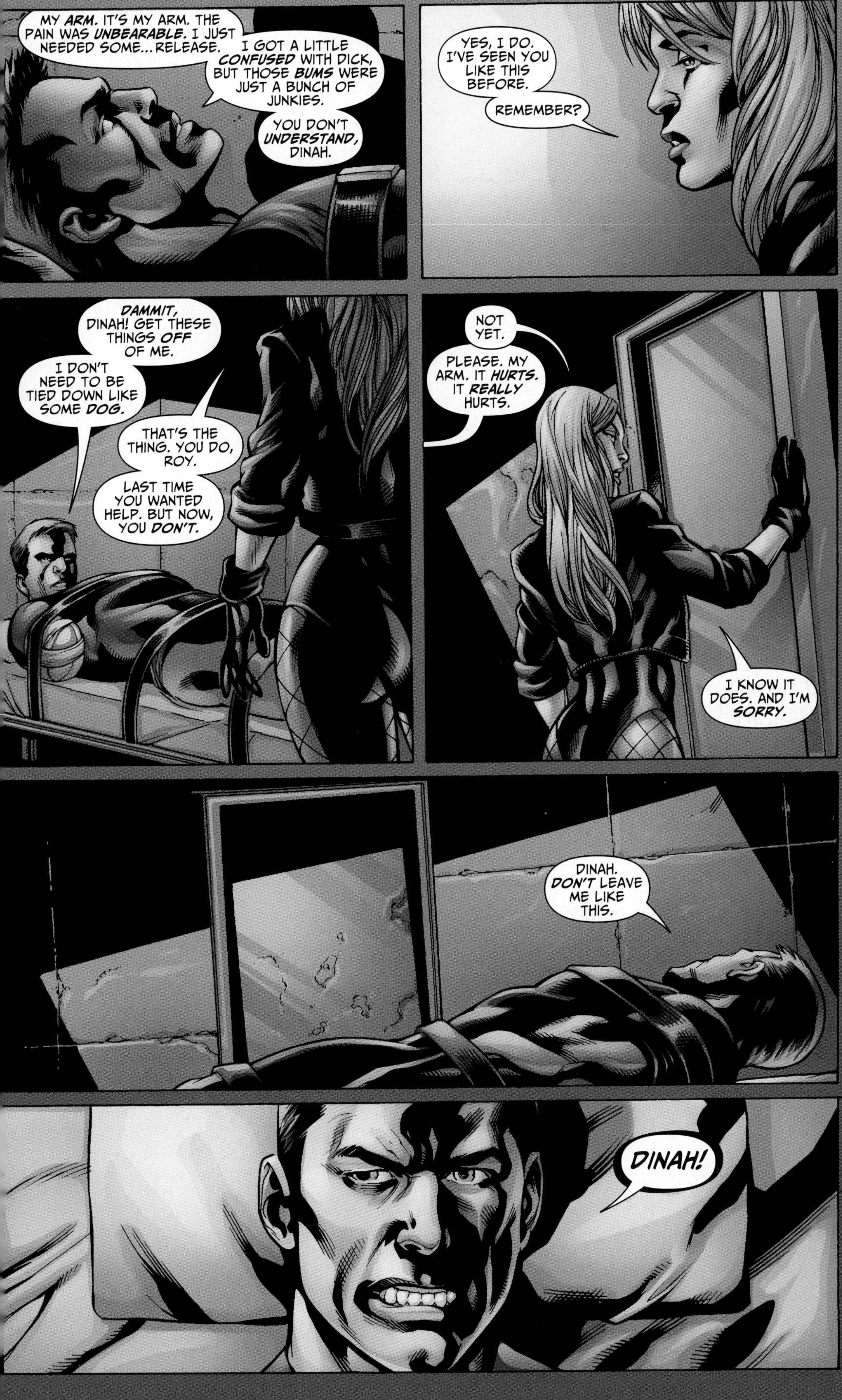
MY ARM. IT'S MY ARM. THE PAIN WAS UNBEARABLE. I JUST NEEDED SOME... RELEASE.
I GOT A LITTLE CONFUSED WITH DICK, BUT THOSE BUMS WERE JUST A BUNCH OF JUNKIES.
YOU DON'T UNDERSTAND, DINAH.
YES, I DO. I'VE SEEN YOU LIKE THIS BEFORE.
REMEMBER?
DAMMIT, DINAH! GET THESE THINGS OFF OF ME.
I DON'T NEED TO BE TIED DOWN LIKE SOME DOG.
THAT'S THE THING. YOU DO, ROY.
LAST TIME YOU WANTED HELP. BUT NOW, YOU DON'T.
NOT YET.
PLEASE. MY ARM. IT HURTS. IT REALLY HURTS.
I KNOW IT DOES. AND I'M SORRY.
DINAH. DON'T LEAVE ME LIKE THIS.
DINAH!

VIRGIL HOUSE

DINAH!

THAT WENT WELL.

THE IMPORTANT THING IS THAT HE'S HERE AND HE'S SAFE.

VIRGIL HOUSE SPECIALIZES IN CONVICTED VILLAINS WITH SUBSTANCE ABUSE PROBLEMS, BUT IT'S THE BEST PLACE FOR ROY RIGHT NOW.

THEN WHY DO I FEEL LIKE WE'RE DUMPING HIM OFF IN *ARKHAM?*

ARKHAM IS FOR THE PEOPLE WITH LITTLE TO NO CHANCE OF RECOVERY. THOSE TOO FAR GONE.

BUT HERE, THERE'S STILL A GOOD CHANCE FOR THESE INMATES.

GUESS THEY DON'T MAKE 'EM AS CRAZY IN STAR CITY AS THEY DO IN GOTHAM.

COUNT YOURSELF LUCKY.

I STILL FEEL LIKE I'M ABANDONING HIM HERE.

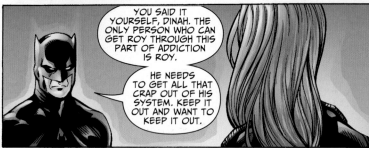

YOU SAID IT YOURSELF, DINAH. THE ONLY PERSON WHO CAN GET ROY THROUGH THIS PART OF ADDICTION IS ROY.

HE NEEDS TO GET ALL THAT CRAP OUT OF HIS SYSTEM. KEEP IT OUT AND WANT TO KEEP IT OUT.

I. KNOW.

BUT I WORRY THAT HE WON'T *EVER* WANT THAT AGAIN.

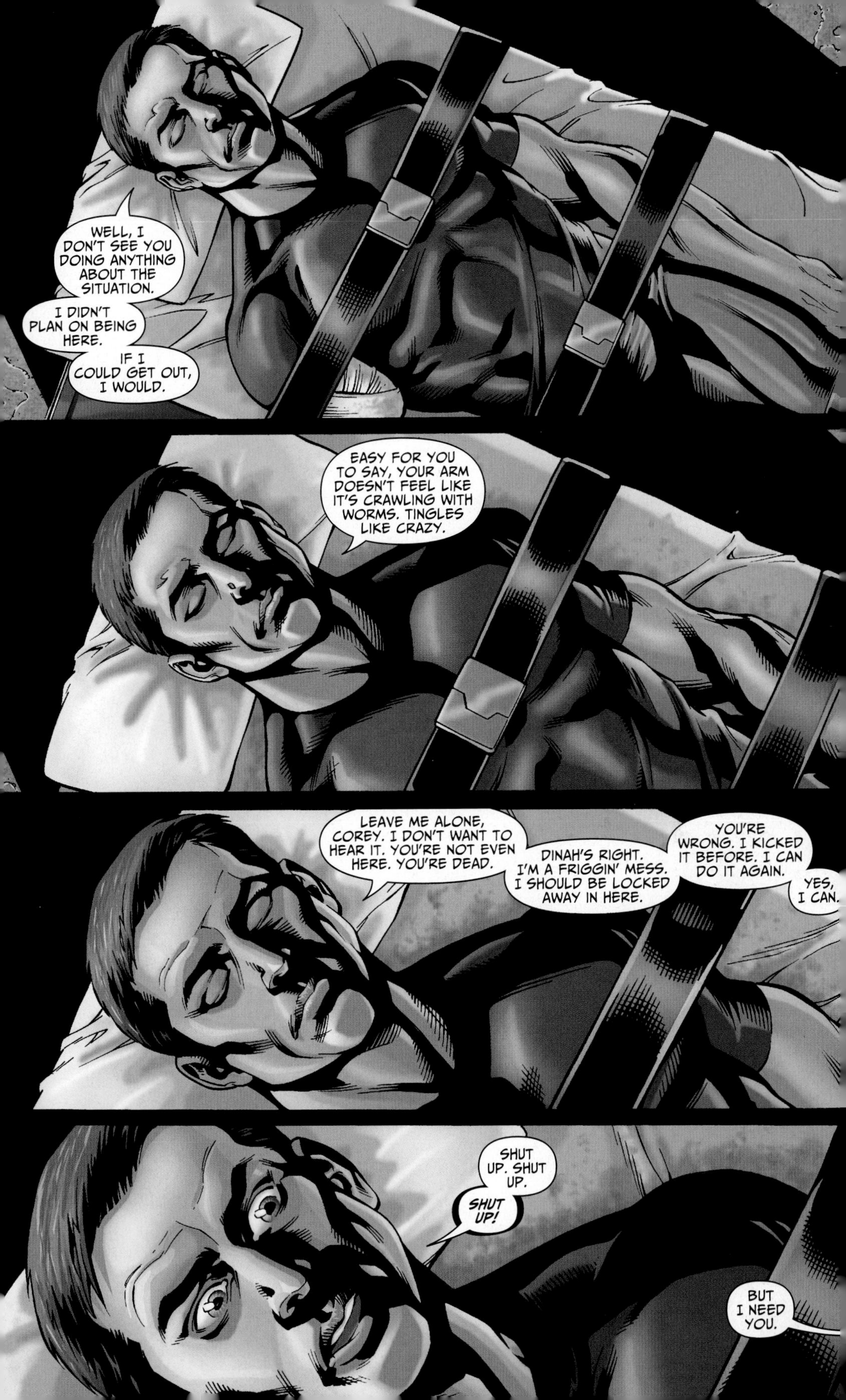
WELL, I DON'T SEE YOU DOING ANYTHING ABOUT THE SITUATION.
I DIDN'T PLAN ON BEING HERE.
IF I COULD GET OUT, I WOULD.
EASY FOR YOU TO SAY, YOUR ARM DOESN'T FEEL LIKE IT'S CRAWLING WITH WORMS. TINGLES LIKE CRAZY.
LEAVE ME ALONE, COREY. I DON'T WANT TO HEAR IT. YOU'RE NOT EVEN HERE. YOU'RE DEAD.
DINAH'S RIGHT. I'M A FRIGGIN' MESS. I SHOULD BE LOCKED AWAY IN HERE.
YOU'RE WRONG. I KICKED IT BEFORE. I CAN DO IT AGAIN.
YES, I CAN.
SHUT UP. SHUT UP.
SHUT UP!
BUT I NEED YOU.

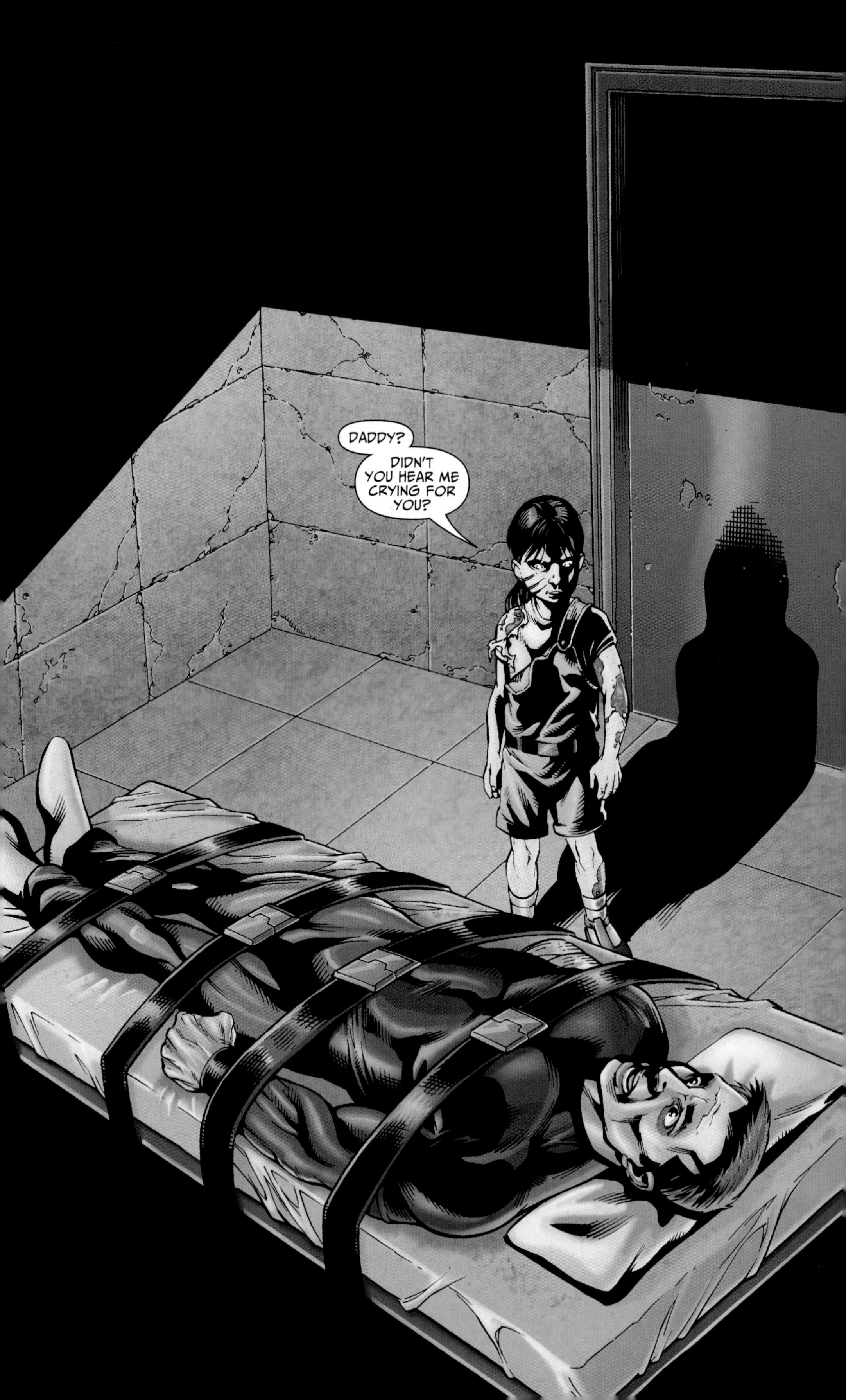
DADDY?
DIDN'T YOU HEAR ME CRYING FOR YOU?

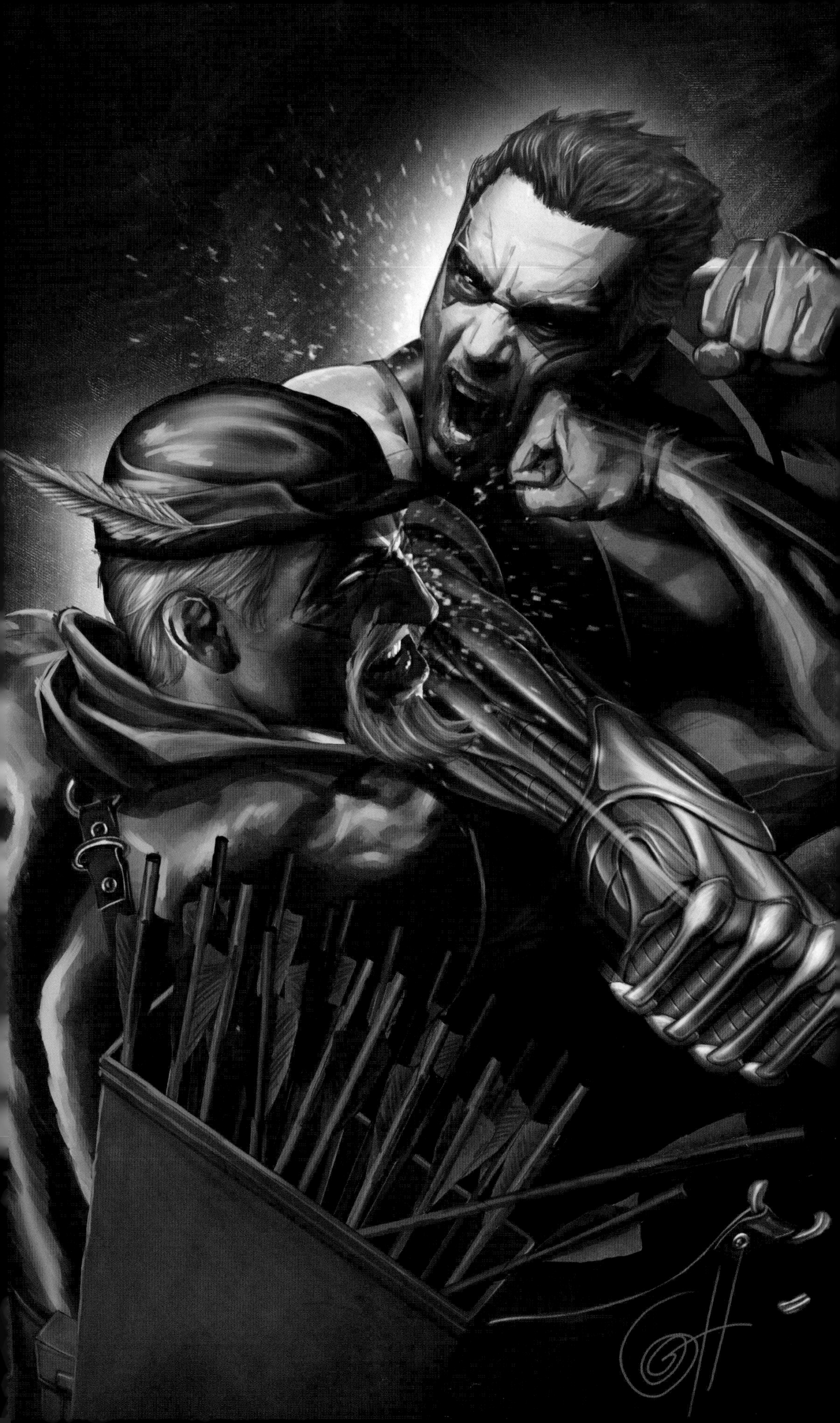

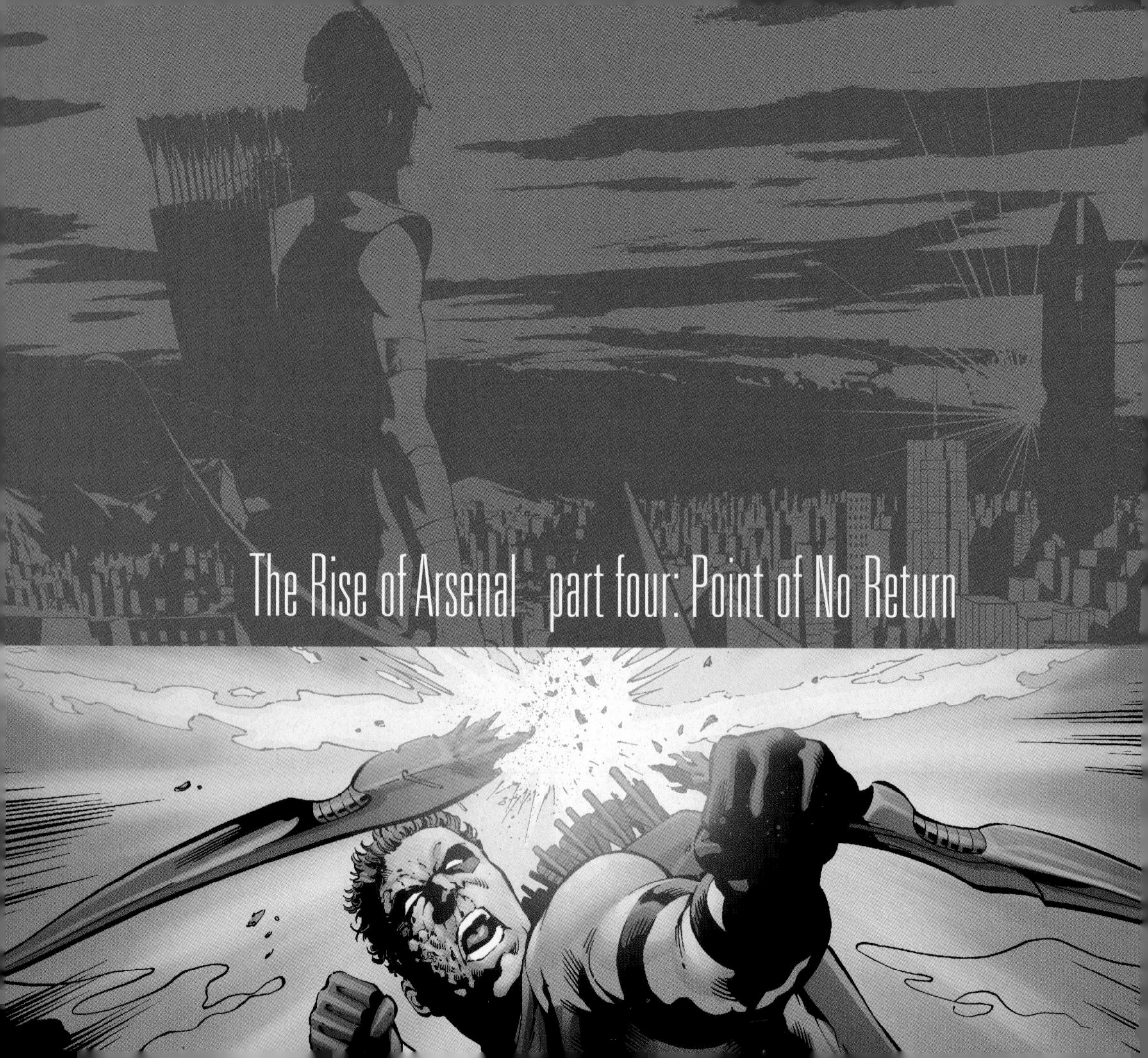
The Rise of Arsenal part four: Point of No Return

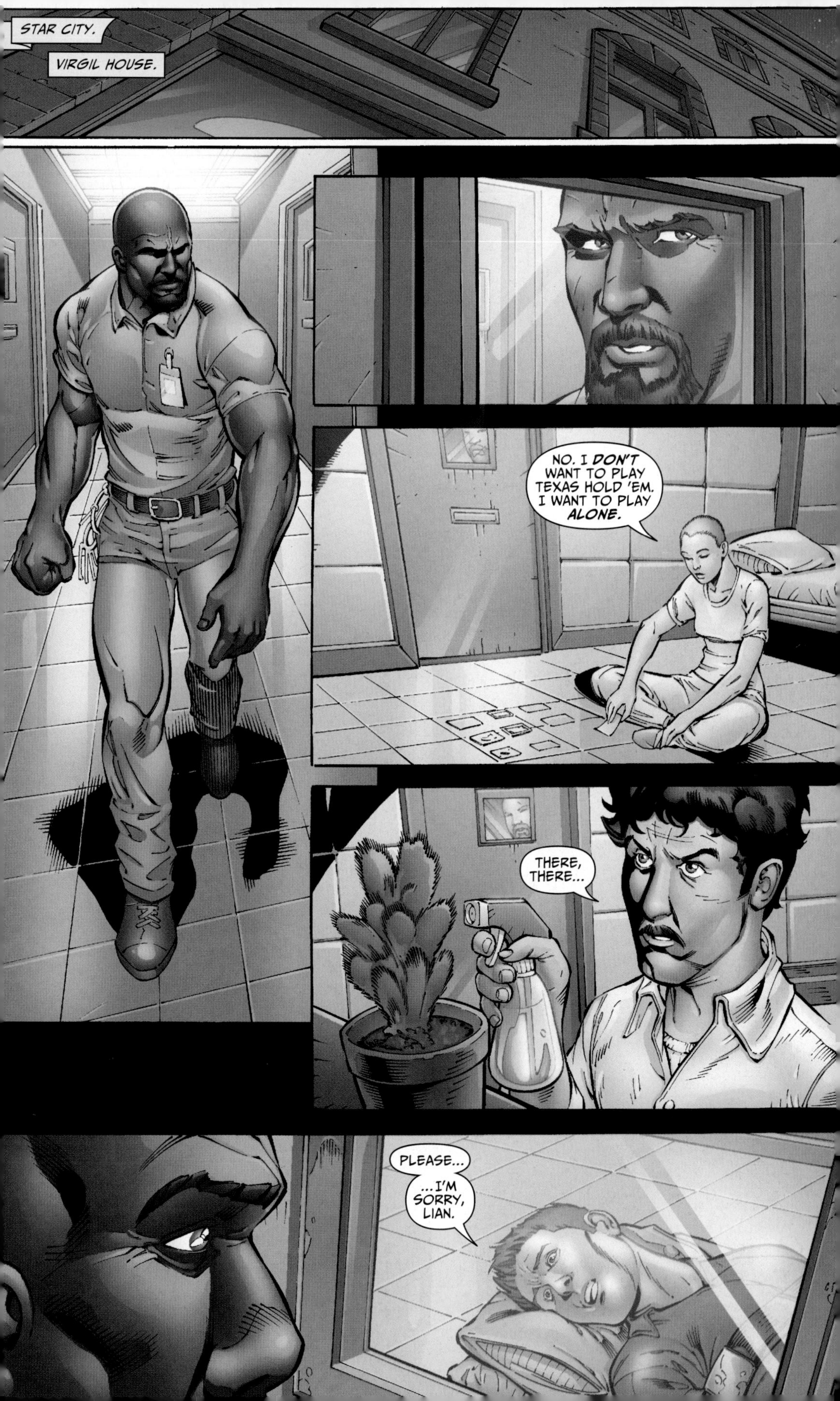
STAR CITY.
VIRGIL HOUSE.
NO. I DON'T WANT TO PLAY TEXAS HOLD 'EM. I WANT TO PLAY ALONE.
THERE, THERE...
PLEASE...
...I'M SORRY, LIAN.

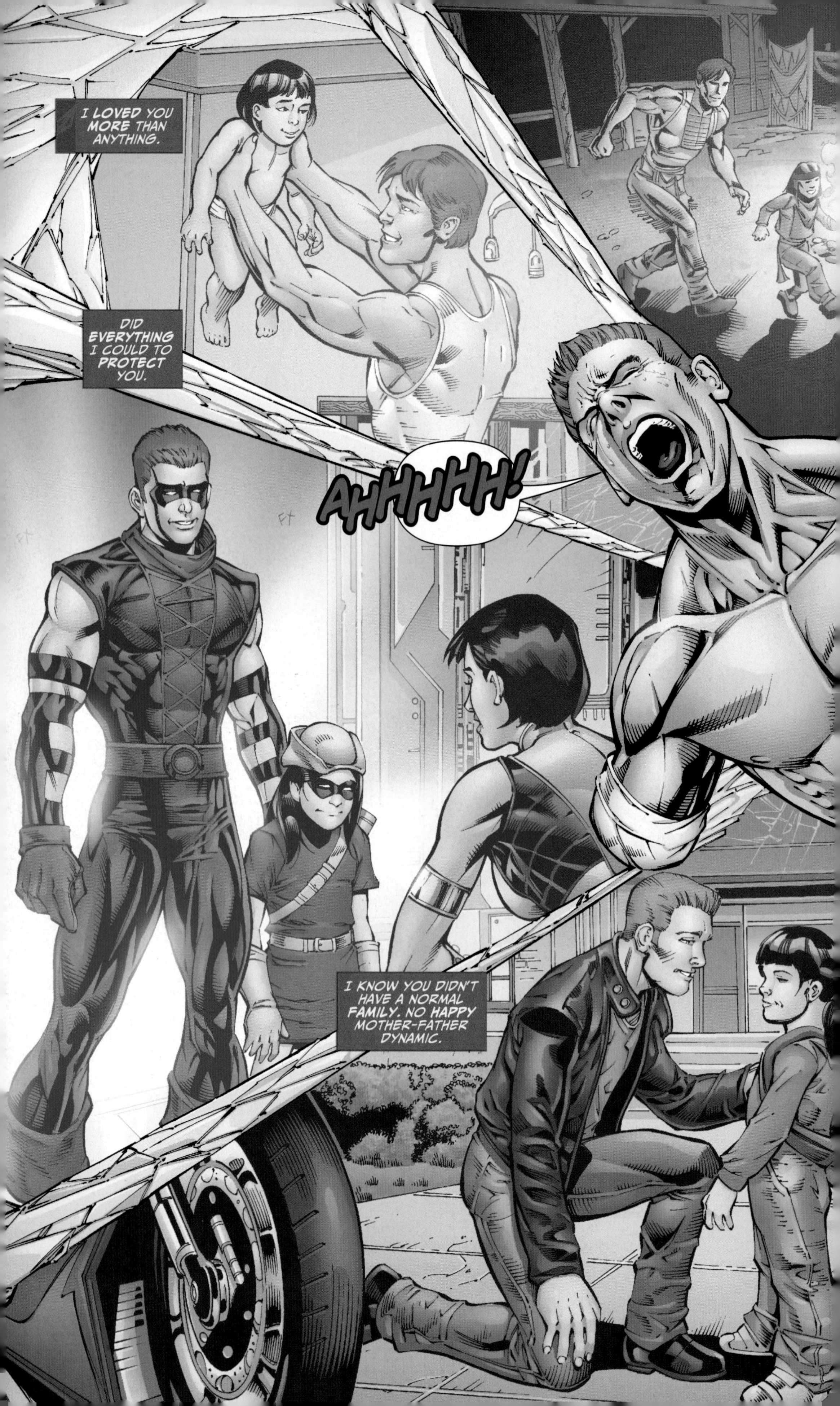

I LOVED YOU MORE THAN ANYTHING.
DID EVERYTHING I COULD TO PROTECT YOU.
AHHHHH!
I KNOW YOU DIDN'T HAVE A NORMAL FAMILY. NO HAPPY MOTHER-FATHER DYNAMIC.

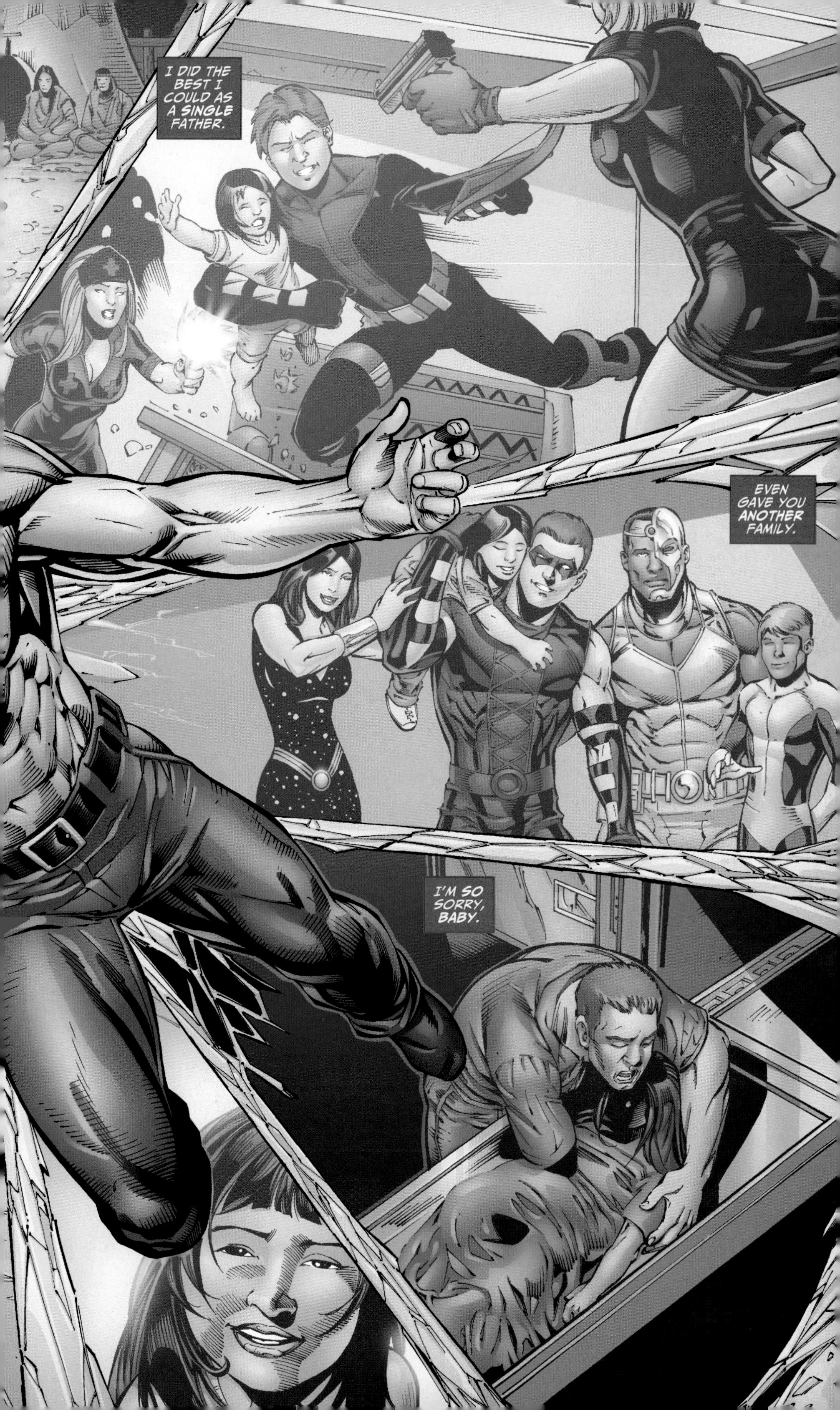
I DID THE BEST I COULD AS A SINGLE FATHER.
EVEN GAVE YOU ANOTHER FAMILY.
I'M SO SORRY, BABY.

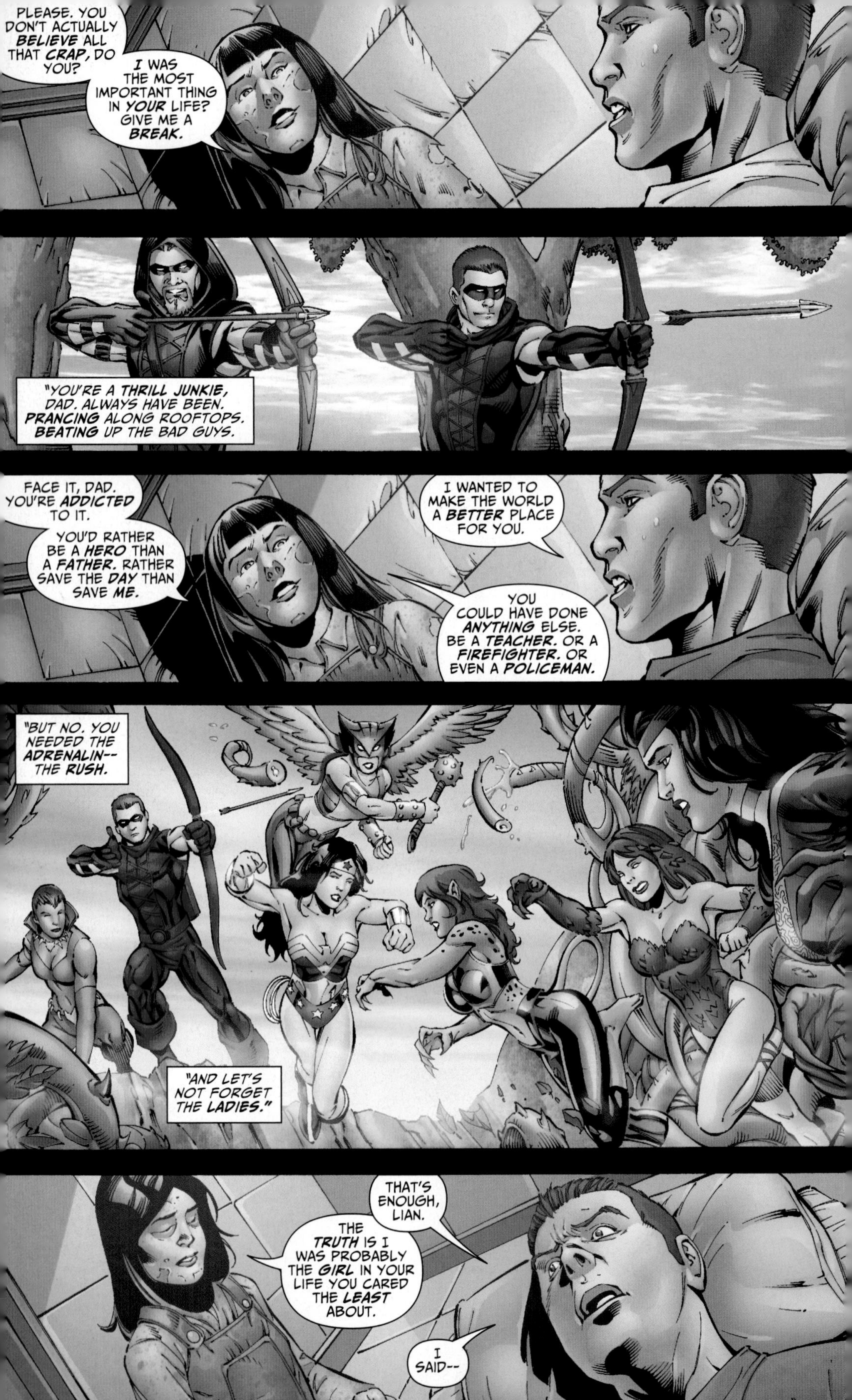
PLEASE. YOU DON'T ACTUALLY BELIEVE ALL THAT CRAP, DO YOU?
I WAS THE MOST IMPORTANT THING IN YOUR LIFE? GIVE ME A BREAK.
"YOU'RE A THRILL JUNKIE, DAD. ALWAYS HAVE BEEN. PRANCING ALONG ROOFTOPS. BEATING UP THE BAD GUYS.
FACE IT, DAD. YOU'RE ADDICTED TO IT.
YOU'D RATHER BE A HERO THAN A FATHER. RATHER SAVE THE DAY THAN SAVE ME.
I WANTED TO MAKE THE WORLD A BETTER PLACE FOR YOU.
YOU COULD HAVE DONE ANYTHING ELSE. BE A TEACHER. OR A FIREFIGHTER. OR EVEN A POLICEMAN.
"BUT NO. YOU NEEDED THE ADRENALIN-- THE RUSH.
"AND LET'S NOT FORGET THE LADIES."
THAT'S ENOUGH, LIAN.
THE TRUTH IS I WAS PROBABLY THE GIRL IN YOUR LIFE YOU CARED THE LEAST ABOUT.
I SAID--

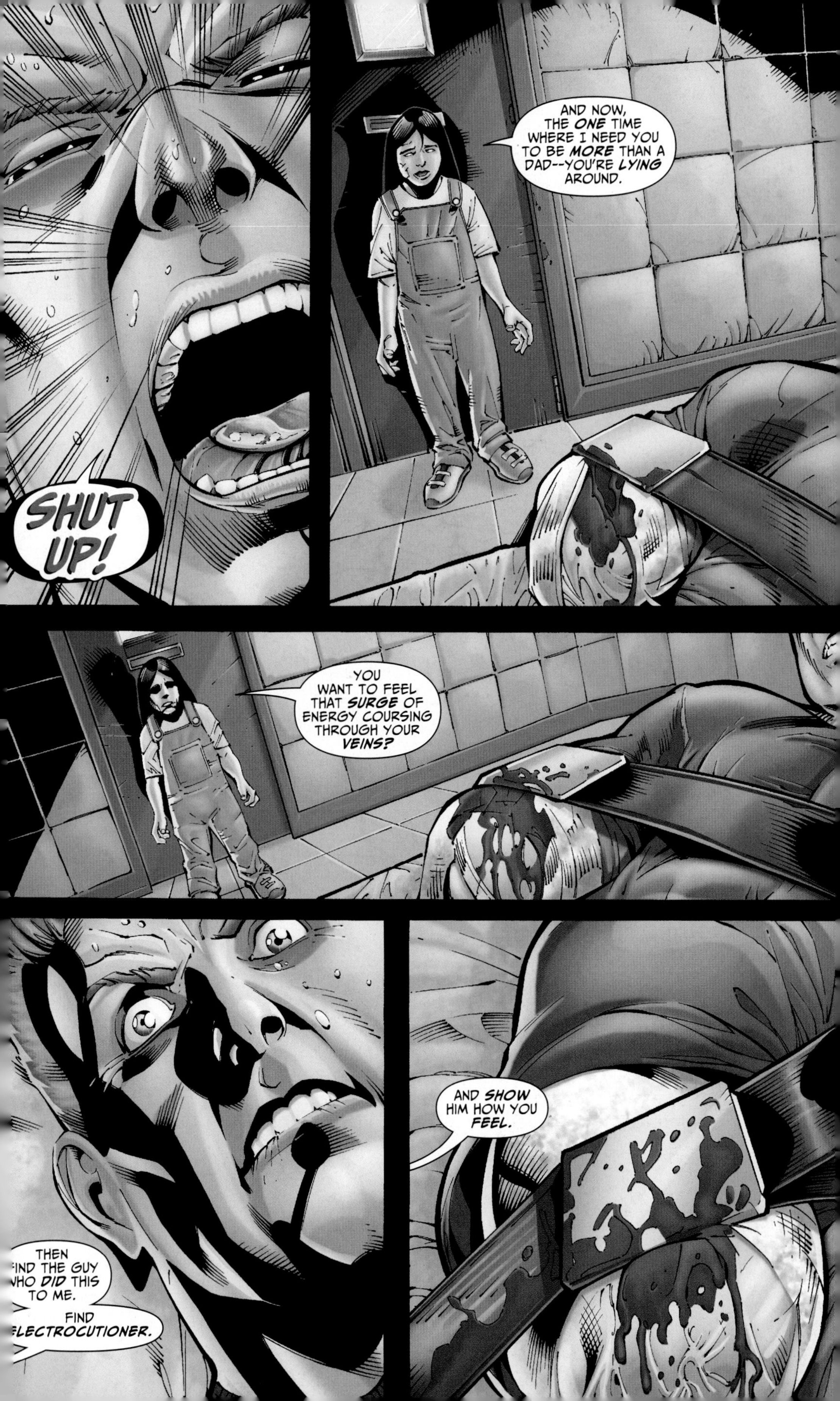
SHUT UP!
AND NOW, THE ONE TIME WHERE I NEED YOU TO BE MORE THAN A DAD--YOU'RE LYING AROUND.
YOU WANT TO FEEL THAT SURGE OF ENERGY COURSING THROUGH YOUR VEINS?
THEN FIND THE GUY WHO DID THIS TO ME.
FIND ELECTROCUTIONER.
AND SHOW HIM HOW YOU FEEL.

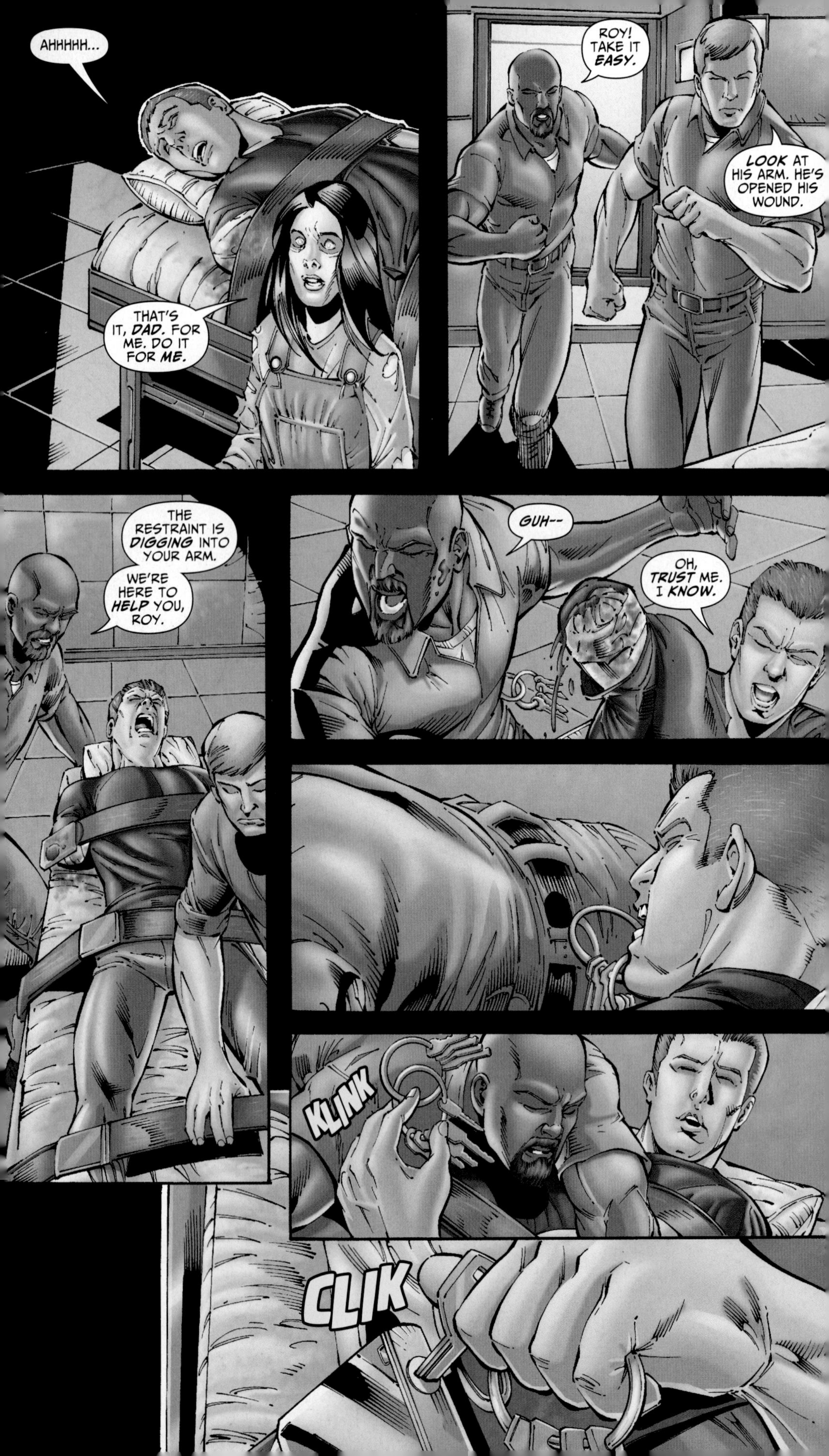
AHHHHH...
THAT'S IT, DAD. FOR ME. DO IT FOR ME.
ROY! TAKE IT EASY.
LOOK AT HIS ARM. HE'S OPENED HIS WOUND.
THE RESTRAINT IS DIGGING INTO YOUR ARM.
WE'RE HERE TO HELP YOU, ROY.
GUH--
OH, TRUST ME. I KNOW.
KLINK
CLIK

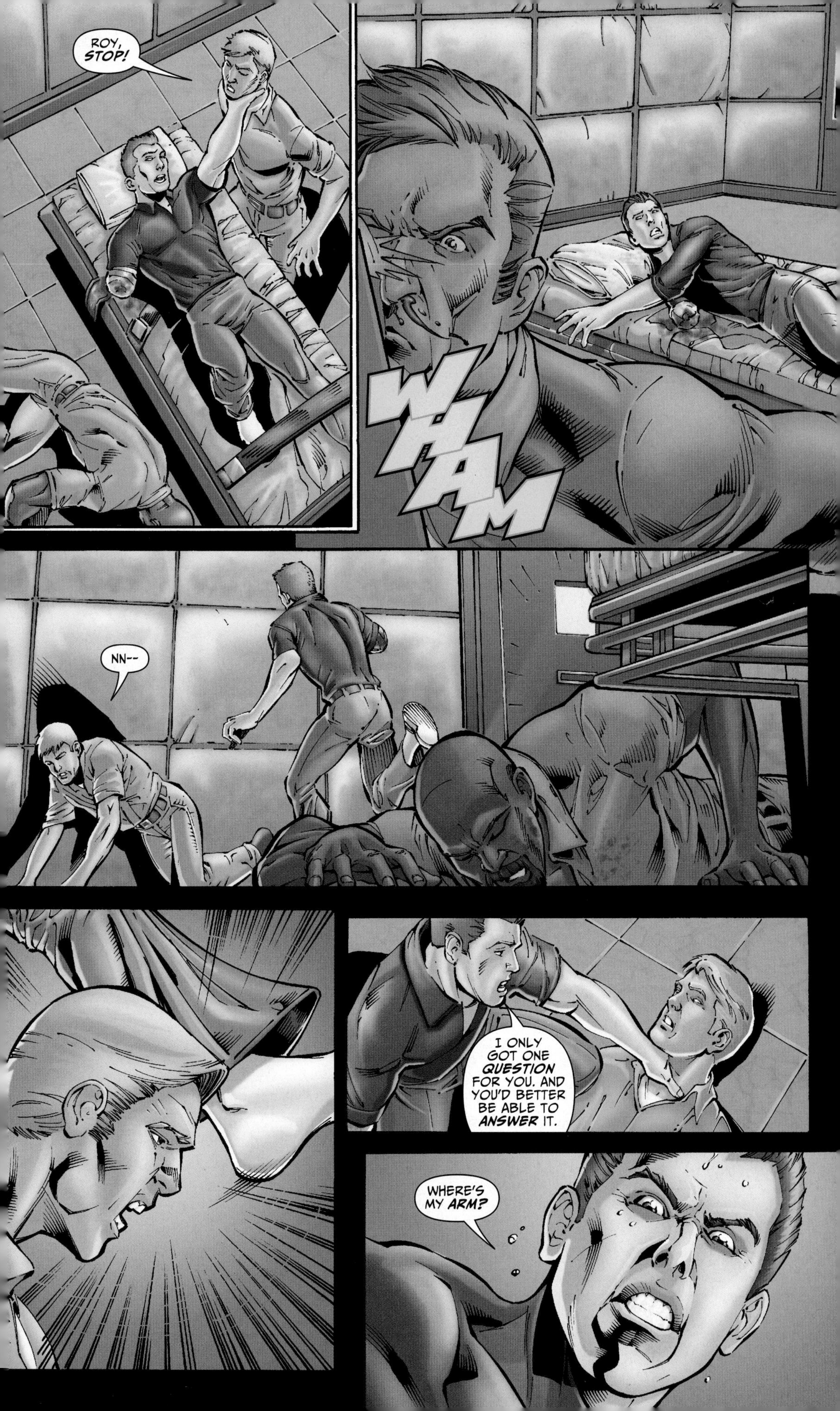
ROY, STOP!
WHAM
NN--
I ONLY GOT ONE QUESTION FOR YOU. AND YOU'D BETTER BE ABLE TO ANSWER IT.
WHERE'S MY ARM?

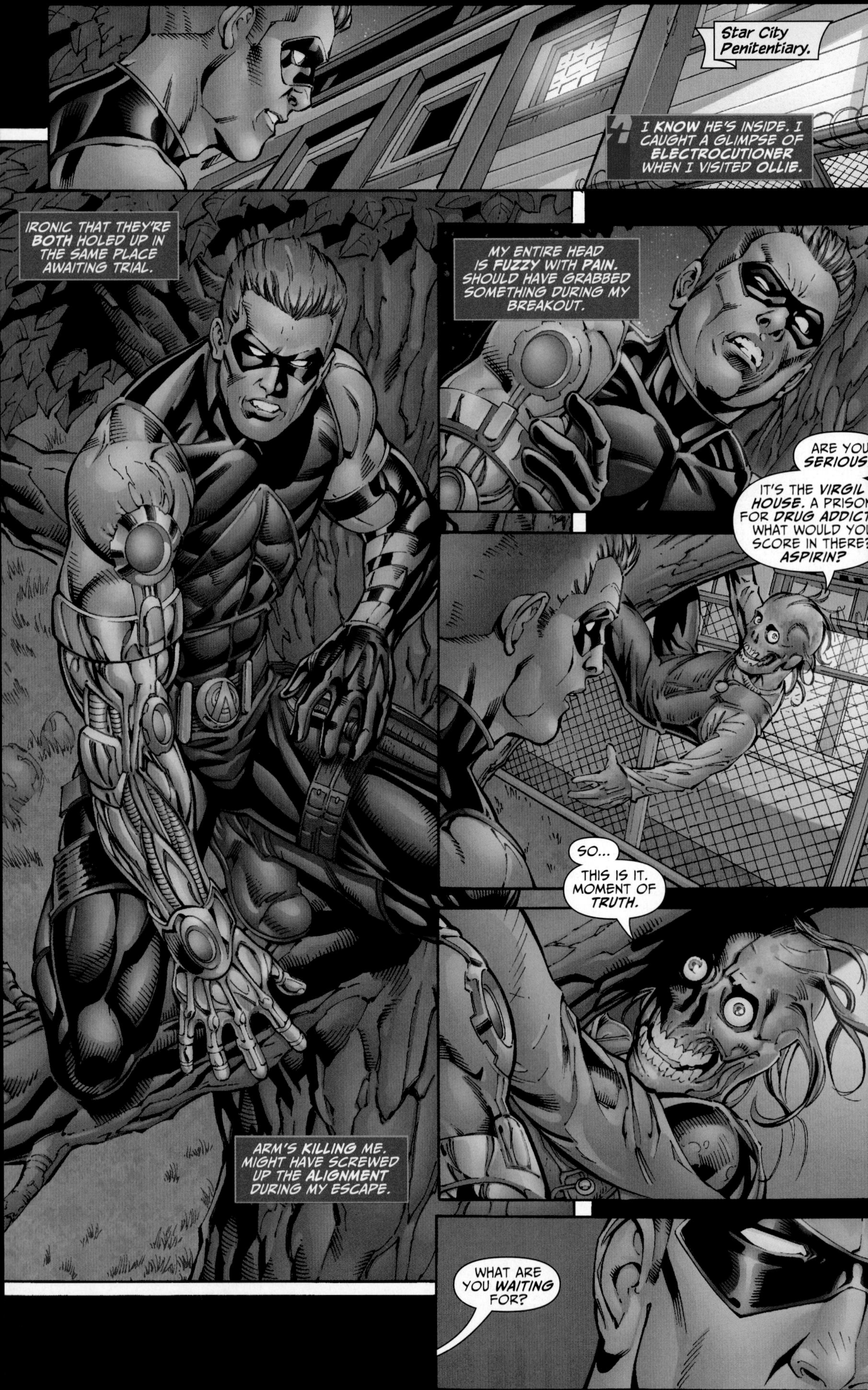

Star City Penitentiary.
I KNOW HE'S INSIDE. I CAUGHT A GLIMPSE OF ELECTROCUTIONER WHEN I VISITED OLLIE.
IRONIC THAT THEY'RE BOTH HOLED UP IN THE SAME PLACE AWAITING TRIAL.
ARM'S KILLING ME. MIGHT HAVE SCREWED UP THE ALIGNMENT DURING MY ESCAPE.
MY ENTIRE HEAD IS FUZZY WITH PAIN. SHOULD HAVE GRABBED SOMETHING DURING MY BREAKOUT.
ARE YOU SERIOUS
IT'S THE VIRGIL HOUSE. A PRISON FOR DRUG ADDICT WHAT WOULD YOU SCORE IN THERE? ASPIRIN?
SO...
THIS IS IT. MOMENT OF TRUTH.
WHAT ARE YOU WAITING FOR?

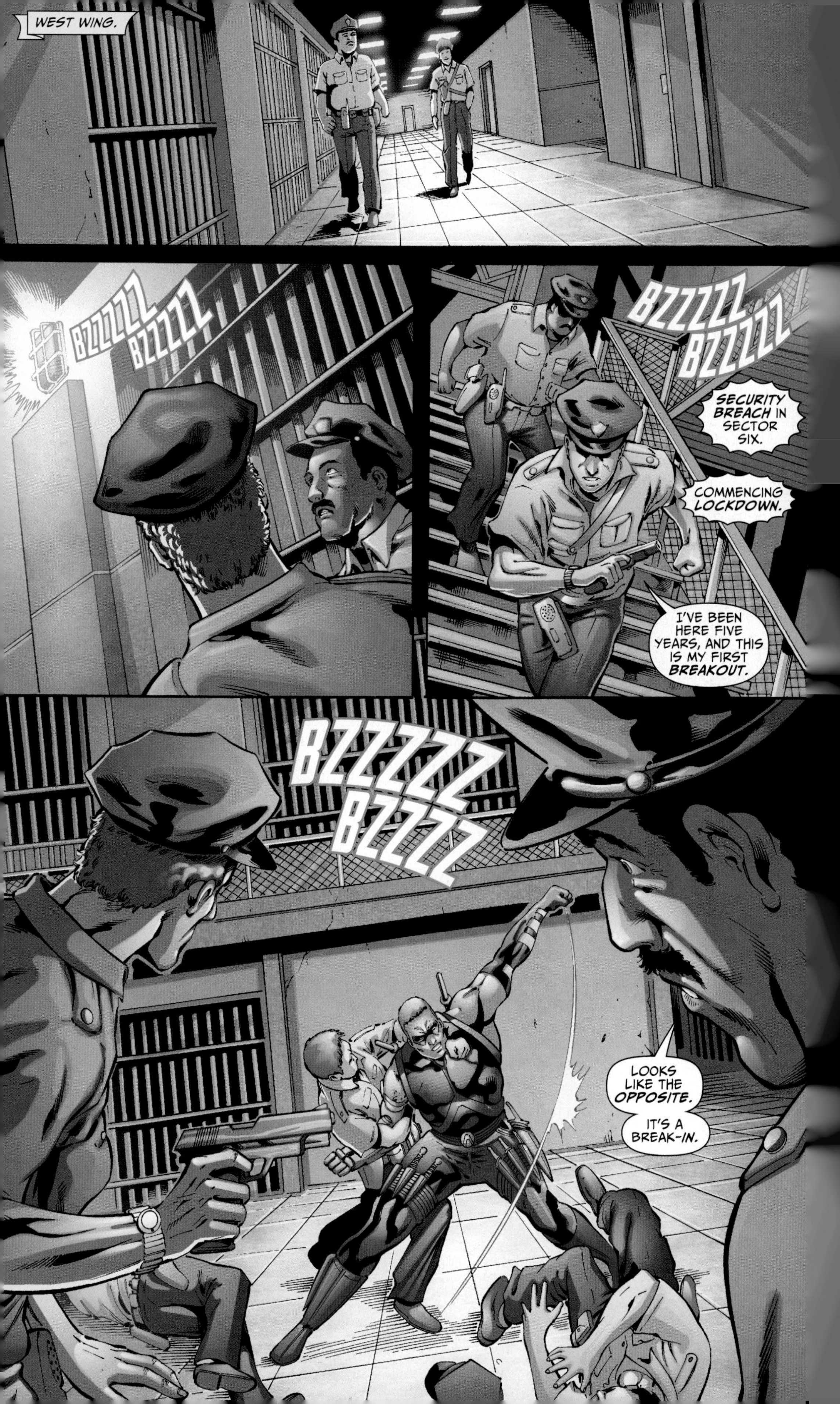
WEST WING.
BZZZZZZ
BZZZZZZ
BZZZZZ
BZZZZZ
SECURITY BREACH IN SECTOR SIX.
COMMENCING LOCKDOWN.
I'VE BEEN HERE FIVE YEARS, AND THIS IS MY FIRST BREAKOUT.
BZZZZZZ
BZZZZ
LOOKS LIKE THE OPPOSITE.
IT'S A BREAK-IN.

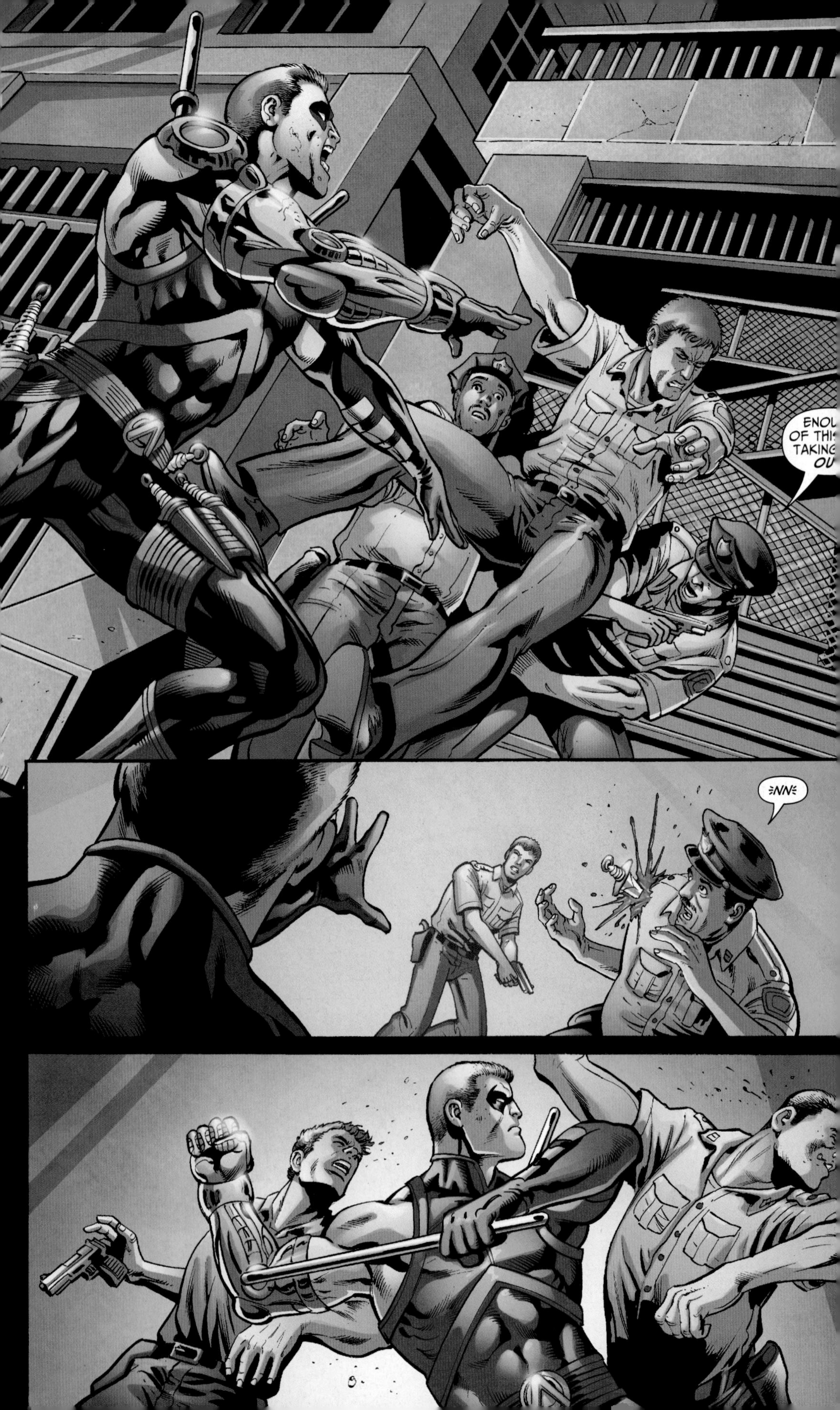
ENOU
OF THIS
TAKING
OU
NN

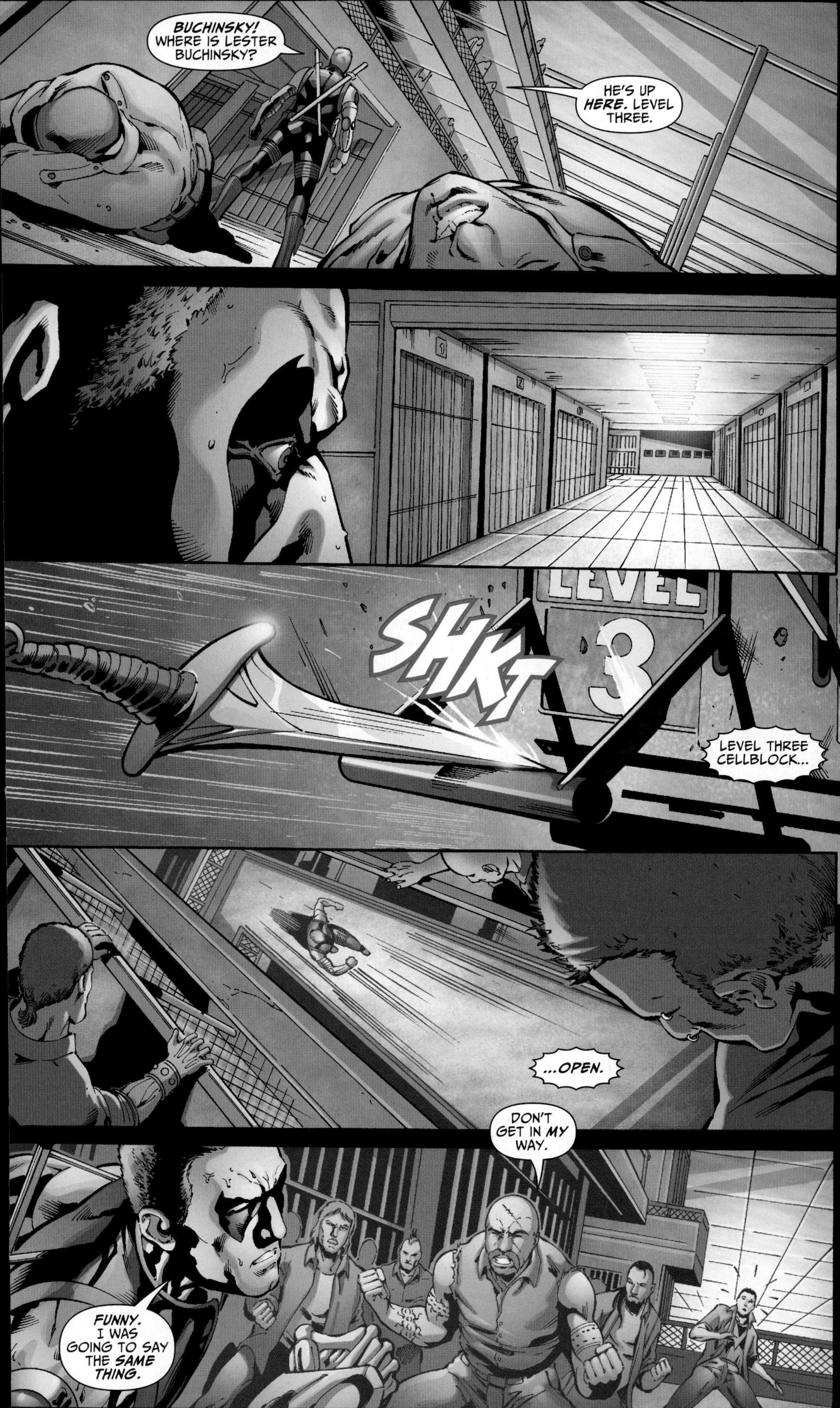
BUCHINSKY! WHERE IS LESTER BUCHINSKY?
HE'S UP HERE. LEVEL THREE.
LEVEL
SHKT
LEVEL 3
LEVEL THREE CELLBLOCK...
...OPEN.
DON'T GET IN MY WAY.
FUNNY. I WAS GOING TO SAY THE SAME THING.

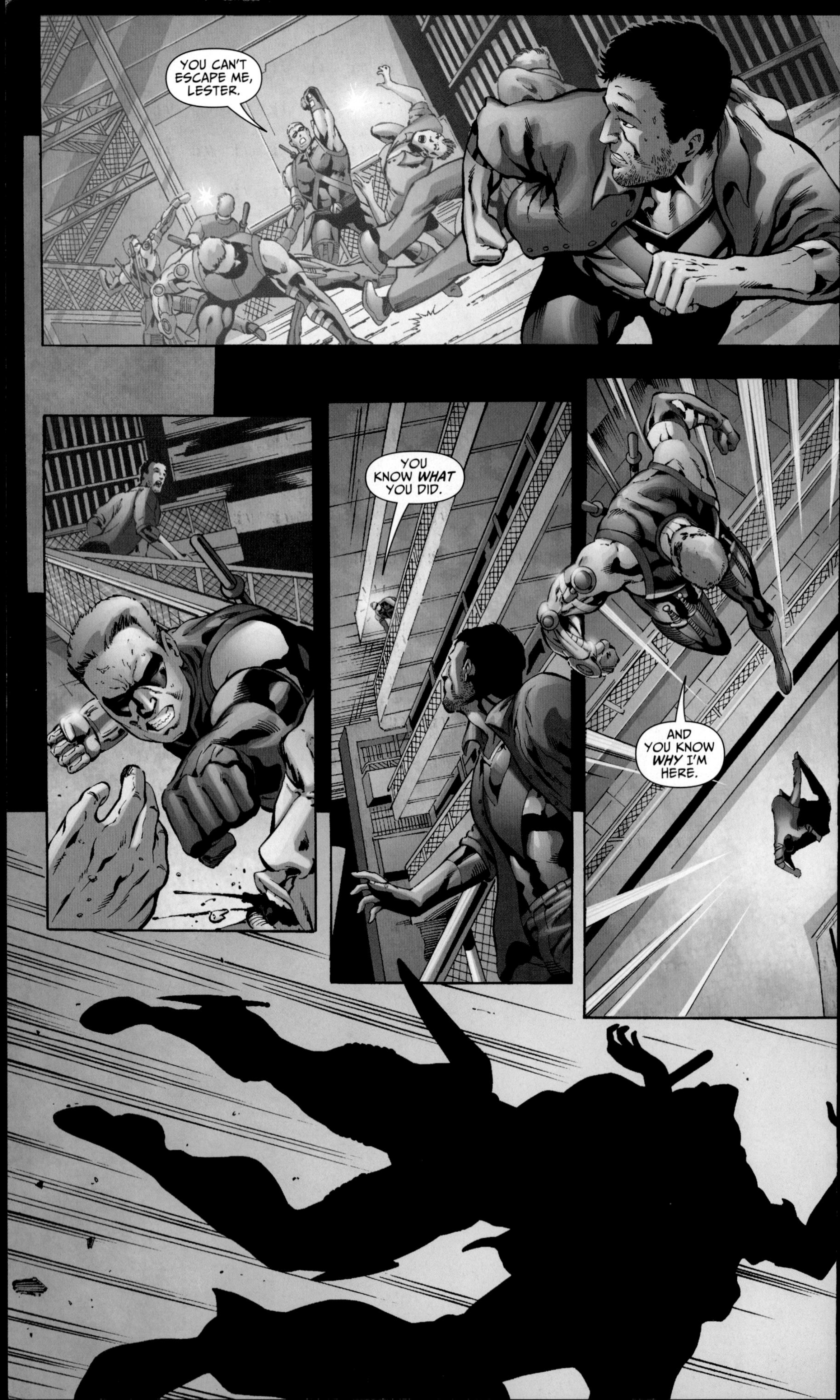

YOU CAN'T ESCAPE ME, LESTER.
YOU KNOW WHAT YOU DID.
AND YOU KNOW WHY I'M HERE.

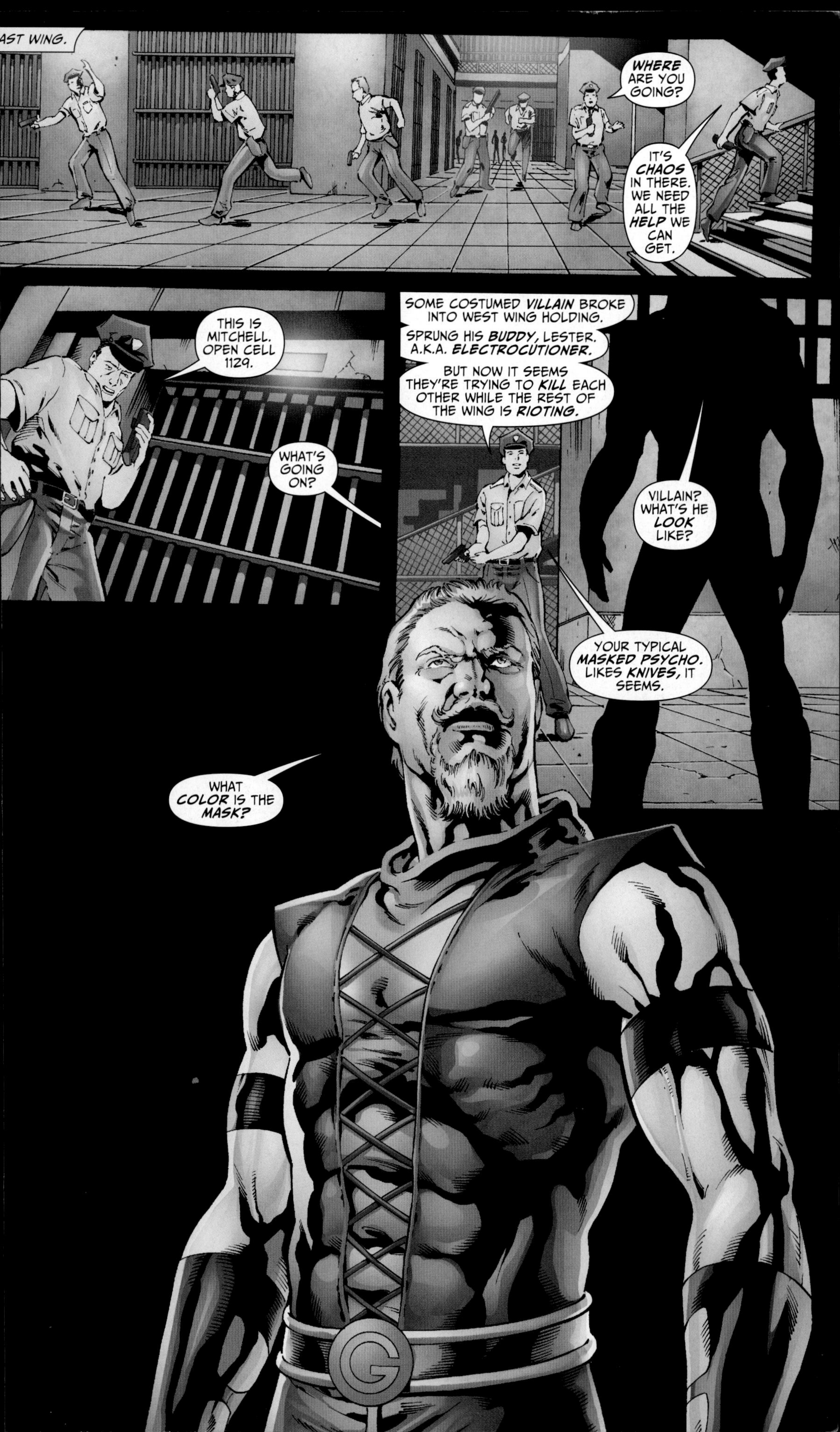

AST WING.
WHERE ARE YOU GOING?
IT'S CHAOS IN THERE. WE NEED ALL THE HELP WE CAN GET.
THIS IS MITCHELL. OPEN CELL 1129.
WHAT'S GOING ON?
SOME COSTUMED VILLAIN BROKE INTO WEST WING HOLDING.
SPRUNG HIS BUDDY, LESTER. A.K.A. ELECTROCUTIONER.
BUT NOW IT SEEMS THEY'RE TRYING TO KILL EACH OTHER WHILE THE REST OF THE WING IS RIOTING.
VILLAIN? WHAT'S HE LOOK LIKE?
YOUR TYPICAL MASKED PSYCHO. LIKES KNIVES, IT SEEMS.
WHAT COLOR IS THE MASK?

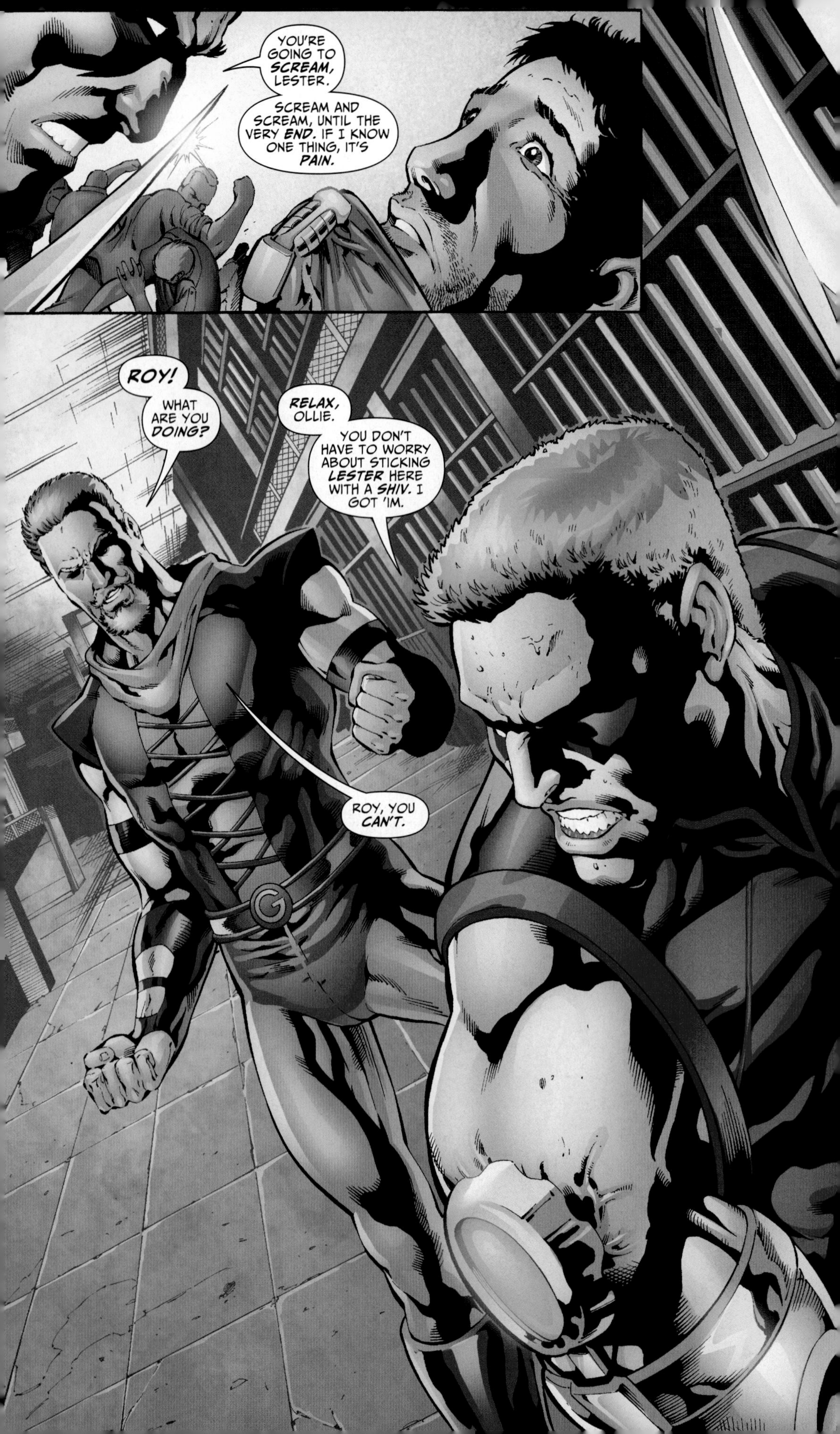
YOU'RE GOING TO SCREAM, LESTER.
SCREAM AND SCREAM, UNTIL THE VERY END. IF I KNOW ONE THING, IT'S PAIN.
ROY!
WHAT ARE YOU DOING?
RELAX, OLLIE.
YOU DON'T HAVE TO WORRY ABOUT STICKING LESTER HERE WITH A SHIV. I GOT 'IM.
ROY, YOU CAN'T.

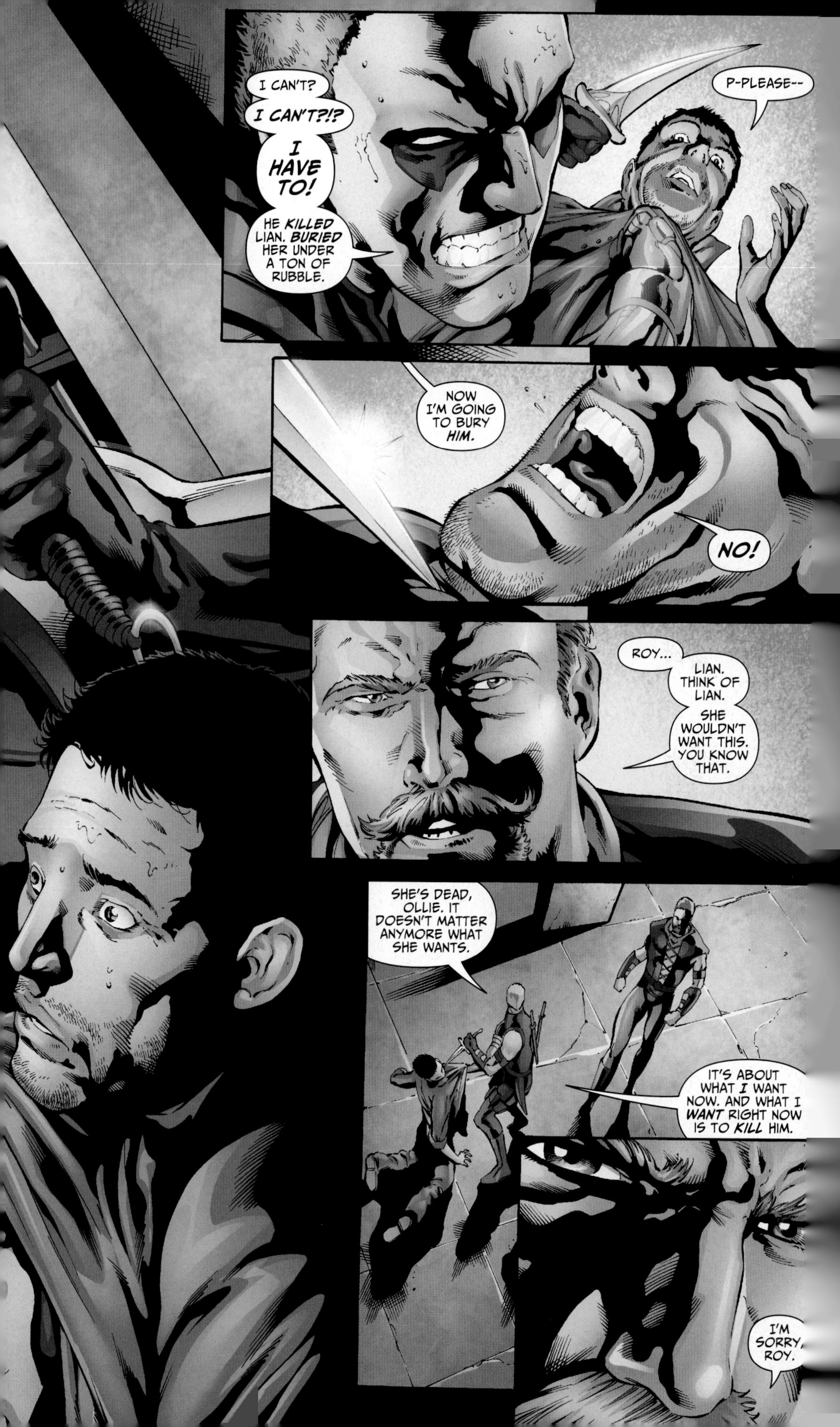
I CAN'T?
I CAN'T?!?
I HAVE TO!
HE KILLED LIAN. BURIED HER UNDER A TON OF RUBBLE.
P-PLEASE--
NOW I'M GOING TO BURY HIM.
NO!
ROY...
LIAN. THINK OF LIAN.
SHE WOULDN'T WANT THIS. YOU KNOW THAT.
SHE'S DEAD, OLLIE. IT DOESN'T MATTER ANYMORE WHAT SHE WANTS.
IT'S ABOUT WHAT I WANT NOW. AND WHAT I WANT RIGHT NOW IS TO KILL HIM.
I'M SORRY, ROY.

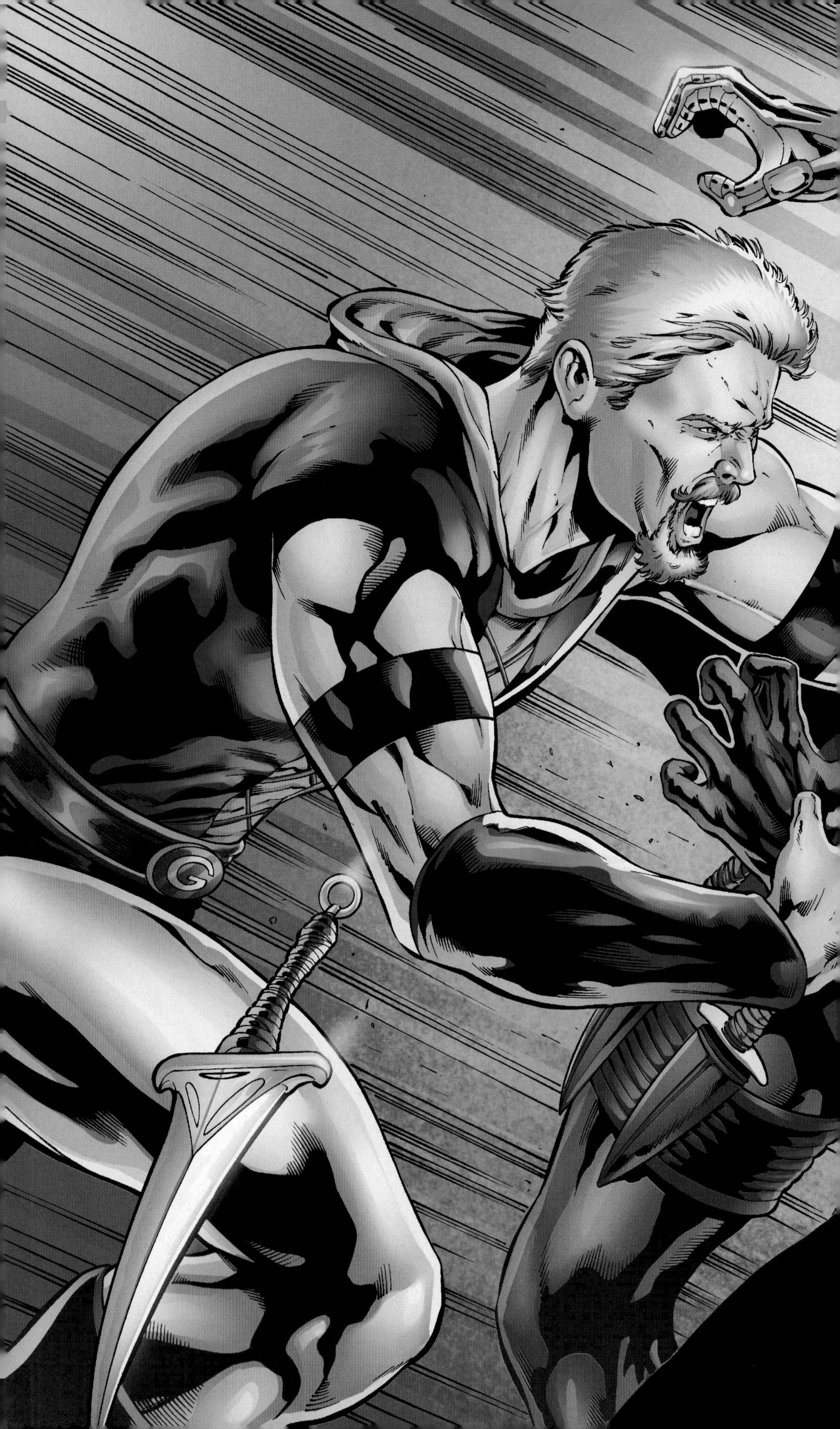

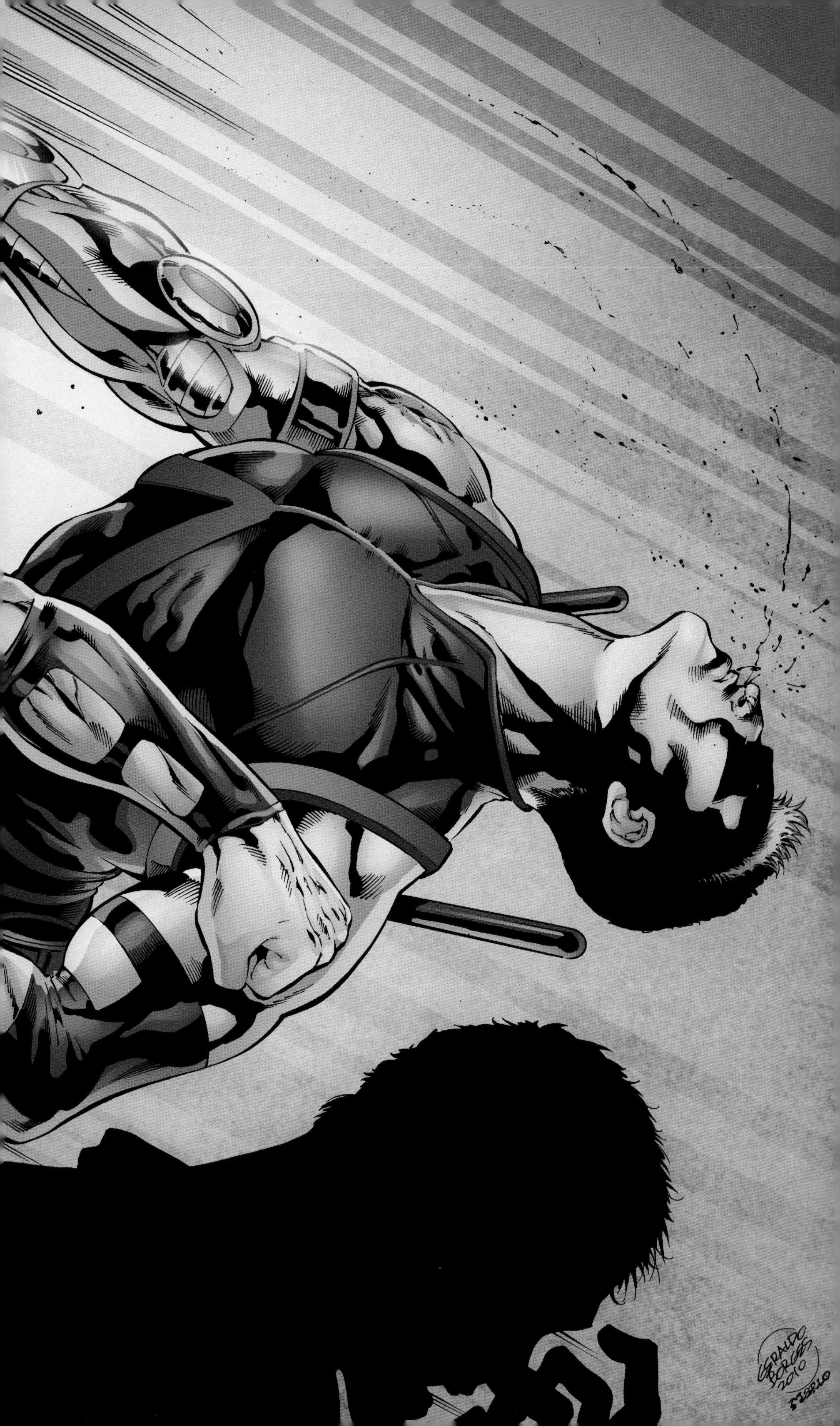
GERALDO BORGES 2010

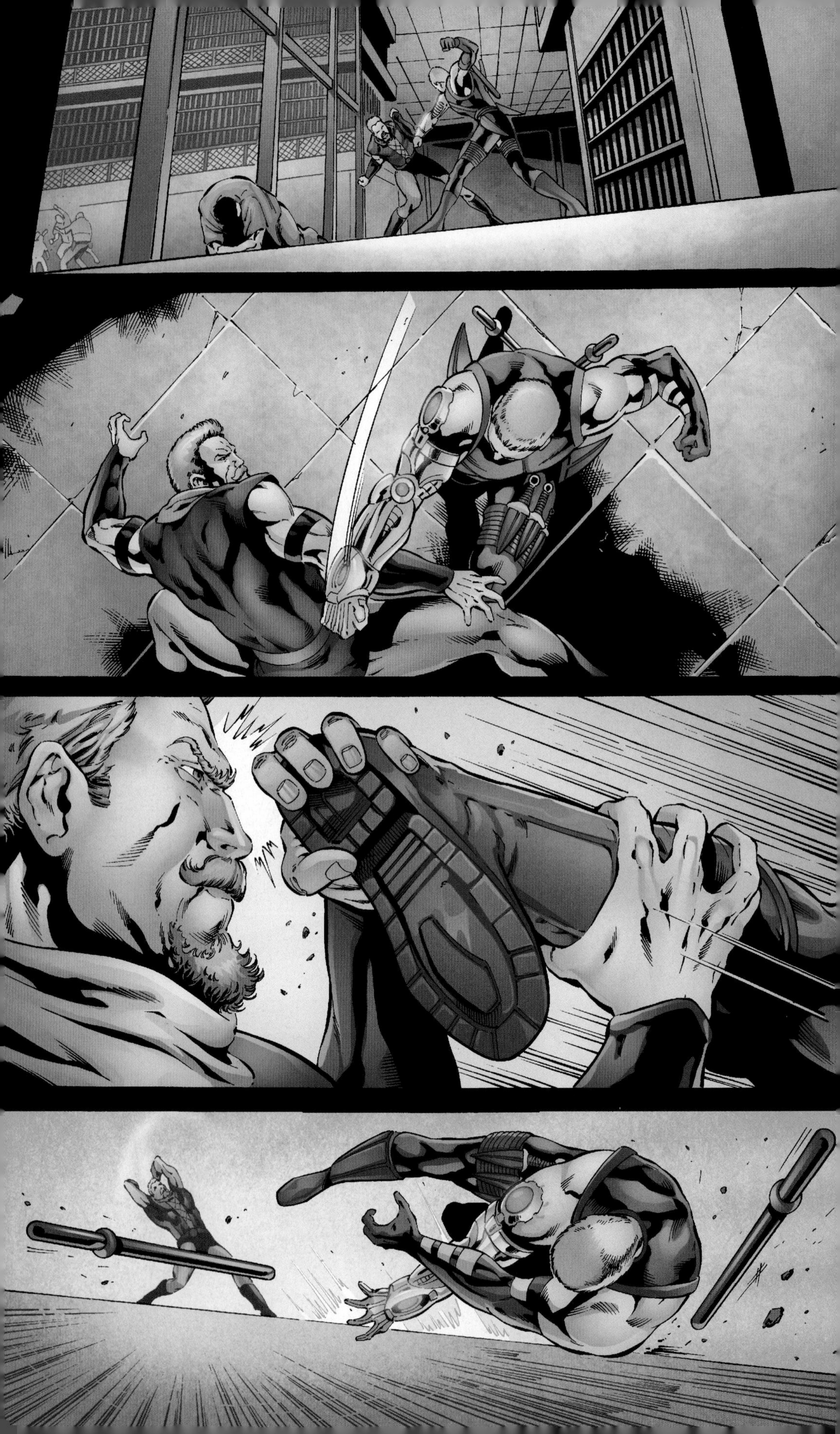

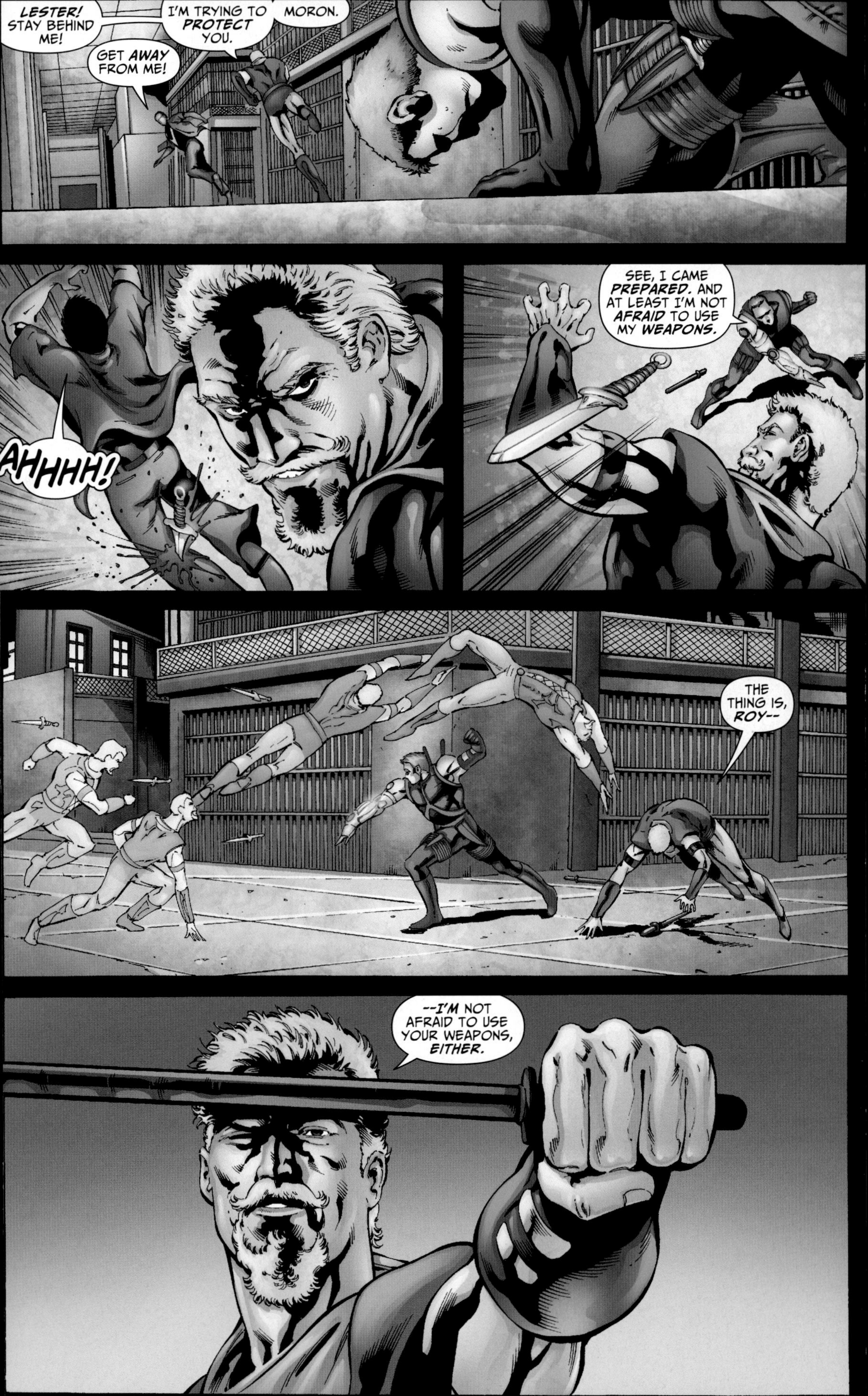
LESTER! STAY BEHIND ME!
I'M TRYING TO PROTECT YOU.
MORON.
GET AWAY FROM ME!
AHHHH!
SEE, I CAME PREPARED. AND AT LEAST I'M NOT AFRAID TO USE MY WEAPONS.
THE THING IS, ROY--
--I'M NOT AFRAID TO USE YOUR WEAPONS, EITHER.

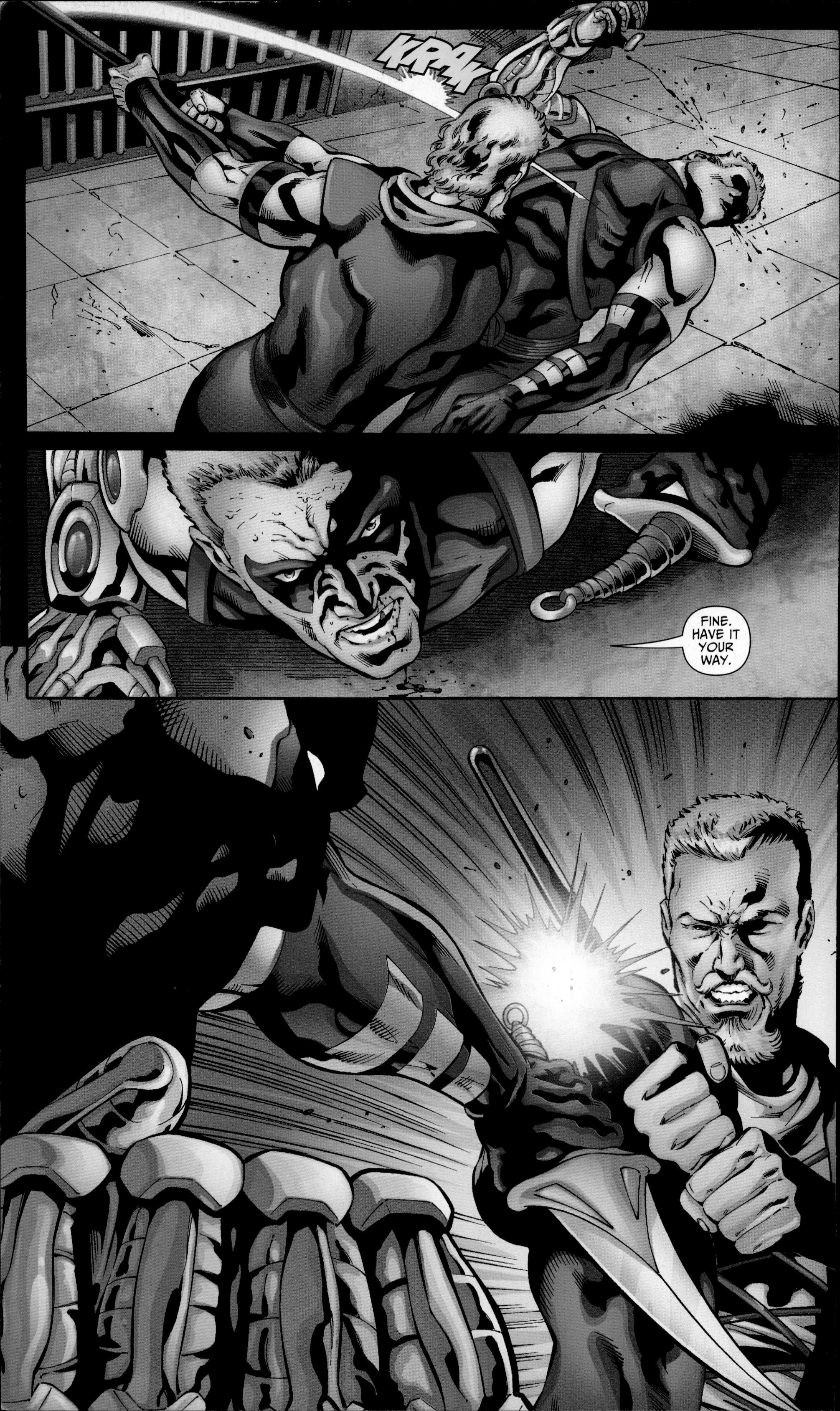
KRAK
FINE. HAVE IT YOUR WAY.

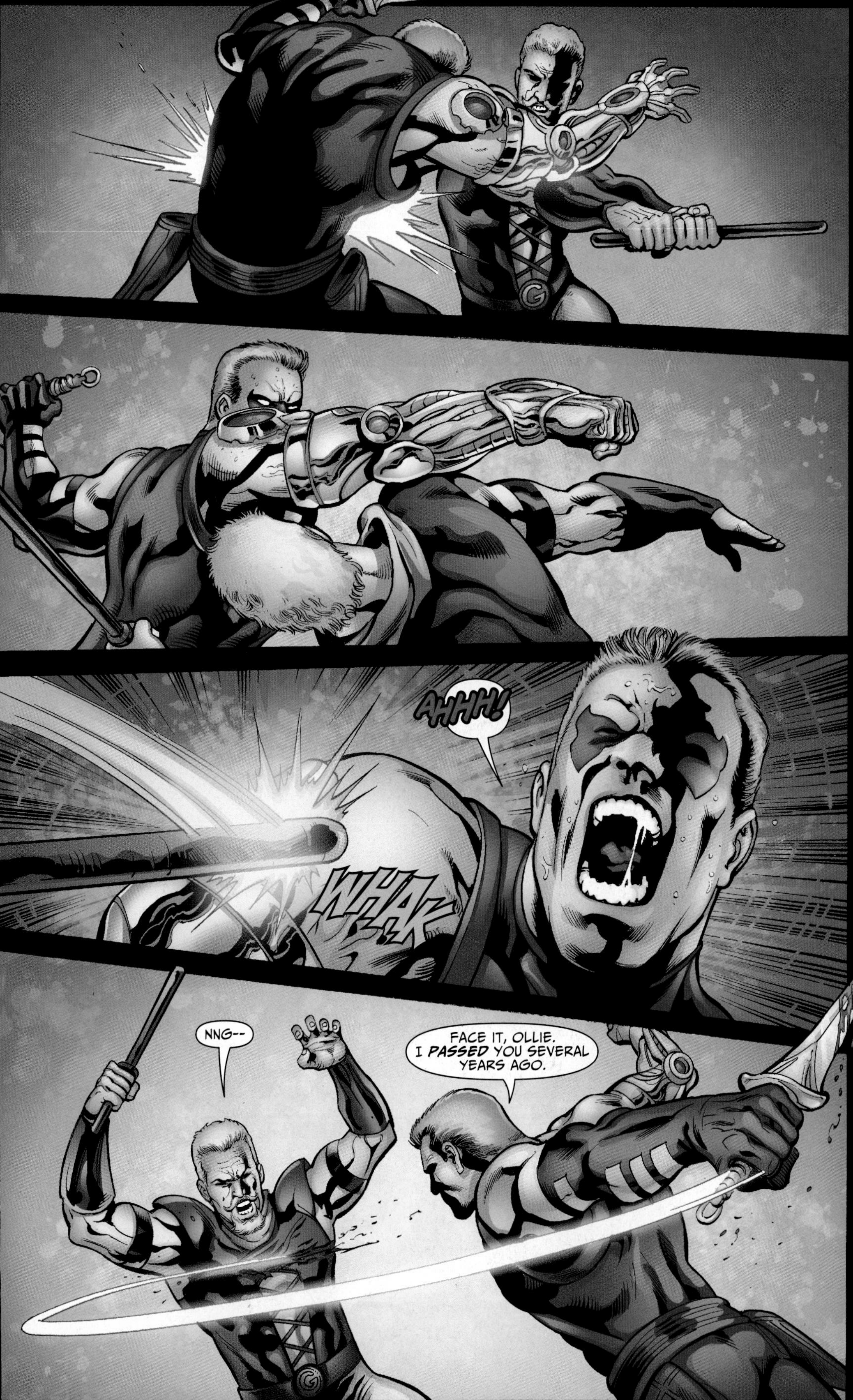

AHHH!
WHAK
NNG--
FACE IT, OLLIE. I PASSED YOU SEVERAL YEARS AGO.

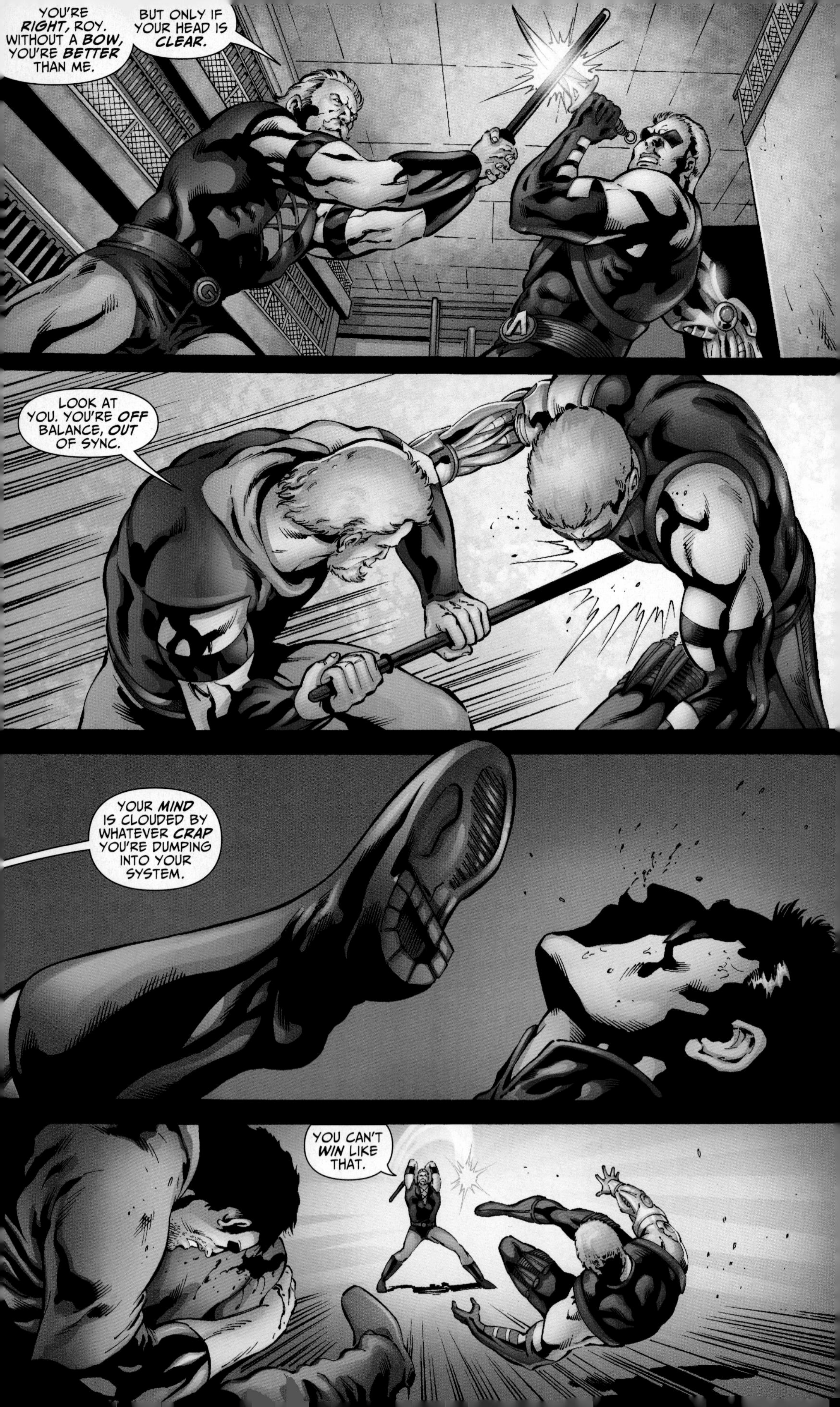
YOU'RE RIGHT, ROY. WITHOUT A BOW, YOU'RE BETTER THAN ME.
BUT ONLY IF YOUR HEAD IS CLEAR.
LOOK AT YOU. YOU'RE OFF BALANCE, OUT OF SYNC.
YOUR MIND IS CLOUDED BY WHATEVER CRAP YOU'RE DUMPING INTO YOUR SYSTEM.
YOU CAN'T WIN LIKE THAT.

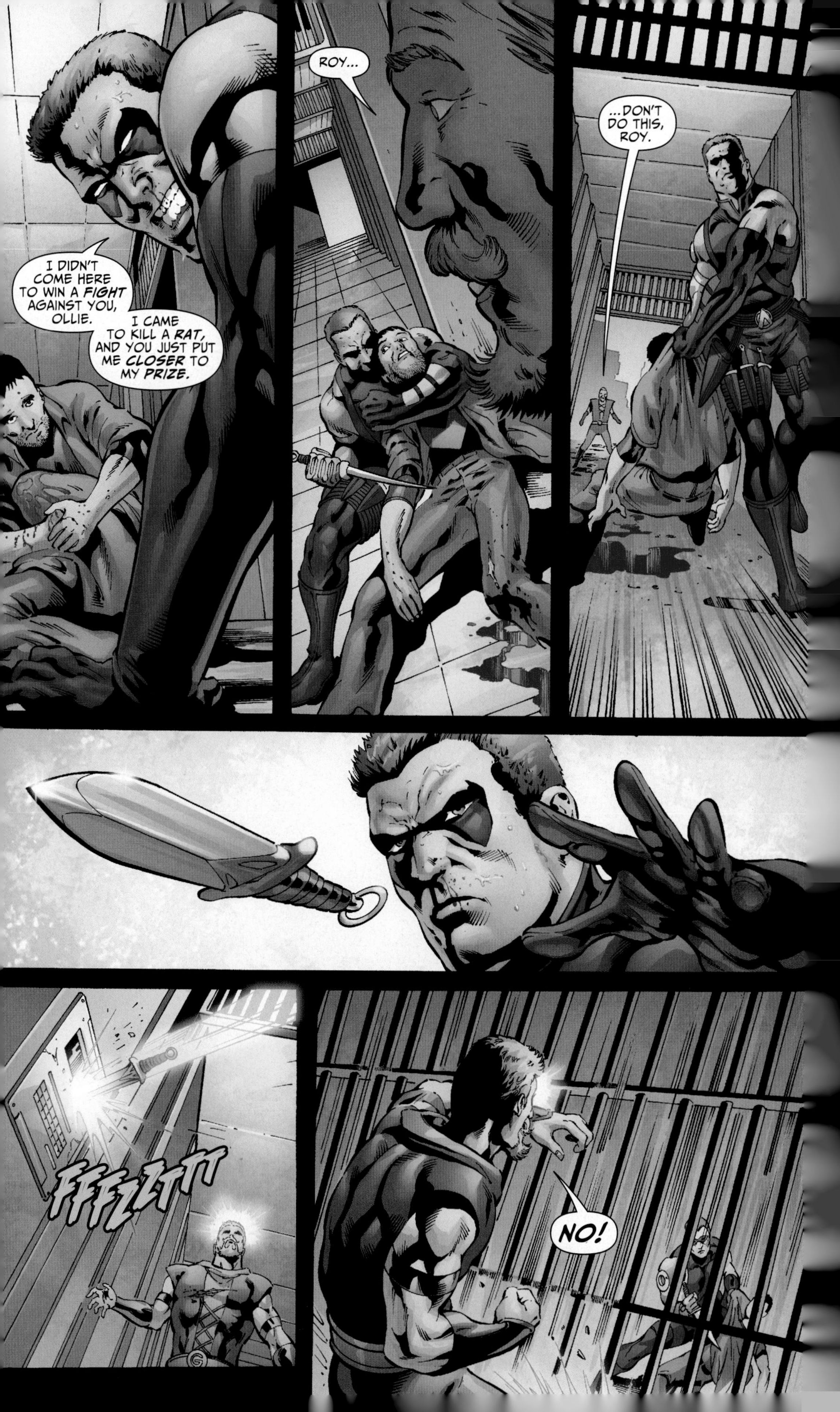
I DIDN'T COME HERE TO WIN A *FIGHT* AGAINST YOU, OLLIE.
I CAME TO KILL A *RAT*, AND YOU JUST PUT ME *CLOSER* TO MY *PRIZE*.
ROY...
...DON'T DO THIS, ROY.
FFFZZTTT
NO!

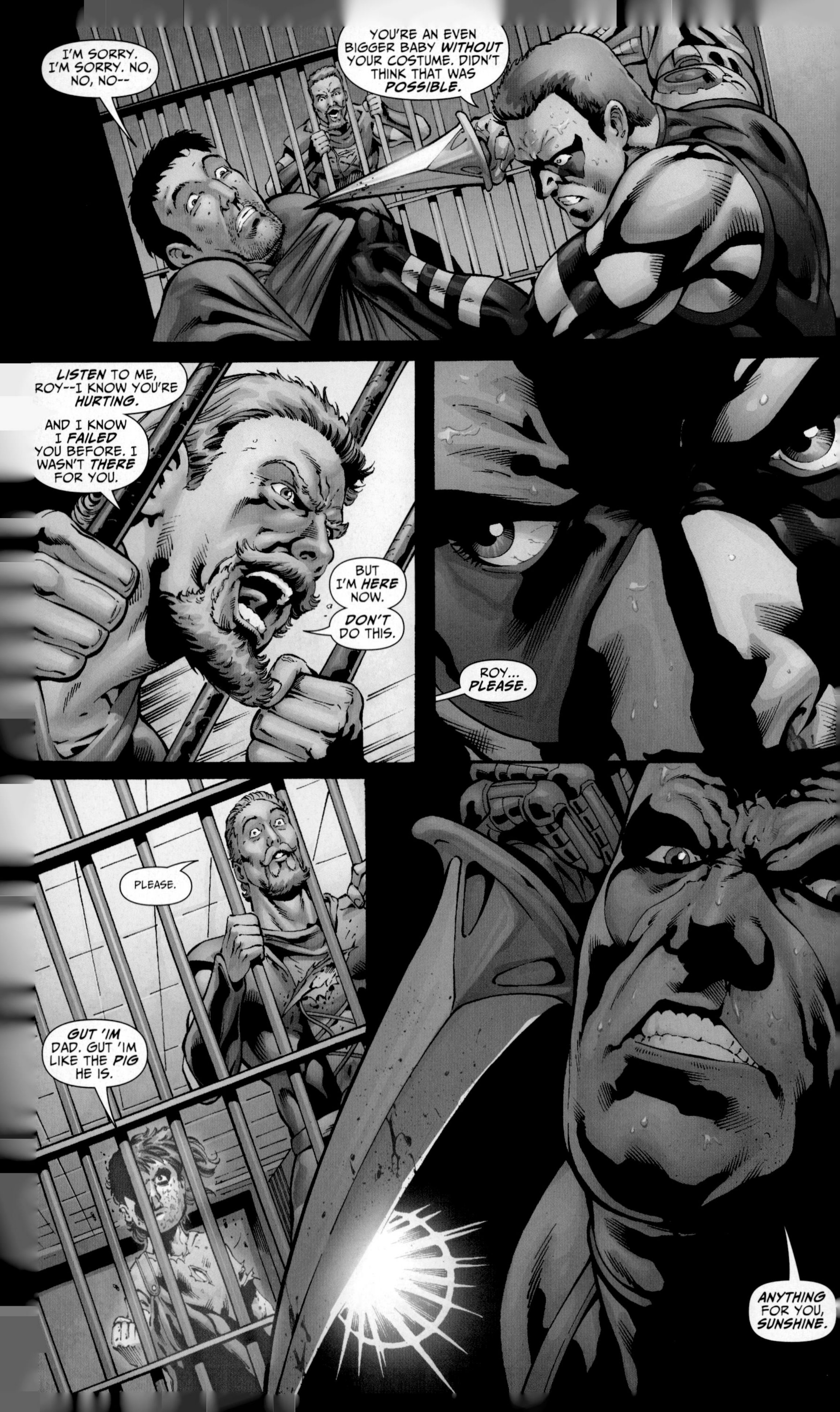
I'M SORRY. I'M SORRY. NO, NO, NO--
YOU'RE AN EVEN BIGGER BABY *WITHOUT* YOUR COSTUME. DIDN'T THINK THAT WAS *POSSIBLE.*
LISTEN TO ME, ROY--I KNOW YOU'RE *HURTING.*
AND I KNOW I *FAILED* YOU BEFORE. I WASN'T *THERE* FOR YOU.
BUT I'M *HERE* NOW.
DON'T DO THIS.
ROY... *PLEASE.*
PLEASE.
GUT 'IM DAD. GUT 'IM LIKE THE *PIG* HE IS.
ANYTHING FOR YOU, *SUNSHINE.*

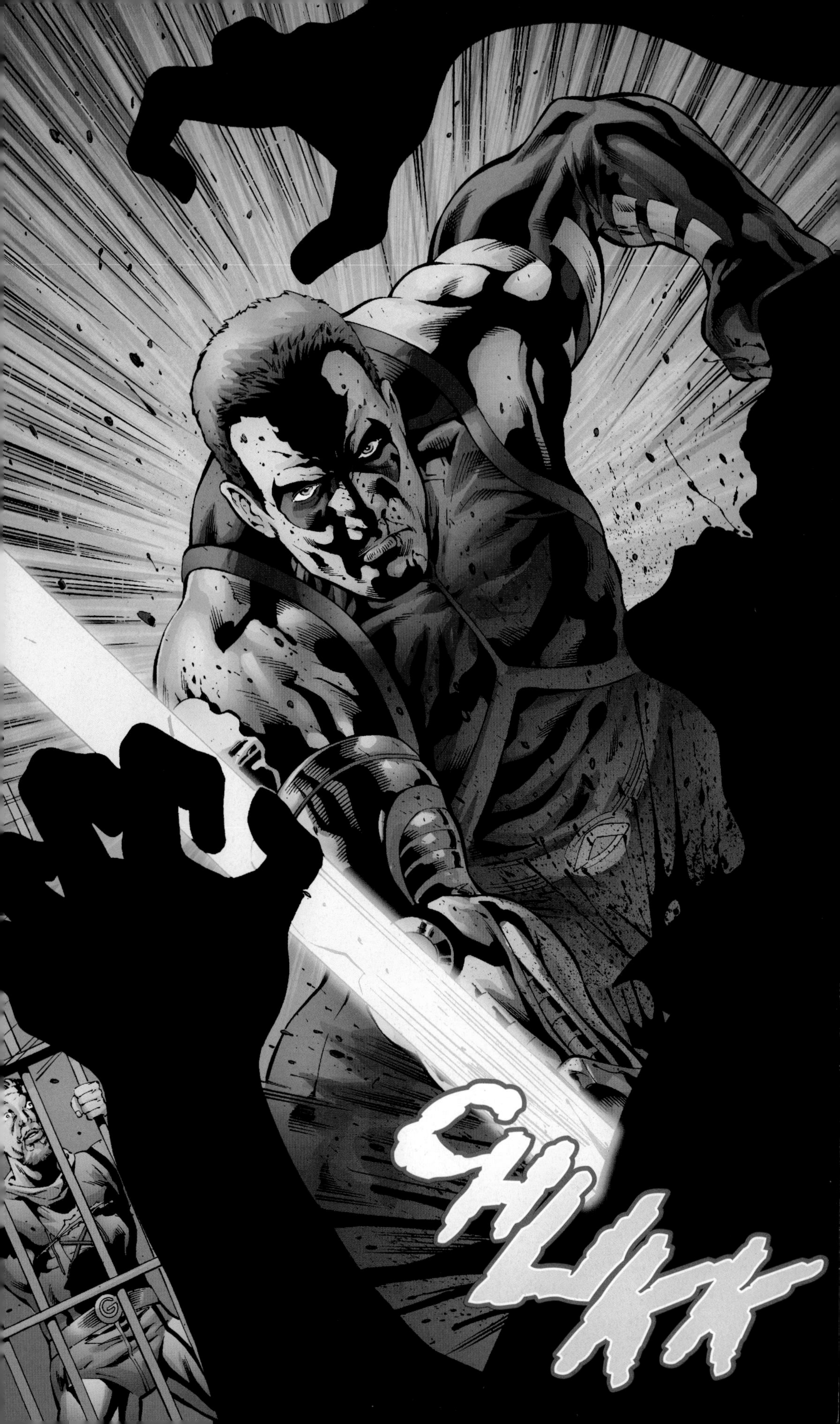
CHUKK

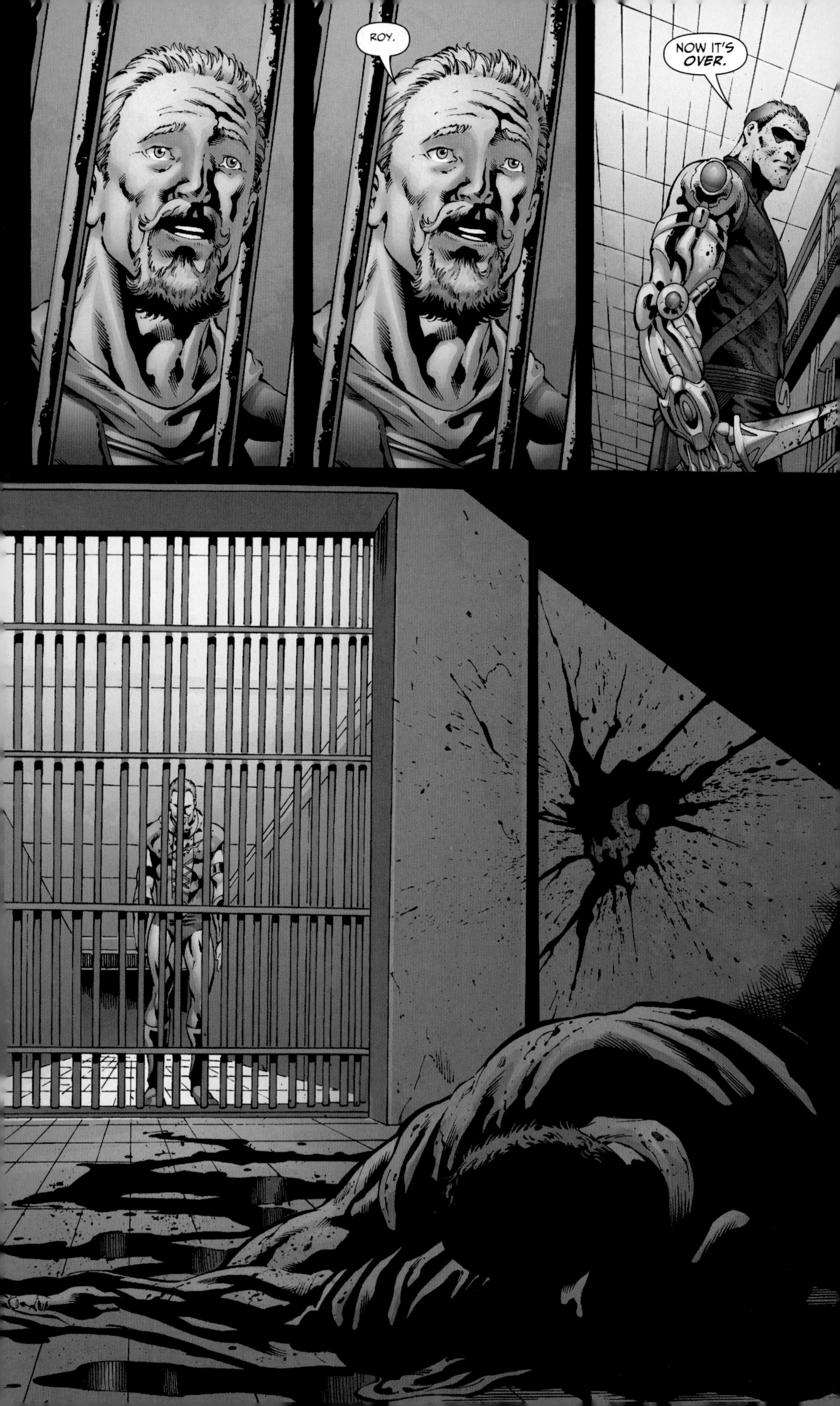

ROY.
NOW IT'S OVER.

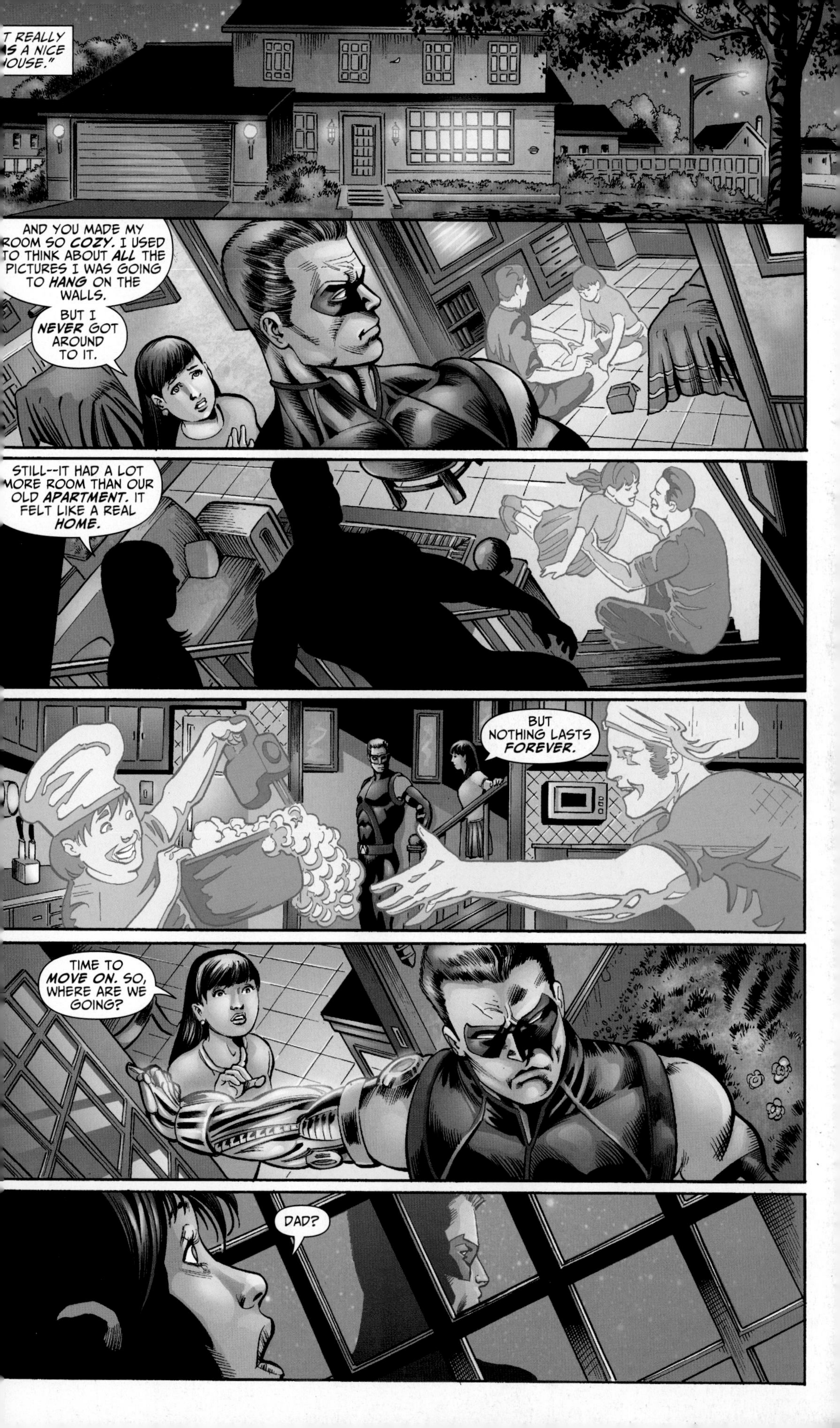
T REALLY
S A NICE
IOUSE."
AND YOU MADE MY ROOM SO COZY. I USED TO THINK ABOUT ALL THE PICTURES I WAS GOING TO HANG ON THE WALLS.
BUT I NEVER GOT AROUND TO IT.
STILL--IT HAD A LOT MORE ROOM THAN OUR OLD APARTMENT. IT FELT LIKE A REAL HOME.
BUT NOTHING LASTS FOREVER.
TIME TO MOVE ON. SO, WHERE ARE WE GOING?
DAD?

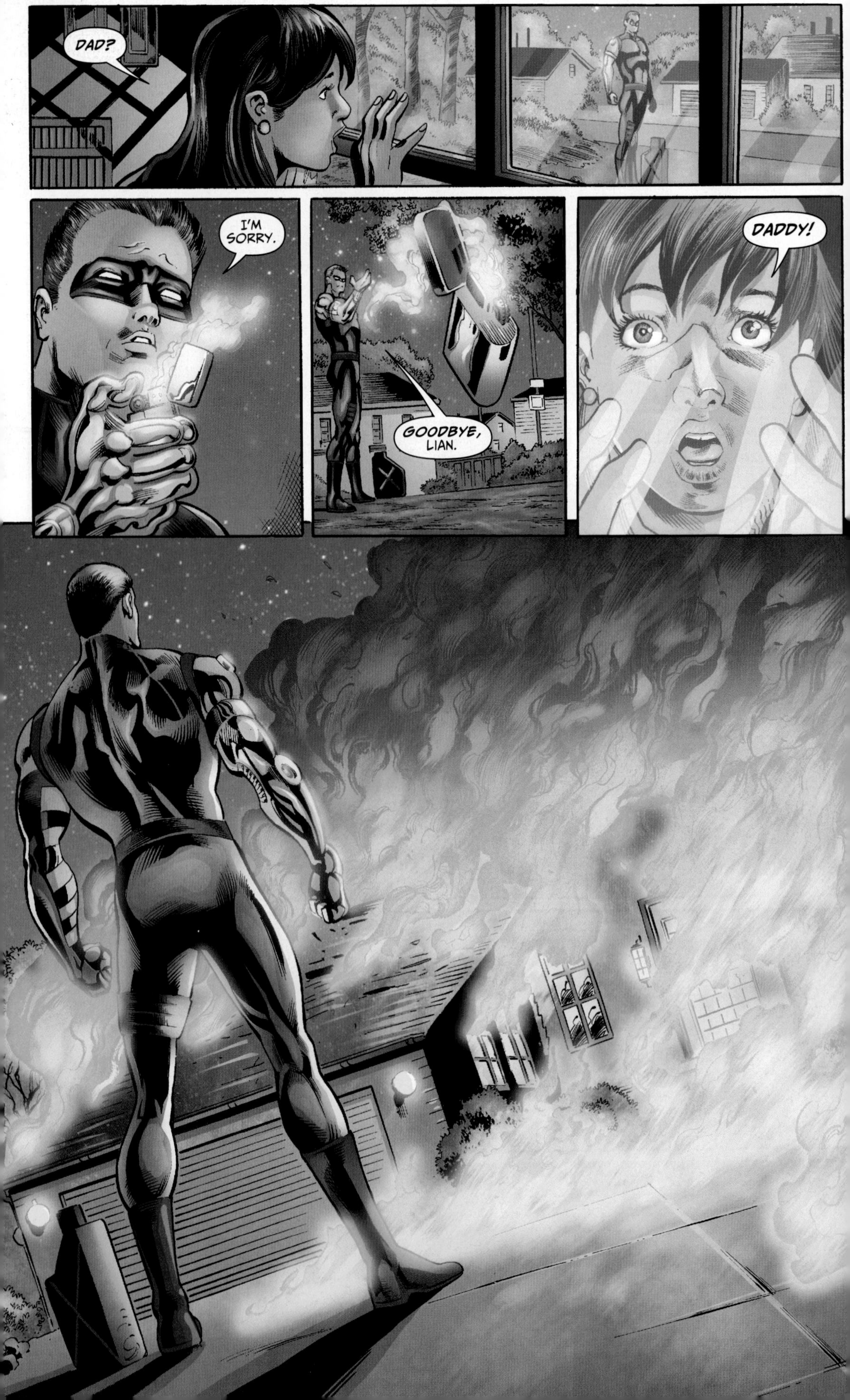
DAD?
I'M SORRY.
GOODBYE, LIAN.
DADDY!

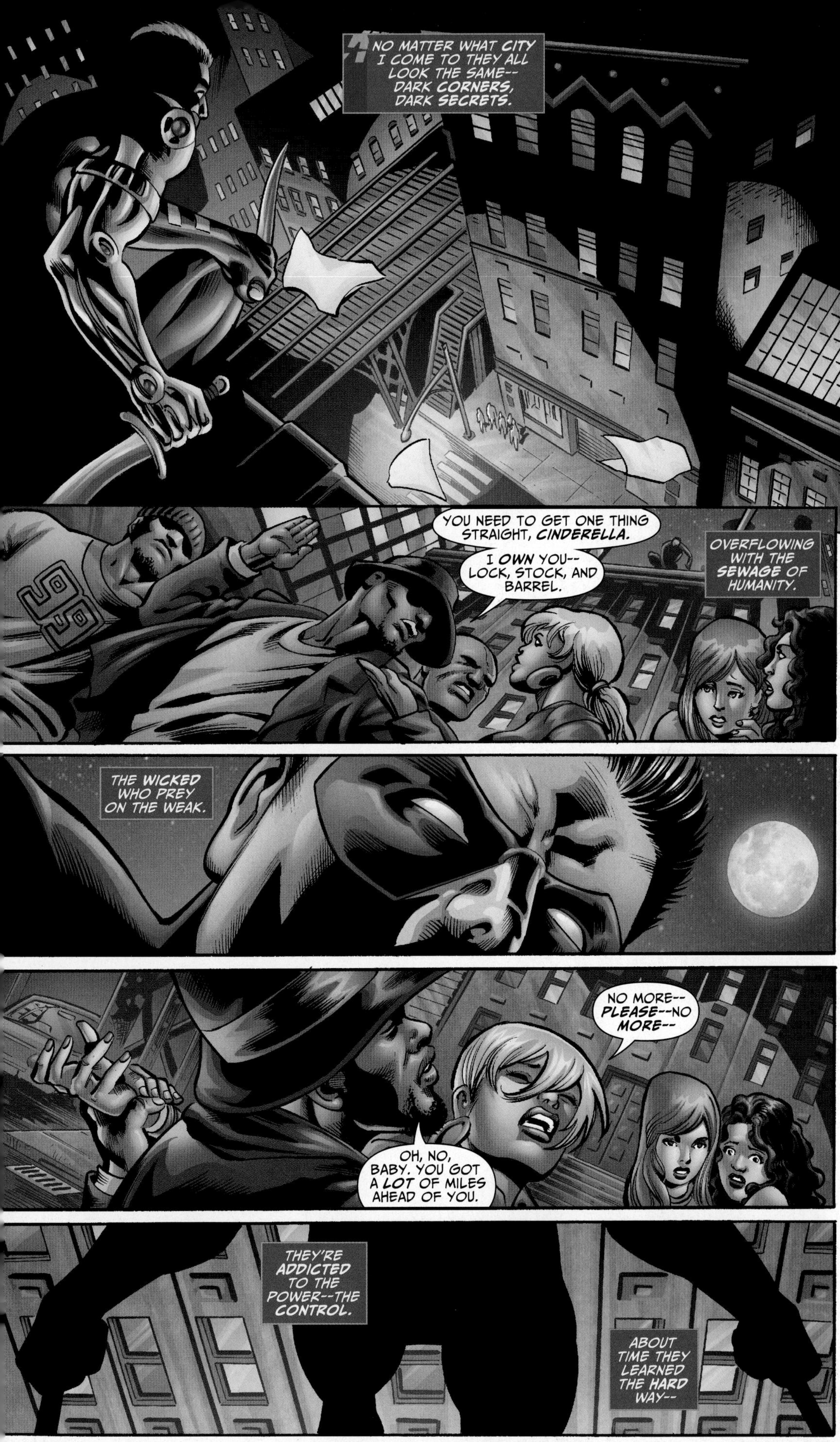
NO MATTER WHAT CITY I COME TO THEY ALL LOOK THE SAME--DARK CORNERS, DARK SECRETS.
YOU NEED TO GET ONE THING STRAIGHT, CINDERELLA.
I OWN YOU--LOCK, STOCK, AND BARREL.
OVERFLOWING WITH THE SEWAGE OF HUMANITY.
THE WICKED WHO PREY ON THE WEAK.
NO MORE--PLEASE--NO MORE--
OH, NO, BABY. YOU GOT A LOT OF MILES AHEAD OF YOU.
THEY'RE ADDICTED TO THE POWER--THE CONTROL.
ABOUT TIME THEY LEARNED THE HARD WAY--

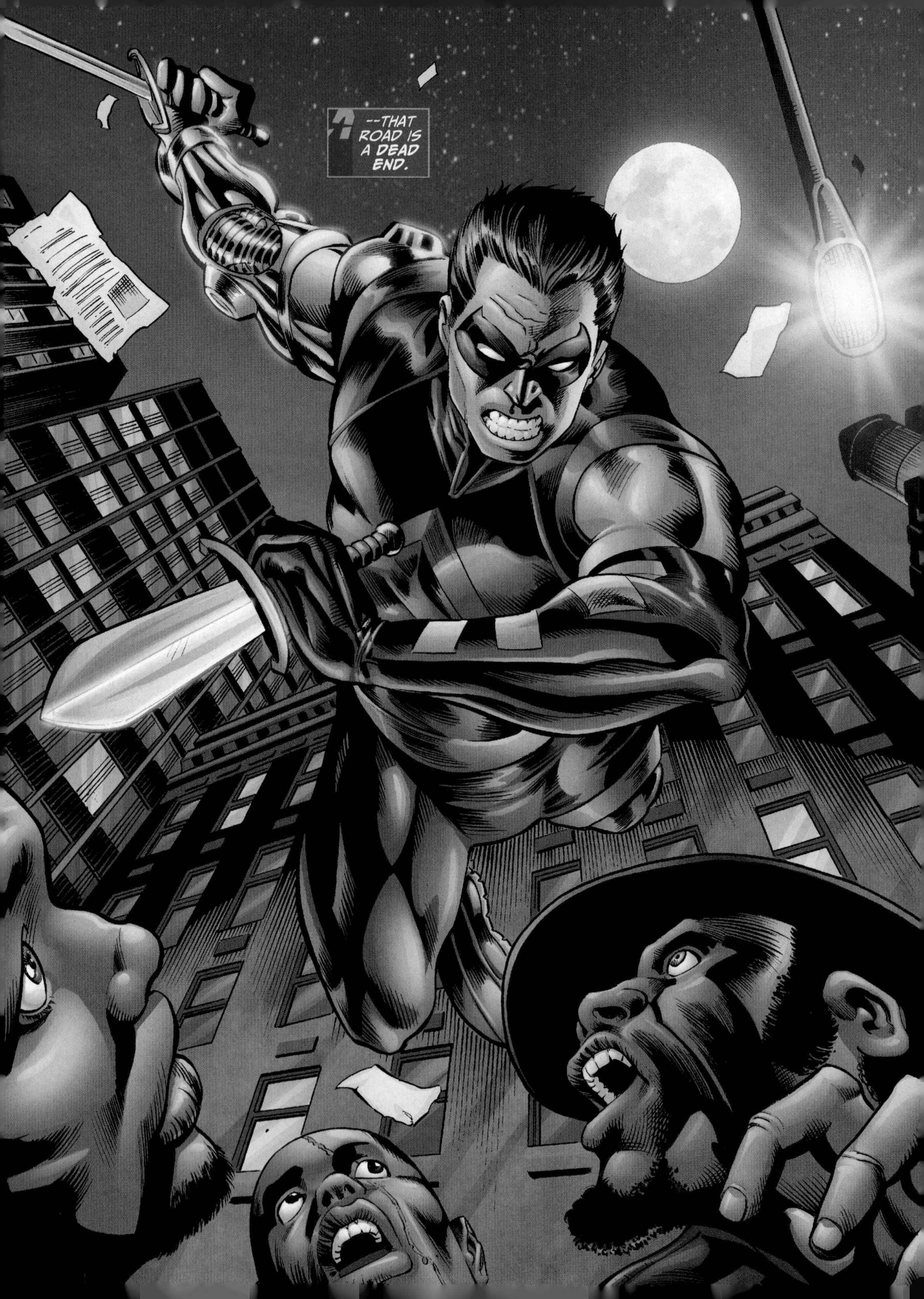
--THAT ROAD IS A DEAD END.

Variant Cover Gallery

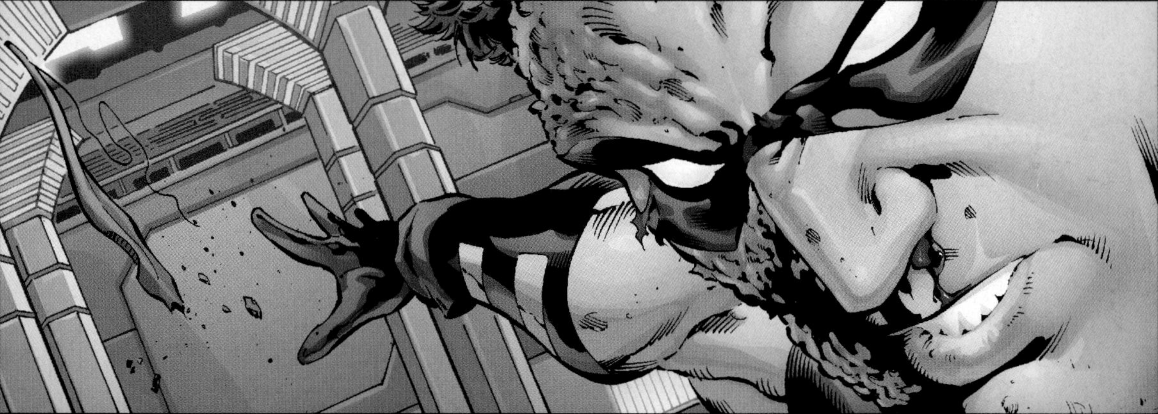

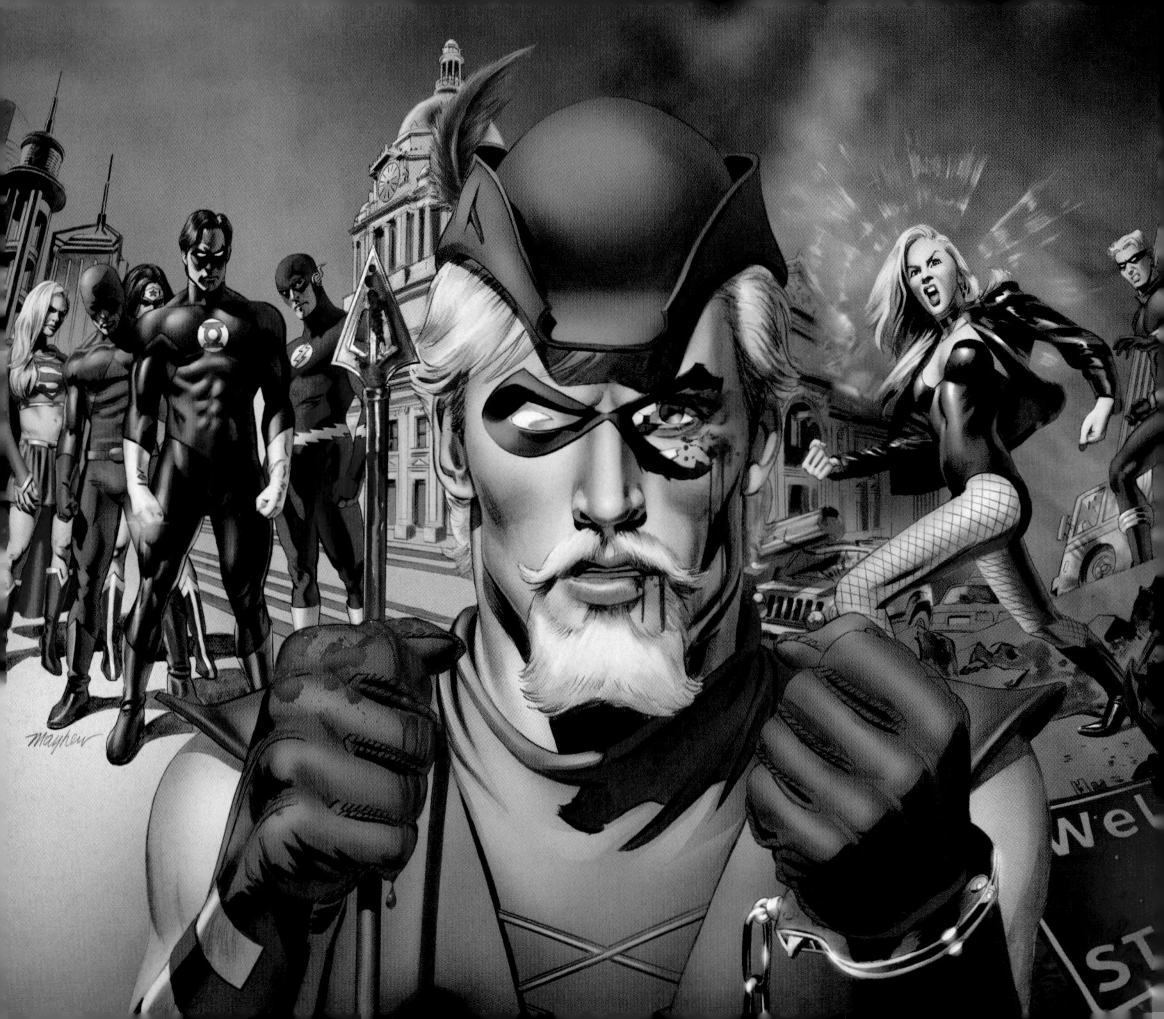
mayhew

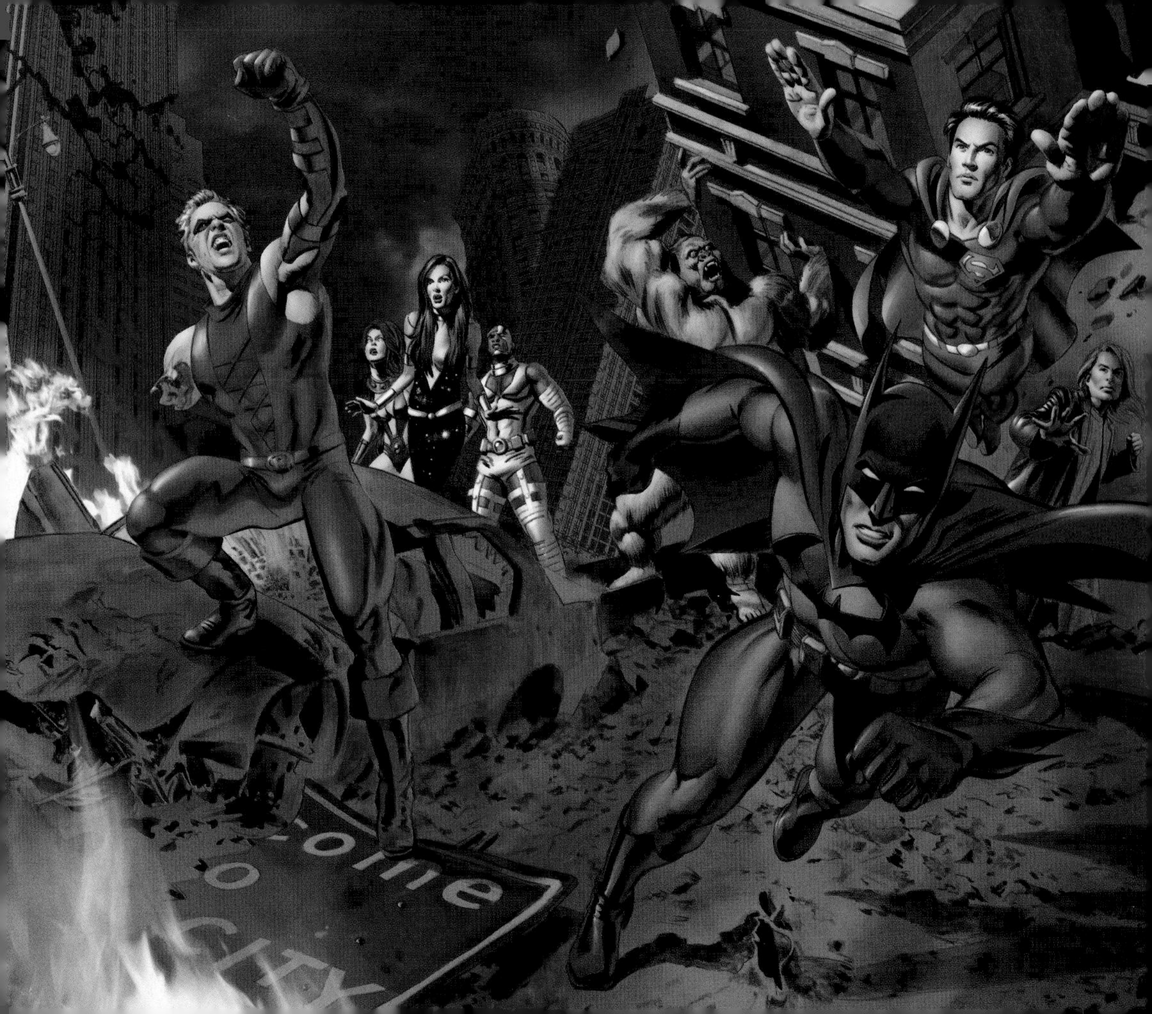

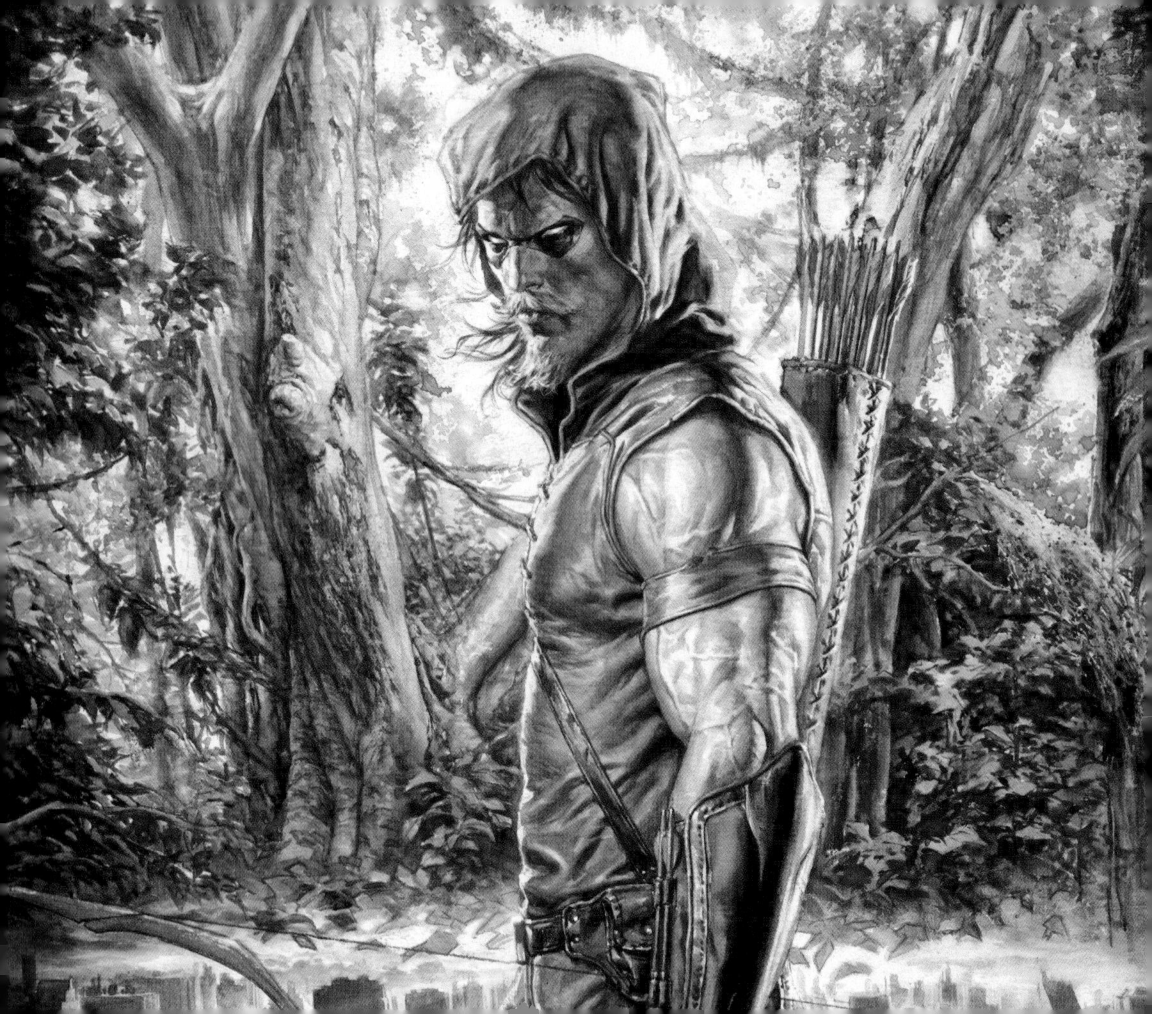

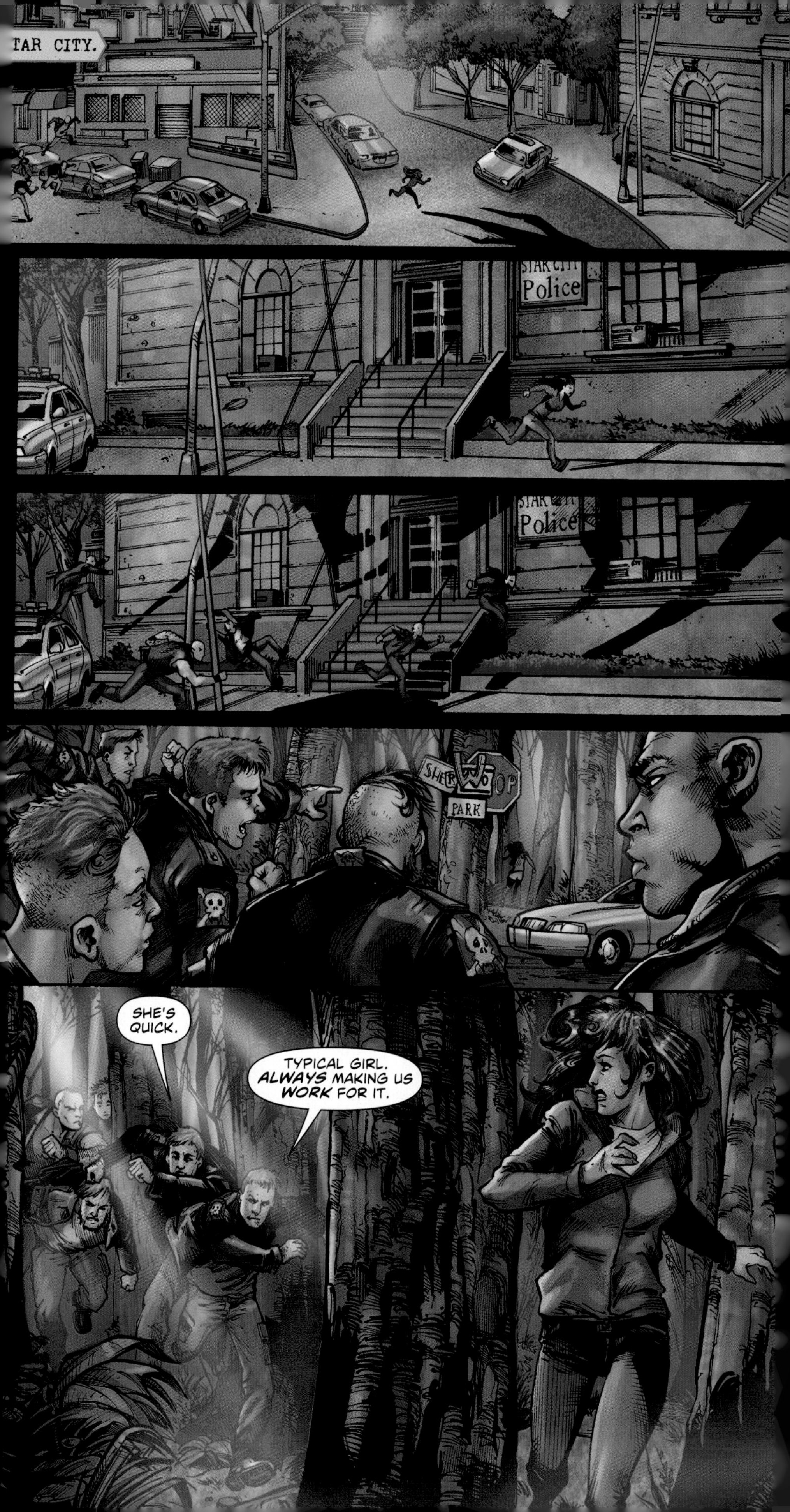
TAR CITY.
STAR CITY Police
STAR CITY Police
SHER
OP
PARK
SHE'S QUICK.
TYPICAL GIRL. ALWAYS MAKING US WORK FOR IT.

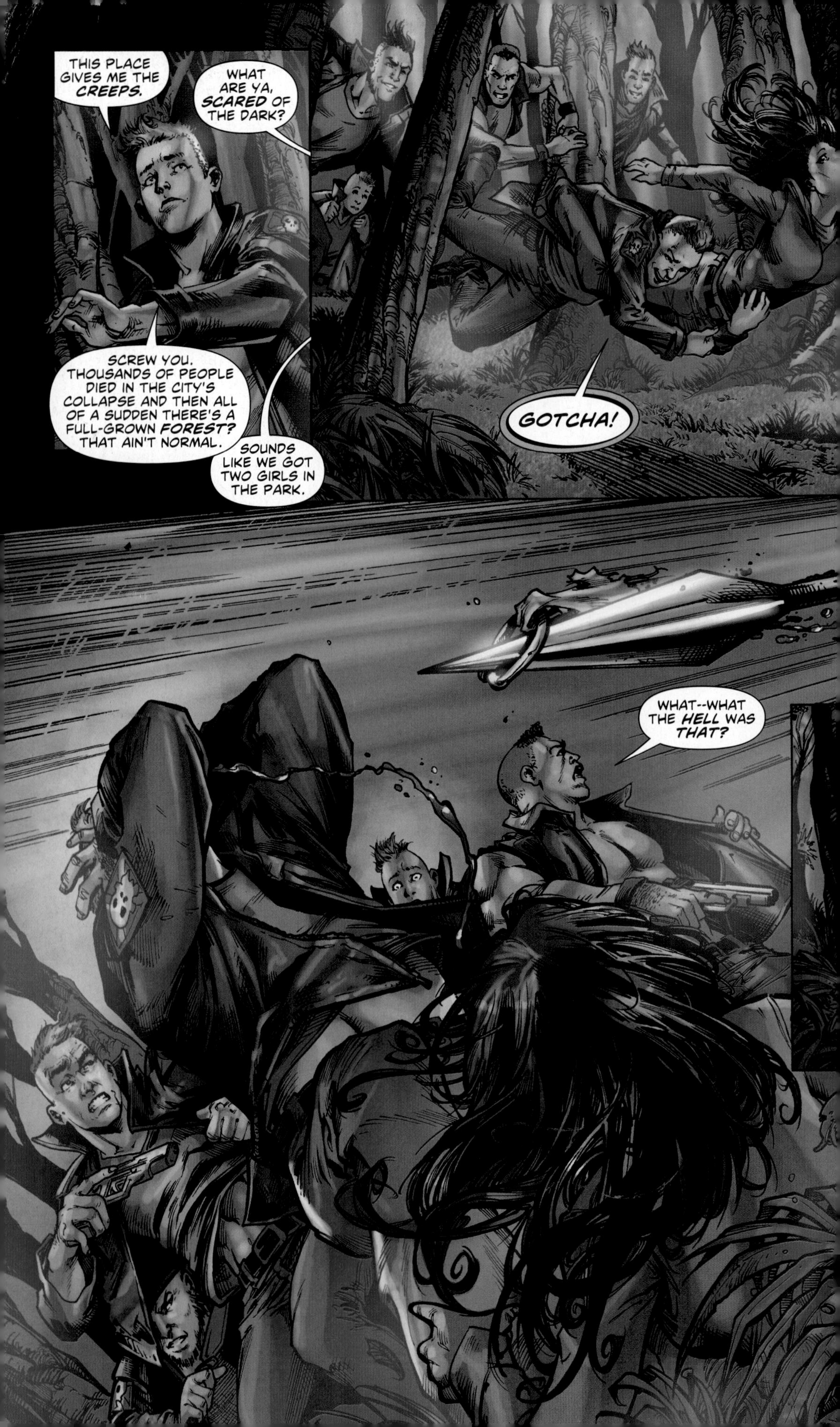
THIS PLACE GIVES ME THE CREEPS.
WHAT ARE YA, SCARED OF THE DARK?
SCREW YOU. THOUSANDS OF PEOPLE DIED IN THE CITY'S COLLAPSE AND THEN ALL OF A SUDDEN THERE'S A FULL-GROWN FOREST? THAT AIN'T NORMAL.
SOUNDS LIKE WE GOT TWO GIRLS IN THE PARK.
GOTCHA!
WHAT--WHAT THE HELL WAS THAT?

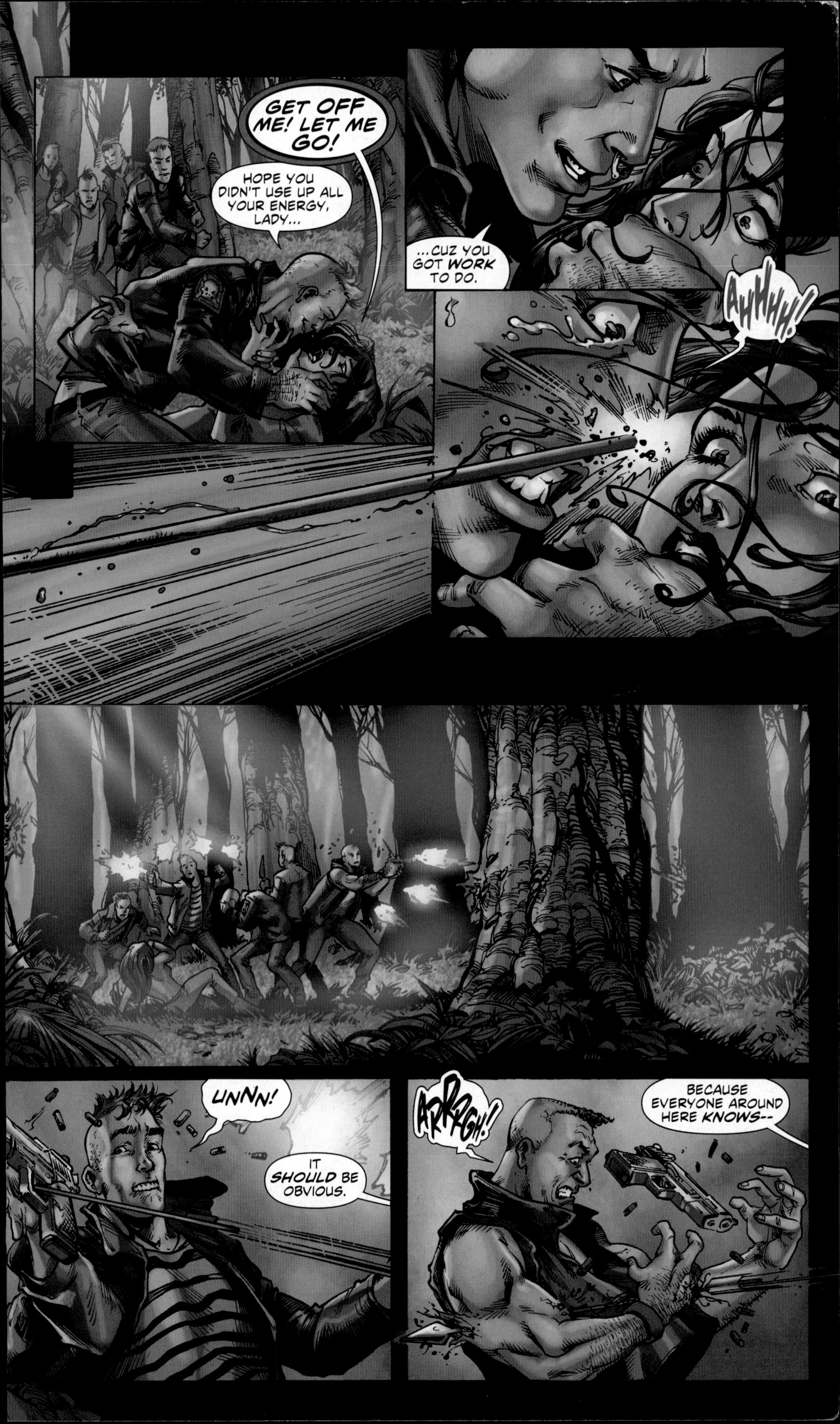
GET OFF ME! LET ME GO!
HOPE YOU DIDN'T USE UP ALL YOUR ENERGY, LADY...
...CUZ YOU GOT WORK TO DO.
AHHHH!
UNNN!
IT SHOULD BE OBVIOUS.
ARRRGH!
BECAUSE EVERYONE AROUND HERE KNOWS--

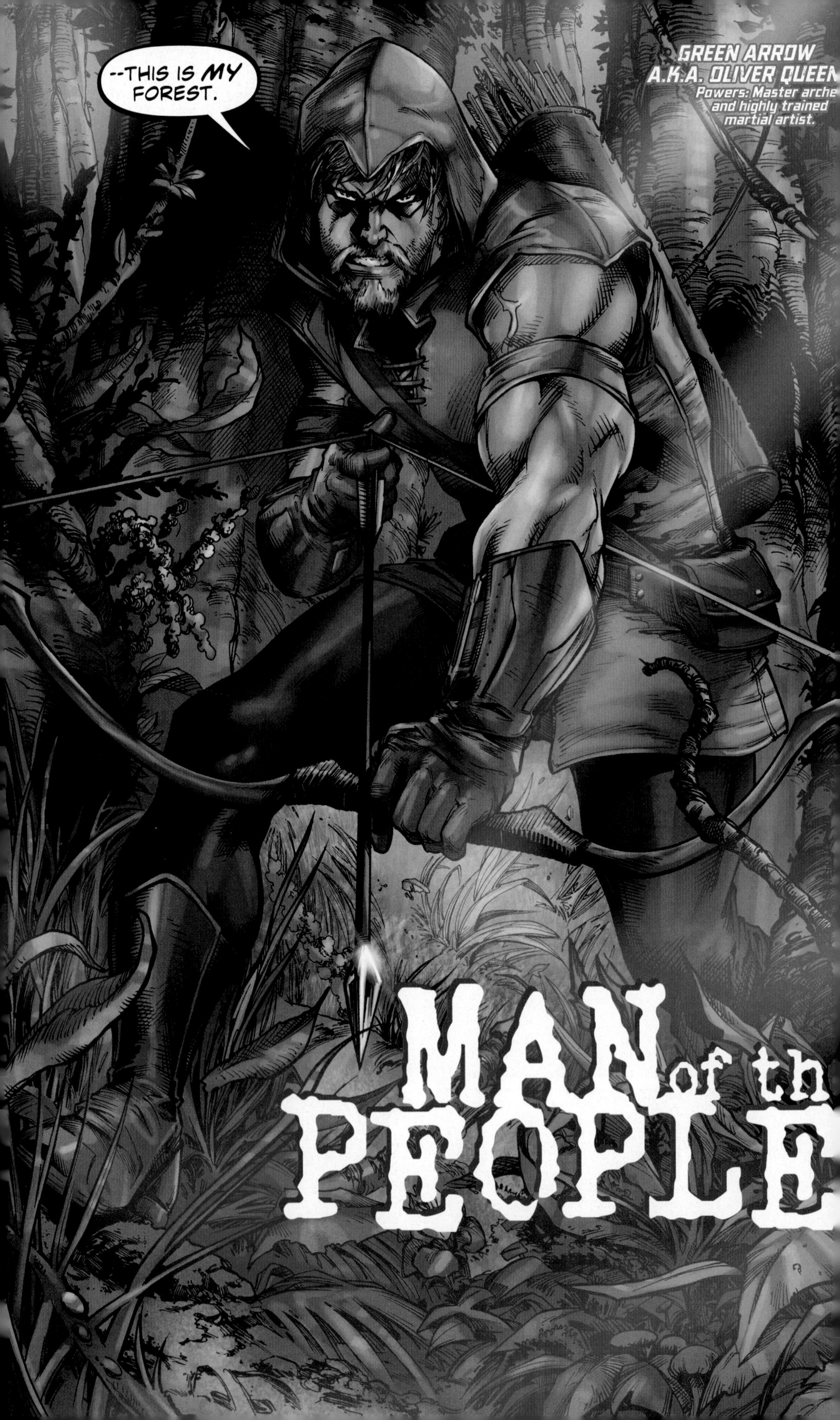
--THIS IS MY FOREST.
GREEN ARROW
A.K.A. OLIVER QUEEN
Powers: Master arche
and highly trained
martial artist.
MAN of th
PEOPLE

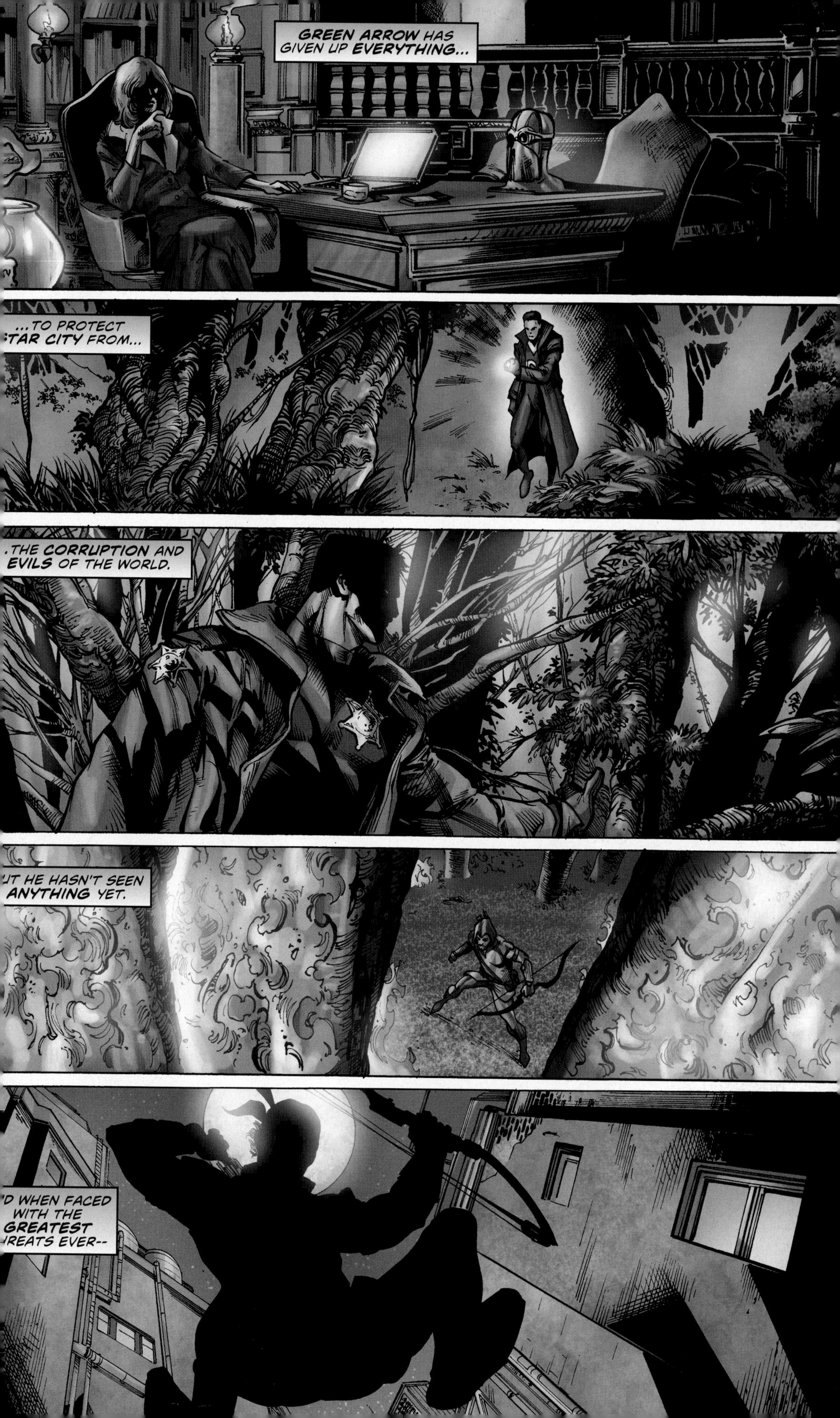
GREEN ARROW HAS GIVEN UP EVERYTHING...
...TO PROTECT STAR CITY FROM...
.THE CORRUPTION AND EVILS OF THE WORLD.
UT HE HASN'T SEEN ANYTHING YET.
'D WHEN FACED WITH THE GREATEST HREATS EVER--

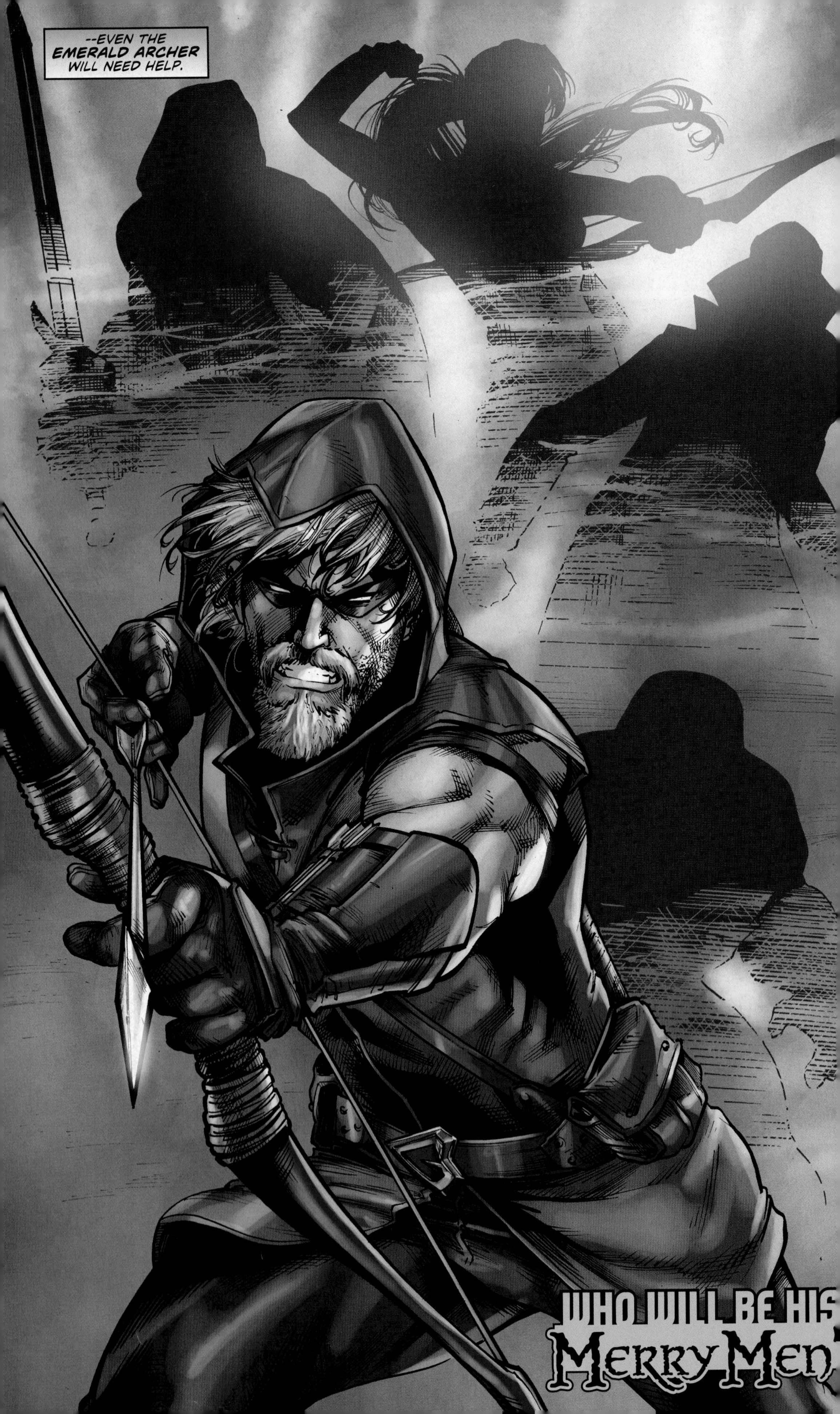
--EVEN THE EMERALD ARCHER WILL NEED HELP.
WHO WILL BE HIS
MERRY MEN

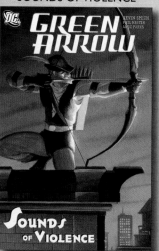